Praise for

REVOLUTIONARY FOUNDERS

"The best essays are small gems of exposition, providing both the context and detail necessary to enable readers to recognize the important contributions of these previously unappreciated and largely unknown individuals. . . . In short, *Revolutionary Founders* is one step . . . toward a comprehensive account of the nation's origins."
—Mary Beth Norton, *The New York Times Book Review*

"In these 22 provocative essays, leading historians highlight Revolutionary-era people and movements that textbooks and standard accounts skip. They recast the making of America as a bottom-up, widespread set of developments, where common folk spearheaded changes. . . . *Revolutionary Founders* aims to test the parameters of what we think we know with new and reinterpreted data and fresh theories." —*American History*

"*Revolutionary Founders* brilliantly restores the struggle for social equality to the central place in the history of American Revolution, and explains how the 'spirit of leveling' shaped the making of the new American Republic. For anyone interested in the sources of popular democracy in the United States, *Revolutionary Founders* is required reading."
—Ira Berlin, author of
The Making of African America: The Four Great Migrations

"*Revolutionary Founders* is, to my mind, one of the best recent books on the American Revolution, and one that, unlike many others, could be of use in the college classroom. Several essays would serve particularly well to complement, deepen, and even bring into question standard textbook accounts, and to demonstrate that some current issues have deep historical roots." —Pauline Maier, author of
Ratification: The People Debate the Constitution, 1787–1788

"Revolutions free the imagination, making many things seem possible that once were deemed wild visions. *Revolutionary Founders* introduces into the pantheon of the American Revolution those rebels, radicals, and reformers who passionately committed themselves to act on the conviction that 'all men are created equal.' "   —Joyce Appleby, author of
The Relentless Revolution: A History of Capitalism

"[A] uniformly strong collection, [by] an impressive array of historians—among them, T. H. Breen, Eric Foner, Jill Lepore and Alan Taylor. . . . Editors Young, Nash, and Raphael have solicited wisely, with each contributor adding an important dimension to the controlling theme: 'We cannot have too much liberty.' "   —*Kirkus Reviews*

"Fast-paced and readable, this remarkable book captures an American Revolution that has long been hiding in plain sight. I emerged with a new set of heroes, a fresh appreciation for complex stories, and a new sense of our own connection to a revolutionary past."
—Linda K. Kerber, author of *No Constitutional Right to Be Ladies: Women and the Obligations of Citizenship*

Revolutionary Founders

Alfred F. Young is Professor Emeritus of History at Northern Illinois University and was senior research fellow at the Newberry Library in Chicago. His most recent books include *Liberty Tree: Ordinary People and the American Revolution* and with Gregory Nobles, *Whose American Revolution Was It?: Historians Interpret the Founding.* He lives in Durham, North Carolina.

Gary B. Nash is Professor of History Emeritus and Director of the National Center for History in the Schools at UCLA. He lives in Pacific Palisades, California.

Ray Raphael is the author of *Mr. President, A People's History of the American Revolution, Founding Myths,* and several other books on the nation's founding. He lives in northern California.

Revolutionary Founders

Rebels, Radicals, and Reformers
in the Making of the Nation

EDITED BY

ALFRED F. YOUNG, GARY B. NASH, AND RAY RAPHAEL

Vintage Books
A Division of Random House, Inc.
New York

FIRST VINTAGE BOOKS EDITION, APRIL 2012

Copyright © 2011 by Alfred F. Young, Ray Raphael, and Gary B. Nash

All rights reserved. Published in the United States by Vintage Books, a division of Random House, Inc., New York, and in Canada by Random House of Canada Limited, Toronto. Originally published in hardcover in the United States by Alfred A. Knopf, a division of Random House, Inc., New York, in 2011.

Vintage and colophon are registered trademarks of Random House, Inc.

Pages 451–52 constitute an extension of this copyright page.

The Library of Congress has cataloged the Knopf edition as follows:
Revolutionary founders : rebels, radicals, and reformers in the making of the nation / edited by Alfred F. Young, Gary B. Nash, and Ray Raphael.—1st ed.
p. cm.
Includes bibliographical references and index.
1. United States—History—Revolution, 1775–1783.
2. Revolutionaries—United States—History—18th century.
3. United States—History—Revolution, 1775–1783—Social aspects.
4. United States—History—Revolution, 1775–1783—Biography.
5. United States—Intellectual life—18th century.
I. Young, Alfred Fabian, 1925- II. Nash, Gary B. III. Raphael, Ray.
E208.R463 2011
973.3—dc22   2010041102

Vintage ISBN 978-0-307-45599-4

www.vintagebooks.com

Printed in the United States of America
10 9 8 7 6 5 4 3 2 1

Contents

و

INTRODUCTION
"To Begin the World Over Again"
Alfred F. Young, Ray Raphael, and Gary B. Nash

3

PART I · Revolutions

ONE
Alfred F. Young
Ebenezer Mackintosh: Boston's Captain General of the Liberty Tree

15

TWO
Ray Raphael
Blacksmith Timothy Bigelow and the Massachusetts Revolution of 1774

35

THREE
T. H. Breen
Samuel Thompson's War: The Career of an American Insurgent

53

FOUR
Gary B. Nash
Philadelphia's Radical Caucus That Propelled Pennsylvania
to Independence and Democracy

67

Illustrations

Revolutionary Founders

"To Begin the World Over Again"

Alfred F. Young, Ray Raphael, and Gary B. Nash

A ll men are created equal," our first founding document declared. Men are "endowed by their Creator with certain unalienable rights," including "life, liberty, and the pursuit of happiness." These truths might be self-evident, as the Declaration of Independence stated boldly, but historically they are enigmatic. A majority of the fifty-six men who subscribed to such noble thoughts enslaved other human beings. Thomas Jefferson certainly did, but he alone is not the puzzle, nor is slavery the only inconsistency. What, exactly, did Jefferson and his colleagues mean by "created equal"? Was a shoemaker's son, at birth, really created equal to the son of a wealthy merchant? Did women have the same unalienable rights as men? Were blacks as well as whites entitled to life, liberty, and the pursuit of happiness? Such notions frightened most of the prominent men we think of today as the Founding Fathers.

Eleven years after the Declaration, when the framers of the Constitution devised "a more perfect union," they did so, in part, to prevent an "excess of democracy" (a phrase they repeated often) from sweeping the young nation. The framers pejoratively labeled threats to their wealth and political power as "leveling" and those to their political power as "democratic." Political, social, and economic equality were not what the framers had in mind.

The disparity between words and deeds presents a particular problem for history-proud Americans who see the founders as guiding, patriarchal exemplars of their most cherished ideals. Searching for a moral resolution to this conundrum, typical American textbooks today assert that though all people were not treated equally in America in 1776, the Declaration of Independence set high goals for equal treatment in the future. This has become our nation's standard fallback response. By treating liberty and equality as "promises" to future generations, we simultaneously acquit the founders of culpability and affirm our national commitment to these high goals. It's a clever remedy, but factually it does not ring true. While some of the men who commanded slave labor hoped the institution would end someday, and a handful freed their slaves in their wills, that was as far as they went. With few exceptions, the gentlemen who drafted and signed our two founding documents opposed popular democracy and social equality. Our high goals were not theirs. They did not hold fundamental values that we accept as common currency today.

Although the Declaration of Independence claimed that people had "the right to alter or abolish" their form of government if they had exhausted all other means to express their grievances, the traditional founders did not wish to "alter or abolish" the institutional structures that protected their claim to rule. Once an elective government was established, traditional founders suppressed political rebellion. They did not want people to significantly alter, much less abolish, the structures they had just created.

By contrast, many of their contemporaries wanted to strike at the heart of existing inequalities and radicalize governmental structures. Our protagonists in this book wanted to extend the lofty principles expressed in the Declaration of Independence to areas of life that the traditional founders never intended. These people *did* have a sense of the promise of the Revolution, and they wanted to fulfill it in their own time. Sharing no single agenda, they acted in the spirit of the words of Thomas Paine: "We have it in our power to begin the world over again." The new nation was "a blank sheet to write upon," Paine wrote,[1] and on that sheet they placed their marks. Their actions were many and varied:

- Common farmers, artisans, and laborers often led the resistance to imperial policies, moving the colonies toward independence while reshaping the character of political life in North America.
- Slaves emancipated themselves by fleeing to freedom, then established their own viable communities.
- Women staked claims to "equality of the sexes" and to retain rights to their own property in marriage.
- Persecuted religious dissenters pushed for, and obtained, "the free exercise of religion."
- Resisting the inequities of rank, soldiers carried democratic values into the military.
- Native Americans claimed sovereignty and fought to defend it, with a spirit of independence that paralleled that of colonists.

- Farmers threatened with the loss of their land resorted to collective action, including taking up arms.
- Printers published what they wanted, overriding attempts to repress them.
- Self-proclaimed democrats, turning that term of derision on its head, won the right of ordinary people to vote, hold public office, and pass judgment on their rulers.

Most of these "Revolutionary founders," as we call them here, were *radicals* in the literal sense of the word: they promoted root changes in the very structure of social or political systems. One of those fundamental changes, of course, was independence from Britain, a goal they shared with the traditional founders, but often they pushed for others. Many of these people can also be considered *rebels,* either because they forcibly challenged British authority or because they confronted old or new hierarchies. Finally, some might best be described as *reformers* who sought to change a particular feature of society while leaving others intact.

Each of these rebels, radicals, and reformers moved the American Revolution in some direction the traditional founders did not want to take, extending it farther and deeper than a separation from the British Empire. They made the Revolution more revolutionary.

~℮

For more than four decades, historians have been investigating the lives of everyday Americans. Unlike their better-known contemporaries, few ordinary people wrote extensively, so at first they were described by some historians as "inarticulate" and their influence deemed inconsequential. As scholars' investigations of popular movements deepened, however, they realized that many of these people were not only articulate but eloquent and politically potent. Historians have uncovered the lives of new and more radical protagonists, revealing individuals who endeavored to write on Paine's "blank sheet" and reshape history.

In *Revolutionary Founders,* we have asked prominent scholars to discuss men and women who are representative of larger historical currents. Most were associated with "popular" movements (a contemporary term meaning broadly based and democratic), either as leaders or as writers who articulated a movement's ideals. Others challenged established structures in their own individual struggles yet were also representative of broader trends. Collectively, their stories highlight the depth and range of our nation's formative radical underpinnings.

Paine is certainly the best-known radical of the times, but, as we shall see, he has been badly misrepresented. He appears prominently in textbooks promoting independence and taking the debate over *Common Sense* to taverns, meetinghouses, and army campfires, but Paine wanted much more than national independence for the Americans. In *Common Sense* he proposed that each state establish a single-house legislature based on a broad suffrage. In *Rights of Man* he advocated social equality, popular sovereignty, and a welfare state that redistributed wealth—not just in the United States but also in Britain, France, and everywhere else. In *The Age of Reason* he wrote that all established churches were no more than "human inventions, set up to terrify and enslave mankind, and monopolize power and profit."[2] These views are not touted in school textbooks; nor are they mentioned by the politicians of conservative persuasions who claim Paine as their own.

Two well-known popular movements of the era, the so-called Shays's and Whiskey Rebellions, have also been distorted. Both names were given to them by their opponents as a way to discredit them. "Shays's Rebellion" in Massachusetts had not one but a host of leaders, each with strong roots in local communities. The "Whiskey Rebellion" of Pennsylvania, a sweeping challenge to Alexander Hamilton's finance program as a whole, was given that label by Hamilton himself in order to caricature his opposition. Following the lead of many of the actual participants, the authors in this book refer to these people as "Regulators," who insisted that their rights did not end with voting and petitioning but included the right of the people to pass judgment on or to "regulate" their alleged rulers. But standard texts, by referring to "Shaysites" who followed a disgruntled leader and "whiskey rebels" who didn't want to pay taxes on the hard liquor they manufactured, demean the protesters and obscure their goals.

This misnaming may seem trivial, but it is suggestive of greater obfuscation. What has been concluded from these summary appellations and distorted renditions of these popular protests is that wild radicals lost out to more reasonable men. Those stories have set the textbook tone. Of little account on their own, dissidents of the founding era serve only as narrative foils to more important protagonists. The subtext is easy to spot: radicals failed and are marginalized. Their only effect on the nation's history and character is to provide an occasion for their betters to shine. "Shays's Rebellion" led to the Constitution, we are told, and the "Whiskey Rebellion" allowed Washington to assert federal authority. Wise and strong men saved the infant nation from anarchy.

The essays here suggest otherwise. There were triumphs as well as defeats. As a group, militant rebels who advocated resistance to imperial policies from 1765 to 1776 were triumphant not only in pushing the country toward independence but also in establishing the ability of "the people out of doors" to shape the actions of men with power "within doors" in legislative chambers and courts of law. Demonstrations in Boston in 1765, led by the shoemaker Ebenezer Mackintosh, established the capacity of the man in the street to shape events. The blacksmith Timothy Bigelow and the people of Worcester declared their readiness for independence a full twenty-one months before the Continental Congress Declaration. In 1775–76 the militant insurgency of Samuel Thompson and poor farmers in Maine intimidated the local Loyalist-leaning gentry. In 1776 a radical caucus in Philadelphia pushed simultaneously for independence and a truly democratic state constitution, and won on both counts.

Stories of reformers who crusaded for freedom of expression add a dimension long missing from the origins of American constitutional liberties. Freedom of religion, freedom of the press, and freedom of speech were cornerstones of liberty that would not have become so deeply embedded in national tradition without the tireless efforts of often-persecuted Americans. While James Madison and Thomas Jefferson are commonly given credit for writing "the free exercise of religion" into Virginia law, and from there into the Bill of Rights, they were pushed from below by Baptists such as James Ireland and John "Swearing Jack" Waller, who were subjected to brutal assaults before their views prevailed. In the new republic editors won hard-fought battles for freedom of the press. The New Yorker Thomas Greenleaf printed his allegedly seditious material despite numerous attempts to shut him down, and when he died, his wife, Elizabeth, followed suit. This grass-roots fight for freedom of speech continued well after passage of the First Amendment. Jedediah Peck, known as the "Plough-Jogger" in upstate New York, was arrested under the Sedition Act in 1798 because he circulated a petition against that very same law, but his proud defiance led the government to drop the case against him. Peck prevailed in elections, became a power in state politics, and became known as "father" of the state's school system.

The hard-to-recover life histories of enslaved individuals force us to re-define slave resistance in the era of the Revolution. An untold number of slaves took advantage of armies clashing on American soil to emancipate themselves. In epic journeys, Harry Washington, Mary Perth, and Moses Wilkinson fled bondage on Virginia plantations in response to the offer of freedom by British generals. They made their way to New York City, were transported to Nova Scotia, and finally sailed to Sierra Leone, where they were among the founders of a new nation. Similarly, Phillis Wheatley, Boston's politically astute African-American poet, in effect managed her own emancipation by publishing her poems in London. After the war, former slaves Richard Allen, Prince Hall, and Daniel Coker founded religious and fraternal institutions that cemented bonds among free African Americans in urban communities.

While there was no organized movement for women's rights in the era of the Revolution, some women, attuned to the currents of change, pushed back the boundaries of patriarchy in their own private realm. When Abigail Adams asked her husband, John, to "remember the ladies" in drafting "the new code of laws,"[3] she got nowhere, but she did not let up. By law and custom, as a married woman she was not supposed to own her own property, but she insisted she could, and she did. She was not supposed to write her own will disposing of that property, but she did. Toward the same end of personal independence, Judith Sargent Murray advocated education for women that would enable them to fend for themselves in the event of widowhood.

Actions challenging the status quo in the personal realm, though, could be thwarted by harsh institutional restraints. Virginia's Richard Randolph, upon his death, provided for the emancipation of the people he held in bondage, but his will was tangled in legal restrictions for years. Several distinguished Virginians in Randolph's circle called for the state to pass a gradual emancipation law, but their demands ran aground on the race prejudice of whites who could not imagine large numbers of free blacks living among them.

Native Americans faced a unique set of circumstances. For most, neutrality would have been the best choice in what they saw as a white man's "cousins war," but that was not an available option. Forced into choosing sides, the various Indian nations, sometimes split internally, acted to preserve the ancestral land still remaining in their hands, to maintain their political sovereignty, and to protect—or restore—ancient lifeways. Their leaders pursued "life, liberty, and the pursuit of happiness" just as avidly as did the white radical revolutionaries. Dragging Canoe, for example, was both a rebel and a reformer, resisting the recurrent white encroachment on ancient Cherokee homelands while urging his people to limit their dependence on white trade goods. Han Yerry and Tyona Doxtader of the Oneida Nation allied with the Americans, but their interest in protecting the Oneida homelands was no less intense than Dragging Canoe's.

Many of these individuals who challenged the roots of authority were anything but inarticulate. Abigail Adams in her letters to John certainly held her own. Judith Sargent Murray's collected essays, which included "On the Equality of the Sexes" and "Observations on Female Abilities," filled three volumes. Private Joseph Plumb Martin's pithy and pungent memoir of his seven years as a Continental soldier is now considered a classic. Herman Husband, leader of two backcountry rebellions, composed a series of stirring pamphlets that laid out his full-blown vision of an egalitarian utopia, down to the finest detail. Robert Coram's pamphlet argued forcefully that "every man should have property," in the form of either land or sufficient training in a trade.

Even when they fell far short of their goals, individuals and groups with radical agendas were often able to force concessions from would-be rulers, and they sometimes paved the way for later successes. In Virginia in the midst of the war, when hardscrabble and tenant farmers forcefully resisted military enlistments on unfavorable terms, they did not escape service; but neither were they punished with any severity, even in the midst of war. Virginia's leaders were forced to accede to some of their demands. In response to the Massachusetts Regulation of 1786–87 and the threat of slave rebellions, the framers of the Constitution granted the federal government powers to suppress "domestic insurrections." But in the face of popular protests, legal as well as illegal, they realized that they would have to accommodate "the genius of the people" (what we would call the spirit or temper of the people), creating a document more open to the expansion of democracy than they might have preferred.[4] The Pennsylvania Regulation of 1794 collapsed when a federal army approached, but the repellent image of armed Americans employed against their countrymen inspired Democratic-Republican opposition at the polls to the Federalists, who in a few years were swept from national office.

Since no victory, and no defeat, was absolute, any discussion of these movements must be nuanced. The emergence of democratic institutions in the new nation engendered deep differences as to tactics among protesters. In western Pennsylvania in 1794, some leaders promoted armed resistance to the federal government's repression, while others insisted on staying within the electoral process. The defeat of such Regulators, combined with Jefferson's victory in 1800, established limits to the scope of popular protest, inhibiting, although not suppressing, radical action. Grassroots Democratic-Republicans supported societies, newspapers, and leaders who pushed for and achieved some reforms through electoral politics, but they turned their backs on rebellion. Was that a victory, a defeat, or a complex evolution of social movements? The form militant protest should take was an issue in itself, which later movements would also face.

Most of the narratives included here reflect the give-and-take of struggle. A common thread among many of our protagonists is a sense of betrayal:

during the war they had fought for liberty and equality, but afterward they received much less. Joseph Plumb Martin was promised land for enlisting in the Continental Army, but fifty years later he was still furious that soldiers "were turned adrift like old worn-out horses, and nothing said about land to pasture them upon."[5] Herman Husband, with a command of history, wrote that "in every revolution . . . the people at large are called on to assist & promised true liberty, but when the foreign oppressor is thrown off, . . . then our own learned and designing men immediately aim to take their places." Yet as a true believer in the millennium, he held that "God set up the true Republican form of right government in which the body of the people will have Supreme power to choose their [governors], and their will [shall] be the supreme law of the land."[6] These driving forces—disillusion and anger, complemented by faith and hope—appear and reappear in radical thought and action.

This complex dynamic between radicals and rulers is registered time and again in the lives of famous founders. Those who aspired to power in the new nation were forced to respond to popular movements and personal challenges, and their reactions ranged across a continuum from accommodation to repression. Consider how George Washington and John Adams, both raised to the height of power in the Revolutionary Era, reacted to movements represented by protagonists in these essays.

Washington, as commander in chief during the war, needed manpower for his army, but a former employee in Virginia, James Cleveland, led his fellow tenant farmers in protesting military enlistments that burdened the poor and excused the rich, and Washington had little choice but to accept soldiers on terms they would agree to. At first Washington was opposed to enlisting former slaves, but when Harry Washington and more than a dozen other enslaved men and women fled from his plantation to fight with the British, he altered his policy to allow free blacks to enlist. He welcomed Phillis Wheatley's poetic tribute to him, arranged for its publication, and even received her at his military headquarters. But in 1783, with victory assured, he was zealous in his efforts to recover his human property, about to be transported on British ships to freedom in Nova Scotia. Only at the end of his life did Washington revise his will to allow for the ultimate emancipation of his slaves.

When Private Martin and his starving "band of brothers," with bayonets pointed at their officers, demanded food, General Washington was forced to weigh his sympathy for the soldiers' demands against the importance of enforcing discipline. As president, too, Washington brooked no defiance to authority. As commander in chief, he led an army to put down the Pennsylvania Regulators of 1794, and he singled out Herman Husband, actually a moderate leader, to be tried for speech inciting rebellion. A jury of his peers found Husband innocent.

John Adams too was forced to deal more often than he liked with various protagonists in this book. Although he supported resistance to imperial policies, he was zealous to contain popular democracy. He welcomed peaceful actions led by street leaders like the shoemaker Ebenezer Mackintosh, but not violence. As a delegate to the Continental Congress in 1774, Adams tried to slow down Timothy Bigelow and the Worcester radicals, whose premature declaration of "independency" threatened to scare off delegates from other colonies. In 1776 Adams welcomed Thomas Paine's *Common Sense* because it argued for independence, but he opposed Pennsylvania's new state constitution, pushed by Paine, which he thought was "democratical without any restraint."[7] Three years later Adams drafted a state constitution for Massachusetts in which those without property were given no vote and the popular will, as expressed through the lower house, was checked by a senate that was apportioned according to property, not population. When Adams became president, he moved from containing to repressing popular democracy. With his sanction, the Sedition Act led to the prosecution of the Democratic-Republican editor Thomas Greenleaf and Jedediah Peck, the "Plough-Jogger," and a score of others. Mere criticism of the president or Congress was grounds for arrest.

Thomas Paine haunted Adams. At every stage of his political career, Adams confronted Paine, author of the three most widely read radical challenges to political and religious hierarchies of the era: *Common Sense* in 1776, and *Rights of Man* and *The Age of Reason* in the 1790s. "History is to ascribe the American Revolution to Thomas Paine," Adams wrote. That wasn't the half of it. For Adams, Paine's later views on government and religion were leading to a new and chaotic world. Defeated in the election of 1800, Adams had to endure the presidency of Thomas Jefferson, who had written, "A little rebellion now and then is a good thing." In 1806 when asked by a correspondent what to call the age they were living through, Adams wrote, "I know not whether any man in the world has had more influence on its inhabitants or affairs for the last thirty years than Tom Paine"—so why not "call it then the Age of Paine"?[8] For all the constitutional barriers he and other traditional founders had erected, Adams acknowledged the triumph of the democratic ideal.

This rich dialectic, in which men in power chose to accommodate or repress threats from below, was central to the forming of the nation. As radicals and reformers pushed their demands, they engaged with those who were trying to gain or keep power. Such is the stuff of history; but that history is lost when we fail to recognize the individuals and movements forcing the issues. In accounts of the era that focus on its best-known leaders, the failure to include radical impulses from below results in a deficient, truncated history.

According to the traditional national narrative of American history, the period of radical change started with "Jacksonian Democracy" in the 1830s, gained steam with the abolitionists and women's rights advocates of the 1840s, and swelled with the labor protests and Populism of the industrial era. Before all this, in historical treatments of the founding era, words such as *reform* or *radical* are rarely used, while the term *revolutionaries* refers to nonradical stalwarts such as Washington and Adams.

These later generations of dissenters in some cases knew of the rebels, radicals, and reformers of the founding era, but because their stories were not well known, they did not point to that tradition when pushing for their goals. Instead, they called forth traditional founding icons, who carried the weight of the Revolutionary generation in the national narrative. This presented them with a dilemma: Should they accept or reject the Revolution's most celebrated men and the documents they created? Some invoked the Declaration of Independence. The women and men at the Seneca Falls Convention in 1848 resolved that "all men and women are created equal,"[9] and they modeled their statement of grievances on the Declaration. Others were ambivalent about the traditional celebrations. On the seventy-sixth anniversary of the nation's birth in 1852, addressing the nation, Frederick Douglass declared, "The fourth of July is yours, not mine. You may rejoice, I must mourn."[10]

Later generations of dissenters faced the same dilemma. The foreshortened view of radicalism in America prevents us from grasping powerful crosscurrents of the founding era. We will never grasp the full scope of the American Revolution until we take seriously its most progressive participants and incorporate them into our national narrative.

PART I

REVOLUTIONS

CHAPTER ONE

Ebenezer Mackintosh:
Boston's Captain General of the Liberty Tree

Alfred F. Young

Wednesday, August 14, 1765, was a day unlike any that Bostonians had ever seen. At dawn two effigies were hanging on the Great Elm in the South End of town on the road that everyone coming into Boston had to take: farmers with produce in their carts, teamsters driving wagons, or visitors on horseback on business at the center of government a half mile down the road. The effigies dangled from the lower branch of the giant tree. A dummy stuffed with straw labeled "A.O." represented Andrew Oliver, recently designated commissioner of the Stamp Act passed by Parliament in March. A high jackboot stood for the king's ministers considered responsible for the act: the Earl of Bute (*boot* a common pun on his name) and Lord George Grenville (represented by the sole of the boot painted green, a "Greenville" sole). At the top of the boot was "the devil crawling out, with a pitch-fork in his hand."

Bostonians were not unfamiliar with effigies. Every November 5—Pope's Day in Boston, Guy Fawkes Day in England—the town's rival North End and South End companies paraded effigies of the Devil, the Pope, and the Stuart Pretender to the throne through town on wagons and engaged in a battle royal to capture and burn each other's effigies. The ceremony originally observed England's deliverance from a Catholic plot on November 5, 1605, to blow up James I and Parliament. The effigies on the Great Elm this day, however, targeted living political figures, one of whom, Oliver, was a wealthy merchant in their midst who held high office as secretary to the provincial government.

Throughout the day Bostonians of all sorts streamed into "Deacon Eliot's corner," the well-known site of the Great Elm, to watch the spectacle.

Observers agreed that "almost the whole town" turned out. At intervals during the day there was comic street theater. As farmers and teamsters stopped their wagons at the tree, the organizers manipulated the effigy of Oliver to "stamp" their wares. At dusk they cut down Oliver's effigy and placed it on a bier, and a "great concourse of people," including "gentlemen," walked behind in a solemn mock funeral procession toward the center of town. At the Town House, the site of royal government, marchers paraded through the first-floor arcade, huzzahing "Liberty, Property, and No Stamps" loud enough for the governor and his council above to hear.[1]

The planned event was only half over. As the main body of marchers disbanded, a designated group of several hundred made their way to Andrew Oliver's dock on the waterfront, where his newly erected office building was thought to house the stamps. They leveled it in less than half an hour with the skill of a fire company trained to pull down a house to keep a fire from spreading. The assemblage then marched to Oliver's nearby house and ceremoniously beheaded his effigy in the street. Rampaging through the mansion, they broke furniture, windows, and a huge mirror, all symbols of Oliver's wealth, and helped themselves to his liquor. The action ended on top of adjacent Fort Hill, where the crowd "stamped" the timber collected from Oliver's office, fences, and coach house before throwing it all into a raging bonfire, along with the headless effigy. It was a daring public execution. Lieutenant Governor Thomas Hutchinson and the sheriff made an appearance but retreated under a hail of stones. The next morning Oliver let it be known that he would not accept the commission as Stamp Act distributor.

For the rest of the year, massive demonstrations against the act continued. In March 1766 Hutchinson explained to a friend in Britain, a former governor of Massachusetts, that a "new model of government" now ruled Boston. Using the metaphor of "branches" of government to describe the distribution of power among different social classes, Hutchinson wrote: "the lowest branch, partly executive, partly legislative . . . consists of the rabble of the town of Boston headed by one Mackintosh . . . When there is occasion to hang or burn [effigies] or pull down houses these are employed." Going up the social scale, he explained that "the rabble" were "*somewhat* controuled by a superior set consisting of the master masons, carpenters &c. of the town." "When anything of more importance" was to be decided, "as opening the custom house or any matter of trade, these are under the direction of a committee of the merchants." However, "all affairs of a general nature, opening the courts of law &c," were "proper for a general meeting of the inhabitants"—that is, the legal town meeting—where James Otis "and his mobbish eloquence prevails in every motion."[2]

"One Mackintosh" was Ebenezer Mackintosh, a shoemaker, known in Boston before the Stamp Act protests chiefly as captain of the South End Pope's Day company. He was conspicuous as a leader in five major actions in 1765. The governor and lieutenant governor described him as "the principal leader of the mob" initated by the Loyal Nine, a social group, on August 14, and "among the most active" and the "ringleader" of the mob that left Hutchinson's house a shell on August 26. Peter Oliver, Andrew's brother, described Mackintosh in vivid detail as leader of the peaceful protest processions of November 1 and 5. And Henry Bass, a member of the Loyal Nine, was delighted that the shoemaker and not they had the "principal credit" for the climactic event of the year, December 17—Oliver's public resignation of his appointment.

In sum, Mackintosh was an indispensable leader of a mass movement whose overall goal was to prevent enforcement of the Stamp Act, nullify it, and force its repeal. In Boston the Great Elm was christened the Liberty Tree and Mackintosh acquired a new fame as "Captain General of the Liberty Tree." Other towns designated liberty trees or erected liberty poles—at least sixty-eight in all—which became places of assembly and often of militant confrontation of patriots with Loyalists and royal authority. The Tree of Liberty rapidly became an icon of the American Revolution.[3]

As candidly as Hutchinson had identified the social classes in Boston politicized by the Stamp Act crisis, he shared the limitations of other class-conscious aristocrats in England and colonial America in understanding the "mob." He would have agreed with Peter Oliver, who, in his history of "the late horrid rebellion," held that "the people in general were like the mobility in all Countries, perfect machines, wound up by any Hand who might first take the Winch." But Hutchinson was more subtle, recognizing that Boston's crowds could act on their own volition. The "rabble" in Boston was "*somewhat* controuled," he wrote, emphasizing *somewhat,* and their "branch" was "partly legislative, partly executive," conceding that it had a hand in making as well as carrying out policy.[4]

In reality, a complicated and fascinating relationship prevailed among Hutchinson's classes, who formed varying powerful partnerships. To understand the dynamics of this interplay requires some sense of the numbers of the "better sort," "middling sort," and "lower sort"—the common colonial terms for class. A town of about 15,500 people, Boston was the third-largest seaboard city in the colonies. There were about 150 merchants, a term reserved for those engaged in the seaport's oceangoing commerce who owned the town's ships, docks, and warehouses and most of its wealth. The "superior set" of masters to whom Hutchinson referred were master artisans skilled in a trade consisting of about 1,100 men (and no more than a handful of women). The August 14 procession, he wrote, was headed by "40 to 50 tradesmen, decently dressed." The "lower sort," Hutchinson's "rabble," was everyone else: artisans in the "inferior" trades like shoemakers (poorer and of lower status); apprentices and journeymen in the employ of masters; day laborers who worked for merchants (such as dockworkers and cartmen) living from hand to mouth; seamen; and Negro "servants," a euphemism for slaves. In 1765 the town counted 800 African American men, women, and children, almost all enslaved and all but a small number household servants or laborers. At any one time several hundred transient seamen might be awaiting their next voyage. Half the white males were under sixteen, making for an especially youthful population. Of about 4,000 boys, perhaps 1,500 were apprentices, and about 1,800 were of school age, only half of whom were enrolled in school. The numbers alone suggest the large pool of laboring men and boys who might be drawn to street events.[5]

In the decade before independence, in seaports with variant arrays of classes—New York, Philadelphia, Baltimore, Charlestown, and Savannah—movements of artisans emerged with identifiable leaders. They often called themselves "the respectable mechanics and tradesmen." A few individuals of the "lower sort" surfaced as leaders in the Stamp Act crisis, but only fleetingly.[6] No one of his status achieved as much prominence as Ebenezer Mackintosh or owed his initial popularity to his leadership in a ritualized observance such as Pope's Day. And no one lasted as long in the public eye or struck such fear in ruling circles.

≈

In 1765 Boston-born Ebenezer Mackintosh was twenty-seven, single, and apparently in partnership with another shoemaker, Benjamin Bass. He was descended from Scots clansmen who had been exiled in 1651–52 by Britain to Massachusetts, where they were put to labor as indentured servants in the colony's ironworks. A generation later Ebenezer's father, Moses, born in nearby Dedham in 1708, was unusually down and out, even for Boston. He had been "warned out" of the town twice, and he defiantly told Boston's keeper of the records that he had been warned out of several other towns. (Towns "warned out" impoverished new arrivals of no known occupation to avoid taking them on as charity wards.) Moses enlisted in the British Army, a continuing alternative for Boston's poor, at least twice.[7]

In 1752, when Ebenezer was about fourteen, his father elsewhere and his mother deceased, he was apprenticed to his mother's brother as a shoemaker. The trade was a refuge for boys whose families could not afford the fee to enter a "higher" trade or who lacked the brawn for a more strenuous one. Late in his life Mackintosh was described as "slight of build, of sandy complexion and a nervous temperament," traits likely true of the young man.[8] In 1758–59, at the end of his apprenticeship, he enlisted in the British Army, once again at war with France on the American continent. He may have heard George Whitefield, the charismatic evangelist, bless Boston's Protestant warriors as they went off to battle the papist foe. With a father named Moses and his own name Ebenezer—associated with Samuel in the Bible—he lived with reminders of Old Testament prophets and warriors.

In the 1760s the shoemaker won recognition of two sorts. He and Benjamin Bass were selected as members of Fire Engine Company No. Nine in the South End, one of ten engine companies made up largely of artisans. To be selected was a sign of respect: a firefighter had to be a "prudent person of known fidelity." Engine men had élan: they sported black leather jockey caps bearing a distinctive emblem and mastered teamwork under pressure.[9] In the 1760s the ex-soldier also acquired a reputation among the lower sort as a leader of the South End Pope's Day company whose members elected him captain in 1764, a clear sign that he had proven himself in their street battles.

Mackintosh (who signed his name this way, but it was commonly rendered Mcintosh in legal records) was one of about fifty neighborhood shoemakers scattered around Boston, making new shoes to order or repairing old ones. It was an honorable trade with rich traditions but hardly offered prospects for economic independence, much less wealth. We cannot be sure that he owned enough property to qualify to vote in town meetings. Mackintosh was literate; indeed, he was known for reciting poetry from memory, including passages from Edward Young's melancholy epic *Night Thoughts on Life, Death and Immortality* (1742–45), a favorite with evangelicals. And he would have shared the fraternity of Boston's neighborhood taverns with a choice of lifting a glass with fellow members of his engine company, his Pope's Day company, or his trade.

While Ebenezer was marginally better off than his father, both their lives unfolded amid a depressed economy. From 1730 to 1765 Boston's population dropped from 17,000 to 15,500, artisans deserting the city in droves. In Britain's Crown Point expedition of 1756 against France, four out of every five Boston recruits were artisans, among them eighteen carpenters, fifteen tailors, and twelve shoemakers. In the late 1750s a seventh of the population was on some kind of poor relief. John Hancock's handsome mansion high on Beacon Hill looked out both on the green landscape of the Common and on a grim almshouse at its edge. When the town's gnawing poverty became an issue in public life, the haughty Hutchinson claimed that the "common people . . . live too well," and James Otis, the town meeting orator he scorned, responded, "I do not think they live half well enough."[10]

In the 1740s, amid such conditions, Pope's Day took on the ritual form it would have later in the 1760s. It had become "a grand gala day" for laboring people and boys of all classes. In England through the seventeenth century Guy Fawkes Day was both a royal and a popular holiday, observing a reigning Stuart monarch's escape from death. In Boston it did not sink deep roots until it could be celebrated as an anti-Stuart holiday, marking the defeat of the efforts of the Stuart descendants so detested in Puritan New England to regain the throne: the "old pretender" in 1715 and the "young pretender" in 1745. At first a festivity organized by a single company in the older North End, home to the shipbuilding trades, only later did it take on its warlike character when South Enders representing a variety of other trades formed their own company.[11]

It was a day when the "rabble" took over the streets. The daytime was for soliciting. Boys of all ages and classes (and some girls) went from house to house demanding money as their right, reciting a rhyme, ringing bells, and threatening broken windows and abuse. The nighttime was for battle. At the end of the workday, artisans and older boys in the two companies rolled out large horse-drawn wagons fitted as a stage on which larger-than-life effigies acted out the political theater of antipopery. The Devil, portrayed with a grotesque carved mask and a tarred body, poked the Pope, who in turn prod-

The North End's Pope wagon was drawn in 1767, when the slogan of the united companies was "Love and Unity." The figures on the wagon from left to right are "Nancy Dawson," the Pope sitting on his throne, a boy blowing a horn, and the grotesque tarred Devil holding Guy Fawkes's lantern. *From a sketch by Pierre Eugène Du Simitière, Courtesy Library Company of Philadelphia.*

ded the Stuart Pretender. Small boys manipulated the giant figures from below. The effigies varied, sometimes including a detested British public figure. Boys, dressed as grenadier soldiers with conical caps or as gentlemen in long coats sporting canes, beat drums or blew horns and conch shells. Each wagon and its display was commonly called a "Pope."[12] At dusk, at the command of their captains bellowing through speaking trumpets, the two companies, each with perhaps seventy-five to one hundred men and older boys, advanced on each other. When they met, a brawl ensued in which each tried to capture the other's effigies, the victor taking the loser's to a high hill, where they were ceremoniously burned in a giant bonfire. Spectators by the thousands cheered on the nighttime warriors.

A ritual of reversal, both class and generational, Pope's Day was a day of comic mocking of authority, even while an official holiday. It was a time when the genteel felt threatened by violence, ear-splitting noise, and licentiousness. There was bawdy play on the stages as young males cross-dressed as "Nancy Dawson" (a London actress of legendary fame and uncertain morals) or as "Pope Joan" (the apocryphal female pope). "Imps," boys in tarred trousers, caressed the effigy of the Devil. Moreover, the nighttime battles were a threat to life and limb.

In 1765 popular resistance to the Stamp Act was structured around the leadership, constituency, and symbolism of Pope's Day. On August 14 members of the two companies were active in every stage of the action and led the attack on Oliver's office and house. The beheading and burning of Oliver's effigy in a bonfire duplicated the public execution at the end of Pope's Day. Clearly the companies had provided organizational experience for Hutchinson's "rabble," who had no other associations in Boston they could call their own. At other public ceremonies the "rabble" were no more than spectators. For Pope's Day they elected officers, who each year had to assign tasks and hold councils of war to map strategy. It was a training ground for direct action and violence. And Ebenezer Mackintosh, notwithstanding his slight size, had qualities of a successful street leader. Hutchinson called him "bold," Peter Oliver described him as "manly and sensible," and John Rowe, a leading merchant and himself a fire warden, praised the members of Mackintosh's Engine Company No. 9 for their "dexterity and clever behaviour."[13]

For good reason, ministers and magistrates were ambivalent about the day. On the one hand, as the Massachusetts riot law put it so emphatically, the day encouraged a "mobbish temper" and "opposition to all government and order." On the other hand, it celebrated the core of the Puritan tradition of anti-Stuart and antipopery sentiment. Typically, when "a gentleman of character" scolded sailors and Negroes for their riotous behavior on the day, it was because it was no way for "a Protestant mob" to behave. It epitomized the threat of "popery," which by the mid-eighteenth century was far more political than religious, a fear less of Catholicism than of Britain's enemies, the Catholic countries, France in particular. The Boston establishment, unwilling and unable to suppress the day, could do no more than regulate its excesses.[14]

Early in 1765 the Pope's Day constituency faced a crisis. On November 5, 1764, the wheel of the North End stage ran over an eight-year-old boy, killing him instantly. Authorities succeeded in halting the event and dismantling both stages, but the South Enders led by Mackintosh recovered and brazenly resumed the fray, capturing the North End Pope in their first victory in memory. The North End captain, Henry Swift, a shipwright, was knocked unconscious for days. In March 1765 a grand jury handed down indictments of Mackintosh, Swift, and a score of others after Thomas Hutchinson (in his capacity as chief justice of the province) lectured them as a "lawless mob" responsible for a "notorious riot." All were identified by their trades, some as apprentices, one as a laborer, and one as a mulatto servant. The charge was "riotous assembly." They were arraigned and freed, each having been required to post a hefty cash bond. Through the spring and summer the threat of a trial hung over them. Thus there was an awareness, low as well as on high, of an acute need to bring the day under control.[15]

In April 1765, with Pope's Day members unsure of their fate, news of the Stamp Act arrived in Boston, a measure with an unusual capacity to excite opposition among all classes. It was an act of taxation by a Parliament in violation of a long-standing tradition of the colonists taxing themselves through their own elected representatives in their assemblies. Its impact was broad. A stamp had to be affixed to (or an official image embossed on) all legal documents, among them ship clearances, liquor licenses, and apprentices' indentures, as well as on all printed matter, including newspapers and playing cards. Amid hard times, it was not far-fetched to charge that the act would "strip multitudes of the poorer people of their property and Reduce them to absolute beggary," as did the lawyer John Adams in a resolution for his town of Braintree, later adopted by some forty towns. The slogan "Liberty and Property, No Stamps" struck a chord with the propertyless as well as the propertied.[16]

Boston's five major organized protests of 1765 against the Stamp Act—August 14 and 26, November 1 and 5, and December 17—were based on different kinds of partnerships among Hutchinson's three branches: rabble, artisans, and merchants. The first and fifth events were initiated by the Loyal Nine, a small group of "superior" artisans, some in the luxury trades, and lesser merchants who met socially and discussed politics in the distillery of a member in the South End near the Great Elm. They had the social connections to reach out to more wealthy merchants and town leaders but not to those below them. Thanks to an indiscreet letter by Henry Bass, we know that the Loyal Nine arranged the formal public resignation of Andrew Oliver as Stamp Act distributor on December 17. The "whole affair" was "transacted by" the group, Bass wrote, as was the "first affair," on August 14. They were pleased, however, that Ebenezer Mackintosh "has the credit of the whole affair," thus masking their responsibility for both events. Bass revealed the steps the group took in managing the December confrontation. They composed the letter to Oliver insisting on a public resignation, printed broadsides summoning people to the event at Liberty Tree, and arranged to have them "pasted up to the amount of one hundred the night before between 9:00 o'clock and 3.00 a.m."[17]

While Peter Oliver's malicious claim—that the leaders "hired a shoemaker"—is simplistic, there is evidence that patriot organizers wielded both a carrot and a club with Mackintosh. The chairman of the Loyal Nine and other members posted bond for at least two apprentices indicted for the 1764 riot. In mid-March 1765 the town meeting, whose appointments were vetted by a political caucus in which Samuel Adams was a member, voted Mackintosh as one of four sealers of leather, a minor office for inspecting the quality of leather—another carrot. In July Adams, who until the year before had been one of the town's four tax collectors and still had responsibility for a huge backlog of uncollected taxes, got a court order serving Mackintosh and Benjamin Bass with a warrant for unpaid taxes of £10.12. It was an unusual action given Adams's customary leniency to tax delinquents. Here was the club. The sheriff served the warrant on August 12, two days before the scheduled August 14 day of protest, but later returned it, marking the document unserved, suggesting that Adams withdrew it, in effect turning a club into a carrot.[18]

The Pope's Day rank and file had their own incentives to join a protest. They wanted to avoid a prosecution in which Hutchinson was their vociferous enemy. Their liberty, personal as well as political, was at stake. Meetings must have occurred between leaders of the companies and between them and delegates from the Loyal Nine to plan the action for August 14: the effigies to be hung, the route of the march, and ways to dramatize the impact of the Stamp Act. After all, the companies, not the Loyal Nine or Adams's political caucus, had experience with street theater. If Mackintosh, as the governor claimed, was "visibly under the command of Persons much his Superior" on August 14, he very likely was carrying out plans he helped to draw up.

On August 26 he may have been acting at the request of still others. Who was responsible for the wild violence that night remains something of a mystery to this day. The private residences of three public officials were targeted: Lieutenant Governor Hutchinson, the registrar of the Court of Vice-Admiralty (the court designated for the trial of violators of the Stamp Act), and the comptroller of customs, associated with new customs laws, another object of merchant anger. The event began at dusk with a bonfire set in a street by boys and an Indian war whoop and whistle, common signals to call a mob. Several hundred men responded, some with blackened faces; hundreds more were spectators. At the first two houses, after destroying glass windows and furniture, the crowd carried the records of the Vice-Admiralty Court to the bonfire. At Hutchinson's mansion a small group hacked away with axes and clubs through the night, destroying whatever they could, leaving the house an empty wreck and scattering his private manuscripts and official papers in the streets. They did more, said Hutchinson, "than was ever done to save a house from fire," a comment suggesting he associated the rioters with fire companies. Uncommon for the Revolutionary Era, the crowd looted, carrying off a fortune in money, silver plate, and other valuables. They were a "rage intoxicated rabble," Josiah Quincy Jr., a young patriot lawyer, wrote.[19]

What accounted for the rage? Governor Francis Bernard was acutely aware of "popular resentments," and Hutchinson of "private resentments" that made him "politically obnoxious." He was blamed (wrongly) for promoting the Stamp Act and was assumed to be in collaboration with Andrew Oliver, his in-law. For years he had been a target of popular hatred as a proponent of abolishing the town meeting and as an opponent of the land bank, both favored by the "popular" party. The intermarried Hutchinson-Oliver families held a near monopoly of high provincial offices. "Private resentments," Hutchinson was convinced, were harbored by a handful of merchants who wanted to destroy "valuable papers of a public kind" that either incriminated them as smugglers (clearly an objective in burning the Vice-Admiralty Court papers) or supported the claims of their rivals to land grants in Maine (records that could have been housed at Hutchinson's). Mackintosh was jailed the next day, but let go by the sheriff after a leading citizen told him that if Mackintosh were not freed, no one would patrol the streets to keep order. Hutchinson was furious because he had been counting on the shoemaker to implicate the higher-ups he assumed had instigated the action.[20]

Underlying the rage of rank-and-file rioters were long-standing class resentments that they vented on a luxuriously furnished mansion owned by an arrogant official who was a symbol of imperial policy. The day after the action, Governor Bernard heard that fifteen more houses "of the most respectable persons" had been targeted. He panicked: "it was now becoming a War of Plunder, of general leveling & taking away the distinction of rich and poor." Two weeks later he feared that if merchants adopted the tactic of halting trade to repeal the Stamp Act and unemployment ensued, "necessity will soon oblige and justify an insurrection of the poor against the rich, those who want the necessities of life against those who have them." Neither additional house attacks nor insurrection materialized, but such class fears hovered over the wealthy for a decade.[21]

Almost immediately the official town meeting disavowed the house assaults as the work of "a lawless unknown rabble." Over the next two months the Loyal Nine and leading merchants went into action to regain control of events. Early in September the Loyal Nine christened the Great Elm as the Tree of Liberty and took charge of the site, taking down effigies they had not authorized. They began calling themselves the Sons of Liberty. The title attached to Mackintosh, "Captain General of the Liberty Tree," burlesqued the full title of the royal governor. In time the name "Sons of Liberty" was used in Boston to refer to the patriot movement as a whole. Every August 14 for years thereafter the Sons would sponsor an elegant dinner in a suburban tavern celebrating their victory over the Stamp Act as the fruit of the allegedly peaceful action of August 14, disavowing the destructive violence of August 26.[22]

In late October leading merchants entered into a visible public collaboration with the Pope's Day leaders. With the Stamp Act officially scheduled to go into effect on November 1 and Pope's Day on its heels, two merchants whom the governor called "the richest men in town" (one of whom was John Hancock and the other very likely John Rowe) invited gentlemen to entertain the Pope's Day officers at a popular tavern. Some two hundred in all attended, Hancock and his co-sponsor flanking Mackintosh and Swift at the head table. Hancock very likely announced that he would foot the bill for uniforms to clothe the officers in style in November. The officers in turn would have renewed their pledge of unity with each other and with the patriot cause that they had made the night of August 14 with Andrew Oliver's liquor.[23]

The result of this alliance was in full display on November 1, a day the whole town observed with a mock funeral. A melancholy blast from a conch shell (called the "Pope horn") and "a funereal tolling of bells" began a well-orchestrated day of mourning for the goddess Liberty. Shops were shut, and ships in the harbor lowered their flags to half-mast. A "vast concourse of people" gathered at the Liberty Tree, "some with weeds in their hats" (the mourners' symbol), others "with downcast eyes." Grenville's effigy was now joined by one of John Huske, a former Bostonian detested for his part in Parliament passing the Stamp Act. At three o'clock organizers cut down the effigies and placed them in a cart. Several thousand people "of all ranks" followed in "regular ranks." The marchers included the Pope's Day companies and members of the militia, with four columns of men on horseback bringing up the rear. They paraded to the center of town, then to the North End and back through the South End to the town gallows, at the far end of town, where the organizers hung the effigies. When they took them down, the crowd "tore them to pieces . . . flinging their limbs with indignation into the air." An order to disperse was given, which was "punctually performed." In the evening all Boston was quiet.[24]

It was Ebenezer Mackintosh's day, bedecked by Hancock's largesse. In the solemn march William Brattle, the official commander of the militia, walked literally arm in arm with the shoemaker, lending him legitimacy. The governor reported he was "dresst in blue & red, in a gold lace Hat & and a gilt gorget on his breast, with a Rattan Cane hanging at his wrist & a speaking Trumpet in his hand to proclaim his orders." Fifteen years later the Loyalist Peter Oliver, writing his history in exile in England, remembered the day vividly. Mackintosh "dressed genteely & in Order to convince the publick of that Power which he was invested he paraded the town with a mob of 2000 men in two files." Oliver was still amazed at the response to Mackintosh's orders. "If a Whisper was heard among his followers, the holding up of his Finger hushed it in a moment and when he had full displayed his authority, he marched his men to the first Rendezvous, & ordered them to retire peaceably to their several homes; & was punctually obeyed."[25]

On November 5 the two companies celebrated Pope's Day as a peaceful political festival with the slogan "Union and No Stamps," portrayals of "Stamp Men" joining the Pope and Devil on the wagons. Musicians accompanied the officers in their new uniforms. To further establish their newfound respectability, they issued a warning to Negroes to stay away from the parade. The two "Popes" met ceremoniously in the center of town, then formed a peaceful caravan to the Liberty Tree, where refreshments were served. At six o'clock "several thousand" joined the companies, marching in rank to Fort Hill, where the pageantry was thrown into the customary bonfire. Once again the huge crowd dispersed without incident. Merchants were so overjoyed with the two events that they emptied their purses to sponsor another joint celebration with the Pope's Day marchers a week later. This time printed tickets set up five ranks of diners with separate rooms for each.

An alliance of classes did not mean that the genteel had to surrender class distinctions.[26]

It is not hard to see why Mackintosh frightened the ruling elite. The mobs stampeding through the mansions of the rich had shaken them with tremors of class war, but the marchers on November 1 and 5 were anything but a "mob." Mackintosh, the governor believed, "has under him 100 or 150 men trained as regular as a military corps." If so, and if two thousand and more marched, this corps would have been less than 10 percent of the total. What was alarming was that the marchers as a whole showed such discipline and were willing to take orders from a shoemaker. Worse yet, the lofty Liberty Tree rapidly became a site of popular justice, usurping the judicial function of government. In February 1766 Liberty Hall, the name adopted for the space beneath its wide-spreading branches, was the scene of a mock trial, attended, it was said, by several thousand who pronounced the Stamp Act guilty of violating the Magna Carta. Towering above the tree was a liberty pole on which a flag could be hoisted to summon Bostonians to a meeting. Within months the tree became a symbol of the cause.[27]

To the Crown-appointed officials, Mackintosh conjured up the terrifying image of Masaniello, the name given Tommaso Aniello, the fisherman who led a bloody proletarian uprising in Naples in 1649. Hutchinson thought the shoemaker "as likely for a Masaniello as you can well conceive." The parallels were remarkable. In Naples the target was also imperial rule (Spain); the provocation was also a tax (on fruit); and the leader had also played a part in the mock battles at the annual ritual celebration of the city's victory over the Turks. Masaniello was also elected "captain general" of his city. Most terrifying, in his nine days of rule, he allegedly executed some 250 enemies before he himself was assassinated. The shoemaker even resembled the fisherman, both of them slight men.[28]

Patriot leaders shared this fear, albeit with less hysteria. John Adams passed on questions from Rhode Island bigwigs who were "very inquisitive about McIntosh. Whether he was a man of Abilities or not? Whether he would probably rise, in Case the Contest [with Britain] should be carried through to any length." Bostonians asked the same questions. After all, no less a Whig authority than "the great Mr. Locke" had warned of the danger of a Masaniello. The name entered the popular political vocabulary, so much so that in 1776 Thomas Paine could warn that unless the colonists set up their own government, "some Masanello [sic]" may "collect together the desperate and the discontented" and "sweep away the liberties of the continent like a deluge."[29]

The fears of the Sons of Liberty are implicit in their efforts in 1765 to co-opt Mackintosh. In 1767–68 when they renewed the conflict with Britain by organizing boycotts against importers of British goods, they seem to have shunted him aside. Now when they wanted to stage some street theater, they commonly turned to one of their own circle, such as Dr. Thomas Young or William Molineux, a lesser merchant. Young, a country doctor new to Boston whose radicalism grew out of his deism and experience in the class wars of tenants and "manor lords" in the Hudson Valley, had skills Mackintosh lacked. He could write articles for Boston's new patriot paper, *The Massachusetts Spy,* and letters to other towns as a member of the Committee of Correspondence, and he could persuade artisans by his oratory in town meetings.[30]

What Mackintosh did politically between 1766 and 1774 is full of uncertainties. He may have had a hand in managing the now-harmonious Pope's Day observances. The truce between the two companies launched in 1765 held until 1773. In 1774, with British troops occupying the city and rumors of the old enmity in the air, patriot leaders fearful of a bloody clash managed to tame the festivity once again. It was to be the last held in Boston. Mackintosh was not reported at major patriot events, possibly fearful of prosecution for the house assaults of 1765. In 1769 an informer claimed that Mackintosh had attended meetings of the Sons of Liberty and "had already been threatened with death" by them in case he revealed their secrets. But he hardly needed such a threat to stay mum since there is no sign that he ever deserted the cause. In 1766 he married Elizabeth Maverick at a ceremony performed by the Reverend Andrew Eliot, conservative minister of the New North Congregational Church. A year later they baptized a daughter Elizabeth, and in 1769 they named a son Pascal Paoli after the leader of Corsica's fight for freedom from rule by Genoa. Paoli was frequently toasted by the Boston Sons of Liberty. William Molineux was called "Paoli Molineux," and John Hancock named a brig *Paoli.* The Corsican general was a conservative liberator. Thus, in naming his son after him, Mackintosh was giving notice that he had no intention of becoming a Masaniello.[31]

Mackintosh may have fallen out with patriot leaders. From 1766 through 1768 the town meeting continued to appoint him sealer of leather but did not in 1769. In 1770 they appointed Benjamin Bass, his erstwhile partner, to the post. About this time there were several lawsuits against Mackintosh, most likely by people distressed by his decisions as a certifier of leather. In July 1770 he was listed on a roll of twenty or so in Boston's debtors' prison, "a most shocking loathsome place," in Hutchinson's opinion.[32] Who came to his aid we do not know. But Peter Oliver's gloss on Mackintosh's woes is naturally suspect. Mackintosh, he wrote, "by neglecting his Business . . . was reduced to part with his last & all [awl], took to hard drinking, was thrown into Jail & died." The shoemaker did not die in prison. He left Boston with his tools in 1774 and by September had resumed his trade in Haverhill, New Hampshire, where he lived until 1816. Yet Oliver's malicious final comment resonated with backhanded praise for Mackintosh's integrity. When he pleaded with his "rich employers for 2 or 3 Dollars to relieve his distress," Oliver claimed, "he was refused the small Pittance because at that Time they had no further Service for him & had he not possessed a soul endowed with superior Honor to any of his Employers, he would have brought several of them to the Gallows."[33]

If Mackintosh was neither present nor visible at major public events after 1765, his Pope's Day constituency had become a distinct presence. The "Boston Massacre" of March 5, 1770, was a chaotic unplanned event at which British soldiers fired into a crowd, killing five working-class Bostonians (among them Samuel Maverick, Mackintosh's brother-in-law, a seventeen-year-old apprentice to an ivory turner). At the trial of the soldiers, their lawyer, John Adams, characterized the "mob" that had taunted them as a "Motley rabble of saucy boys, negroes and molottoes, Irish Teagues, and outlandish Jack tars"—a description that could have easily applied to Pope's Day activists. So too could Thomas Hutchinson's description of a "tea party" meeting in November 1773 at which leaders let down the property bars that restricted attendance at official town meetings, jamming Old South Meeting House to the rafters. The audience, he wrote, was composed principally of "the lower Ranks of the People & even Journeymen Tradesmen . . . & the Rabble were not excluded."[34]

As to the men who boarded the three ships and destroyed the tea, Mackintosh in his old age boasted to a boy of ten that "it was my chickens that did the job." It was a reasonable claim, given the number of apprentices, former apprentices, and established artisans identified at the event. The other claim for his presence came from an old Bostonian who in 1835 compiled the first list of participants and put down "——— Mcintosh" (with a blank instead of a first name). This more than likely was Ebenezer.[35]

In actuality, the laboring men in Boston's many spur-of-the-moment crowds after 1765 did not need Mackintosh. In 1768 a waterfront riot of several thousand against an attempt at impressment into the British navy, which took place in the evening "when the lower class of people were returning from work," was led from within by unknown individuals. So too were the several tar-and-featherings aimed at customs officials with whom seamen had their own grievances. Indeed, "the only clue" the historian Peter Oliver could find as to "the Origin of this Invention" was the tarred Pope and Devil in the "pageant" every November 5. He was observant.[36]

However active or inactive he may have been after 1766, Mackintosh's reputation as a leader persisted. In 1770 a Loyalist merchant reported that "McIntosh, [James] Otis & [Samuel] Adams are our demagogues." In April 1774 a patriot paper printed a rumor from Britain that "a sloop of war" on the high seas would seize and return four Bostonians—Samuel Adams, John Hancock, John Rowe, and Ebenezer Mackintosh—explaining that "the latter has been very active among the lower order of people, and the other [three] among the higher." Later in the year an unnamed Boston letter writer told a British correspondent that "a Scotch shoemaker was the leader of all our mobs during the time of the Stamp Act and has ever since continued a leading man among us." *"Very active among the lower order of people"* may be as good a contemporary summary of Mackintosh's political role in Boston as we are likely to find.[37]

With troops on the way, Mackintosh had cause to take the British threat seriously. He fled the city, probably early in 1774, by lore walking to Haverhill, New Hampshire, in the Connecticut River valley (more than 150 miles), with his two children, Elizabeth, aged seven, and Pascal, aged five. (His wife had died of a prolonged illness.) He served two short military stints in the Revolutionary War and in 1784 married a widow with three children, who bore two more sons. He lived out his life as a shoemaker and, occasionally, the village sealer of leather, and as far as the record shows, he remained poor and landless. With his children scattered, he died in the local poor farm, aged seventy-nine, and was buried in the North Haverhill cemetery. The grave marker is since lost.[38]

In the twentieth century, a state roadside marker near the cemetery recognized Mackintosh as "a known participant in the Boston Tea Party" and as "a soldier." "He was a shoemaker by trade and practiced his vocation here for the rest of his life"—the only historical marker in the United States honoring a shoemaker for his services in the American Revolution.

❧

Historians weighing the sources of the American Revolution have rarely found a place for Ebenezer Mackintosh. But he had a measurable impact. He helped make political action by "leather apron" men acceptable and by shoemakers in particular. The "gentry" often singled them out for derision, invoking the proverb "Shoemaker, stick to thy last." A patriot aristocrat in Charleston offered the condescending rationale: men who knew little more than "to cobble an old shoe in a decent manner or to build a necessary house" lacked the education or leisure to participate in government.[39]

Not so Boston's patriot leaders. In 1772 "Crispin"—the name of the patron saint of shoemakers—began an anti-Loyalist article in the *The Massachusetts Spy* (a paper aimed at working people) by avowing, "I am a shoemaker, a citizen, a free man and a freeholder." The printer Isaiah Thomas added a postscript justifying "Crispin's" performance: "it should be known what common people, even *coblers* think and feel under the present administration." The rise to active citizenship by mechanics was also the theme of another Boston shoemaker, George Robert Twelves Hewes, whose memoirs recounted one episode after another in which he cast off deference to his betters. "We are all from the cobbler up to the senator become politicians," a Bostonian could claim in 1774.[40]

Mackintosh also influenced the leaders who emerged in the Stamp Act crisis, more perhaps than they could afford to say. It was a time when John Adams, Samuel Adams, and John Hancock, the three men who became Massachusetts's principal figures in the Revolution, learned different strategies for accommodating "the people out of doors" who were challenging those "within doors" with power in legislative chambers. "The year," John Adams confided to his diary at the end of 1765, "has been the most remarkable year of my Life." He was moved that "the People, even to the lowest ranks have become more attentive to their Liberties"—but he was also furious at the threats to individuals and property, and he undertook a lifelong commitment to maintain a due sense of "rank and subordination" in "the lowest ranks." For Samuel Adams, 1765 was the year he learned the importance of associations, committees, and the town meeting as a means of organizing ordinary people. John Hancock—twenty-seven, newly rich, and new to politics—learned in 1765 how he might use his fortune to advance both a cause and himself. His entertaining and outfitting Pope's Day officers while displaying all the trappings of great wealth began a style of patrician patronage that over time would make him the most popular politician in Massachusetts. He also discovered how crucial it was to keep the allegiance of his fellow merchants in the patriot coalition. In the final crisis, in 1775–76, a large proportion of the town's merchants and most of its men of greatest wealth would favor independence. This presence of merchants in the patriot coalition helps explain why in Boston the class feeling of the poor against the rich was more or less absorbed within the conflict with Britain.[41]

All three leaders subscribed to the strategy expressed by the two rallying cries posted on the Liberty Tree late in 1765: "Vox populi, vox dei" and "Good Order and Steady" (which would reappear later as the slogan "No violence or you will hurt the cause"). The large, more or less peaceful demonstrations Mackintosh led gave them the confidence to claim "The Voice of the People is the Voice of God." At the same time they learned that the mere threat of violence to property and the symbolic violence to people implicit in hanging effigies could effectively intimidate enemies. Mackintosh's success lay in organizing the people "out of doors" to a sense of their potential, drawing on rituals of popular culture familiar to them. The success of the Sons of Liberty leaders lay in bringing such people, newly aroused, literally indoors and into a political system that would be enlarged by their presence. The Revolution in Boston owes much to both.

FOR FURTHER READING

Most of the known details about Ebenezer Mackintosh's life are in George P. Anderson, "Ebenezer Macintosh: Stamp Act Rioter and Patriot" and "A Note on Ebenezer Macintosh," in Colonial Society of Massachusetts *Publications* (1924–26): 15–64, 348–61. A short summary of his career is in William Pencak, "Ebenezer Mackintosh," in *American National Biography* (New York, 1999), 14:261–62. Two of my articles provide a context for Mackintosh: "Liberty Tree: Made in America, Lost in America" and "The Mechanics of the Revolution: 'By Hammer and Hand All Arts do Stand,' " in Alfred F. Young, *Liberty Tree: Ordinary People and the American Revolution* (New York, 2006), 325–94, 28–99. My book *The Shoemaker and the Tea Party: Memory and the American Revolution* (Boston, 1999) follows another Boston shoemaker, George Robert Twelves Hewes, through the Revolution.

For Pope's Day, the fullest descriptions are in reminiscences by contemporaries: Isaiah Thomas, *Three Autobiographical Fragments* (Worcester, Mass., 1962), and articles in the (Boston) *Daily Advertiser*, November 5, 8, 9, 1821, and (Boston) *Columbian Centinel*, November 10, 1821. The best visualization is in J. L. Bell, "Notes and Comments: Du Simitiere's Sketches of Pope's Day in Boston, 1767," in *The Worlds of Children, 1620–1920, Annual Proceedings of the Dublin Seminar for New England Folklife*, ed. Peter Benes (Boston, 2002), 207–15, and Bell, "The Fifth of November in Boston," a virtual exhibition online at Boston Historical Society, 2009 (http://rfi.bostonhistory.org).

For the politics of the Stamp Act, Edmund S. and Helen M. Morgan, *The Stamp Act Crisis: Prologue to Revolution*, rev. ed. (Chapel Hill, N.C., 1963), remains standard, giving "special attention" to Loyalists as "the sufferers" from patriot resistance. For correctives of scholarship dealing with history "from the bottom up," see Jesse Lemisch, "Jack Tar in the Streets: Merchant Seamen in the Politics of Revolutionary America," *William and Mary Quarterly*, 3rd ser., 25 (July 1968): 371–407, the seminal work; Gary B. Nash, *The Urban Crucible: Social Change, Political Consciousness and the Origins of the American Revolution* (Cambridge, Mass., 1979);

and Benjamin Carp, "Fire of Liberty: Firefighters, Urban Voluntary Culture and the Revolutionary Movement," *William and Mary Quarterly*, 3rd ser., 58 (2001): 781–818. Dirk Hoerder, *Crowd Action in Revolutionary Massachusetts, 1765–1780* (New York, 1977), has the most fully researched descriptions of crowds.

The Loyalist sources, often the only ones for an event, are *Peter Oliver's Origin & Progress of the American Rebellion: A Tory View,* ed. Douglass Adair and John A. Schutz (Stanford, Calif., 1961); Thomas Hutchinson's manuscript letters, Massachusetts Archives and Massachusetts Historical Society, which John W. Tyler is editing for the Colonial Society of Massachusetts; and Francis Bernard, manuscript letters, in Sparks Mss., Letterbooks, Houghton Library, Harvard University.

For help in tracking Mackintosh, I am indebted to J. L. Bell (keeper of the blog at http://boston1775.net), George Quintal, Benjamin Carp, and Walter Wallace. My thanks to Elizabeth Bouvier, Head of Archives, Massachusetts Supreme Judicial Court Archives, for court records, and to John W. Tyler for transcripts of the Hutchinson Papers.

CHAPTER TWO

Blacksmith Timothy Bigelow
and the Massachusetts Revolution of 1774

Ray Raphael

B oston set the pace, we know that. During the Stamp Act crisis, several cities copied Boston's August 14 street theater deed for deed. The Massachusetts "Circular Letter" of 1768, sponsored by Boston Whigs, challenged other colonies to resist Parliament's new round of taxation, the Townshend duties. In 1770, although New York beat Boston to the punch with its (almost forgotten) Battle of Golden Hill, which pitted common citizens against British redcoats, the Bostonians bid them up a few weeks later by dubbing their own battle with redcoats a "massacre." And after Boston activists dumped tea into the harbor on December 16, 1773, patriots in Newport, New York, Philadelphia, and Charleston were able to reject shipments headed to their cities merely by threatening to follow suit.

But in 1774 the people of the Massachusetts countryside, not the instigators in Boston, summarily cast off British rule, the first colonials to do so. Precisely because Bostonians played but a small role in this seminal event, we hear very little about it. How strange that our core national narrative leaves out the initial transfer of political and military authority from British officials to American political activists.

Boston's Whig leadership did help set the stage. In the fall of 1772 the Boston Town Meeting sent a lengthy pamphlet to each and every community in Massachusetts, urging town meetings to create "committees of correspondence" to promote the resistance movement outside the major port cities. Less than two years later these committees, together with the town meetings that sponsored them and the local militia companies that added military might, engineered a revolution unique in its power, breadth, and truly democratic style—so robust a revolution, in fact, that Boston's most famous and effective patriots tried to slow it down.

ᴄᴇ

When Boston's pamphlet arrived in the town of Worcester early in 1773, a revolution of sorts was already in the works. Ever since Worcester, forty-five miles west of Boston, had become the "shiretown" of the newly formed Worcester County in 1731, John Chandler II, followed by his son John Chandler III and grandson John Chandler IV, along with various close relations, had dominated the local political scene by commandeering the lion's share of public offices. In one year alone, the list of positions occupied by four members of the Chandler clan included Massachusetts councilman, town representative to the assembly, chief justice of the court of common pleas, clerk for that court, probate judge, register of probate, register of deeds, assessor, county sheriff, county treasurer, town treasurer, town clerk, moderator of the town meeting, town selectman, and colonel of the county militia. This concentration of power did not sit well with a number of citizens, who in the 1760s mounted an opposition to the Chandlers. During the Stamp Act crisis, the challengers succeeded in electing one of their own as the town's representative to the General Court, and in a written set of instructions, they asked him to push for an end to multiple officeholdings. But current members of the Chandler clan—John Chandler IV and his fifteen adult offspring; John's younger brother Gardiner, the sheriff, with his six offspring; the Chandlers' brother-in-law Timothy Paine, with his ten offspring; the powerful attorney James Putnam, John Adams's mentor, also married to a Chandler—retained most court positions and continued to control patronage. For the next seven years, during an uneasy truce, neither faction moved aggressively to subdue the other. That's where matters stood when the Boston pamphlet arrived, upsetting the delicate balance.[1]

At Worcester's town meeting on Monday, March 1, 1773, after a public reading of Boston's pamphlet, the town chose five men to draft a response: three former selectmen associated with the anti-Chandler wing; Stephen Salisbury, a prominent merchant who was John Chandler's chief economic competitor; and a relative newcomer to politics, thirty-three-year-old blacksmith Timothy Bigelow.[2]

Bigelow had firm roots within his community. His great-grandfather, also a blacksmith, had emigrated from England sometime before 1655 and settled in Watertown, just outside Boston. His grandfather had fought in King Philip's War in 1675, and his father, a cordwainer, had settled in Worcester before it was designated the shiretown and had participated in town affairs.

Timothy too was an active member of the town meeting, having served previously as hog reeve, tithing man, surveyor of highways and collector of highway taxes, and fence viewer. He was reasonably well-off, ranking in the second quarter of assessed valuation on the 1771 Worcester tax rolls, but his assets were dwarfed by those of John Chandler IV, who possessed seven times as much property within Worcester alone and still more in neighboring towns. Bigelow had learned to read and write in the local school and even possessed a small library, but he lacked the high learning of the courthouse crowd, several of whom had been educated at Harvard.[3]

Even so, Bigelow was versed in the politics of the day. In 1762 he had moved into the family home of his wife, across the street from the county courthouse, where he set up his shop. There he shod horses and oxen, mended tools, and fashioned nails for almost everyone in town, certainly farmers but also merchants and tradesmen who tended gardens, raised stock, rode horses, or had any need to melt and shape metal. He came to occupy a central role in the workaday world of Worcester, and he earned his neighbors' trust. They could evaluate the quality of his work and assess his character. They also discussed with him matters of public concern, not only local issues but the looming imperial crisis as well. Certainly they would not have called on this hog reeve and fence viewer to elucidate Worcester's position on controversial issues unless they had already heard him hold forth on these topics with some authority and style. And they would not have been able to load the committee with anti-Chandler men unless a majority were already opposed to British imperial policies and local placemen beholden to the royal governor.

The letter Bigelow and the committee drafted was weak on particulars but strong on basic Whig principles and on words in general—some two thousand of them in scarcely a dozen sentences. More significantly, when the town meeting endorsed the letter, it also appointed Bigelow and two others to serve as a standing committee of correspondence, charged with transmitting "the earliest intelligence to the inhabitants of this Town, of any designs that they shall discover at any time against our natural and constitutional rights." In response, one of the Chandler faction complained that Bigelow and his ilk were "devils" and a "sett of cussed venal worthless raskalls." The dispute over British imperial policies was adding a new and critical dimension to the struggle for local power. Henceforth politics in the provincial town of Worcester would be inalterably linked to tumultuous events that spanned the Atlantic Ocean.[4]

The deepening divisions came to a head the following year, in the aftermath of the Boston Tea Party. On January 3, 1774, thirty-one men from

Worcester, solid members of their community but not the wealthy and well connected, founded the American Political Society (APS), a radical caucus that met in advance of town meetings to plot strategies, determine agendas, and put forward candidates for public office. While the committee of correspondence, as a public body, reported back to the town as a whole, the APS, avowedly partisan from the outset, could do and act as it pleased. Bigelow and two cohorts were charged with drafting a mission statement and a set of rules. The document they created, which other members approved, pledged to oppose "the machinations of some designing persons in this Province, who are grasping at power and the property of their neighbors," to repose "special trust and confidence in every other member of the society," and to limit their liquor expenses to sixpence per man at monthly meetings and two shillings per man at quarterly meetings. These men might drink but not to excess, for they had serious business to transact: deposing "designing persons" like the Chandlers and furthering the province-wide resistance movement. Within a year, membership in the organization would grow to seventy-one, almost one-third of the enfranchised citizens of the town. Since these men could be counted upon to show up at every town meeting, ensuring a majority, the APS became in effect a shadow government.[5]

Through the spring of 1774 the APS battled the Chandler faction for control of the town meeting. Repeatedly, Bigelow and the APS presented radical resolutions and actions that the Chandlers opposed; each time the APS emerged victorious by a narrow margin. We know from the town records and minutes of the APS that Timothy Bigelow had a hand in drafting the winning position statements and resolutions, and we suspect, from oral accounts passed on for generations, that he figured prominently in the debates. According to a nineteenth-century rendition of one meeting, "Timothy Bigelow at length arose, without learning, without practice in public speaking, without wealth—the Tories of Worcester had, at that day, most of the wealth and learning—but there he stood upon the floor of the Old South Church, met the Goliath of the day, and vanquished him."[6]

In June, frustrated by a string of defeats, the "government men" (as they called themselves) or "Tories" (as labeled by their opponents) drafted a dissenting opinion, which the town clerk, Clark Chandler, entered in the official record and published in the Boston press. With a haughty manner that contributed to their own undoing, they groused that uneducated militants like Timothy Bigelow had been "spending their time in discoursing of matters they do not understand" while "neglecting their own proper business and occupation, in which they ought to be employed for the support of their families." The APS agitators were "enemies to our King and Country, violators of all law and civil liberty, the malevolent disturbers of the peace of society, subverters of the established constitution, and enemies of mankind."[7]

Although patriots had confirmed their majority status, the Tories remained firm and unrepentant. The two sides might have continued that way for months or years, tugging over words and resolutions, but suddenly, in an instant, the terms of engagement shifted. To retaliate for the destruction of tea in the Boston Harbor, Parliament revoked the Massachusetts Charter of 1691, the very rules that governed the province. Town meetings, the basis of self-government, could not convene without special consent from the Crown-appointed governor, who had to approve all agenda items. Members of the powerful Council, formerly elected, would now be appointed by the king, while judges, sheriffs, justices of the peace, and grand jurors, previously subject to approval by elected representatives, would be selected by Crown-appointed officials. These oppressive measures irrevocably altered the political landscape in Worcester and throughout the province. Before, government men had presented a cogent, albeit controversial, case for submitting to imperial authority. Now they could not reasonably argue that the people of Massachusetts would be better off without any say in their own government. "Soft" Tories switched sides, giving the men who considered themselves patriots an overwhelming majority. "Hard" Tories were faced with two choices: bow to the powerful and sometimes vengeful will of the majority, or flee their homes as refugees.

With their constitution revoked, radicals in Worcester and throughout the province moved beyond protests to armed resistance. At its July 4 meeting, the American Political Society declared "that each, and every, member of our Society, be forth with provided, with two pounds of gun powder each 12 flints and led answerable thereunto." Timothy Bigelow agreed to provide more than the minimal share and also volunteered to serve on a two-person committee "to equally divide and proportion" the donated powder among all members. For the next two months he turned his workshop into a local armaments factory, mending guns and casting bullets. With an arms race under way, members of the APS somehow managed to smuggle four cannons from under British watch in Boston. Six months later, but still two months before the march on Lexington and Concord, two British spies reported that in Worcester patriots had accumulated fifteen tons of powder, thirteen small cannons (displayed proudly but mounted poorly in front of the meeting-house), and various munitions in the hands of a merchant named Salisbury and "un grand chef" named Bigelow. (The report was written in French.)[8]

The town's militiamen, meanwhile, stepped up their training schedule and elected a new captain, Timothy Bigelow, whom they expected to lead them against British regulars if the town were attacked. It's easy to imagine why they chose him. Bigelow was energetic and committed, strong and tall (six feet, some five inches taller than the average adult male at the time). He was a problem solver, as he proved daily at his forge. He was also able to communicate with townsmen in ways that mattered. Militia days had always been social affairs, but "social," in these trying times, meant political. As they gathered to drill on the town common, and when they regrouped in taverns at day's end, militiamen hashed out the issues and debated how to proceed. Captain Bigelow, no stranger by now to political discourse, would no doubt encourage this process, thereby deepening the commitments of his men.

The American Political Society, now in firm command of the town meeting, escalated the resistance politically as well as militarily. On Thursday, August 18, meeting at a tavern run by the widow Mary Stearns, members instructed Timothy Bigelow, his cousin Joshua Bigelow, and five others to suggest "something that they shall think proper for the town to act upon at our next town meeting." This committee settled on a devilish plan. They would round up the fifty-two Tories who had written the cranky dissent and have them sign a statement admitting they had "given the good people of this Province in general, and the inhabitants of the town of Worcester in particular, just cause to be offended with each of us . . . and we hereby beg their forgiveness, and all others we may have offended." Then, in full public view, they would force each of the miscreants to strike out his signature on the Tory dissent, which Clark Chandler had entered in the town record. The APS had little difficulty implementing this plan: by now, the group was electing the town moderator at its own meetings and even issuing instructions to the town's selectmen. So in the meetinghouse the following Wednesday, one at a time, each of the dissenters stepped forth and drew a line through his signature. Then the town meeting ordered Clark Chandler to "obliterate, erase or otherwise deface the said recorded protest . . . in the presence of the town," first by a scratch of the pen through each and every line, and then, since some words could still be deciphered, by a series of tightly looped spirals. Finally, for full humiliation, they commanded that the clerk for the town of Worcester—John Chandler's son—dip his own fingers into a well of ink and drag them over the first page of the offending document. The original town record book, stored today in the basement of Worcester's City Hall, reveals short, irregular changes of direction in the defacements, indicating that Chandler's hand was forced.[9]

The battle with local Tories was over, but not the larger fight over imperial abuse. To figure out how to wage that war, politically and perhaps militarily, committees of correspondence from twenty-two towns across Worcester

County convened at Stearns's tavern. Their overarching goal was simple but bold: to shut down the government, which had lost all claim to legitimacy because of the Massachusetts Government Act. Their tactics: force all Crown-appointed officials to resign and close the county courts, the farthest outreach of imperial authority, which were slated to convene on September 6.[10]

First up: the three local men whom the king had appointed to serve as provincial councilors. The committees dispatched riders throughout the county, and on Saturday morning, August 27, somewhere between 1,500 and 3,000 men (estimates vary) swarmed into town to confront Councilor Timothy Paine, who had little choice but to comply. The high-flown lawyer who was ranked fifth in his class at Harvard (according to social standing), and who preferred riding in a "handsome green coach, trimmed with gilding and lined with satin," was made to walk the length of the town to the common, where he submitted his resignation before the assembled patriots of Worcester County. Ever since 1765, when Ebenezer Mackintosh led Andrew Oliver to resign his post as Stamp Act commissioner before several thousand people, protesters of the Revolutionary Era had not deemed a resignation complete without public witness and humiliation.

The crowd then ventured to John Murray's residence in nearby Rutland. When Murray's son claimed the councilor was not at home, the crowd aggressively searched his house, and somebody punched a hole through the wig on Murray's portrait. In fact, Murray had already fled to Boston, where he could be protected by British troops. Timothy Ruggles, the final councilor on the list that day, had already been abused several times for his intractable support of imperial policies. He no longer dared show his face at home, and angry patriots tormented him wherever he went. Earlier that week, when he turned up in Dartmouth, his prize English stallion "had his Mane and Tail cut off, and his Body painted all over." If this sounds ugly, it was also restrained. Recalcitrant councilors, like the Tory dissenters in Worcester, were intimidated, not tortured or killed, while those who complied, such as Timothy Paine, were incorporated back into their communities. Almost every document that emerged from the sweeping rebellion included a disavowal of riots and mobs.[11]

Intimidating individual councilmen proved easy enough, but closing the courts was another matter. General Thomas Gage, the new governor and military commander of the province, vowed to draw the line there: "In Worcester, they keep no terms, openly threaten resistance by arms, have been purchasing arms, preparing them, casting ball, and providing powder, and threaten to attack any troops who dare to oppose them," Gage wrote to

Secretary of State Lord Dartmouth. "I apprehend that I shall soon be obliged to march a body of troops into that Township, and perhaps into others, as occasion happens, to preserve the peace."[12]

As soon as Timothy Bigelow and the Worcester County Committees of Correspondence got word that Gage intended to send troops their way, they moved to garner support from outside the town and county. If Worcester patriots stood alone against British regulars, the committee feared, they might well be crushed, but if they gained the assistance of freedom fighters from elsewhere, they could keep the regulars at bay. So they wrote to the Boston Committee of Correspondence, urging a multicounty convention to deal with the developing crisis and impending showdown in Worcester. The Boston Committee consented, and on August 26 representatives from the province's most populous counties—Suffolk (which included Boston), Middlesex, Essex, and Worcester—convened at Faneuil Hall, hallowed meeting place for Boston's patriots over the previous decade. Threatened with attack, Worcester had assumed a leading role in mobilizing and coordinating the resistance.[13]

Representing Worcester at the multicounty meeting were Timothy Bigelow and Ephraim Doolittle, the town's former representative to the assembly, who had moved to Petersham, still within the county. Representing Boston were a host of patriot heavyweights, including Joseph Warren, Benjamin Church, William Molineux, Joseph Greenleaf, and Dr. Thomas Young. (John Adams and Samuel Adams had left to attend the First Continental Congress in Philadelphia.) Although the Worcester pair were clearly outranked, Timothy Bigelow, who had been instrumental in calling the meeting, was honored with a position on the five-man committee charged with drafting resolutions. Eighteen months earlier Bigelow's highest political position had been that of fence viewer; now he was hobnobbing with Boston's most influential Whigs and preparing a document for them to adopt.

The document that the committee created, and the convention approved, urged each county to shut down its courts: "Every officer belonging to the courts" who acted under the authority of the Massachusetts Government Act was to be considered "a traitor cloaked with the pretext of law," and they "ought to be held in the highest detestations by the people, as common plunderers." Knowing the British would not sit idly by, the authors then advised all patriots to learn "the military art . . . as necessary means to secure their liberties against the designs of enemies whether foreign or domestick." Finally, they called for a special provincial congress, to meet the first week of October, to provide some sense of order for the escalating opposition to the Massachusetts Government Act.[14]

Bigelow quickly returned home to report the results of the multicounty convention and mobilize resistance at the local level. On August 30, one week before the courts were slated to convene, Bigelow and the Worcester County Committees of Correspondence held another convention in Mary Stearns's tavern—or at least they tried to, but they couldn't comfortably fit. Immediately after their opening prayer, the 130 delegates resolved "by reason of the straitness of the place, and the many attending, to adjourn to the county court house." The seat of government, they assumed, was already theirs for the taking. Once reconvened, delegates declared "that it is the indispensable duty of the inhabitants of this county, by the best ways and means, to prevent the sitting of the respective courts." Then, since Gage seemed likely to send his troops, they suggested that the citizenry of the county should arm and show up in Worcester, ready to fight.[15]

But would General Gage make good on his pledge to protect the courts? On August 31, six days before the anticipated showdown, Tory councilors who had retreated from outlying regions to Boston, and who had experienced firsthand the power and fury of the people, told Gage, "It would not be for His Majesty's service to send any Troops into the interior parts of the province." This warning caused Gage to waver.

Two days later, on September 2, an unprecedented torrent of patriots forced his decision. Four thousand "Freeholders and Farmers of the Country" (Gage's phrase) met on the Cambridge Common to protest the recent seizure of gunpowder by British troops and force two more councilors to resign. Six of Boston's Whig leaders, hoping to avoid a premature confrontation, scurried to Cambridge to control the crowd, only to find that the crowd was controlling itself well enough without them. Country leaders rejected the Bostonians' invitation to retreat to a nearby tavern to strategize; braving "the scorching sun of the hottest day we have had this summer," they stayed outside with their people. Meanwhile, tens of thousands of additional patriots, spurred by a false rumor that British regulars had killed six men and burned down the city, were on the march toward Boston. (Contemporary estimates for participants in the "Powder Alarm," as it was called, ranged from 20,000 to 100,000.) That settled the matter: Gage would not dispatch his troops. "The flames of sedition," he conceded that day to Secretary of State Lord Dartmouth, had "spread universally throughout the country beyond conception."[16]

Once Gage pulled back, all power defaulted to the patriots. Without opposition, they would close the courts and shut down the government— but how would they dramatize this momentous occurrence?

Before dawn on September 6, local activists entered the courthouse and boarded the doors to prevent officials from entering. Then, with the break of day and through the morning, militiamen "with staves and fife" marched into town with great fanfare. The previous day, having gleaned intelligence that no British regulars were on the move from Boston, the APS "voted, not to bring our fire-arms into town the 6 day of Sept." So the mood was festive, not anxious.[17]

Breck Parkman, one of the participants, recorded the turnout in each company: 45 men from Winchendon on the New Hampshire border, 156 from Uxbridge on the Connecticut line, and so on, a total of 4,622 citizen-soldiers from thirty-seven distinct townships. Yes, the revolution had truly spread "beyond conception." Half the adult males of a rural county, many walking and riding through the night, showed up at one place and time to shut down a government they regarded as oppressive.[18]

The first militia companies to arrive went straight to the common, just as they would muster in their hometowns. But the common proved too small a venue for the largest gathering ever to assemble in Worcester, so by midmorning, companies started marching north along Main Street to an open expanse behind Stephen Salisbury's store, catercorner to the courthouse and proximate to the committees of correspondence from each town that were meeting inside Timothy Bigelow's house to coordinate the event.

Soon Bigelow and the committeemen moved their proceedings outside "to attend the body of the people," the only legitimate source of authority. Here in the countryside, though, the "body of the people" was a composite, broken into thirty-seven discrete units, each its own master, and this complicated the proceedings. Each company had to elect a special representative (distinct from the military captain it had already elected) "to wait on the judges," who huddled inside Daniel Heywood's tavern, halfway between the courthouse and the meetinghouse, wondering what the militiamen would force them to do. This ad hoc committee met with the court officials to hammer out a formal recantation, which Breck Parkman characterized as "a paper . . . signifying that they would endeavor &c"—that's all Parkman noted about the document, which he seemed to regard as no more than an empty promise. The draft was then taken back to the separate companies for their approval—or disapproval, as it turned out. The judges' statement, in Parkman's words, "was not satisfying." The people, like Parkman, were not content with a promise of good faith, so they sent their representatives back into Heywood's tavern with instructions to prepare a stronger document. The process was democratic but cumbersome, and when some militiamen evidenced impatience, the committees of correspondence appointed three men to inquire about the delay.[19]

Finally, by midafternoon, the stage was set. The militiamen arranged themselves along Main Street, half on the Mill Brook side and the other half under the embankment to the west. The lines stretched for a quarter mile between the courthouse and Heywood's tavern, each company in formation, Uxbridge in front of the courthouse, Westborough next, and so on, down to Upton and Templeton, stationed outside Heywood's tavern. When all were in place, each of the two dozen court officials emerged from the tavern with his hat in his hand, reversing the traditional order of deference. Each recited his disavowal of British authority to the first company of militiamen, then walked to the next and repeated his recantation there, and in this manner made his way slowly through the gauntlet, all the way to the courthouse. Over thirty times apiece, so all the militiamen could hear, the judges, justices of the peace, court attorneys, and others whose power had been sanctioned by the Crown pledged "that all judicial proceeding be stayed . . . on account of the unconstitutional act of Parliament . . . which, if effected, will reduce the inhabitants to mere arbitrary power."[20]

That should have sufficed, but it did not: the militiamen then demanded that those who had signed the Tory dissent back in June, and inked through their signatures to that document in August, walk through the lines as well, reciting their own recantations. As Tories made their way meekly through the ranks, delivering their lines again and again, militiamen fumed but kept good order. High Sheriff Gardiner Chandler, John's brother, required an extra guard of four men to ensure he would not be abused. Years later, exiled in England, a bitter John Chandler IV complained to the British government:

> In September A.D. 1774 a mob of several thousands of Armed People drawn from the neighboring Towns assembled at Worcester for the purpose of Stopping the Courts of Justice then to be held there which having accomplished they seized your memorialist who in order to save himself from immediate death was obliged to renounce the aforesaid Protest and Subscribe to a very Treasonable League and Covenant.[21]

With this humiliating submission, all British authority, both political and military, as well as the power of the Chandler faction, disappeared forever from Worcester County.

ﭻ

Key to this revolutionary upheaval was an infrastructure for political action peculiar to the countryside, including town meetings, committees of correspondence, political caucuses, militia companies, and taverns.

At town meetings, enfranchised citizens (approximately 90 percent of adult males) came together several times a year to govern themselves in local matters. (Estates and widows with property also had the franchise.) There, following a tradition dating back well over a century, communities had discussed how to keep hogs from overtaking the streets, which fences needed fixing, and how to ensure tithing and collect taxes. Citizens knew how to work together to promote the public good; now, although their decisions had greater consequences, they were not starting from scratch.[22]

Committees of correspondence gave political activists like Timothy Bigelow an official standing within the town meeting structure, while private groups like the American Political Society, unfettered by any need to include or placate Tories, pushed the most radical agendas. These organizations, more focused than the town meeting, could plot, strategize, and in the end mobilize a wider base. With the termination of British rule, the committees of correspondence filled the governmental vacuum, performing for a brief time the ad hoc administration of public affairs.

Militia companies provided a military heft that political activists in Boston lacked. Militia training during this moment of crisis was politically empowering, with the men, not their officers, making key decisions. Two weeks after the closing of the courts in Worcester, a county convention of the committees of correspondence suggested that each town enlist one-third of its men between sixteen and sixty "to be ready to act at a minute's warning." That's when the Minutemen were born. The convention also recommended that the militia for Worcester County be reorganized into seven regiments, that the company for each town choose its officers, and that these company officers come together to choose field officers to command the newly formed regiments. This was to be a thoroughly democratic army of citizens, from bottom to top, with each company functioning as a mobile town meeting.[23]

Most frequently, at informal gatherings in taverns, hardworking men shed traditional constraints while downing a mug of hard cider or a shot of grain whiskey. In Boston or other cities, citizens might meet and talk at the marketplace or some other central venue, but country folk had no public place to come together on a daily basis. There was a tavern for every forty to fifty adult males in Worcester County, and these served as important venues for discourse on public affairs.[24]

And in Worcester men also gathered at Timothy Bigelow's house and shop. In his front room, Bigelow hosted meetings of the town's committee of correspondence, the American Political Society, and even the county convention of committees of correspondence. In his basement, he would soon house Isaiah Thomas's printing press (the official press for the Revolutionary provincial congress), which he helped smuggle from Boston two nights before British regulars marched on Lexington and Concord. At his shop, while Bigelow toiled, neighbors informally talked and schemed. Strategically located near the courthouse, Bigelow provided a physical address for the Revolution-in-the-making, an actual place where people could come to spread or receive information and ideas.[25]

In other towns as well, we might conjecture, blacksmith shops functioned as hubs for Revolutionary activity. In the early stages, they served as venues for debates and communications; by the late summer of 1774, when armed conflict appeared imminent, their forges assumed additional importance. Every active patriot with a firearm cleaned his musket, checked his flintlock, and rolled cartridges. Some needed their guns repaired; all needed to mold shot. For blacksmiths like Bigelow, the workday came to be dominated by preparations for war, and it is no coincidence that blacksmiths participated in the resistance with extra verve.

Timothy Bigelow certainly understood the pivotal role that blacksmiths could and did play. Two days after the September 6 court closure, while men from across the county still lingered in town, Bigelow organized a unique trade convention for blacksmiths only. Leveraging their position as dispensers of a necessary service, forty-three smiths of Worcester County vowed not to "perform any blacksmith's work or business of any kind whatever for any person or persons whom we esteem enemies of this country, commonly known by the name of tories." Going further, they pledged to withhold services from any "mechanick, tradesman, labourer or others" who did business with "said enemies to this country." Finally, Bigelow and company encouraged "all denominations of artificers"—and even "husbandmen, labourers, &c."—to follow their example and "call meetings of their respective craftsmen in their several counties" to devise collective sanctions. By encouraging such groups to organize within their trades, Bigelow and his fellow blacksmiths were offering leading roles to ordinary folks who worked with their hands.[26]

All these rural venues—town meetings, militia training days, committees and caucuses, informal gatherings in taverns or at blacksmith shops—fostered politicized relationships among people who recognized one another, whose families in many cases were connected through genealogy or geography, and who had set roles in their communities that everyone recognized. This made for a different, more personal style of Revolutionary activity. There were no "crowds" in the urban sense, assemblages of unaffiliated individuals. The 4,622 men who gathered in Worcester on September 6 were comparable in number to the largest crowds Boston had to offer, but here each man functioned within the familiar context of his militia company.

Together with men he knew, he elected a representative for the day, debated the wording of the judges' recantations, and lined up in formation along Main Street for the ritualistic capitulation.

This corporate mode had deep roots in congregational Massachusetts, where ordinary men had chosen their pastors and their political representatives for generations. The people, in concert, determined public policies, both religious and secular. In the political realm, at the annual town meeting, townsmen drafted specific instructions to their elected representative, who was expected only to facilitate the popular will, not determine or define it. The bottom-up chain of command was clear, and it was repeated in various ways, shapes, and forms in the various Revolutionary organizations that stemmed from and emulated colonial town meetings.

Timothy Bigelow played dual roles in this process, and that is how we can best view his brand of leadership. In 1773 and 1774 he served on virtually every committee that drafted instructions or set agendas for the Worcester Town Meeting and the American Political Society. Then, once his townsmen elected him to positions we normally categorize as "leadership"—militia captain and representative to the Massachusetts Provincial Congress—he no longer drafted instructions but received them.

One instruction was of particular consequence. On October 4, 1774—six months and two weeks before British regulars would attack Lexington and Concord—the town meeting told Bigelow, whom it had just chosen as its representative to the forthcoming provincial congress:

> You are to consider the people of this province absolved, on their part, from the obligation therein contained [the 1691 Massachusetts charter], and to all intents and purposes reduced to a state of nature; and you are to exert yourself in devising ways and means to raise from the dissolution of the old constitution, as from the ashes of the Phenix, a new form, wherein all officers shall be dependent on the suffrages of the people, whatever unfavorable constructions our enemies may put upon such procedure.[27]

The people of Worcester were telling their representative it was time to start a new government, no matter what British authorities or anybody else might say. It would take exactly twenty-one months for the Continental Congress to catch up with the town of Worcester and declare independence.

⚬

Worcester's Revolutionary tale is not unique. Of every twenty people in Massachusetts, nineteen lived outside Boston. In the late summer and early

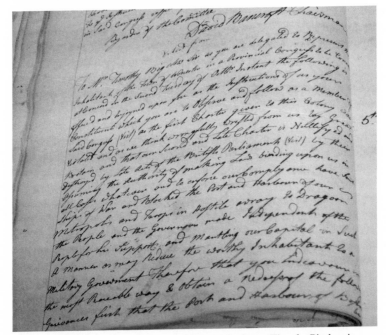

These instructions from the Worcester Town Meeting to Timothy Bigelow, its representative to the provincial congress, tell him to push for a new form of government. Dated October 4, 1774, twenty-one months before Congress followed suit, this is the first known declaration from a public body advocating a clear break from British authority. *Courtesy of the Worcester City Clerk.*

fall of 1774, these people, in overpowering numbers, brought down the government in every shiretown in contiguous Massachusetts. Only in Boston, which General Gage protected by fortifying the Neck (the only land entrance to the city), did British soldiers manage to enforce some vestige of imperial rule. In Springfield, more than three thousand militiamen marched "with staves and musick" as they unseated British-appointed officials. In Plymouth, after four thousand patriots had forced a court closure similar to that in Worcester and Springfield, the victors were so excited they gathered around Plymouth Rock and tried (in vain) to move it to the courthouse.[28]

Meanwhile, in Philadelphia, delegates from twelve colonies had just come together in what we now call the First Continental Congress. Their job was to coordinate the opposition to imperial abuse, but delegates were not of one mind as to what this meant. Some, like Joseph Galloway and John Dickinson of Pennsylvania, wanted to focus on conciliatory measures; others, including Samuel and John Adams of Massachusetts, wanted to apply more pressure through the coordinated efforts of the various colonies. The two sides seemed evenly matched for the first two weeks, but then in mid-September Paul Revere rode into town bearing news of the sweeping rebellion in Massachusetts and carrying a copy of the "Suffolk Resolves," which defiantly pledged "no obedience" to the Massachusetts Government Act and the Boston Port Bill. (Ironically, this celebrated document, written by Joseph Warren and the Boston Whigs, came from the only county that *failed* to throw off British rule in 1774.) Congress unanimously endorsed the resolves, a political victory for delegates who favored continued resistance over accommodation. Even moderates like Galloway and Dickinson were forced to give verbal support to the Massachusetts rebellion, so as not to appear unpatriotic. After the vote John Adams exclaimed: "This was one of the happiest days of my life. In Congress we had generous, noble sentiments, and manly eloquence. This day convinced me that America will support the [province of] Massachusetts or perish with her."[29]

But John Adams quickly softened his praise for the Massachusetts rebels, who his informants soon reported were getting out of control. Country radicals, like Timothy Bigelow and his constituents, were proposing "independency," a concept that no patriot leader had yet embraced in public. They favored "setting up a new form of government of our own," based on the model of the original 1629 Massachusetts charter, in which the people elected their own governor, rather than on the 1691 charter, in which the power of the people could be checked from above. Worse yet, some country radicals were suggesting that all patriot residents leave Boston so the insurgents could shell the city and send the British troops packing. These were ideas that "startle people here," Adams responded, almost in a panic.[30]

Samuel Adams, like his cousin John, wrote urgently to his friends back home: slow the Revolution down, he said, or it will alienate important allies. Perhaps he was correct: moderates in other colonies might well have withdrawn support if radicals in Massachusetts had assumed an offensive posture. Back home, this message set up a contentious debate within the newly assembled provincial congress. Although Bigelow and western radicals were well represented, delegates from Boston and the seaboard towns, better educated and more experienced within chambers, assumed most of the leadership roles and were able to moderate the actions of this body, which was now directing the Revolutionary movement on a province-wide level. It would collect taxes and secure arms to defend the Revolution, but it would not yet proclaim itself a new and independent government, despite the wishes of

Timothy Bigelow and the people of Worcester, and it would not marshal an attack on British troops in Boston.[31]

Here again is an ironic twist: Boston's Whig leaders, whom we celebrate today for prompting the Revolution, were no longer in the vanguard. Country people were. They were the ones to force the issue, while their famous compatriots tried to rein them in. It was the country people who challenged General Gage and forced him to back off. Then, unimpeded, they shed British rule, and now they wished to solidify their authority before British regulars had a chance to mount a counterrevolution, while cool-headed leaders, including the alleged firebrand Samuel Adams, argued for a more tempered approach.

This dynamic is hardly unusual for revolutionary movements: leaders who initially push for resistance or rebellion often back off a bit when others go farther than they would like. This is what happened in 1774. But since we pay so little attention to the upheaval that swept the countryside in the wake of the Massachusetts Government Act, we overlook this key dynamic and misrepresent the roles of our most cherished leaders.

Worse yet, we underestimate the importance and misrepresent the character of popular resistance at such a critical moment in our nation's founding. The militiamen who overthrew British authority across Massachusetts more than half a year before Lexington and Concord epitomized all that is best in political movements: overwhelming support; overpowering participation; grassroots control by the people, not by charismatic leaders; appropriate restraint (no blood was shed, which helps explain the movement's obscurity); and last but certainly not least, success. Often popular movements are squashed. Even at their best, they can take years to achieve their goals. Not this time. Timothy Bigelow, the citizens of Worcester, and their counterparts throughout Massachusetts succeeded beyond the wildest dreams of most radicals: democratically, with all due force but no loss of life, they cast off an oppressive government.

FOR FURTHER READING

The monographic narrative of the Massachusetts Revolution of 1774, highlighting events in Worcester, is Ray Raphael, *First American Revolution: Before Lexington and Concord* (New York, 2003). In *Founders: The People Who Brought You a Nation* (New York, 2009), I take a more biographical approach, featuring Timothy Bigelow as one of seven characters whom I follow through the Revolutionary Era. Earlier biographies, based on oral tradition and not very reliable, are Charles Hersey, *Rem-*

iniscences of the Military Life and Sufferings of Col. Timothy Bigelow (Worcester, Mass., 1860), and Ellery B. Crane, *Services of Colonel Timothy Bigelow in the War of the American Revolution* (Worcester, Mass., 1910). For Bigelow's family history, see Patricia Bigelow, *Bigelow Family Genealogy* (Flint, Mich., 1986), and Charles Nutt, *History of Worcester and Its People* (New York, 1919). Other relevant histories of Worcester include Kenneth J. Moynihan, *A History of Worcester: Worcester, 1674–1848* (Charleston, S.C., 2007); Albert A. Lovell, *Worcester in the War of the Revolution* (Worcester, Mass., 1876); Donald Johnson, "Worcester in the War for Independence" (Ph.D. diss., Clark University, 1953); and William Lincoln, *History of Worcester* (Worcester, Mass., 1862).

Bigelow left few letters, but his participation in town politics can be traced through the minutes of the American Political Society at the American Antiquarian Society and records of town meetings, reprinted in *Worcester Town Records from 1753 to 1783,* ed. Franklin P. Rice (Worcester, Mass., 1882). The original town records are at the city clerk's office, Worcester City Hall. On a broader level, his participation in the county conventions and the provincial congress can be traced in *The Journals of Each Provincial Congress of Massachusetts in 1774 and 1775 . . . Containing the Proceedings of the County Conventions,* ed. William Lincoln (Boston, 1838), and L. Kinvin Wroth, *Province in Rebellion: A Documentary History of the Founding of the Commonwealth of Massachusetts, 1774–1775* (Cambridge, Mass., 1975). A key source for the September 6, 1774, event in Worcester is Ebenezer Parkman's diary, based on his son Breck's firsthand account, housed at the American Antiquarian Society. Bigelow's property transactions are detailed in Holly V. Izard, "The Andrews-Bigelow-Lincoln-Court Mills Site," Worcester Historical Museum, 2001. For his later military career, see the town histories listed above; *Massachusetts Soldiers and Sailors in the War of the Revolution,* 17 vols. (1896), 2:26–27; and Kenneth Roberts, ed., *March to Quebec: Journals of the Members of Arnold's Expedition* (New York, 1940).

CHAPTER THREE

Samuel Thompson's War:
The Career of an American Insurgent

T. H. Breen

A s early as 1774, General Thomas Gage, commander of the British Army, realized that his forces in America were confronting a new kind of enemy. By September, ordinary people throughout New England had driven royal officeholders from the countryside. Angry farmers, acting outside a clearly delineated command structure, terrorized neighbors who defended the king's government. A few months later, surveying the situation beyond the security of occupied Boston, Gage observed that the Americans, "deriving confidence from impunity, have added insult to outrage; have repeatedly fired upon the King's ships and subjects, with cannon and small arms, have possessed the road, and other communications by which the town of Boston was supplied with provisions." On the distant frontier of empire, this veteran officer faced a rising of the people. The colonists "make daily and indiscriminate invasions on private property, and with a wantonness of cruelty . . . carry depredation and distress wherever they turn their steps." Government ministers in London, such as Lord Dartmouth, convinced themselves that Gage exaggerated. They did not want to hear such disturbing intelligence from the ground, and in any case, like the military officers whom they dispatched to America, parliamentary leaders had no understanding of insurgency.[1]

The term *insurgency* used in the American context has an unsettling quality. We have come to regard it as a foreign and unpleasant phenomenon, certainly not as a category of political analysis that we readily apply to our own Revolutionary experience. The problem, of course, is that denial about the popular character of resistance serves largely to distort our understanding of the nation's origins. For ordinary Americans experiencing the crisis of imperial rule between 1774 and 1776, discussions of insurgency occurred all the time. This was the period when people who had long viewed themselves as loyal subjects of the British Crown reached a breaking point, a moment of political reckoning no doubt different for each person, but whatever the individual circumstances may have been, it was a traumatic decision that profoundly changed their world.

Gage's complaint reminds us that the sine qua non of our Revolution—indeed, of any successful revolution—was the willingness of a sufficient number of people to take up arms against a state that no longer served the common good. This moment occurred in America sometime in late 1774. If we cannot explain why reasonably contented colonists suddenly decided to resist the representatives of the king's government, with violence when necessary, then we will not fully understand the revolutionary character of our own Revolution. After all, had it not been for the insurgents, we might not even be an independent nation today.

From this perspective, the revolution of the people calls forth a strikingly innovative interpretive vocabulary. We would be well advised to drop some traditional words. *Patriot* might be the first to go. Of course, Americans who resisted the empire were courageous and often high-minded, but by labeling them patriots, we separate their experiences from those of ordinary men and women in other places and at other times who have stood up against the exercise of arbitrary power. If we insist that our Revolution was somehow exceptional—fundamentally unlike all other revolutions—then we shall not make much progress in comprehending how revolutions actually work. For the sake of thoughtful comparative analysis, we should substitute *insurgent* or *militant* for *patriot*.[2]

Once we make this move, others soon follow. Insurgencies are not movements for the faint of heart. They involve a lot more than a commitment to a set of abstract intellectual principles. What is demanded, it would seem, is a greater appreciation of the kinds of passions that have energized insurgencies throughout world history. Our revolutionary lexicon should include popular anger and rage, a desire for revenge, and a feeling of betrayal—harsh concepts perhaps, but ones that better reflect the actual revolutionary process than do those encountered in the academic histories of political thought.

Contemporaries were well aware of this grittier aspect of political action. A respected minister in Brookfield, Massachusetts, Nathan Fiske, for example, explained the emotional calculus of revolution to a New England congregation soon after a British army of occupation closed the Port of Boston to all commerce. Anger rather than enlightened debate defined the political moment. "When any act of injustice is practiced upon us," Fiske observed, "we feel ourselves injured, we feel ourselves imposed on and dishonored; and we cannot help feeling our resentments kindle, our anger rise, our grief excited." There was nothing surprising about this. Fiske identified the well-spring of successful political resistance. As he argued—using rhetoric that has for a long time gone missing from studies of the American Revolution—"sometimes, when the injury is great or long continued, we feel the workings of revenge."[3]

Fiske's voice was not an exceptional case. Thomas Paine, for one, believed that such a visceral sense of wrong gave life to insurgency. In *Common Sense*—the most popular publication of the entire Revolutionary Era—he explained how anger could mobilize political discontent. He urged those Americans who in early 1776 still contemplated reconciliation with the rulers of Great Britain to "examine the passions and feelings of mankind." Could anyone at this late date really advocate reasoned negotiations with the enemy? To those who answered in the affirmative, Paine asked, "Hath your house been burnt? Hath your property been destroyed before your face? Are your wife and children destitute of a bed to lie on, or bread to live on? Have you lost a parent or a child by their hands, and yourself the ruined and wretched survivor?" If one could experience such atrocities and still accept the king and Parliament as legitimate symbols of political authority, "then, you are unworthy the name of husband, father, friend, or lover, and whatever your rank or title in life, you have the heart of a coward."[4] This is the language of personal revenge.

By any standard, Samuel Thompson was an American insurgent. The passage of time has obscured the personal qualities of leadership that poor farmers living in backwoods communities of Maine—then part of Massachusetts—saw in this man. Thompson certainly made other people, especially those who fancied themselves his social betters, uncomfortable. He still has that capacity today. Born in Brunswick, some twenty miles northeast of modern-day Portland, to a Scots-Irish family in 1735, he managed a modest tavern in the town. Although Thompson has slipped from the pages of the history of the Revolution, he sparked a crisis during the spring of 1775 known as Thompson's War, a moment of insurgency that exposed the raw, violent side of popular resistance to the British Empire.[5] The aggressive militancy that Thompson and his irregular followers brought to the conflict not only frightened prosperous American merchants who lived in Falmouth (now Portland), then a flourishing Atlantic port, but also triggered a horrible act of revenge by the British navy. Those who crossed Thompson quickly learned that they might fall "prey to the Sons of Rapine and lawless Violence."[6]

Thompson could have come from any colony. He was a product of his times, a charismatic figure who blended his own values and aspirations so persuasively with the Revolutionary cause that others of his social background accepted his leadership without second thought. Dr. David Ramsay, a Revolutionary officer who wrote an insightful account of the Revolution, observed in 1789, "The great bulk of those, who were active instruments in carrying on the revolution, were self-made, industrious men. Those who by their own exertions had established or laid a foundation for establishing personal independence, were most generally trusted, and most successfully employed in establishing that of their country."[7] Thompson fit Ramsay's general description. At the end of the day, he may have been a medium-sized fish in a very small pond, but he managed to support a large family in a community that offered even hardworking people meager economic opportunities.

Since Thompson's personal papers were destroyed sometime during the early nineteenth century, we know the man largely through the observations of contemporaries, many of whom were implacable opponents. The problem of reaching a balanced assessment of this person seems to be a function of the fact that he never learned to show deference to those who regarded themselves as his social betters. He spoke his mind. Material success apparently did not impress him. One person who found Thompson obnoxious described him as "a portly man, not of very tall stature, but somewhat corpulent, and apparently of a robust constitution." This particular commentator added in a condescending manner that probably tells us more about class bias than about Thompson, "Nature had furnished him [Thompson] with strong mental powers and a capacity, which, if it had been rightly directed and employed, might have rendered him a useful member of society, but his mind needed cultivation."[8]

Even so, Thompson could at times be extraordinarily persuasive. To be sure, detractors noted that whenever he became excited—a situation that occurred with regularity—he stuttered quite noticeably. We must assume that the extraordinary passion of his pronouncements riveted public attention. He spoke the language of Brunswick's hardscrabble farmers. Not surprisingly, political adversaries characterized his speeches as "impetuous, noisy, and sometimes even furious." Confessing a failure to comprehend his ability to inspire the ordinary people of his town, one antagonist concluded that "owing to his [Thompson's] outspoken and vehement manner, he made so many enemies that it is difficult to know the truth of some statements made in regard to him."[9] Wit and intelligence, no doubt, helped elevate Thompson above the level of populist demagogue.

Another curious element in the story was Thompson's bizarre domestic situation. Sometime after he married Abial Purinton in 1757, she began to show signs of mental instability. A crisis in their relationship occurred after Abial murdered an adopted five-year-old boy with a steelyard (a scale used for commercial transactions). But the details of Thompson's personal life—surely the stuff of gossip in a small frontier town—never eroded his standing with the insurgents who followed him during the Revolution.

Thompson communicated to these men a passionate contempt for special privilege and a willingness to resist—with violence, if necessary—those who either exploited or patronized the smallholders who struggled to make a living off the land. He proclaimed a radical vision of social equality. He did not draw his ideas from political philosophers who had explored republican theories of government for more than two centuries. He may not even have been able to identify John Locke, let alone Algernon Sydney or James Harrington.

To comprehend the assumptions and beliefs that energized his militancy and that resonated so powerfully among American colonists of his background and experience, we must search in other directions. Three separate mental strands seem to have shaped Thompson's vision of political society. They provided a coherent ideological framework that gave meaning to the crisis that overwhelmed the British Empire in America. This bundle of ideas and opinions helps explain Thompson's furious reaction at the time of the Revolution to what he interpreted as the abuse of power. His views—a product of religious radicalism, ethnic memories, and class antagonism—may have lacked the elegance of more intellectual explanations for American resistance to George III, but they do open a window onto the world of the insurgents who made independence possible.

One source of Thompson's absolute commitment to social equality may have been Universalism, a Protestant sect that flourished in New England before the American Revolution. At the time many people looked upon the members of this group with suspicion. But as with other aspects of his life in Brunswick, Thompson threw himself into religion with unreserved enthusiasm. People of this persuasion took inspiration directly from the Bible. They taught that it is the purpose of God, through the grace revealed in Jesus Christ, to save every member of the human race from sin. Universalists accepted no institutional authority beyond the locally gathered congregation, and when a local minister preached doctrines that ran counter to those held by the majority of his parishioners, he lost his job. Within these churches one person's opinion deserved as much respect as another's. Thompson claimed to believe "in the Trinity, in a day of general judgment for all mankind, and in the punishment of the wicked in a literal hell-fire." He also expressed conviction "in the final salvation of all."[10] Modern accounts of the Revolution tend to discount the power of religion to trigger, and then to sustain, political resistance. This is a mistake. For people like Thompson, no clear line separated spiritual from political concerns.

Thompson had not the slightest doubt that God had a plan for everything that happened in human society. He often responded to questions—not only about British policy—with the observation, "It is all right in the great plan." He never spelled out the precise contours of the great plan. All that mattered was that Thompson understood the divine scheme. He assumed that he—unlike his enemies—was in harmony with God's program. This is the stuff of radical resistance. Such a belief can give a person a powerful sense of moral certainty; those who obstruct the plan or who fail to see the logic of the Lord's blueprint deserve little sympathy. When great plans become guides to revolutionary politics—as they have repeatedly over the last several centuries—they encourage the violent suppression of dissent. People living in Brunswick seem to have known about Thompson's "great plan." One intrepid shoemaker even joked with Thompson about God's blueprint. When Thompson complained about an ill-fitting pair of boots he had ordered, the tradesman responded, "It is all right in the great plan." Thompson replied sharply, "The great plan has nothing to do with these boots."[11]

The second element that may have informed Thompson's politics was his Scots-Irish heritage. People living in the small inland communities of Maine knew which families could trace their genealogies back to Ireland. These people tended to live together, intermarry, and keep a certain distance from English neighbors. How much Thompson's political sentiments reflected long-standing ethnic grievances against Great Britain remains unclear. Other Ulster migrants whose background paralleled Thompson's thoroughly disliked the British government for the poverty and oppression it had visited upon the people of the northern counties of Ireland, upon Presbyterians as well as Catholics. One Irishman living in Virginia on the eve of the Revolution reminded his brother in a letter published in a colonial newspaper, "You know why I left *Ireland;* you saw the miserable situation of my family, by a rise in my rent *to the double* of what was paid before, and by the enclosure of the *only ground* where I could graze my few cattle; you saw the numerous companions of my misery spoiled, insulted, and abused."[12]

Thompson knew how Parliament had passed trade laws that systematically undermined the Ulster economy. The sense of wrong ran deep. One Hessian soldier who fought for the British declared that the Revolution was "not an American Rebellion; it is nothing more or less than an Irish-Scotch Presbyterian Rebellion."[13] He had a point. It would not be a great exaggeration to claim that the American Revolution was also Ireland's revolution in America. Most of the time, however, the betrayals that had occurred in Ireland lay buried deep in the past, dry seeds of a shared identity capable under certain conditions of energizing resistance in a new land.[14] The O'Briens, for example, had come to hate the British long before the Revolution. They had moved originally to Brunswick from County Cork. In 1765 the members of this clan relocated to Machias, a small port far to the northeast on the coast of Maine. They had a long history of resistance. Before moving to Cork, Morris O'Brien, the patriarch of the family, had run afoul of the law in Dublin for "having actively participated in a revolt against British tyranny."[15] In America he regaled younger O'Briens with stories of a great-grandfather who had fought at the Battle of the Boyne. Morris took pride in a portrait of Brian Boru, supposedly an Irish king "who as early as the year 978, reigned in regal pomp in Munster, Ireland."[16] And when they had the chance in June 1775 to even old scores, Morris and his sons—like Thompson, insurgents— boldly captured the HMS *Margaretta*, a British schooner assigned to protect local timber merchants who flouted the American boycott by supplying Gage's troops with building materials.

A third factor shaping Thompson's political outlook was an edgy resentment of the inequalities of class. The people living in the inland towns of Maine—Brunswick, Scarborough, and Gorham, for example—had long resented their economic dependence upon merchants in ports like Falmouth who controlled the flow of commerce. By the standards of Boston or Philadelphia, the gentry of this region never amassed huge fortunes. Nevertheless, they looked after their own interests, even when that meant turning a blind eye to fellow traders who did business with the British. Although most of these families eventually supported the American cause, they did so in a slow, begrudging manner that irritated men of Thompson's temperament.

Thompson sensed that the Falmouth gentry viewed him as an uncouth upstart. He certainly knew when he was being patronized. When a person who thought highly of himself once exclaimed that if Thompson had had a proper education, he would have been a great man, Thompson replied, "If I had your education, I could put you in my pocket." On another occasion a member of the Massachusetts General Court expressed pity for Thompson's lack of formal education. To which Thompson observed, "If I have no education perhaps I can furnish some ideas to those who have."[17]

This brew of radical religion and personal resentment reached a boiling point in 1774. Before that time Thompson had served in a number of town offices, and although he clearly enjoyed the respect of his neighbors, he had not aggressively taken a lead in the imperial controversy. All that changed quite suddenly after militants in Boston called for a boycott of British imported goods. Known as the Solemn League and Covenant, the proposal called not only for an end to British trade but also for the public humiliation of anyone who refused to sign the agreement. The plan generated muted enthusiasm throughout Massachusetts. The story was quite different in Maine. Thompson and his armed followers took it upon themselves to enforce the covenant. They did not restrict their activities to Brunswick. The insurgents targeted alleged enemies, usually hapless people who openly expressed support for Great Britain. It is possible that Thompson terrorized vulnerable individuals as a means to warn the merchants of Falmouth—for whom he had no love in any case—that they had better sever ties with those continuing to supply Gage's forces with timber, often in the form of masts for ships.

Thompson may have taken the lead in enforcing the Revolution, but the men who joined him in these forays did not need much persuading. A number of his most zealous partisans lived in Gorham. At a formal town meeting held early in 1774, they recorded their political views in no uncertain terms. They resolved that "our small possessions, dearly purchased by the hand of labor, and the industry of ourselves, and our dear ancestors, with the loss of many lives, by a barbarous and cruel enemy, are, by the laws of God, nature and the British Constitution, *our own,* exclusive of any other claim under heaven." To seize the profits of their lawful labor amounted to "State robbery." They had had enough of petitioning Parliament and the Crown. Such appeals yielded nothing of value. And so, in the strong language of the insurgency, the men of Gorham declared that "we of this town have such a high relish for Liberty that we, all with one heart, stand ready sword in hand, with the Italians in the Roman Republick, to defend and maintain our rights against all attempts to enslave us, and join our brethren, opposing force to force, if drove to the last extremity, which God forbid." For those members of the community who may have harbored personal misgivings about the militancy of Gorham's "Italians," the final resolution must have had a chilling effect. The town declared that anyone who dared "condemn, despise, or reproach" its resolves "shall be deemed, held, and adjudged, an enemy to his country, unworthy the company or regard of all those who are the professed sons of freedom, and shall be treated as infamous."[18]

Thompson's followers soon demonstrated exactly the risks a person took by opposing the cause of freedom. Thompson's "armed mob" were doubtlessly members of the local militia.[19] The term *mob* makes sense only if we remember that eighteenth-century mobs did not engage in random violence. They defined specific political objectives. Mobs generally targeted people who had flouted community values. In this case, the individuals whom Thompson and his friends visited had openly defended the empire to anyone prepared to listen. By silencing such figures, Thompson sent a powerful message to those people in Maine who had not yet taken sides and who probably hoped that the entire controversy would be resolved without armed confrontation. Not content to monitor the activities of his own town, Thompson took to the road, and like a political evangelist eager to ferret out sin, he humiliated dissidents. The group appeared in Wiscasset, Pownalborough, and Georgetown.

Anyone who refused to sign the Solemn League and Covenant might suffer physical abuse. The Reverend Jacob Bailey, an Anglican minister, fled when he heard that his pro-British comments had come to Thompson's attention. The forms of intimidation varied from place to place. The insurgents almost drowned one man who refused to sign. Another person was made to stand on a hogshead. Surrounded by Thompson's followers who aimed cocked rifles at the offender, the man was asked if he might like to confess his ideological errors. He did. So too did the pariah who was forced to dig his own grave. When he had completed the task, the militants aimed their guns, demanding an abject apology for failing to abide by the political will of the people. Again, the threat of death brought forth remarkable conversions. No one died. But then, no one had the courage to call Thompson's bluff, and royal officials did not have the resources needed to secure the region.[20]

Thompson's great opportunity came during the spring of 1775. He had watched with growing impatience as small-time merchants working out of Falmouth loaded masts for the British navy. No one in the town showed the slightest willingness to intervene, even though such commerce directly violated the directives of the Continental Congress. When British commanders learned that Thompson might attempt to intimidate a trader who was busy assembling a prohibited cargo, they dispatched a warship to Maine under the command of Lieutenant Henry Mowat. The captain of the HMS *Canceaux* was a tough, seasoned officer, not the sort to be intimidated by a few backwoods insurgents. Indeed, during a short period in May, Thompson and Mowat transformed the imperial conflict into a kind of duel. During a moment known in local history as Thompson's War, they assessed each other's strengths and weaknesses. Neither wanted to lose face by backing down; neither anticipated how far his rival was prepared to go to win the contest. As tensions mounted in March, insurgent leaders in Boston urged the reluctant gentry of Falmouth to show proper resolve. The Boston Committee of Inspection declared in words worthy of John Winthrop that "the eyes of the whole Continent" were now focused on this one small port town. "The tools of power wish for an opportunity to charge us with negligence, and are watching for it, to make a division between this Province [Massachusetts] and the other Colonies."[21] The burden was too much for the local gentry. They dithered, complaining that forceful action might jeopardize the safety of the entire community. If they were too aggressive in enforcing the boycott, Mowat might bomb their homes.

Thompson had no sympathy for such tremulous behavior. The tipping point may have been news of the Battle of Lexington and Concord that had occurred on April 19, 1775. Writing from Brunswick as a member of the local committee of safety to the head of the committee at Cambridge, Thompson announced that "having heard of the Cruill murders they have don in our Province, makes us more Resolute than ever, and finding that the Sword is drawn first on their side, that we shall be animated with that noble Spirit that wise men ought to be, until our Just Rights and Libertyes are Secured to us . . . My heart is with every true Son of America, though my Person can be in but one place at once, tho very soon I hope to be with you on the spot."[22] Thompson's initial foray was a total failure. His plan involved hiding sixty Americans on a barge and then, after maneuvering it next to the *Canceaux,* making a successful strike. It all came to naught. Someone alerted Mowat to the danger before Thompson's followers had made much progress.

A less fervent militant might have quit the operation, interpreting the setback as part of the great plan. But Thompson was not so easily discouraged. Without really having a clear backup scheme, he ordered about fifty armed followers to take up positions in a heavily wooded area near Falmouth harbor. No one in town seems to have noticed. The insurgents wore no uniforms. Their only mark of identity was a sprig of spruce attached to their hats. For their standard they carried a small evergreen tree, stripped of all its branches except for a few at the very top. They waited. Even with their target so close at hand, the men grumbled that the citizens of Falmouth did not have the courage to make a proper stand against the British. Then Thompson's little army had an extraordinary piece of luck. Unaware that the Americans were lurking nearby, Mowat and another naval officer came ashore for a meeting with local leaders, and as the party strolled through town, Thompson seized them. For him, the capture was an act of war. In any case, sensing that he now had the upper hand, Thompson demanded that the *Canceaux* immediately depart from Falmouth waters in exchange for the release of the two officers.

The British, however, showed not the slightest interest in bargaining with the insurgents. An officer left in charge of the ship threatened to bomb the town. To which Thompson responded, "Fire away! Fire away!" He declared that for every shot that the *Canceaux* fired, "I will cut off a joint," a threat that he was prepared to dismember Mowat, piece by piece. If Thompson expected the townspeople to applaud his tenacity, he was disappointed. They rushed about in utter panic. Many residents threw whatever possessions they could carry onto wagons and fled Falmouth as fast as they could. One witness to the event reported that the confrontation "frightened the women and children to such a degree that some crawled under wharves, some ran down cellar and some out of town. Such a shrieking scene was never before presented to view here."[23] The leading gentlemen of Falmouth visited Thompson in the woods, begging him to stand down, and when he appeared unwilling to compromise, several local spokesmen promised that if Thompson allowed Mowat to return to his ship on parole, they would take his place as prisoners. The captain was supposed to return the next day. The parties sealed the deal; Mowat made for the *Canceaux* as swiftly as possible. He later ignored the agreement, claiming in his defense that he feared for his life, a fair, if cowardly assessment of the situation.

Mowat's exit did not signal the end of Thompson's War. The insurgents, who had been joined by hundreds of other inland militiamen, took their disappointment out on the townspeople. They stole food and liquor from those who had spoken in favor of avoiding violence. According to one report, "The soldiery thought nothing too bad to say of the Falmouth gentry. Some of them were heard to say as they walked the streets yesterday, 'this Town ought to be laid in Ashes.'"[24] By May 10 the crisis was over. The leaders of Falmouth apologized profusely to Mowat for the impertinent behavior of Thompson and his friends. This unattractive crew, they insisted, had almost brought about the destruction of the entire town. In a letter addressed to the provincial government of Massachusetts, they whined that insurgency was not the proper way to resist British oppression. "We are afraid that if any number of men at any time, and in any manner, may collect together, and attack any thing, or any person they please, every body may be in danger."[25] They did not want to take the risk that armed resistance to British colonial rule might destabilize the traditional order of society.

The Falmouth gentry soon learned that they misplaced their bets. In October 1775 Mowat reappeared in the harbor, and despite the townspeople's assumption that he came as a friend, the *Canceaux* proceeded to bomb the defenseless town. British marines came ashore and burned those buildings that the ship's guns had not already destroyed. As with most atrocities of this sort, Mowat's revenge only served to strengthen the insurgency. As *The New-England Chronicle* reported on November 23, "The savage and brutal barbarity of our enemies in burning Falmouth, is a full demonstration that there is not the least virtue, wisdom, or humanity in the British court; and that they are fully determined with fire and sword, to butcher and destroy the whole American people."[26] News of the atrocity spread rapidly throughout the colonies. The incident had precisely the opposite result from what Mowat had intended. Instead of intimidating the insurgents, the burning of Falmouth strengthened popular resistance to British rule.

However much some gentry leaders disliked Thompson, the provincial congress of Massachusetts praised his passion for the American cause. To be sure, he sometimes let his emotions get the best of him. But at least he brought courage and energy to the conflict. To the dismay of his detractors in Maine who assumed that good breeding and college education should automatically translate directly into high command, Thompson received an appointment as brigadier general in the Continental Army. A short piece that appeared a few years later in a Boston newspaper helps us to better understand Thompson's popular appeal. In an address before the members of his brigade, he stated "that there had been Stories reported that the Officers and Soldiers in his Brigade were against him; therefore, if it was the case, he never would rule over a People, if he could not rule in their Hearts, [and he] therefore desired the commanding Officers to try a vote." They did. Not one

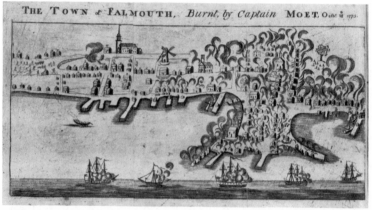

The British navy responded to the growing insurgency in the coastal towns of Maine by destroying Falmouth in October 1775. No doubt Captain Mowat still harbored a grudge against Samuel Thompson. However, by burning the entire town—an act that Americans saw as an unprovoked atrocity—British forces achieved what they most wanted to avoid, broad popular support for resistance to imperial rule.

officer cast a negative ballot. When he learned the result, Thompson pledged to the rank and file, "I never will forsake you." The person taking down Thompson's word that day wrote, "It was enough if he could at his Death see his Country Free, and it was a Pleasure to Die for the Rights of this People rather than submit to the cruel Hand of Tyranny, and if we go back we Die twice." Thompson asked only one concession from his troops. If on "the Day of Battle" he held back, "slay me . . . for it will be just."[27]

After the Americans had won independence, Thompson returned to Maine and held many elective offices, and as a delegate to the Massachusetts ratifying convention in 1788, he spoke passionately against the Constitution of the United States. He demanded annual elections for senators and congressmen. When his critics chided him for his radicalism, Thompson responded, "We cannot have too much liberty."[28] He was particularly bothered by the Constitution's failure to outlaw racial slavery in the new republic. As a Revolutionary insurgent, he had fought for equality, and after sacrificing so much for independence, he asked those who still remembered Thompson's War, "Shall it be said, that after we have established our own independence and freedom, we make slaves of others?"[29]

Once again in his own blunt manner, Thompson had spoken truth to power. Perhaps for this reason obscurity was his reward. To be sure, Thompson, who died in 1798, had the honor of having a single gun battery bear his name a century later. It was located in a fort constructed in the late nineteenth century to protect the citizens of Maine from possible attack during the Spanish-American War.[30] We can do more. It is time to reconsider the stories we tell ourselves about our own revolution and to restore Thompson and thousands of other American insurgents to the history of national independence.

FOR FURTHER READING

The spread of popular militancy before 1776 is the topic of T. H. Breen, *American Insurgents, American Patriots: The Revolution of the People* (New York, 2010). Breen examines the Irish contribution to American radicalism in his "An Irish Revolution in America?" *Field Day Review* (2006): 275–84. Hermann Wellenreuther, Maria Gehrke, and Marion Stange explore the infrastructure of insurgency in *The Revolution of the People: Thoughts and Documents on the Revolutionary Process in North America, 1774–1776* (Göttingen, 2006). A valuable introduction to the topic is Ray Raphael, *Founders: The People Who Brought You a Nation* (New York, 2009). David Ammerman provides a useful analysis of the local committees of safety and observation in *In the Common Cause: American Response to the Coercive Acts of 1774*

(New York, 1975). Anyone interested in the history of Maine during the American Revolution should start with James S. Leamon, *Revolution Downeast: The War for American Independence in Maine* (Portland, Me., 1993). Also of value is Donald A. Yerxa, *The Burning of Falmouth: A Case Study in British Pacification* (Portland, Me., 1975). In *Liberty Men and Great Proprietors: The Revolutionary Settlement on the Maine Frontier, 1760–1820* (Chapel Hill, N.C., 1990), Alan Taylor provides insight into class tensions that long characterized social relations in Maine. The best biographical study of Thompson remains Nathan Goold, "General Samuel Thompson of Brunswick and Topsham, Maine," Maine Historical Society *Collections* 1 (1904): 423–58.

CHAPTER FOUR

Philadelphia's Radical Caucus That Propelled Pennsylvania to Independence and Democracy

Gary B. Nash

Sitting in the East Room of Pennsylvania's statehouse on July 15, 1776, one week after the Declaration of Independence had been read before a carpet of jubilant Philadelphians in the statehouse yard, Continental Congress members were busily directing the war and organizing the new national government. They paused to watch a motley group of Pennsylvanians filing into the West Room across the hall. These were the men just elected for the weightiest political task assigned in Pennsylvania since William Penn had drafted the Frame of Government for his colony ninety-five years before. Their job was to write a constitution specifying the rights and responsibilities of the state's three hundred thousand citizens.

The delegates numbered ninety-six. Most were farmers, a few were merchants and lawyers, and others were artisans, shopkeepers, and schoolteachers. A majority were immigrants or sons of immigrants from Ireland, Scotland, England, and Germany. An ironmonger born in Upper Silesia filed in along with an Ulster-born farmer and an Alsatian-born shopkeeper. With hardly a powdered wig in sight, the delegates took their seats. Many were in their mid-twenties. All but eight represented the rural counties outside Philadelphia. About half had joined up as militiamen, called Associators, and most of them had been elected officers by the rank and file.

Nowhere in the world had such a plainspoken, largely unschooled group of men with work-toughened hands been charged with such a portentous matter. Francis Alison, Philadelphia's Presbyterian minister, called them "mostly honest well-meaning country men, who are employed; but entirely unacquainted with such high matters [and] hardly equal to the task to form a new plan of government." That was a mild dig compared to the view of one lawyer member of the convention. Only a few had served in the Pennsylvania legislature, he remarked ruefully; some had not even held a local office such as hog reeve or fence viewer; and "not a sixth part of us ever read a word on the subject" of government. The voters had apparently decided that "any man, even the most illiterate, is as capable of any office as a person who has had the benefit of education; that education perverts the understanding, eradicates common honesty, and has been productive of all the evils that have happened in the world." It was time to begin the world anew, he spouted: "We are resolved to clear every part of the old rubbish out of the way and begin on a clean foundation."[1]

Clearing away the "old rubbish" and building from a new foundation had long been under way, and by late 1775 a set of Philadelphia men, whom we will meet shortly, had taken form as an informal caucus. Though never entirely stable, never meeting on a regular schedule, and always jockeying for position with a variety of better-established politicos, this cadre featured people of widely different backgrounds and distinctly different personalities. Religion, age, occupation, or ethnic background did not bind them together, nor did family connection. Their glue was reform ideas. Previously unknown in the art of governing, they believed in the worth of ordinary people and regarded the people at large as the ultimate source of political authority. They produced no popular movement; rather, they tapped into the democratic energies of a mass of Philadelphians below them. They channeled ideas bubbling up from the streets, taverns, and docks and devised strategies for accomplishing what ordinary men had been striving for since the early 1760s.

~e

A decade of spirited debate and dramatic events had brought common people into the arena of politics and step by step prepared the way for the emergence of the radical caucus of 1775–76. Swirling arguments with Great Britain over taxes and imperial management of the colonies had meshed with the internal tensions that had surfaced in Philadelphia as class distinctions sharpened and class animosity increased. In 1770, when merchants wanted to abandon nonimportation of British manufactures, which had advantaged artisans working to gain a market for their locally produced articles, they lectured the artisans that they had "no right to give their sentiments respecting an importation" and called the craftsmen "a rabble." Artisans responded in kind. In a broadside passed around the city, they charged that merchants, chasing gold, regarded workingmen as "two-legged pack horses . . . created solely to contribute to the ease and affluence of a few importers" and "a kind of beast of burden, who . . . may be seen in a state but should not be heard." Two years later "Brother Chip" rallied the artisans and other "useful and necessary inhabitants of this Province"—a side slap at those who did not work with their hands—and insisted that the end was coming for "those Gentlemen [who] make no scruple to say that the mechanics . . . have no right to *speak* or *think* for themselves."[2]

Laboring Philadelphians were on the march by late 1774, when radical artisans and shopkeepers began to win election to the Committee of Observation and Inspection that was charged with enforcing boycotts against British imported goods. Previously, Presbyterian, Quaker, and Anglican artisans had tangled on political issues just as had German, Scots-Irish, and English craftsmen. Overcoming the religious and ethnic factionalism that had split them during the Stamp Act crisis, and aided by the withdrawal of violence-shy Quakers from political positions, the workingmen had developed their own consciousness and organizational base. At this point the radical cadre took form. Their success in working with the city's laboring classes was aided by the partial vacuum of political leadership created by the withdrawal of Quakers from power and the decision of the Society of Friends in December 1774 to enforce a policy of passive obedience and non-resistance, which soon led to disowning any Quaker serving on the quasi-governmental committees of observation and safety.

A glimpse at the backgrounds of six particularly energetic members of the radical caucus might cause one to wonder how such a mixture could emerge to shape the popular sentiment that had been gaining momentum and find strategies for hammering out both prongs of the Revolutionary movement—the war for independence and the struggle to re-create America.

Here are the six:

- James Cannon: A mathematics teacher at the College of Philadelphia, the thirty-six-year-old Cannon had been schooled at Edinburgh University. He could match minds with many of the delegates to the Continental Congress, but whereas most of them leaned to the right, Cannon inclined to the left. He had arrived in Philadelphia from Scotland in about 1765, seemed to worship nowhere, and had played no part in politics for his first ten years in Pennsylvania. Developing a talent for biting prose, he became the journalistic wheelhorse of the caucus, writing petitions, broadsides, and newspaper screeds.
- Christopher Marshall: The oldest of the group at sixty-five, the Irish-born Marshall made a modest living as a druggist. Disowned years before by the Society of Friends for "attempting the transmutation of metals" (which put him at risk of conviction for counterfeiting),

he remained a devout man. Hyperactive for a man his age, he liked the rough-and-tumble of urban politics and became an effective go-between among different groups.

· Timothy Matlack: A birthright Quaker, Matlack was a brewer and a brawler. About forty-six in 1776, he had known hard times and like his father had landed in debtors' prison during the Stamp Act crisis. Irreverent and outspoken, he fell out with the Society of Friends, who were generally moderates and conservatives as the issue of independence arose. He curried favor among the lower ranks and drew curses from proper Philadelphians for his involvement in cockfighting and horse-racing. Impressive in stature, mercurial in temperament, and fast with his fists, Matlack found in politics the success that eluded him in business.

· Thomas Paine: Thirty-seven years old upon arrival in Philadelphia in late 1774, Paine was an epistolary whirlwind, discharging from his pen lightning bolts against corrupt England and against slaveholders, exploiters of Native Americans, wife-abusers, purse-proud merchants, and property aggrandizers. An artisan and a deist, his opposition to ill-gained fortune and exploitation of the common man gained him friends among men of various religious commitments. Scruffy in his dress, with a chiseled, sallow face, he fit easily into the cobblestone street culture of the city's workingmen.

· Daniel Roberdeau: Jovial and dangerously overweight, Roberdeau was a merchant of middling success. Tepid in his Presbyterianism, he was chosen to moderate town meetings in the fateful days of 1775–76, a sign that people of different political sensibilities trusted him. Forty-nine in 1776, he became progressively radical as the moment of separation with England neared and as he became a favorite officer of Philadelphia's militiamen.

· Thomas Young: To a conservative Philadelphian, the forty-four-year-old Young was "a certain bawling New England man of noisy fame."[3] A doctor steeped in caucus politics who figured prominently in the resistance movements in Albany, Boston, and Newport, Rhode Island, he alighted in Philadelphia in May 1775, full of radical ideas. Doctoring largely to working-class families, he earned only a modest income to support his large family. Burning with zeal to reform the colonial political system, he was the caucus's most effective outdoor speaker.

This cadre could lead, but they also had to follow. In a constantly changing situation, they had to respond to the ordinary people, who already were

Charles Willson Peale was an artist-patriot who took the image of important officers, politicians, and diplomats. But mindful of the political risks, he seldom painted radicals such as his friend Timothy Matlack. He never displayed his first portrait of Matlack; but many years later, in 1826, Peale took the image of his old friend again and this time, when both he and Matlack were aged, displayed it. *Courtesy of the Library of Congress.*

finding their own voice. The caucus members also had to interact with the shifting politics playing out in the Continental Congress that was riven by pro- and anti-independence states. The caucus had no officers, no constitution, kept no minutes, and held no regular meetings. But writing newspaper essays, broadsides, and petitions; organizing mass meetings; and drawing up slates of candidates for quasi-governmental committees that ruled the street, the caucus strategized adroitly to unseat the elected Pennsylvania legislature, to propel Pennsylvania toward independence, and to help engineer the most radical state constitution written in the thirteen states.

☙

Thomas Paine landed unnoticed in Philadelphia in December 1774. But he did not remain unnoticed for long. Making friends with Benjamin Rush, he plunged into the local scene, using his crimson-dipped pen to expose flaws, especially the enslavement of Africans in the City of Brotherly Love. In January 1775 Paine witnessed the founding of the United Company of Philadelphia for Promoting American Manufactures, formed to employ hundreds of laboring Philadelphian women to produce coarse textiles. The board of directors, including Christopher Marshall, chose Daniel Roberdeau as president and James Cannon as secretary. This was a locus of political discourse among Philadelphia's lower ranks and the first appearance on the political stage for Marshall, Roberdeau, and Cannon.

Only a few days after hearing of the bloody skirmishes at Concord and Lexington, thousands of Philadelphians gathered in the statehouse yard on April 25, 1775. There they formed thirty-one neighborhood militia companies that enlisted most of the city's able-bodied men, including apprentices and artisans who lived hand to mouth. Unauthorized by the legislature, they took matters into their own hands. They called themselves Associators, mimicking Benjamin Franklin's ploy during the Seven Years' War for ordinary citizens to associate among themselves for common defense when the Quaker-dominated assembly had refused to authorize a compulsory militia. Among the three colonels elected by the enlisted men—in itself a democratic process that today is unimaginable—was Daniel Roberdeau. Timothy Matlack was elected a brigade colonel. Shortly thereafter, the rank-and-file Associators formed the Committee of Privates to lobby for an all-community commitment to "the glorious cause" and fair treatment of their families if they were pressed into battle. Cannon became their secretary and spokesman.[4]

Thomas Young's arrival in May 1775 added an important figure to the emerging radical cadre. Young quickly found kindred spirits in Cannon, Matlack, and Marshall, who for months had been conferring with the pro-independence delegates to the Congress from Massachusetts—John Hancock, John Adams, and Samuel Adams—the latter with whom he had worked for years in radical Boston politics. Now operating for the first time as a self-conscious group, radical artisans and their friends began to grasp the levers of political action. In August 1775 Philadelphians elected Marshall and Matlack to the Committee of Inspection and Observation, the strong right arm and face of popular sentiment that was taking control of the streets, setting control on prices of scarce commodities, and pushing the colony's legislative assembly to oppose British policies.

Of the many issues the radical caucus and the Committee of Privates confronted in 1775, the most important was a General Militia Law. No society can go to war without nearly unconditional commitment of its people, especially in a war against the world's most powerful military juggernaut. Yet Pennsylvania had been founded by pacifist Quakers, whose peace testimony had left Pennsylvania, alone among all the North American British colonies, with no militia law providing for trained, able-bodied men for defensive or offensive military campaigns. Now, in the autumn of 1775, with the undeclared war fully under way, Pennsylvania's legislature could wait no longer to establish a military capability.

Two questions dominated the intense debate: Should Pennsylvanians be subject to compulsory militia service? If so, should noncompliers, pleading conscientious objection, as did most Quakers, be required to pay fines substantial enough to support the families of laboring men away at war, or the widows and orphans they left behind if they died in battle?

In October 1775 the Committee of Observation and the Committee of Privates lobbied strenuously as the provincial assembly deliberated. With schoolmaster Cannon composing their petitions, the Committee of Privates urged mandatory militia service and substantial fines against non-Associators. The Committee of Observation, where Matlack served on a petition-drafting committee, followed suit. The Associators, wrote one of their officers, were mostly "of the poorer sorts of people, whose public spirit far exceed their abilities in point of fortune" and that "a vast number of substantial inhabitants . . . are sitting at their ease and bearing no part in the expense or labor of the Association."[5]

Caught between the Associators and the Quakers, who were supported by many anti-independence men, the legislature hammered out new "Rules and Regulations for the Better Government of the Military Association" and "Articles of Association" in late November 1775. For the next six months the Committee of Privates met twelve times to plot strategy to revise the Militia Law and to forge links to rural militiamen. While restively waiting for the legislature to satisfy their demands, they appointed a committee of correspondence and began circulating a public letter, almost certainly written by Cannon, to plead their case. By now the Philadelphia militia had become a school of political education, much in the manner of Oliver Cromwell's New Model Army in the mid-seventeenth-century English Civil War, where soldiers debated the future of the political system. They had elected Matlack and Roberdeau as colonels of the Second and Fifth battalions. Young had signed on as surgeon to the Philadelphia Rifle Battalion, where he became the political counselor of the largely untutored citizen-soldiers.

In January 1776, writing anonymously, Paine unleashed *Common Sense*. It took the city by storm with its pungent language calling for independence and more democratic governance in America. For the next five months, as New Englanders increased the pressure for the states to line up behind independence, Young, Cannon, and Paine dueled with conservatives such as William Smith, provost of the College of Pennsylvania, in the Philadelphia newspapers. In a barrage of long newspaper essays, Young, writing as "Elector," Paine as "Forester," and Cannon as "Cassandra" schooled the public in how to bring off their high perch those who opposed independence and defended the old elite-controlled provincial politics. Writing as "Cato," Smith did his best to discredit Paine's *Common Sense* and reviled "Cassandra" as "an enthusiast or a madman," a "barbarian," and "a drunken independent."[6]

Beginning to resemble a well-oiled political machine, the radical caucus turned its attention in February to forging links between the city and the countryside. In York County they cultivated James Smith, part lawyer, part iron manufacturer. In Cumberland County they drew Robert Whitehill, a farmer from Carlisle who was on the Committee of Privates there, into their orbit.

By this time Cannon's and Young's houses had become the nerve centers of the Philadelphia radical caucus, pushing for independence and internal reform. Marshall's diary gives the flavor of the incessant caucusing and coordinating. At Young's house on March 13, Marshall listened to Dr. Young read *Plain Truth,* a conservative attack on Paine's *Common Sense,* and examined Cannon's latest newspaper retort to Provost Smith's defense of British policies. Two days later Marshall was at Cannon's house with Matlack to hear how Smith vowed that "Great Britain would mortgage America for as much money as would enable her to conquer it." On April 1: "Went to James Cannon's. Spent good part of this afternoon and evening till eight there in conversation with Thomas Paine, Dr. Young, James Wigdon, and Timothy Matlack." Four days later Marshall reflected on the escalating tempo of activity as the fateful decision on independence neared and the city bustled with war preparations: "Dined at home with James Cannon. We then went to Paine's, stayed some time; thence Cannon and I went to Dr. Young's not at home. We went up to Kensington, found him and several friends there at work on board the frigate building by Messrs Eyre. We joined them in assisting what we could till night."[7] Druggist, schoolteacher, doctor, journalist, and brewer—all plotted political tactics by day and raised upper and lower deck beams by night on the two frigates at the shipyard of Jehu Eyre in the outlying artisan village of Kensington.

In April 1776 the assembly amended the Militia Law to meet half of the radicals' demands: Associators could send substitutes if leaving their families created great hardship; militia fines would be reserved to aid Associators wounded in battle and the families of those who paid the ultimate sacrifice; masters refusing to allow their apprentices to serve would pay the non-Associators' fine; and the fine for non-Associators was raised to three and a half pounds per year. But the assembly failed to increase the number of training days; fund the militia equitably; provide arms for poor Associators; allow the annual election of officers; or levy extra taxes on the property of non-Associators. Still, the amendments to the General Militia Law were a partial victory for the radicals.

By now, after news of the British burning of Norfolk, Virginia, on New Year's Day in 1776, and after four months of journalistic fusillades, every Pennsylvanian who cared about the workings of government knew where matters stood. Those for independence adamantly backed expanding the franchise to include every man paying even the slightest tax, while those who held out against independence stood as guardians of the old political order, fearing the widening of the franchise as a recipe for anarchy. On April 24, in his memorable third "Forester" letter, Paine stitched together a call for independence with a call for social and political reform. First, he attacked the "false light of reconciliation" with England. "'Tis gone! 'Tis past! he wrote. "The grave has parted us—and death, in the persons of the slain, has cut the thread of life between Britain and America." Then he issued an invitation to reform: "Can America be happy under a government of her own? The answer is short and simple: as happy as she please; she hath a blank sheet to write upon."[8]

On May 1, 1776, the pressure exerted by the radical caucus to push the foot-dragging Pennsylvania legislature into the pro-independence camp reached a critical juncture. The radicals pinned their hopes on a victory for their slate of four Philadelphia leaders at a special election on May 1 to enlarge the assembly. If they won, this would tilt the legislature toward independence and end the sway of the anti-independence stalwarts, and Pennsylvania, the keystone state, would join the pro-independence New England states and Virginia in the Continental Congress.

With the radical cadre in full throat, Marshall and Cannon helped choose the pro-independence ticket, one of whom was Roberdeau. But fierce electioneering by the conservatives and the exclusion of most Germans from the polls carried the day; three of the four seats went to conservative candidates. Stunned, Marshall, Young, and Cannon met on May 3. Then they repaired to the lodgings of Samuel and John Adams to lay the groundwork for destroying through public outrage what it could not control—the political will of the Pennsylvania Assembly. Since the ballot box had failed them, they could take recourse in the streets. The people "out of doors" would trump the legislators indoors, even if they had been legitimately elected.

If the British had intended to aid the radicals in pushing Pennsylvania into the pro-independence camp, their timing couldn't have been better. Six days after the election newspapers screamed with news that the British were sending thousands of Hessian and Hanoverian mercenaries to bring the rebellious colonists to their senses. Two days later word reached the city that two British warships that had been blockading American coastal commerce up and down the Delaware River were sailing upriver to pummel Philadelphia. On May 8–9 a dozen Pennsylvania row galleys dueled with the deep-drafted forty-four-gun *Roebuck* and twenty-eight-gun *Liverpool* within earshot of the city. Despite great naval superiority, the British ships retreated after the mariners peppered the *Roebuck,* which had run aground on a shoal. Though Philadelphians savored this half victory, many fled the city, most believing that "a larger force will come against us."[9]

As war came to Philadelphia's doorstep, public opinion shifted rapidly.

Capitalizing on this development, John Adams moved boldly in Congress on May 10, offering a resolution that every state resisting independence should reconstitute itself. It was a dagger aimed at the heart of the recalcitrant Pennsylvania Assembly, and the radical cadre made sure it was read aloud at the London Coffee House, a popular gathering place.

On May 15, 1776, Congress not only endorsed Adams's resolution but strengthened it with a preamble proclaiming that "the exercise of every kind of authority under the . . . crown should be totally suppressed." Already Marshall, Paine, Matlack, Rush, and others had met to concoct a plan for a mass citywide meeting in anticipation of Congress passing John Adams's resolution. Thereafter they gathered to coordinate further with the Committee of Observation and then called for a provincial conference to replace the assembly. On Sunday, May 19, a broadside with the blaring headline "The Alarm," probably authored by Thomas Paine, and printed also in German, blanketed the city, urging the people to support a move for a provincial conference that would establish a new government "on the authority of the people." All the pieces were falling into place.

On May 20 four thousand Philadelphians—more than four times the number who had voted in the May 1 by-election—walked through pouring rain to the statehouse yard. There Daniel Roberdeau, by agreement of the radical caucus, read the resolve of the Continental Congress and then yielded to Thomas McKean, chairman of the Committee of Observation, who argued that a conference "chosen by the people" must establish a new government. When Colonel John Cadwallader urged moderation, the crowd shouted him down. Timothy Matlack finished up with rousing oratory that touched off roars of approval for independence and avowals that the sitting assembly must disband. The "Protest of the Inhabitants . . . of Pennsylvania," constructed by the radical caucus, was read and approved. "This meeting," scribbled the young militia captain William Bradford Jr. in his diary, "gives the coup de grâce to the King's authority in this province."[10]

The radical caucus, again coordinating with the Committee of Observation, made sure that the rest of the province fell into line behind Philadelphia. Immediately after the hot-tempered crowd at the statehouse yard dispersed, Marshall and his friends composed a circular letter to spread their resolves to the countryside. "Liberty and slavery is before you; take, then, your choice," wrote the radicals. "For us, we are determined to be free, and invite you to partake of that freedom which all are entitled to."[11] Dr. Young rode west to York and Lancaster to rouse farmers and artisans to endorse the dismissal of the assembly and to select representatives to a conference that would settle on plans for the constitutional convention to meet in July. Cannon sallied forth to Bucks County. Others set off for more distant counties with warnings that the province's militiamen, ready to fight for independence, would "have to contend" against proprietary placeholders and their supporters, "joined by all the avowed as well as secret enemies of the cause of American freedom." Many of those accustomed to holding power left the city, "disgusted at the present proceedings, fearful of the people, and railing at men in office on account of their low birth and little fortune," as the visiting Dr. James Cliterall observed.[12]

To make sure that they hobbled the now-rebuked assembly, the radicals took further steps. The Committee of Observation petitioned the city courts to suspend all operations until the people formed a new government. The court justices complied, bringing the judicial process to a halt. Next, militia privates rejected the assembly's selection of two brigadier generals for the Pennsylvania militia, calling instead for each battalion to send two privates and two officers to Lancaster on July 4, 1776, to elect the brigadier generals.

Going further, radical and moderate legislators began absenting themselves from legislative sessions in order to prevent a quorum. The Committee of Privates, aided by Cannon, added to the legislative paralysis by polling each of the city's five battalions as to their support for the "Protest" and the plan to convene the provincial conference. The three battalions led by Colonels Roberdeau, McKean, and Matlack were nearly unanimous in favor; and even in the other two battalions, the conservative colonels got nowhere in trying to persuade the militiamen to oppose the "Protest." A day later Philadelphians read a pithy warning in *The Pennsylvania Evening Post:* "Take heed, Tories, you are at your last grasp!"[13]

Now Pennsylvanians began choosing conference delegates. Already in high gear, the radical cadre in Philadelphia leveraged its influence with the Committee of Observation, which now was the only effective government in the city. The committee named five of its members, among them Marshall, Matlack, Rush, and McKean. Outside Philadelphia, Germans and other backcountry people, who had never factored much in provincial politics, were selected for the conference.

Meeting for a week from June 18 to 25, the conference did not shrink from acting as a Revolutionary body. It elected Thomas McKean as its president and declared Pennsylvania's support for independence. Then it organized an election for a constitutional convention. Deciding that the city of Philadelphia and each of the state's seven counties should have eight seats at the convention, the provincial conference set July 8 as the day for electing delegates. That done, it made a momentous decision, mingling the call for independence with the insistence on internal reform. Supported by Cannon and his compatriots, the Committee of Privates had urged that in the forthcoming election all Associators of any age and any social status should be able to vote. The conference moderated this unprecedented broadening of voting rights, enjoyed nowhere in the English-speaking world, by extending the ballot to Associators twenty-one years and older who had paid some tax, even if it was merely the small poll tax levied on those without so much as a square yard of land to call their own. Even with these restrictions, the conference enlarged the electorate by at least half in some counties and in others by as much as 90 percent. It passed one other qualification: only those ready to swear allegiance to the independence movement could vote. This test of loyalty, along with the widened suffrage, proved crucial in composing the convention's delegates. By neatly disenfranchising Tories and moderates (those still opposed to an outright declaration of independence), the conference paved the road for a body that was representative not of Pennsylvania's people in their entirety but of those committed to independence and internal change. Though enraging their opponents, the radicals had a strong argument: if Pennsylvania was to have a new constitution, then those called upon to defend it should have a voice in its creation.

Cannon and his radical friends prepared carefully for an election of tremendous import—the selection of delegates who would write Pennsylvania's new constitution. On June 22 a provincial conference committee on which Matlack sat stressed the seriousness of what lay before them. "Divine providence is about to grant you a favor," they wrote, "which few people have ever enjoyed before, the privilege of choosing Deputies to form a government under which you are to live."[14] Four days later reform-minded Philadelphians plastered the city with a broadside as radical as any produced during the American Revolution. The task at hand was to shape the composition of the constitutional convention. Cannon, addressing a broadside to the "Several Battalions of Military Associators," most of whom would vote for the first time in their lives, warned that "great and over-grown rich men will be improper to be trusted . . . They will be too apt to be framing distinctions in society, because they will reap the benefits of all such distinctions . . . Though we have several worthy men of great learning among us, . . . we would think it prudent not to have too great a proportion of such in the Convention." What should be preferred to deep learning and professional status? "Honesty, common sense, and a plain understanding, when unbiased by sinister motives." These qualities, counseled Cannon, "are fully equal to the task."[15]

On July 3, one day after the Continental Congress voted for independence, Cannon, Matlack, and Young helped choose a slate of eight persons well qualified and "steady in their integrity, zeal and uprightness" to represent Philadelphia at the convention.[16] On July 8, after Philadelphia's sheriff read the Declaration of Independence, the crowd jubilantly tore down the king's arms from the courtroom. The voters then elected eight delegates, including Benjamin Franklin, David Rittenhouse, Matlack, and Cannon—the latter two of the caucus. "There were bonfires, ringing bells, with other great demonstrations of joy upon the unanimity and agreement of the declaration," wrote Marshall.[17]

Outside Philadelphia, Pennsylvanians elected constitution writers who looked like themselves, thought like themselves, and promised to act accordingly. This astounded—and frightened—many of the congressmen across the hall in the statehouse. Undaunted, the Pennsylvania Constitutional Convention began its deliberations on July 25, 1776, just after the Philadelphia militiamen had been called out to move north to face the British in New Jersey. The delegates appointed Cannon and Matlack to a seventeen-man drafting committee along with Robert Whitehill and James Smith, two rural representatives aligned with the caucus's political agenda. Within four days a draft was ready and printed up with a copy for each of the ninety-six delegates to consider. This rapidity of work suggests that Cannon and Matlack had come prepared with the principal features of their desired constitution. But they had to win over less radical members than themselves, including David Rittenhouse, George Bryan, and George Clymer. As the convention met in July and August, amid great apprehension over the huge British force poised to take New York City, members of the radical caucus also had to jockey with men from outside Philadelphia.

Working for eight weeks, the constitution drafters rejected three of the most honored elements of English republican thought. First, they scrapped the idea of a two-house legislature, where the upper house traditionally reflected men of wealth and the lower house mirrored the common citizens. The case for unicameralism rested primarily on long historical experience that upper houses in the colonies had reflected the interests of the wealthy and given institutional form to a contest of interests that did not, at least in the minds of most ordinary people, serve the common good. Other precedents fortified the unicameralist argument: town meetings, the Continental Congress itself, and almost a century of one-house rule in Pennsylvania. Hardly a radical, Benjamin Franklin supported unicameralism, seeing an upper house as a vestige of the aristocratic English system against which the Americans were rebelling.

In a second departure from conventional wisdom on a balanced government, the convention abandoned the idea of an independent executive branch with extensive power, especially to veto legislative bills—a governor's authority commonly found in British colonies. Instead, the convention provided for an elected weak plural executive branch, composed of a president and a council. It was empowered to appoint important officers, including the state's attorney general and judges, but it was given no legislative veto power. Its duty was to implement the laws passed by the legislature, not to amend or veto them.

Finally, the constitution drafters scuttled the old franchise, which had allowed the vote only to free white property-owning males, and created in its stead the most liberal franchise in the Western world. Colonies varied on how much property conferred voting rights on men, but they varied only modestly from the ancient English election laws limiting the vote to landowners whose property could yield an annual rent of forty shillings (about one month's wages for an ordinary worker). But in the radical view, political rights must now be vested in the people at large. Only apprentices and the deeply impoverished (excused from paying any tax) were excluded. This was a flat-out rejection of the hoary idea that only a man with "a stake in society" would use the vote judiciously. And was not risking one's life on the battlefield evidence of having a stake in society? Making voters out of ordinary men put the broadened franchise at the center of democratized polity.

One proposed feature of the constitution went beyond the wishes of the full convention. Radical caucus leaders urged a clause in the bill of rights that gave the state the power to limit private ownership of large tracts of agricultural land or urban property. Knowing that the gap between the very wealthy and the very poor had grown in Philadelphia, the radicals reasoned that "an enormous proportion of property vested in a few individuals is dangerous to the rights and destructive of the common happiness of mankind; and therefore every free state hath a right by its laws to discourage the possession of such property." Franklin himself may have offered this ultrademocratic proposition, for it echoed similar statements he had earlier made—that "what we have above what we can use, is not properly *ours,* tho' we possess it."[18] The convention, however, did not endorse this bold idea, perhaps because of its vagueness about how the state could limit the accumulation of wealth without actually confiscating private property and perhaps because the delegates were unwilling to tamper with the inclinations of many Pennsylvanians. Yet in agreeing on clauses abolishing imprisonment for debt and providing for public education supported by taxes on property holdings, the delegates took important steps toward achieving a more equitable society.

If limiting the concentration of wealth proved unacceptable, the convention reached consensus on erecting hedges to prevent concentrated political power. The constitution continued the annual elections by ballot used in the colonial period so that the power to make laws returned annually, as Cannon stressed, to the hands of the people. It also guaranteed that the doors of the legislative house would remain open to "all persons who behave decently," so the people from whom government derived its authority could monitor their elected legislators. Printing the legislative debates and votes on legislation in English and German allowed for greater transparency. In a final check against unresponsive and corrupt legislators, every piece of approved legislation had to be printed "for the consideration of the people" and then in the next session to be finally approved. One shocked Continental Congress delegate declared that this made "the mob . . . a second branch of legislature—laws subjected to their revisal in order to refine them, a washing in ordure by way of purification."[19]

Four final provisions nailed down this radical democracy. First, they imposed term limits that restricted a man from serving more than four one-year legislative terms every seven years—a provision adopted in no other state for the lower house. This rotation of legislative seats jibed with the idea that many citizens were capable of performing well in public office. Second, they specified the popular election of a "Council of Censors" once every seven years to review the constitution to ensure that it had "been preserved inviolate in every part; and whether the legislative and executive branches of government have performed their duty as guardians of the people."[20] Third, the convention stipulated the reapportionment of the legislative assembly every seven years on the basis of census returns. This provision was followed by only three other states. Lastly, the constitution specified that officials should be unsalaried.

After completing its work in early September, as Washington's army was preparing to withdraw from New York City, the convention ordered the distribution of four hundred copies of the new constitution for public consideration and debate. This in itself was a radical innovation—to send back to the people the fruit of their elected delegates so they could endorse or reject it. The process was left vague, however, so the invitation was more of an informal public opinion poll than a request for formal ratification. The constitutional convention proclaimed that the document was adopted on September 28, 1776.

The constitution was a victory for small farmers, especially German and mostly Presbyterian Scots-Irish frontiersmen with small holdings of land; for urban artisans, many of whom previously could not vote because they owned no property; and for radical reformers who dreamed of holding the rich at bay in the interest of a more equitable society. It was a heavy blow to wealthy merchants, large property owners, and assorted conservatives who wanted to retain the old political system, which they feared was slipping from their grasp. By shifting the center of political gravity downward, the 1776 constitution capped a move toward a democratized polity that had gained momentum as Revolutionary leaders saw the necessity to mobilize all but the very bottom of society. Here was the idea that the bone, sinew, and muscle of the producing classes were the future of the republic and that the wealthy nonproducers, who lived by manipulating money and land, were to be valued the least.

While people "out of doors" regarded the constitution as the dawn of a new era, conservatives and some moderates, both inside and outside Pennsylvania, looked at it with horror. Departing radically from conventional political thought, the constitution shocked and dismayed such Pennsylvania patriot leaders as John Dickinson, James Wilson, and Robert Morris. Even Benjamin Rush, who had stood with radicals a few months before, called it "our rascally constitution" that made the state government as dreaded as "the government of Turkey." Though he had grown up under a unicameral legislature, Rush now complained that "a single legislature is big with tyranny."[21] "Good god!" gasped John Adams after seeing the full constitution. "The people of Pennsylvania in two years will be glad to petition the crown of Britain for reconciliation in order to be delivered from the tyranny of their Constitution."[22]

No element of the constitution appalled conservatives and some moderates more than the enlargement of the electorate. "The most flourishing commonwealths that ever existed, Athens and Rome," wrote an anonymous Philadelphian, "were RUINED by allowing this right to people without property."[23] For Adams, the unprecedented extension of the franchise was nothing short of a perversion of good republican government. Adams had applauded the Philadelphia town meeting on May 20, 1776, which overthrew the Pennsylvania Assembly that had blockaded the road to independence with the vocal support of people who never before had been given a claim in public affairs. But that much done, he wanted propertyless citizens to disappear from the political stage and surrender it to men of means. Adams saw the Revolution as a "people's war," but he was unwilling to have a people's war produce a people's polity.

Less than a month after the legislature declared that the constitution was Pennsylvania's organic law, conservatives and some moderates borrowed a page from the radicals' playbook, calling for a town meeting on October 21. Their intention was to sharply revise the constitution. Ridiculing the constitution "because a certain Schoolmaster [James Cannon] had a principal hand in forming it," conservatives argued that the next elected assembly should amend or rewrite it. About fifteen hundred Philadelphians gathered. Working people and most of the militiamen who had returned from service in New Jersey stayed away. There to represent them, however, were James Cannon, Timothy Matlack, Thomas Young, and Colonel Smith of York County, who defended the constitution in opposition to Thomas McKean and John Dickinson, who railed against its most democratic features.

The battle continued for nearly a year, with accusations filling the pages of the Philadelphia press. Radicals charged that the conservatives' real objection was that they "would not be governed by leather aprons" and hated to see an end to the right to hold multiple offices and enrich themselves through officeholding. They also reminded readers that the aging Franklin had presided at the convention and had fully approved its handiwork.[24] Conservatives returned fire with charges that the radicals were "coffee-house demagogues" who would bring anarchy to William Penn's peaceable kingdom and that the "strange innovations . . . differ unnecessarily . . . from every [state] government . . . lately established in America on the authority of the people."[25] Only when the British Army drove northward from the Chesapeake Bay region to capture Philadelphia in September 1777 did the opponents of the constitution temporarily quit their attempts to scuttle the document. The argument was far from over, but while the British Army occupied Philadelphia until June 1778, the constitutionalists held their fire.

If the state constitution of 1776 embroiled Pennsylvania in controversy, it had a positive reception in a few other states and in some European capitals. In October 1776 Benjamin Franklin, the convention's president, sailed from Philadelphia for Paris, where the Continental Congress hoped he could convince France to recognize the American revolutionaries and come to their side. With him, Franklin took the newly minted state constitution. French Enlightenment intellectuals read it with wonder, and most found it breathtaking. "Mr. Turgot, the Duke de la Rochefoucauld, Mr. Condorcet, and many others," John Adams wrote ruefully, "became enamored with the Constitution," which was "immediately propagated through France" as the work of Franklin.[26] What enraged conservative and more moderate revolutionists in Philadelphia delighted the *salonistes* in Paris, who were looking for inspiration in their own attempts to begin their world anew.

Closer to home, the budding state of Vermont—Young gave it its name—closely modeled its constitution on Pennsylvania's after Young sent his friends there the Pennsylvania state constitution that he had worked so hard to forge. Other states, particularly North Carolina and Georgia, adopted some of the democratic elements embedded in Pennsylvania's organic law. Franklin defended it to his last days.

꧃

When Thomas Paine returned to America in 1802 after an absence of fifteen years, he penned a series of letters "To the Citizens of the United States." In what he called "sparks from the altar of '76," Paine reminded Americans that independence "was the opportunity of *beginning the world anew* . . . and of bringing forward a *new system of government* in which the rights of *all* men should be preserved."[27] Now he saw the work of his caucus friends sullied. After years of inveighing against it, conservatives—on their fourth attempt—had finally gained enough legislative clout to scuttle the radical constitution of 1776. In 1790 they replaced it with a new constitution that ripped out some of the original's most democratic features. The new constitution installed a strong governor with extensive patronage privileges and a veto power over legislation. Scrapping a unicameral legislature, the constitution sanctioned a two-house assembly with the upper-house members serving for four years.

Though replaced, the ideas embedded in the radical constitution of 1776 lived on. Reflecting the full flowering of democratic thought in the Revolutionary Era and standing as a prime example of the revolution within the Revolution, it inspired lawmakers around the world. Unicameralism, with its insistence that a true democracy should make no distinctions between the haves and have-nots as represented in upper and lower legislative houses, spread around the world. It was acclaimed and implemented in revolutionary France and is how law is made today in Nebraska, Guam, the Virgin Islands, and Hong Kong; in all of Australia and Canada's provinces; in the legislative bodies of Scotland, Wales, and Northern Ireland; in Italy and Spain; and in almost all socialist states. Most important, the broadened franchise, in which land ownership is not required for first-class citizenship, in time became the gold standard nationwide and gradually spread abroad as the most important legacy of the sparks from Pennsylvania's altar of '76. Philadelphia's radical caucus had changed Pennsylvania's position on independence at a crucial moment in the summer of 1776, and in the process had turned Pennsylvania into a people's republic.

FOR FURTHER READING

Philadelphia's radical group that waged the double struggle for independence and internal reform has attracted the attention of many historians. Among recent insightful books are Richard Alan Ryerson, *The Revolution Is Now Begun: The Radical Committees of Philadelphia, 1765–1776* (Philadelphia, 1978); Steven Rosswurm, *Arms, Country, and Class: The Philadelphia Militia and the "Lower Sort" During the American Revolution* (New Brunswick, N.J., 1987); Eric Foner, *Tom Paine and Revolutionary America* (New York, 1976); and my *The Unknown American Revolution: The Unruly Birth of Democracy and the Struggle to Create America* (New York, 2005). Other figures in the radical group are understudied, but for Thomas Young see Pauline Maier, *The Old Revolutionaries: Political Lives in the Age of Samuel Adams* (New York, 1980), chap. 3. For many years the standard work on Pennsylvania's 1776 constitution was Paul Selsam, *The Pennsylvania Constitution of 1776* (New York, 1971). But for a modern reading of it in a comparative treatment of state constitutions, see Marc W. Kruman, *Between Authority and Liberty: State Constitution Making in Revolutionary America* (Chapel Hill, N.C., 1996).

Some of the convoluted political machinations that led to independence and the radical constitution of 1776 can be followed in the official legislative proceedings: *Journals of the House of Representatives of the Commonwealth of Pennsylvania, 1776–81, with the Proceedings of the Several Committees and Conventions Before and at the Commencement of the American Revolution,* ed. Michael Hillegas (Philadelphia, 1782), and *Proceedings Relative to Calling the Conventions of 1776 and 1790* (Harrisburg, Pa., 1825).

CHAPTER FIVE

A World of Paine

Jill Lepore

I n the winter of 1776, John Adams read *Common Sense,* an anonymous, fanatical, and brutally brilliant forty-six-page pamphlet that would convince the American people of what more than a decade of taxes and nearly a year of war had not: that it was nothing less than their destiny to declare independence from Britain. "The cause of America is in a great measure the cause of all mankind" was *Common Sense*'s astonishing and inspiring claim about the fate of thirteen infant colonies on the edge of the world. "The sun never shone on a cause of greater worth. 'Tis not the affair of a city, a county, a province, or a kingdom; but of a continent—of at least one-eighth part of the habitable globe. 'Tis not the concern of a day, a year, or an age; posterity are virtually involved in the contest, and will be more or less affected even to the end of time, by the proceedings now."[1] Whether these words were preposterous or prophetic only time would tell, but meanwhile everyone wondered: Who could have written such stirring stuff?

"People Speak of it in rapturous praise," a friend wrote Adams. "Some make Dr. Franklin the Author," hinted another. "I think I see strong marks of your pen in it," speculated a third. More miffed than flattered, Adams admitted to his wife, Abigail, "I could not have written any Thing in so manly and striking a style." Who, then? Adams found out: "His Name is Paine."[2]

Thomas Pain was born in Thetford, England, in 1737 (he added the *e* later and was called "Tom" only by his enemies), the son of a Quaker journeyman who sewed the bones of whales into stays for ladies' corsets. He left the local grammar school at the age of twelve, to serve as his father's apprentice. At twenty he went to sea on a privateer. In 1759 he opened his own stay-making shop and married a servant girl, but the next year both she and their child died in childbirth. For a decade Pain struggled to make a life for himself. He taught school, collected taxes, and in 1771 married a grocer's daughter. Three years later he was fired from his job with the excise office; his unhappy and childless second marriage fell apart; and everything he owned was sold at auction to pay off his debts. At the age of thirty-seven, Thomas Pain was ruined. He therefore did what every ruined Englishman did, if he possibly could: he sailed to America. Sickened with typhus during the journey, Pain arrived in Philadelphia in December 1774 so weak he had to be carried off the ship. What saved his life was a letter found in his pocket: "The bearer Mr Thomas Pain is very well recommended to me as an ingenious worthy young man."[3] It was signed by Benjamin Franklin. It was better than a bag of gold.

How an unknown Englishman who had been in the colonies for little more than a year came to write the most influential essay of the American Revolution—no matter that he had once caught Franklin's eye during a chance meeting in London—is a mystery not easily solved. Paine is a puzzle. Lockean liberalism, classical republicanism, and Leveller radicalism all can be found in his work, though whether he ever read Locke, or anyone else, is probably impossible to discover. His love for equality has been traced to Quakerism, his hatred of injustice to growing up next door to a gallows. Good guesses, but guesses all the same.

"I offer nothing more than simple facts, plain arguments, and common sense," Paine wrote, but this was coyness itself: *Common Sense* stood every argument against American independence on its head. "There is something absurd in supposing a continent to be perpetually governed by an island," he insisted. As to the colonies' dependence on England, "We may as well assert that because a child has thrived upon milk, that it is never to have meat." And hereditary monarchy? "Nature disapproves it, otherwise she would not so frequently turn it into ridicule by giving mankind an ass for a lion."[4]

Adams, who had been the colonies' most ardent advocate for independence, refused to accept that Paine deserved any credit for *Common Sense*. "He is a keen Writer," Adams granted, but he'd offered nothing more than "a tolerable summary of the argument which I had been repeating again and again in Congress for nine months." The longer John Adams lived, the more he hated Thomas Paine, and the more worthless he considered that forty-six-page pamphlet. Adams believed, with many of his contemporaries, that democracy was dangerous and that the rule of the mob was one step away from anarchy; the rabble must be checked. Paine's notion of common sense, he believed, was "democratical without any restraint." By the end of his life, the aging and ill-tempered ex-president would call *Common Sense* "a poor, ignorant, Malicious, short-sighted, Crapulous Mass."[5]

◡ͼ

Thomas Paine is, at best, a lesser founder. In the comic-book version of history that serves as our national heritage, where the Founding Fathers are like the Hanna-Barbera SuperFriends, Paine is Aquaman to Washington's Superman and Jefferson's Batman; we never find out how he got his superpowers, and he shows up only when they need someone who can swim. That this should be the case—that Americans have proven ambivalent about Paine— seems, at first, surprising, since Paine's contributions to the nation's founding would be hard to overstate. *Common Sense* made declaring independence possible. "Without the pen of the author of *Common Sense,* the sword of Washington would have been raised in vain," Adams wrote.[6] But Paine lifted his sword too and emptied his purse. Despite his poverty—he was by far the poorest of the founders—he donated his share of the profits from *Common Sense* to buy supplies for the Continental Army, in which he also served. His chief contribution to the war was a series of essays known as the *American Crisis.* He wrote the first of these essays by the light of a campfire during Washington's desperate retreat across New Jersey, in December 1776. Making ready to cross the frozen Delaware River—at night, in a blizzard—to launch a surprise attack on Trenton, Washington ordered Paine's words read to his exhausted, frostbitten troops: "These are the times that try men's souls. The summer soldier and the sunshine patriot will, in this crisis, shrink from the service of their country; but he that stands it now, deserves the love and thanks of man and woman. Tyranny, like hell, is not easily conquered; yet we have this consolation with us, that the harder the conflict, the more glorious the triumph."[7] The next morning the Continentals fought to a stunning, pivotal victory.

It's hard to believe anyone thought Adams could have written lines like these; Paine wrote like no one else: he wrote for everyone. "As it is my design to make those that can scarcely read understand," he explained, "I shall therefore avoid every literary ornament and put it in language as plain as the alphabet."[8] So gripping was Paine's prose, and so vast was its reach, that Adams once complained to Jefferson, "History is to ascribe the American Revolution to Thomas Paine."[9] But history has not been kind to Paine, who forfeited his chance to glorify his role, or at least to document it: at the end of the war, Congress asked him to write the history of the Revolution, but he declined. And the person who did write that history, John and Abigail Adams's close friend, the Massachusetts poet and playwright Mercy Otis Warren, relegated Paine to a footnote—literally—in her magisterial 1805 *History of the Rise, Progress, and Termination of the American Revolution.*[10] By the time Paine died in 1809, all of the surviving founders had renounced him. (Jefferson even refused to allow his correspondence with Paine to be printed. "No, my dear sir, not for this world," he told an inquirer. "Into what a hornet's nest would it thrust my head!")[11] And nearly no one showed up to see him buried. As Paul Collins observed in *The Trouble with Tom: The Strange Afterlife and Times of Thomas Paine,* "There were twenty thousand mourners at Franklin's funeral. Tom Paine's had six."[12]

Disavowed by his contemporaries, Paine left little behind in his own defense; the bulk of his papers, including notes for an autobiography, were destroyed in a fire. (Even his bones have been lost; they were stolen, stashed, smashed, and finally probably thrown out with the rubbish.) Paine enjoyed a brief revival in the 1940s, after FDR quoted the *American Crisis*—"these are the times that try men's souls"—in a fireside chat in 1942, three months after the attack on Pearl Harbor; and an excellent two-volume set, *The Complete Writings of Thomas Paine,* was published in 1945, edited by Philip Foner. But Paine has never much enjoyed the esteem of academics who, on the whole, have shared John Adams's view of him, whatever the rest of America might think. The eminent early American literary scholar Perry Miller believed that Paine's obscurity was well deserved. In a review of *The Complete Writings* in *The Nation* in 1945, Miller sneered, "The price of popularizing for contemporaries is temporary popularity." In 1980 Ronald Reagan inaugurated a second Paine revival when, accepting the Republican Party nomination for president, he quoted *Common Sense*: "We have it in our power to begin the world over again." In the wake of that revival, Princeton historian Sean Wilentz agreed with Miller's assessment; in *The New Republic* in 1995, Wilentz called Paine "hopelessly naïve." Gordon Wood finds him to be merely "a man out of joint with his times," but Paine emerges in most academic accounts as a kind of idiot savant: savvy about adjectives but idiotic about politics. *Common Sense* is "a work of genius," Bernard Bailyn concluded in 1990, but next to men like Adams, Jefferson, and Madison, Paine was "an ignoramus."[13]

Thomas Paine left the United States in 1787. "Where liberty is, there is my country," Franklin once said, to which Paine replied, "Wherever liberty is not, there is my country."[14] In England in 1791 he wrote the first part of *Rights of Man,* a work he considered an English version of *Common Sense.* Defending the French Revolution from English critics, he argued that France had "outgrown the baby clothes of count and duke, and breeched itself in manhood." Americans had weaned themselves of milk, and the French had put on pants; now it was time for the British to grow beards. "It is an age of revolutions, in which every thing may be looked for." The next year Paine wrote *Rights of Man, Part the Second,* his most important statement of political principles, in which he explained and insisted on natural rights, equality, and popular sovereignty. He went further: "When, in countries that are called civilized, we see age going to the work-house and youth to the gallows, something must be wrong in the system of government."[15] By way of remedy, Paine proposed the framework for a welfare state, providing tax tables calculated down to the last shilling.

The first part of *Rights of Man* sold fifty thousand copies in just three months. The second part was outsold only by the Bible. But British conservatives didn't want to follow France, especially as the news from Paris grew more gruesome. Paine was charged with seditious libel, and, everywhere, his ideas were suppressed and his followers persecuted. "I am for equality. Why, no kings!" one Londoner shouted in a coffeehouse, and was promptly sent to prison for a year and a half.[16] Meanwhile, William Pitt's government hired hack writers to conduct a smear campaign, which asserted, among other things, that Paine—horribly ugly, smelly, rude, and relentlessly cruel, even as a child—had committed fraud, defrauded his creditors, caused his first wife's death by beating her while she was pregnant, and abused his second

By the time Thomas Paine left the United States in 1787, he was attracting the venom of conservatives on both sides of the Atlantic. In this 1791 print, *Mad Tom, or the Man of Rights,* Paine sits on a sheet of his *Rights of Man* and scribbles "Riots, treasonous plots, conspiracies, civil war" on the paper on his writing table.

wife almost as badly, except that she wasn't really his wife because he never consummated that marriage, preferring instead to have sex with cats.

"It is earnestly recommended to Mad Tom that he should embark for France and there be naturalized into the regular confusion of democracy," the London *Times* urged.[17] In September 1792, that's just what Paine did, fleeing to Paris, where he had already been elected a member of the National Assembly, in honor of his authorship of *Rights of Man*. In France he faltered and fell, not least because he spoke almost no French but mostly because he argued against executing Louis XVI, suggesting instead that he be exiled to the United States, where, "far removed from the miseries and crimes of royalty, he may learn, from the constant public prosperity, that the true system of government consists not in kings, but in fair, equal, and honourable representation."[18]

Back in England, Paine's trial for *Rights of Man* went on without him; he was found guilty and outlawed. "If the French kill their King, it will be a signal for my departure," Paine had pledged before he left for France, but now he had no choice: not only could he not return to England, he couldn't venture an Atlantic crossing to the United States, for fear of being captured by a British warship. Instead, he stayed in his rooms in Paris and waited for the worst. As the Reign of Terror unfolded, he drafted the first part of *The Age of Reason*. In December 1793, when the police knocked at his door, he handed a stash of papers to his friend, the American poet and statesman Joel Barlow. Barlow carried the manuscript to the printers; the police carried Paine to an eight-by-ten-foot cell on the ground floor of a prison that had once been a palace. There he would write most of the second part of *The Age of Reason* as he watched his fellow inmates go daily to their deaths. (In six weeks in the summer of 1794, more than thirteen hundred people were executed.)[19]

When the U.S. government failed to secure his release, Paine at first despaired. Then he raged, writing to the American ambassador, James Monroe, "I should be tempted to curse the day I knew America. By contributing to her liberty I have lost my own."[20] Finally, after ten months, he was freed. But he left prison an invalid. Ravaged by typhus, gout, recurring fevers, and a suppurating wound on his belly, he would never really recover. He convalesced at Monroe's home in Paris and, for years, at the homes of a succession of supporters. After Jefferson defeated Adams in the election of 1800, the new president invited Paine to return to the United States. He sailed in 1802.

◡

"The questions central to an understanding of Paine's career do not lend themselves to exploration within the confines of conventional biography,"

Eric Foner argued in 1976, in *Tom Paine and Revolutionary America.*[21] You can say that again. What with the burned papers, the lost bones, and Paine's role in three revolutions, not to mention tabloid allegations of wife-beating, it's hard to know how to write about Paine. What Foner called "The Problem of Thomas Paine" has a lot to do with the very thing about him that contributed most to his obscurity in the first place: his uncompromising condemnation of all of the world's religions. In *The Age of Reason,* published in 1794 and 1795, Paine wrote: "All national institutions of churches, whether Jewish, Christian, or Turkish, appear to me no other than human inventions, set up to terrify and enslave mankind, and monopolize power and profit. Each of those churches accuses the other of unbelief; and for my own part, I disbelieve them all." Theodore Roosevelt once called Paine a "filthy little atheist," but as Paine was at pains to point out, he did believe in God; he just didn't believe in the Bible, or the Koran, or the Torah; these he considered hearsay, lies, fables, and frauds that served to wreak havoc with humanity while hiding the beauty of God's creation, the evidence for which was everywhere obvious in "the universe we behold." In *The Age of Reason,* Paine offered his own creed:

> I believe in one God, and no more; and I hope for happiness beyond this life. I believe in the equality of man; and I believe that religious duties consist in doing justice, loving mercy, and endeavoring to make our fellow creatures happy. But . . . I do not believe in the creed professed by the Jewish Church, by the Roman Church, by the Greek Church, by the Turkish Church, by the Protestant Church, nor by any church that I know of. My own mind is my own church.[22]

"Paine's religious opinions were those of three-fourths of the men of letters of the last age," Joel Barlow observed, probably overstating the case only slightly.[23] Paine's views were hardly original; what was new was his audience. Not for nothing did Sean Wilentz call *The Age of Reason* a "*Reader's Digest* rendering" of the Enlightenment.[24] But while other Enlightenment writers wrote for one another, Paine wrote, as always, for everyone. To say that Paine was vilified for doing this is to miss the point. He was destroyed.

Mark Twain once said, "It took a brave man before the Civil War to confess he had read the *Age of Reason.*"[25] But that didn't mean it wasn't read. In Britain, sales of *The Age of Reason* outpaced even those of *Rights of Man,* though, since it was banned as blasphemous, it's impossible to know how many copies were actually sold. London printer Richard Carlisle, who called his bookstore The Temple of Reason, was fined a thousand pounds for selling it and sentenced to two years in jail. (During an earlier trial on similar charges, Carlisle had read aloud from *Rights of Man*, a ploy that allowed him to publish it again, as a courtroom transcript.) After Carlisle's wife fell into the trap of selling *The Age of Reason* to a government agent posing as a bookstore browser, she—and her newborn baby—followed her husband to prison. Eventually, in order to avoid exposing anyone inside the bookstore to further prosecution, there appeared outside The Temple of Reason an "invisible shopman," a machine into which customers could drop coins and take out a book.[26]

But *The Age of Reason* cost Paine dearly. He lost, among other things, the friendship of Samuel Adams, who seethed, "Do you think that your pen, or the pen of any other man, can unchristianize the mass of our citizens?" Even before Paine returned to the United States in 1802, Federalists used him as a weapon against Jefferson, damning the "two Toms" as infidels while calling Paine "a loathsome reptile." Ministers and their congregants, caught up in the early stages of a religious revival now known as the Second Great Awakening, gloried in news of Paine's physical and mental decline, conjuring up a drunk, unshaven, and decrepit Paine, writhing in pain, begging, "Oh Lord help me! Oh, Christ help me!"[27]

Some of that fantasy was founded in fact. Even at his best, Paine was rough and unpolished—and a mean drunk. In his tortured final years, living in New Rochelle and New York City, he displayed signs of dementia. (Scurrilous rumors about cats aside, Paine's behavior throughout his life appears erratic enough that Eric Foner wondered if he suffered from crippling bouts of depression, while Nelson offers a tentative diagnosis of bipolar disorder.) At home he was besieged by visitors who came either to save his soul or to damn it. He told all of them to go to hell. When an old woman announced, "I come from Almighty God to tell you that if you do not repent of your sins and believe in our blessed Savior Jesus Christ, you will be damned," Paine replied, "Pshaw. God would not send such a foolish ugly old woman as you."[28]

Admirers of Paine's political pamphlets have long tried to ignore his religious convictions. In 1800 a New York Republican Society resolved: "May his *Rights of Man* be handed down to our latest posterity, but may his *Age of Reason* never live to see the rising generation."[29] That's more or less how things have turned out. So wholly has *The Age of Reason* been forgotten that Paine's mantle has been claimed not only by Ronald Reagan but also by the Christian Coalition's Ralph Reed, who has quoted him, and North Carolina senator Jesse Helms, who in 1992 supported a proposal to erect a Paine monument in Washington, D.C. Nor have liberals who embrace Paine, including the editors of TomPaine.com, and Barack Obama, who quoted him—without mentioning him by name—in his 2009 inaugural address, had much interest in the latter years of his career. Maybe that's what it means to be a lesser SuperFriend: no one cares about your secret identity. They just like your costume.

Historians too have tried to dismiss *The Age of Reason,* writing it off as simplistic and suggesting either that Paine wrote it to please his French jailers or that, in prison, he went mad. This interpretation began with Mercy Otis Warren, who called *The Age of Reason* "jejune," explained that Paine wrote it while "trembling under the terrors of the guillotine," and concluded that, "imprisoned, he endeavoured to ingratiate himself."[30] But Paine himself considered his lifelong views on religion inseparable from his thoughts on government. "It has been the scheme of the Christian Church, and of all other invented systems of religion, to hold man in ignorance of the Creator, as it is of Governments to hold man in ignorance of his rights." Writing about kings and lords in *Common Sense,* he wondered "how a race of men came into the world so exalted above the rest, and distinguished like some new species." In *The Age of Reason* he used much the same language to write about priests and prophets: "The Jews have their Moses; the Christians have their Jesus Christ, their apostles and saints; and the Turks their Mahomet, as if the way to God was not open to every man alike." He wrote *Common Sense, Rights of Man,* and *Age of Reason* as a trilogy. "Soon after I had published the pamphlet 'Common Sense,' in America," he explained, "I saw the exceeding probability that a revolution in the system of government would be followed by a revolution in the system of religion."[31]

That Paine was wrong about the coming of that revolution, oh, so very wrong, doesn't mean we ought to forget that he yearned for it. In 1806 John Adams railed that the latter part of the eighteenth century had come to be called "The Age of Reason": "I am willing you should call this the Age of Frivolity, and would not object if you had named it the Age of Folly, Vice, Frenzy, Brutality, Daemons, Buonaparte, Tom Paine, or the Age of the Burning Brand from the Bottomless Pit, or anything but the Age of Reason." But not even Adams would have wished that so much of Paine's work—however much he disagreed with it—would be so willfully excised from memory. "I know not whether any man in the world has had more influence on its inhabitants or affairs for the last thirty years than Tom Paine," Adams admitted, adding, with irony worthy of the author of *Common Sense,* "Call it then the Age of Paine."[32]

Adams wrote those words in 1806 as if Paine were already dead. He was not. That year a neighbor of Paine's came across the old man himself, in a tavern in New York, so drunk and disoriented and unwashed and unkempt that his toenails had grown over his toes, like bird's claws. While Adams, at his home in Quincy, busied himself reflecting on the Age of Paine, Paine hobbled to the polls in New Rochelle to cast his vote in a local election. He was told that he was not an American citizen and was turned away. So much for the rights of man. Three years later, as the seventy-two-year-old Paine lay dying in a house in Greenwich Village, his doctor pressed him, "Do you wish to believe that Jesus Christ is the Son of God?" Paine paused, then whispered, "I have no wish to believe on that subject."

FOR FURTHER READING

The bulk of Paine's letters were destroyed by fire. His published writings and his scant letters were collected by Philip Foner and published in two volumes as *The Complete Writings of Thomas Paine* (New York, 1945). That edition remains authoritative. A very useful edition of *Common Sense* is that edited and introduced by Thomas Slaughter (Boston, 2001). The very many comprehensive biographies of Paine include John Keane, *Tom Paine: A Political Life* (Boston, 1995). The best single-volume study of Paine's American career is still Eric Foner's *Tom Paine and Revolutionary America* (New York, 1976). In *Thomas Paine: Enlightenment, Revolution, and the Birth of Modern Nations* (New York, 2006), Craig Nelson places Paine in a transatlantic context; his book is as much a primer on the Enlightenment as the story of the stay-maker from Thetford. Paine's strange fate in American cultural memory is the subject of Harvey J. Kaye's deeply researched and revealing *Thomas Paine and the Promise of America* (New York, 2005). Paul Collins's *The Trouble with Tom: The Strange Afterlife and Times of Thomas Paine* (New York, 2005) is a somewhat glib and whimsical but ultimately powerful account of the fate of Paine's reputation and, especially, of his bones.

CHAPTER SIX

Phillis Wheatley: The Poet
Who Challenged the American Revolutionaries

David Waldstreicher

homas Woolridge couldn't believe his ears. Traveling in Boston, he'd heard about the nineteen-year-old African woman who wrote excellent English verse to suit any occasion. On October 10, 1772, following an already well-worn path, he made his way to the home of John Wheatley, King Street, near the Long Wharf and a few blocks from the center of town, to meet the poet in person.

Phillis Wheatley was already famous in New England. Her elegy to the great revivalist George Whitefield had been printed on both sides of the Atlantic. Nevertheless, after seeing some of her manuscripts, Woolridge didn't believe his eyes either. He doubted whether the slave girl could have written them. He asked her to show him what she could do, on the spot. Phillis replied that "she was then busy and engaged for the Day," but he could "propose a Subject" and return for the results in the morning.[1] Woolridge proposed his patron and correspondent William Legge, Lord Dartmouth, who just six weeks earlier had accepted the position of secretary of state for the colonies.

When Woolridge came back the next day, Wheatley wrote out for him one of her boldest and most political poems, in praise of Dartmouth. The poem's first two sets of twelve lines described New England, a traditional place of "*Freedom,*" rejoicing at the "happy day" when Dartmouth assumed his post:

> No more of grievance unredress'd complain;
> Or injur'd Rights, or groan beneath the chain,

> Which Wanton Tyranny with lawless hand,
> Made to enslave, O Liberty! thy Land.[2]

Wheatley was apparently well aware not only who Dartmouth was but also that Massachusetts patriots were congratulating themselves that a reputed friend of the colonies had been appointed.

To compare a change in administration to emancipation from tyranny was to perform colonial politics and do it well. Yet Phillis Wheatley has rarely been considered politically savvy, much less effective. Historians of the American Revolution consider her as at best lobbing a quiet if profound antislavery broadside or two from the pious, feminine margins—even though she successfully addressed, and garnered telling responses from, the likes of Dartmouth, George Washington, Benjamin Franklin, and Thomas Jefferson.

What if we consider Phillis Wheatley in the cauldron of 1760s and 1770s Boston? What if she read the newspapers and followed events as they unfolded in buildings or on the streets that were but a few blocks from her master's house: the Town House (center of government), Faneuil Hall (the place of the town meeting), and Old South Meeting House (the scene of protests)? If she did so, she knew more about her era's politics, as well as her Bible and her Virgil, than all but a few of us ever will.

Placing Wheatley within the American Revolution shifts our sense of her historical importance. She understood the subtle and overt relationships between religion and politics in new and old England, and participated in them. She intervened as a writer to free herself and to advance the antislavery cause. She was a committed patriot, early and late—but at key moments, like so many Africans in the colonies, she entertained the notion that the king's government might be more sympathetic to black freedom than the colonial resistance movement. She challenged the American Revolutionaries, as well as their English counterparts, to respond to her political as well as poetic genius. Had she not mastered their words, their ideas, their song, she could not have sent their calls for liberty back to them, inside out and publicly, with such real consequences for herself and her fellow slaves.

By the early 1770s Wheatley and other black Bostonians had developed ways of publicly linking religion, politics, antislavery, and antiracism. She was well prepared to make the most of a visit from a friend of Lord Dartmouth's. In addition to understanding Dartmouth's place in the government, she knew his reputation as a pious reformer mocked by some as a "Psalm-singer."[3] Of all the colonial secretaries who served in her time, none would have been as likely to take an interest in a Christian slave poet as Lord Dartmouth. That was why she took an interest in him.

Wheatley was also quite aware that her poems would be understood as African, with relevance for the question of slavery. The second half of the Dartmouth poem answers the question she imagines an enlightened Dartmouth asking, in effect turning Woolridge's question—can African slaves write English verse?—into another set of questions entirely. Why had Wheatley chosen to write this particular "advent'rous Song" on this occasion? Was it because the issues of colonial liberties and African slavery were linked? *What was the relationship between the rhetoric and the reality of slavery?*

> While you, my Lord, read o'er th' advent'rous Song
> And wonder whence Such daring boldness Sprung:
> Hence, flow my wishes for the common good,
> By feeling Hearts alone, best understood.
>
> From Native clime, when Seeming cruel fate
> Me snatch'd from Afric's fancy'd happy Seat,
> Impetuous.—Ah! what bitter pangs molest,
> What Sorrows labour'd in the Parent breast!
> That more than Stone, ne'er Soft compassion mov'd
> Who from its Father Seiz'd his much belov'd.
> Such once my Case.—Thus I deplore the day
> When Britons weep beneath Tyrannick sway.

In these twelve lines Wheatley accomplishes something of a revolution. From being suspect as a poet or a freak of nature, she becomes a republican who wishes for the "common good" with a heart as feeling as any in British America. She feels deeply, however, not in spite of her race but because of her father's African experience of having his daughter snatched away. She equates with her father's grief the anguish of patriots faced with loss of liberty. Her heritage, as much as that of any British colonist, explains her good citizenship. Awareness of chattel slavery's wrongs makes Phillis a poet of British and New England liberties.

Like patriots' crowd actions and the best of their rhetoric, the Dartmouth poem is bold and theatrical, yet artful. The poem's final twelve lines take the edge off Phillis's boldness by again thanking the powerful cabinet minister and wishing him "heaven'ly grace" and immortality—not just in secular, "fleeting Fame" of the kind bestowed by poets, but also, "like the Prophet," in heaven. Just in case Dartmouth did not get the message, or read the poem carefully, Wheatley wrote out a cover letter that summarized the argument. The occasion excused the "freedom from an African" to write him, since all of "(now) happy America" rejoiced at the appointment of one of America's "greatest advocates." She wished him God's blessing—and signed her name. She also wrote out a brief biographical sketch of herself that was verified by her owners.[4] In less than a year she would sail to England with her manuscript poems and meet Lord Dartmouth himself. That written proof, and her actual presence, led to the publication of her *Poems on Various Subjects, Religious and Moral* (1773) and her own emancipation by the Wheatleys. Wheatley challenged her contemporaries to imagine Africans as full participants in their culture and politics. She challenges us, in turn, to imagine a wider cast of characters for the American Revolution: to broaden our understanding of who successfully engaged in Revolutionary politics.

Phillis Wheatley was bought by Susanna Wheatley off a slaving vessel called the *Phillis* in July 1761. Mrs. Wheatley, the wife of a merchant successful enough to own his own ship for trade with England, was looking for a young female to augment the aging enslaved staff the Wheatleys already owned, to take care of her and her house in her later years, anticipating also the departures of her twin eighteen-year-olds, Mary and Nathanael. Something about Phillis's face and manner interested her, according to an account written by Susanna's niece. We do not know exactly how, or how quickly, Phillis demonstrated remarkable gifts. But within a year the eight-year-old girl had been taught to read by Mary Wheatley and had taught herself to write. By 1765, at the age of twelve, she was writing poems and not hesitating to show them. At about this time she began to be relieved of the most taxing sorts of household work, as the Wheatleys recognized they had a genius on their hands.[5]

Why, though, did she choose poetry as her vocation, and what were the consequences of that choice? The answer probably has something to do with poetry's acceptability as a female accomplishment, and its concision: the possibility of finishing something in a short time when one is liable to be asked—commanded—to do something else, for someone else. Poetry, slavery, and womanhood were surprisingly compatible in an eighteenth-century merchant household.

Just as important to understanding Wheatley is knowing something of the particular uses of formal verse in her world. A poem, before the advent of Romanticism, was not thought to be the exquisite expression of an individual soul (although it could be that) but rather an entry into a world of polite letters in which participants displayed a mastery of the techniques of praise, mourning, and adornment of people and things valued by the culture. There were varieties of poetry for everybody: from tavern songs sung by anyone to classical verse studied by the children of the elite. In between these popular and high favorites were political and pious verses, read and declaimed in church and printed in the newspapers and on broadsides—the single sheets hawked about town by printers' apprentices. Poems were public: they connected people and also marked distinctions among them.

Poetry's integrating functions were particularly important. Ambitious would-be laureates celebrated notable events and anniversaries, glorified the empire and their patrons, sought to demonstrate or inspire salvation, or even had their occasional verse tacked onto effigies of detested public figures during protests likely to be staged on festival days. What might seem like a restricting choice today—especially the iambic pentameter Wheatley favored—would, for her, have been a gateway of connections and, especially, aspirations. No one could say that a good poem wasn't a beautiful, important, or true thing. No one could deny poetry's religious and political significance (although Thomas Jefferson, in response to Wheatley, would try). Nor could those attuned to cultural traditions deny the poet the right to reflect on the glory, and significance, of her own efforts, however much in the service of patrons, kings, or God.

What sort of poems did Wheatley choose to write at first? In her earliest proposal for a book in 1772, she listed as having written in 1765 a version of a poem anticipating the death of Joseph Sewall, the aged pastor of Old South Church. Sewall's father, Samuel Sewall, had been one of the first New Englanders to publicly and repeatedly denounce the institution of African slavery. Later, at least a third of Wheatley's poems took the forms of elegy: encomiums to the recently departed that sent messages to their survivors. By the eighteenth century, elegy was so familiar and important a genre of writing that it was both satirized and still performed in honor of dead worthies, as well as women and children. The teenaged Wheatley's ability to write for specific occasions gained her the admiration and appreciation of women and men in Boston.

The association of Wheatley with elegy, however, can obscure the fact that she was experimenting with several kinds of occasional verse—experiments that led directly to her encounter with Lord Dartmouth. Her first published poem in 1767 depicted the shipwreck and providential rescue of two Nantucket Quaker merchants who had described the incident as she served them at the Wheatleys' table. In being so moved by their harrowing experience at sea, was she remembering her own middle passage six years before? Was she reaching out to men who belonged to the one sect that had disowned human bondage?

By 1768 she was writing in response to secular political as well as sacred events. Her 1772 book proposal also lists a 1768 poem praising the king for the repeal of the Stamp Act. Why would she write about a two-year-old event? The repeal of the Stamp Act on March, 18, 1766, was a major achievement of the patriot movement and was celebrated by a good part of Boston. On March 18, 1768, a rank-and-file group seized the occasion of the anniversary of the repeal to protest the recent arrival in Boston of the customs commissioners with a parade that went through King Street. This procession with "a considerable mob of young fellows & Negroes" only yards from the Wheatley house would have been hard not to see or hear.

Events on the street—as often as not, Wheatley's street—linked the question of slavery to the political crisis. The British troops who came to Boston in 1768 and marched off the Long Wharf past her house on King Street included a significant number of Africans, often especially visible in parades as drummers. (Wheatley wrote a poem, which like her Stamp Act repeal poem has not survived, "On the Arrival of the Ships of War, and the Landing of the Troops.") These drummers were chosen to administer the lash publicly to punished soldiers. If the presence of two thousand troops made some Bostonians feel enslaved, the presence of seven hundred Africans in town raised for British troops the possibility that a forceful imposition of military rule might be welcomed by and find support from slaves and former slaves. Soon after the regiments arrived, an ostensibly drunken officer named John Wilson, already angered at the reception of his company by the locals, approached a group of blacks in the street and told them to go home and cut their masters' throats. Magistrates and selectmen "were in an uproar," and a series of newspaper articles accused the British of plotting emancipation for their own ends.[6]

The presence of slaves also exacerbated a sense of conflicting rules at workplaces. At least twice in 1769 British soldiers were convicted of petty crimes and actually sold into indentured servitude by the local courts. On the Friday before the Boston Massacre, an off-duty soldier sought employment at a Boston ropewalk, only to be told by a worker that he could go clean the privy. A fight ensued. Later a justice of the peace shouted at a black drummer at the head of forty troops who rushed out of the barracks without orders to confront their citizen tormentors, "What have you to do with white people's quarrels?" The drummer was said to have replied, cagily, "I suppose I may look on."[7]

In February 1770 Wheatley memorialized the death of Christopher Seider, an eleven-year-old member of a crowd confronting a nonparticipant in the boycott movement, as "the first martyr for the cause." She compared him to "Achilles" killed "in his mid career" and described his death as directed by "heavens eternal court." The two thousand people who participated in the funeral procession (John Adams wrote that he "never beheld one like it") passed through the scene of Seider's death, a side street near King Street. Two weeks later Phillis Wheatley wrote a similar poem, which may have appeared in the *Boston Evening Post,* about the Boston Massacre, also known as the riot in King Street. For the subsequent funeral-cum-demonstration, four hearses began at the homes of the victims and converged at the scene of the crime for the formal march. Thousands from the countryside turned out for this event, the biggest procession in Boston's history. Nineteen days later the troops were gone. Wheatley could certainly have concluded that the mix of protest, publicity, and elegy she had participated in actually worked.[8]

In this, Wheatley had company among Boston blacks, who participated actively in such demonstrations. Crispus Attucks, also known as Michael Johnson, was one of the patriot martyrs, and three blacks would testify when the soldiers were tried for murder. John Adams, while defending the troops at trial, repeatedly described the crowd as a "motley rabble of saucy boys, negroes and molattoes, Irish teagues, and out landish Jack Tarrs." Meanwhile, Samuel Adams and his fellow writers for the patriot press ignored Attucks or depicted him as white.[9] In the short run Wheatley supported the patriots more than we might expect, given their attempts to keep the issues of slavery and home rule separate.

Participation, for Wheatley, raised the stakes of poetry. Even before the Seider and Boston Massacre elegies, in 1769, she attempted something more ambitious: a moving, though unfinished, poem called "America." It is a mini-epic that begins with a by-then-traditional invocation of New England's "destin'd" growth from a "wilderness" into a "continent" despite Native American opposition. The remarkable, providential growth of these colonies "e're yet Brittania had her work begun" was a common theme in both Puritan histories and Whig protests. She turned it into a parable about God's will, which she then allied with her own, and Africa's, poetic achievement.

> Thy Power, O Liberty, makes strong the weak
> And (wond'rous instinct) Ethiopians speak
> Sometimes by Simile, a victory's won
> A certain lady had an only son

The son at first evokes Jesus—comparing his rise from insignificance to captive Africans speaking (or writing poetry). But the lady and her son turn out to be an allegory for Britain and America, cast in the popular metaphor of the mother country and her colonial children. Britain, "keeping down / New English force," causes the feeling child to lament his "Iron chain," and inspires Wheatley to call for Britain to "Turn" and "claim thy child again."[10] The message is clear. Africans can be brought out of invisibility by God. A godly America too can be liberated from its chains.

The personifications of liberty, the presence of child figures, and the play of national identities in "America" testify to Wheatley's increasingly informed, as well as imaginative, political consciousness. The poem, like the era's politicized funerals and the sermons pronounced at them, has a narrative force, but it is even more impressive in its epigrammatic, even sloganeering, boldness. Wheatley served a political as well as a literary apprenticeship in Boston.

⚯

Between 1765 and September 1770, then, Wheatley was experimenting not only with religious but also with patriotic verse that explicitly as well as implicitly raised the question of blacks' voice in the colonies. Could artful similes win victories against state policies? Against slavery? Could the debate over liberty "make strong the weak" as well as help Africans speak?

Publication, however, did not lead directly or automatically to fame for Wheatley. The return of George Whitefield for the fourth time to New England, and his death at Newburyport in September, provided a special opportunity for elegists in general and Wheatley in particular. Whitefield had been a hero among working people for his direct addresses to them since the 1740s, and they turned out in droves for his sermons even as Whitefield deemphasized his critiques of wealth and authority. Phillis had a special proximity to the great evangelist. Her mistress, Susanna Wheatley, was part of an evangelical network of women who were especially interested in converting Native Americans and slaves, and who were drawn to his message. She probably heard him in the Old South Church. Whitefield's funeral permitted Wheatley to introduce a less partisan, more religious linkage of issues, even as she cast Whitefield as pro-American and, in a London version of her elegy, against slavery. The Boston version was published as a much-reprinted broadside complete with an engraving of Whitefield lying in state. She had the dying revivalist address Africans, asking them to embrace the "Impartial SAVIOUR," who would make them "sons, and Kings, and priests to GOD." The London broadside read: "He'll make you free, and Kings, and Priests to God."[11]

Wheatley dedicated the Whitefield poem to Selina Hastings, the Countess of Huntingdon, the wealthiest and most influential of the female evangelicals. Huntingdon had sponsored Native and African preachers like the

Wheatleys' friend Samson Occom, who had toured England to raise thousands of pounds for the Indian Charity School (later Dartmouth College) and had stayed in the Wheatley house. After some initial effort to raise subscriptions for printing her poems in Boston, and a spell of ill health, Phillis and Susanna Wheatley used the excuse of Phillis needing sea air, along with the encouragement of friends, who had already shown the countess some of the poems, to justify her passage to England during the summer of 1773, with the hope of having the poems published there with the countess's support.

It is tempting, but inaccurate, to call this Wheatley's Tory phase. Rather, as a politically astute person aware that there were people of good intentions, and opponents of slavery, on both sides of the colonial conflict, she was hedging her bets. The disinclination of patriot presses to print her work in 1772 probably derived from the stalemate both in the patriot movement and in the politics of slavery that year. Not only had the organized radicals in Boston like Samuel Adams begun to distance themselves from the linkage of the slavery and patriot issues; the nascent antislavery movement had also embarrassed the patriots by calling attention to the hypocrisy of slave drivers shouting for liberties. These complaints played out decisively that year, with a distinctly anticolonial bias, in the case of *Somerset v. Steuart,* in which Lord Mansfield, a staunch supporter of parliamentary supremacy, ruled that since slavery had no place in English law, an American slave who ran away from his master (another colonial customs officer) while in London could not be forcibly recaptured and returned to servitude in America. Wheatley must have known about the *Somerset* case, and her writings and actions in 1772 and 1773 reflect her understanding of the resulting possibilities.[12]

Consequently, she toned down or eliminated the pro-patriot poems for her 1773 *Poems on Various Subjects, Religious and Moral.* Just as important, she allowed her sympathizers to make her a celebrity in England. Lord Dartmouth and Brook Watson, the Lord Mayor of London, invited her to visit and gave her books. Granville Sharp, the moving force behind the *Somerset* case, took her on what must have been a highly visible tour of the Tower of London, a kind of living museum of British monarchy and empire, where she saw the crown jewels, exotic animals from Africa, and famous artifacts from English history. She was urged to stay for an audience with the king and a visit to Countess Huntingdon's Welsh estate, but her owner, Susanna Wheatley, was on her deathbed, while her son Nathanael, with whom Phillis had traveled, was busy conducting family business and courting an English lady. She returned alone after six weeks in London, having secured the publication of her book.

Before she left, however, she had a consequential visit from Benjamin

Franklin, then agent for several of the colonies in London. This visit is usually viewed as an antislavery act by Franklin, but it was certainly more complicated than that. Franklin had been in a double game, on the one hand defending the Americans against charges of hypocrisy while on the other hand assuring Granville Sharp that he would "act in concert" with him on the matter of slavery. He leveled his own charge of hypocrisy against the British for "freeing one slave," in the *Somerset* case, to counter the charge that freedom-loving Americans, as slave drivers, were hypocritical tyrants.

Meanwhile, Susanna Wheatley had implored Franklin's Massachusetts cousin, Jonathan Williams, to get Franklin to visit Phillis while in London. No doubt aware of the legitimacy that would be conveyed by a visit from Franklin, a literary figure himself, the Wheatleys were persistent, and Franklin obliged with what he construed, in a letter to Williams, less as an endorsement than as a social call, offering, like the diplomat he was, "any services I could do her."

Franklin could hardly ignore Wheatley, especially if he knew that her poems were soon to hit the London bookshops. But he made quick work of the visit, departing in short order because, he told Williams, Nathanael Wheatley had treated him rudely. Since there is no evidence that young Mr. Wheatley was temperamentally rude, or (as some have presumed) a Tory who disliked Franklin's politics, but plenty of evidence that Franklin was treading very carefully where it concerned the slavery issue, it seems most likely that the ever-politic Franklin was doing damage control.[13] From a patriot's political perspective (and he was the official representative of Massachusetts), that was exactly what he needed to do. He could neither embrace the poet publicly, for that might play into anti-American hands, or spurn her, which would have fed into the critique of American hypocrisy on slavery.

What is important here is that Wheatley had forced a careful, equivocal response from Franklin, a leading patriot and the most famous American in the world. He made a gesture in the direction of Lord Dartmouth's patronage—and Franklin was desperately seeking Dartmouth's support at this moment. He did not publicize it, but he did not take any chance of being accused of spurning the slave poet either. From Wheatley's perspective, Franklin was important—but not necessarily more important than Lord Dartmouth. She and Susanna succeeded in making Franklin at least not contradict Dartmouth's endorsement.

People were watching. Several reviews of Wheatley's volume, appearing later in 1773 in Great Britain, explicitly pointed out the hypocrisy of the Americans in holding people like Wheatley in bondage. That same year Philadelphia patriot Benjamin Rush, with whom Wheatley later corresponded, published a pamphlet in which he argued that Wheatley's genius was proof positive against any racial justification of slavery. Franklin and Wheatley manipulated each other politically in a scene that could not have occurred if Wheatley had not previously secured the approval of Lord Dartmouth as well as Granville Sharp and the Countess of Huntingdon.[14]

Wheatley may have already negotiated her freedom as a condition for her return to take care of Susanna. After the commentary in the London papers and in the wake of her rising fame, her proud owners would be personally embarrassed if she remained enslaved. She looked actively for other patrons so she could continue her work. In an October 1773 letter to New Havenite David Wooster (whom she would later elegize after he fell in battle), she described being shown around London and Lord Dartmouth's "gift of 5 guineas" for buying books (including Milton and Pope). At the end of the same paragraph she described how her freedom papers had been "drawn, so as to secure me and my property from the hands of Executurs.[,] administrators, &c. of my master, and secure whatsoever Should be given me as my Own. A copy is sent to Isra[el] Mauduit, Esqr.," sometime agent for Massachusetts whom she had met in London. Britain had become Wheatley's emancipating agent and her insurance policy, even as she returned to Massachusetts. Americans on both sides of the Atlantic were being enlisted in her network. The Boston merchant John Andrews, who had been following her career, perceived this when he complained jokingly in January 1774 that Wheatley, an "artful jade," had withheld some of her poems from her book in anticipation of the demand for a second volume.[15]

To understand Wheatley's strategy on the eve of the Revolution, it is crucial to appreciate the way she became famous as a slave poet. Her celebrity status amid a braided, increasingly tortured controversy about American liberties and African slavery also suddenly made her free. Like other political actors in the imperial crisis, even her seemingly private thoughts became, in 1773, matters of public interest. She was quite aware of this and probably also of the increasing boldness of other Africans in New England who petitioned for their freedom in the early 1770s. *The Connecticut Gazette* published her March 11, 1774, letter to the Mohegan preacher Samson Occom—a letter Occom himself solicited by writing her on the subject of the "natural Rights" of Africans. She replied that "those who invade them"—that is, slaveholders—could not with any consistency applaud, or even contemplate, the Christian conversion of Africa. "Otherwise, perhaps, the Israelites had been less solicitous for their Freedom from Egyptian slavery," she commented, and proceeded to elaborate in an expert linkage of Judaism and Christianity's "African" past to its present prospects: "I do not say they would have been contented without it, by no means, for in every human Breast, God has implanted a Principle, which we call Love of Freedom; it is impatient of Oppression, and pants for Deliverance; and by Leave of our Modern Egyptians I will assert, that the same Principle lives in us." The American patriots simply had to expect the present time to be an age of slave liberation, for "how well the Cry for Liberty, and the reverse Disposition for the Exercise of oppressive Power over others agree,—I humbly think it does not require the Penetration of a Philosopher to determine."[16]

Through her own actions, Wheatley's private liberties became publicly consequential, and it is hard to separate political and personal events in her life and their effects. She became controversial and outspoken—one not easily handled or muffled. Parliament's closure of the Port of Boston during the spring of 1774 worsened an already-troubled economy and began to cut her off from English patrons, leading some scholars to argue, with justification, that Wheatley was ultimately a victim of the American Revolution more than a participant (though the same argument could be made for many who fought in the war). During the occupation of Boston by a British army after mid-1774, she stayed on in the house of the Wheatleys, but the family was experiencing its own transformations. Susanna died in 1774; Nathanael Wheatley had married the Englishwoman he was courting and stayed in England. In the occupied city, Phillis kept her options open. In late 1774 and early 1775 she received poems from British officers and published replies in verse. In these works she introduced a more Romantic identification with "pleasing Gambia," her native country.[17]

After the war started in April 1775, she moved out of town with Mary Wheatley and her husband, John Lathrop, one of the patriots' firebrand preachers. She decided to reach out to the new patriot officialdom with poems of praise. A poem for George Washington, written in Providence in October 1775 and sent to him at his headquarters in Cambridge, hit its mark and led to a third shaping encounter with high officialdom—and another occasion in which Wheatley won a victory through simile.

The occasion, as with the Dartmouth poem, was Washington's appointment as commander of the Continental Army. Once again Wheatley sent the poem with a careful, signed cover letter demonstrating her joyous "sensations not easy to suppress." The poem praises Washington literally to the skies and ends by wishing him "a crown, a mansion, and a throne."

The desire to crown Washington seems odd, but Wheatley's monarchical celebration of Washington predated Thomas Paine's popular attack on monarchy in *Common Sense* by several months. Traditionally, the laying on of such laurels was the poet's role, to be repaid by elite praise and patronage.

The suggestion of a kingship for Washington comes after Wheatley has made it clear that he fights for "freedom," against Great Britain's "thirst of boundless power." Like others in 1775, including Washington himself, Wheatley participated in an attempt to adapt tradition to the republican cause. Washington was, in fact, already becoming the substitute for the patriot-king, beloved for his very refusal of political power.[18]

The timing of Wheatley's letter and poem is striking. It arrived at Washington's camp a month after the general had given executive orders barring the enlistment of African Americans, but before Lord Dunmore, the royal governor of Virginia commanding the army there, issued his November 7 proclamation inviting slaves to secure their freedom by joining the British. During this interval Wheatley heard nothing from Cambridge. On December 30, 1775, Washington partially reversed his decision, allowing free blacks, but not slaves, to enlist.

Meanwhile, she kept her options open. In a recently discovered letter of February 14, 1776, to her good friend Obour Tanner, Wheatley wondered whether the British "thirst of Dominion" might be God's "punishment of the national views" of "this seemingly devoted Country." While English abolitionist leader Granville Sharp was coming to the conclusion "that the developing civil war within the empire in part originated and represented divine punishment for public toleration of the slave trade and chattel slavery," Wheatley, who had spent at least an afternoon with Sharp, was developing an American version of the same outlook. Because of his preference for liberation, God punished those who failed to practice what they preached. The Lord armed their enemies—and liberated their slaves. The patriots might or might not be true to their vision of liberty. Wheatley, like other African Americans, watched carefully and took what actions she could.[19]

There is no better measure of Wheatley's Revolutionary and wartime experience than its pattern of contingency and reversal. Two weeks after her letter to Tanner, Washington had invited Wheatley to visit him at headquarters, praised her "poetical genius," and sent the poem that lauded him to his highest assistant, Joseph Reed, to get it published, after which it appeared in Thomas Paine's *Pennsylvania Magazine* and in *The Virginia Gazette*.[20]

Whether or not she had changed Washington's mind about anything, Wheatley had been part of a diplomatic coup on the part of northern African Americans. When Washington invited Wheatley to camp and incorporated and enlisted her as an ally (and he needed them amid rivalries with other generals), he confirmed the official sanction he had given to free black participation in the American Revolution. As in her encounters with Dartmouth and Franklin, she had chosen her moment well. Poetic appeals led to personal encounters that had real political effects. Sometimes a simile can be as effective as demonstrating in the street.

ॱૐ

Revolutions inspire genius but also destroy it. Wheatley continued to write during the war even as she suffered the war's privations. She published proposals for a longer, second volume of poems, dedicated to Benjamin Franklin. It showcased political verses like "Thoughts on the Times" and included thirteen of her letters. The book, however, never appeared, partly because of the awful economy but also because, absent the well-connected Wheatleys, her former patrons held back.[21] Over the objection of some of her friends, she married John Peters, a "remarkable looking" free black grocer of "talent and information" who spent his spare time studying law and representing Africans in the Massachusetts courts. His prospects soured like almost everyone else's during the war, and the newly formed family lost their house in Boston. John and Phillis Peters moved several times within Massachusetts over the next several years and had to spend much time apart in an effort to support three young children. Her health had always been frail, but the challenge became too much after Peters was arrested and thrown in debtors' prison, a common practice designed to get people or their friends to pay what they owed. (And why wouldn't creditors expect that John Peters could get a loan from his wife's wealthy friends or former owners?) Phillis Wheatley and two of her children died in December 1784, two months before John Peters got out of jail.[22]

Patriots who die as a result of the wars are usually considered heroes, not the kind of tragic figure Phillis Wheatley is often made out to be. There can be no doubt that at the time of her death Phillis Wheatley Peters was a success. While the starving artist suffered poverty in freedom, others were seeing her portrait on the cover of *Bickerstaff's Boston Almanack for the Year of Our Redemption 1782*. Black and white contemporaries wrote poems about *her* during the war.[23] Her 1784 poem celebrating "Liberty and Peace," published as a broadside, sought to put the distresses of the war behind her and behind America. It depicted freedom as universal and international, and looked forward to a renewal of communication across the Atlantic. Allusively, it described the British soldiers who had been "Sent from th'Enjoyment of their native Shore / Ill-fated—never to behold her more," knowing that her readers would be reminded of people like the author, forcibly uprooted from her native shores.[24] If war and slavery had this much in common, perhaps war's end could mean a new birth of liberty.

Praising and shaming America into becoming a true agent of "Heavenly

This image served as the fron-
tispiece for Phillis Wheatley's
*Poems on Various Subjects, Religious
and Moral,* published in London in
1773. The painting on which it was
based was by her Boston African-
American friend Scipio Morehead.

Freedom," Wheatley posed a special problem for slaveholding patriots like
Thomas Jefferson. He must have been aware that enlightened figures like
Voltaire and Benjamin Rush had already cited Wheatley's poetry in the
ongoing, international debate about race, nature, and slavery. When Jefferson entered into this debate with his *Notes on the State of Virginia* (1787), he
attacked her as a pious hack: "Religion, indeed, has produced a Phillis
Whatley; but it could not produce a poet."[25]

In the same book Jefferson was trying to argue that an end must be made
to slavery, while positing black racial inequality as a way of explaining why
emancipation had been put off for the present. His comments on Wheatley
were offered as proof of an absence of African genius: an argument against
those for whom Wheatley meant the very opposite—the absurdity of slavery
when justified by racism. Jefferson had another reason to denigrate Wheatley with this particular inflammatory but precise insult. In the *Notes,* Jefferson also insisted on a separation of church and state. Wheatley's mixing
of the sacred and secular, her linkage of religion and revolution to both
antiracism and antislavery, stood in direct opposition to Jefferson's post-
Revolutionary agenda—his justification of a revolution that had promoted
equality, and allied Puritan Massachusetts with Anglican Virginia, but had
not freed the slaves. His vituperative response to Wheatley suggests the
threat that Wheatley's poems and her public actions—not just the fact of her

existence—posed for Jefferson, who did own a copy of her book. There could be no more creative a misreading of Wheatley than to imagine that she was not a poet, or failed to make a case against slavery, because she was religious. By the time Jefferson completed *Notes on the State of Virginia,* Wheatley was dead and thus in no position to respond.

Others did, shaping a two-hundred-year battle over Wheatley's meaning and reputation. More than her patrons or even her audiences, Wheatley herself made this happen. She created the circumstances that led Lord Dartmouth, Benjamin Franklin, George Washington, and Thomas Jefferson to take her seriously. The African-American poet who seems a prisoner of eighteenth-century conventions wrote for the Revolutionary present and the American future. In doing so she made the Revolution that much more revolutionary.

FOR FURTHER READING

This essay draws on a work in progress, *The Worlds of Phillis Wheatley: A Biography,* as well as on my earlier writings on political festivity, Benjamin Franklin, Thomas Jefferson, and the politics of slavery. See David Waldstreicher, *In the Midst of Perpetual Fetes: The Making of American Nationalism, 1776–1820* (Chapel Hill, N.C., 1997); Waldstreicher, ed., *Notes on the State of Virginia by Thomas Jefferson with Related Documents* (Boston, 2002); Waldstreicher, *Runaway America: Benjamin Franklin, Slavery, and the American Revolution* (New York, 2004); and Waldstreicher, *Slavery's Constitution: From Revolution to Ratification* (New York, 2009).

The most complete and accessible modern edition of Wheatley's writings is Phillis Wheatley, *Complete Writings,* ed. Vincent Carretta (New York, 2001). Three other editions contain important information: Julius Mason's *The Poems of Phillis Wheatley,* 2nd ed. (Chapel Hill, N.C., 1989); John C. Shields, ed., *The Collected Works of Phillis Wheatley* (New York, 1988); and William H. Robinson, ed., *Phillis Wheatley and Her Writings* (New York, 1984), which has the best biographical essay and includes manuscript and print sources not written by Wheatley.

In addition to the work of editors Robinson and Mason, key works by historians that began the modern reassessment of Wheatley include James A. Rawley, "The World of Phillis Wheatley," *New England Quarterly* 50 (December 1977): 657–77; Charles W. Akers, " 'Our Modern Egyptians': Phillis Wheatley and the Whig Campaign Against Slavery in Revolutionary Boston," *Journal of Negro History* 60 (July 1975): 397–410; Sidney Kaplan and Emma Nogrady Kaplan, *The Black Presence in the Era of the American Revolution,* rev. ed. (Amherst, Mass., 1987); and David Grimsted, "Anglo-American Racism and Phillis Wheatley's 'Sable Veil,' 'Length-'ned Chain,' and 'Knitted Heart,' " in *Women in the Age of the American Revolution,* ed. Ronald Hoffman and Peter J. Albert (Charlottesville, Va., 1989), 338–444. More recently there has been an outpouring of articles and book chapters by literary scholars, too numerous to list here. For an introduction to the contexts for black writing, see especially Dickson D. Bruce Jr., *The Origins of African American Literature, 1680–1865* (Charlottesville, Va., 2001). For poetry in Wheatley's America, see David S. Shields, *Oracles of Empire: Poetry, Politics and Commerce in British America, 1690–1750* (Chicago, 1990); Shields, *Civil Tongues and Polite Letters in British America* (Chapel Hill, N.C., 1997); and Max Cavitch, *American Elegy: The Poetry of Mourning from the Puritans to Whitman* (Minneapolis, 2007). For Wheatley's Boston, see Alfred F. Young, *The Shoemaker and the Tea Party* (Boston, 2000); Young, *Liberty Tree: Ordinary People and the American Revolution* (New York, 2006); Dirk Hoerder, *Crowd Action in Revolutionary Massachusetts, 1765–1780* (New York, 1977); Hiller B. Zobel, *The Boston Massacre* (New York, 1970); G. B. Warden, *Boston, 1689–1776* (Boston, 1970); Patricia Bradley, *Slavery, Propaganda, and the American Revolution* (Jackson, Miss., 1998); and Benjamin L. Carp, *Defiance of the Patriots: The Boston Tea Party and the Making of America* (New Haven, Conn., 2010).

PART II

WARS

"Adventures, Dangers and Sufferings": The Betrayals of Private Joseph Plumb Martin, Continental Soldier

Philip Mead

In November 1777, about 450 Continental soldiers at Fort Mifflin on Port Island on the Delaware River withstood a five-day siege of British land and sea batteries, one of the most devastating artillery bombardments of the Revolutionary War. Americans defended the fort as part of an attempt to cut off supplies from reaching British-controlled Philadelphia and thus force the British out of the city. In a memoir published anonymously in 1830, entitled *A Narrative of Some of the Adventures, Dangers and Sufferings of a Revolutionary Soldier; Interspersed with Anecdotes of Incidents that Occurred Within His Own Observation. Written by Himself,* Connecticut Private Joseph Plumb Martin remembered the heroism of his fellow soldiers and the "appalling" gore and misery of the siege. "The enemy's shot cut us up. I saw five artillerists belonging to one gun cut down by a single shot, and I saw men who were stooping to be protected by the works, but not stooping low enough, split like fish to be broiled." Martin lost his own "most intimate associate I had in the army," whose body he identified by his canteen, and whom he found "in a long line of dead men who had been brought out of the fort to be conveyed to the main, to have the last honors conferred upon them." At the end of the siege, "the whole area of the fort was as completely ploughed as a field. The buildings of every kind [were] hanging in broken fragments, and the guns all dismounted, and how many of the garrison sent to the world of spirits, I knew not. If ever destruction was complete, it was here." On the night of November 15–16, Martin and the other Continentals retreated from the island in small boats, the whole time under continued British fire.[1]

For Martin, the defense of Fort Mifflin was "as hard and fatiguing a job, for the time it lasted, as occurred during the Revolutionary War." He knew what he was talking about. A seven-year veteran of the Continental Army, he had been at nearly every major battle and encampment of Washington's main army from 1776 to 1782. In his seven years' service, he had served six months in the Connecticut state troops; three years in the Continental Army's Eighth Connecticut Regiment, including seven months with the Pennsylvania Light Infantry; three years in the Engineering Corps' Sappers and Miners; and two months in a Massachusetts Continental Line Regiment. For Martin, historians' neglect of the Siege of Fort Mifflin proved that, even in a republic, the heroism of common men received little attention:

> I was at the siege and capture of Lord Cornwallis, and the hardships of that were no more to be compared with this than the sting of a bee is to the bite of a rattlesnake. But there has been but little notice taken of it, the reason of which is, there was no Washington, [Israel] Putnam, or [Anthony] Wayne there. Had there been, the affair would have been extolled to the skies. No, it was only a few officers and soldiers who accomplished it in a remote quarter of the army. Such circumstances and such troops generally get but little notice taken of them, do what they will. Great men get great praise; little men, nothing. But it always was so and always will be.[2]

Martin's narrative of Fort Mifflin captures the power of his written voice as well as his audacity in criticizing the dominant narrative of the Revolutionary War in the first decades of the nineteenth century. Among several hundred memoirs of Revolutionary War soldiers, Martin's stands out both for the intimacy with which he reveals his emotions and personal transformations during the war, and for the intensity of his anger at those who disregarded the role of enlisted soldiers like himself. Martin filled his memoir with acerbic comments about the failures of other Americans during the war to support him and the other common soldiers of the army. He scolded the populace for failing to supply food, and officers for taking more food and better shelter than their men. In a sense, Martin's story provides an angry counterpoint to the histories that held sway late in his life, particularly those that focused on the hierarchical Continental Army. Perhaps because his message contradicted the image many Americans wanted of their Revolutionary origins, Martin's book seems never to have achieved a single review during his own lifetime. In the late twentieth century, however, the book became a classic among military historians and Revolutionary War enthusiasts as a unique insight into the mind of a soldier of the Revolution.

But Martin's narrative raises as many questions as it answers. As a memoir written many years later, how much of what he wrote reflected his experiences and perceptions during the war, and how much reflected the influence of his later life? Did he bear resentment for the abuses of officers during the war itself, or did that emerge during his later experiences in frontier Maine, fighting for land rights often against men who had once been Continental Army officers? Since Martin was apparently so well read and wrote with such a strong sense of narrative, can we even be certain that the events he described actually happened and were not simply novelistic inventions? In short, what can Martin's narrative tell us about the mentality of a Revolutionary War soldier and about the postwar disappointments that shaped his understanding of the conflict?

Throughout his life Martin may have had more sensitivity to issues of class and rank than many Continental soldiers. While many enlisted soldiers came from the lowest ranks of American society, particularly after 1777, Martin spent his whole life on the edge of the great social division that separated eighteenth-century America, between commoners and gentry. Born in 1760, the son of a Yale-educated but unsuccessful minister, young Martin watched as two congregations dismissed his father, apparently for contracting bad debts with his parishioners. He learned that in New England elites who misbehaved faced little rebellions, and that one gave deference only to those who earned it. At eight years old he went to live in Milford, Connecticut, with his maternal grandmother and grandfather, whom Martin remembered as "a gentleman" for "he was wealthy, and I had everything that was necessary for life and as many superfluities as was consistent with my age and station." But his grandfather had a large family and could offer Martin few prospects of an inheritance or an adult living. Like many young New England men, Martin joined the military partly to escape limited prospects at home. In the army he reached the rank of sergeant and was part of the elite Sappers and Miners, but as a noncommissioned officer he remained a commoner. After the war he settled in frontier Maine, but any expectations he had for independent wealth were dashed in a legal conflict over land ownership with Henry Knox, a former Continental Army general turned land speculator. While Martin achieved many honorific distinctions—sergeant, captain of militia, esquire, town clerk, representative to the state legislature— the minister's son turned soldier and frontier settler never reached the gentry status that his minister father once had.[3]

Martin began his memoir partly because of the disparagement of regular, or Continental, army veterans during the controversy over the 1818 pension act; partly because his neighbors were curious for his memories; and quite clearly out of a feeling that the historical record had to be set straight. In his epilogue, he urged Americans to continue supporting Revolutionary veterans despite the high cost, and despite the contention of some pension opponents that the Continental Army had been superfluous to the American victory and that militia could have won the war alone. "It is cruel as the grave to any man," he wrote, "when he knows his own rectitude of conduct, to have his hard services not only debased and underrated, but scandalized and vilified." Yet like so many military memoirs—from those of Julius Caesar to those of Ulysses S. Grant—Martin's narrative grew well beyond a case for compensation into a richly detailed treatment of the joys and sorrows, the "adventures, dangers and sufferings" of a soldier's life. In his mid-sixties when he wrote, Martin found, like many memoirists, that his memories were much better than he expected. "In truth," he wrote, "when I began this narrative, I thought a very few pages would contain it, but as occurrences returned to my memory and one thing brought another to mind, I could not stop, for as soon as I had let one thought through my mind, another would step up and ask for admittance."[4]

A reader who compares Martin's narrative to other contemporary sources becomes amazed at the incredible accuracy of his memories. Most nineteenth-century autobiographies began with a preface that insisted the author spoke the "unvarnished truth," but the verifiability of even the smallest details of Martin's tale shows that he was committed to telling the story of his war as well as he could remember it, and that was remarkably well. The weather patterns at battles were almost always exactly as Martin described. Archaeologists at Monmouth Battlefield have been surprised to find that their surveys confirm details of Martin's account not found in contradictory versions of the battle by contemporary historians like David Ramsay. Martin's descriptions of towns and houses are so accurate that numerous industrious local historians have been able to identify his path through their towns. His description of Mount Holly, New Jersey, can almost be used for directions, even today.[5]

An amazing number of the very personal anecdotes in his narrative can also be verified. In his account of the Valley Forge winter, Martin includes a story about a tavern in "The Welch Mountains," which run through the counties of Chester and Lancaster, Pennsylvania, where he discovered that "the landlord and I bore the same name, and upon further discourse I found that he had a son about my age, whose given name was the same as mine. This son was taken prisoner at Fort Lee, on the Hudson River, in the year 1776, and died on his way home." The family took Joseph Plumb Martin in as their adopted son, "almost willing to persuade themselves that I was their son," an oft-noted response to mourning in wartime. A survey of tavern owners in these counties confirms that the owners of "Martin's Tavern" in West Bradford (present-day West Chester), Chester County, Pennsylvania, had a son named Joseph Martin who served in the army but disappeared when Fort Lee was captured in 1776. Martin did not know, however, that this other Joseph had been taken captive and was only presumed dead; he returned home in 1780.[6]

Even the most apparently sentimental stories of Martin's tale turn out to be consistent with other evidence. Martin wrote that he received his only wound during the war from one of his former hometown "playmates"—a man who had served with him during the campaign of 1776. During a battle with some Loyalist militia, Martin remembered, "I could see him through the fence and knew him. He was, when we were boys, one of my most familiar playmates, was with me, a messmate, in the campaign of 1776, had enlisted during the war in 1777, but sometime before this, had deserted to the enemy, having been coaxed off by an old harridan, to whose daughter he had taken a fancy." This Loyalist militiaman was probably Angus McPhee, who was raised with Martin in Milford, served with him in Peck's company in 1776, and joined the first Connecticut Regiment "for the war" in 1777 but deserted to join the Regiment of Westchester Loyalists and wed Deborah Wheaton, the daughter of a New York Loyalist family.[7]

Thus, while we do not know much about Martin as a writer, we know enough to trust that his narrative was his own, and that he worked deliberately to represent his war as authentically as he could. As he put it in his introduction, "I wish to have a better opinion of my readers, whoever they may be, than even to think that any of them would wish me to stretch the truth to furnish them with wonders that I never saw, or acts and deeds I never performed." Martin's writing reflects the influence of the wide range of literature available to most common New Englanders by the early nineteenth century; his book includes references to *Don Quixote,* Homer, the scientific works of Benjamin Silliman, John Trumbull's poem *McFingal,* and the Revolutionary histories of David Ramsay. The conventions of narrative he found in these sources helped Martin sharpen his own storytelling and broaden its significance beyond the small scale of his own experience. His final memoir is not only the most comprehensive and intimate view of the war from the perspective of a common soldier, but also a profound meditation on the timeless dangers and costs of war. While his descriptions reveal his experience in serving in the Revolutionary army, his anger at the "vilification" of his service suggests the ways that Revolutionary veterans saw their nation during the first decades after its independence.[8]

～ℓ

Why did Joseph Plumb Martin join the army, not once, but twice? He first enlisted in June 1776 at age fifteen in a Connecticut Regiment, a unit raised for a six-month term to defend New York City from British attack. Martin remembered his reasons for enlisting: to impress his friends; to gather stories of adventure; to rebel against his grandparents and guardians; and because he considered himself "as warm a patriot as the best of them." Moreover, by joining, he became "the possessor of one dollar." After a short time at home in the winter of 1776–77, Martin enlisted again in the Eighth Connecticut Regiment, part of the "new formation" of the Continental Army that Washington modeled after the standing armies of Europe. Pressured by local recruiting companies, Martin shopped for an enlistment bounty. With Martin's two enlistments, he served in two different armies: the one of 1775–76, which was voluntary, dominated by short-term enlistments, and organized by colonial and town governments; the second raised in 1777, which was filled by a draft, required long-term service, and was organized by a distant Continental Congress. His different reasons for joining reflect the way the Revolutionary War had changed Martin and American society.[9]

In 1776 the war seemed exotic and thrilling to Martin, and he could not wait to gain the "bewitching name of a soldier." Like many generations of young New England men living in a cash-poor and increasingly land-scarce economy, he felt the allure of the army bounty. At a recruiting scene immediately after news of the first battle of Lexington and Concord, Martin remembered, "A dollar deposited upon the drumhead was taken up by someone as soon as placed there, and the holder's name taken . . . O, thought I, if I were but old enough to put myself forward, I would be the possessor of one dollar, the dangers of war to the contrary notwithstanding." For most of the eighteenth century, New England was a "family labor" economy, in which families traded labor as currency, and young sons contributed to their own inheritance by laboring for the family well into their twenties. As the grandson of the homeowner, Martin had fewer prospects than a son and may have seen the hard currency of the army as a path to manhood, if not personal independence.[10]

Martin considered his first enlistment voluntary and patriotic. He admitted that until the war broke out, he had only a limited knowledge of the issues. During the Stamp Act controversy of 1765, "I was so young that I did not understand the meaning of it," and after the "destruction of the tea at Boston and elsewhere," he remembered, "I was then thirteen or fourteen years old and began to understand something of the works going on." In the winter after the war began, however, he paid closer attention: "by hearing the conversation and disputes of the good old farmer politicians of the times, I collected pretty correct ideas of the contest between this country and the mother country (as it was then called). I thought I was as warm a patriot as the best of them." Martin believed that "we had joined the issue, and it would not do to 'put the hand to the plough and look back.' I felt more anxious than ever, if possible, to be called a defender of my country." Once he enlisted, he wanted "to prove myself equal to the profession."[11]

The hardships of Martin's 1776 campaign dissolved much of this early enthusiasm. It was not the violence that most disturbed him. Of his first experience of cannon fire, he remembered, "I rather thought the sound was musical, or at least grand," and when he met wounded men, "another sight I was unacquainted with," the "sight of these a little daunted me, and made me think of home, but the sight and thought vanished together." Rather, Martin described himself as feeling betrayed by poorly trained officers who repeatedly exposed, abandoned, and dispirited him and his fellow soldiers. After the Battle of Brooklyn, he saw a man nearly hung because orders from one officer conflicted with those given by another, a consequence of the American army's unclear chain of command. At Kips Bay an officer ordered him to abandon a wounded man, saying, "If he dies the country will be rid of one who can do it no good." Martin stood shocked. "Pretty fellow! Thought I, a very compassionate gentleman! When a man has got his bane in his country's cause, let him die like an old horse or dog, because he can do no more!" Martin did not wonder at the loss of New York to the British. "How could the men fight without officers," he asked.[12]

When Martin returned home in the winter of 1776–77, he saw enlistment differently, with less enthusiasm to be "called a soldier" and more skepticism of recruiters. The country as a whole was more war weary. Like Martin, Washington and Congress had learned from the losses around New York that the army needed restructuring. Their solution of increasing the term of enlistment from one to three years promised to increase the army's professionalism but made recruiting more difficult. Martin described the quota system developed to draft men: "The inhabitants of the town were about this time put into what were called squads, according to their ratable property . . . Each of these squads were to furnish a man for the army, either by hiring or by sending one of their own number." When one of the squads "attacked me front, rear and flank," Martin decided to "endeavor to get as much for my skin as I could." When he enlisted, Martin remembered no feeling of elation, but rather "*I* felt miserably," and "now I was hampered again. The men gave me what they agreed to, I forget the sum . . . They were now

Many Continental soldiers shared Joseph Plumb Martin's anger at their treatment by the new American governments and by "an ungrateful people." This 1777 cartoon from an American pamphlet, titled *The Downfall of Justice,* shows a conversation between several Continentals. The first soldier says, "Keep up courage, my boys, we will soon bring these villains to terms." The second says, "These d—d Extortioners are the worst enemies to the country." The third says, "I serve my country for sixteen pence per day, pinched with cold." *With permission from the American Antiquarian Society.*

freed from any further trouble, at least for the present, and I had become a scapegoat for them."[13]

Martin's rage at his countrymen's lack of material support for their "scapegoats" burns through the remainder of his narrative. "Almost everyone has heard of the soldiers of the revolution being tracked by the blood of their feet on the frozen ground," he wrote in 1830, and "this is literally true, and the thousandth part of their sufferings has not, nor ever will be told." In page after page Martin did his best to give his readers some idea of this untold suffering, though he often found his narrative inadequate, concluding that "no one who has never been upon such duty . . . can form an adequate idea of the trouble, fatigue and dangers." In every chapter terrible, gut-wrenching hunger dominated his memory of the war. Martin referred to hunger as the soldier's "faithful companion" that "stuck by us as close as ever." Even late in the war, when supplies had improved, soldiers often faced shortages and relied on "the old system of starving."[14]

Food shortages during the war were caused largely by the armies destroying crops and disrupting trade, but for Martin and his fellow soldiers, there was no explanation but the selfishness of "an ungrateful people." One example captures his anger. After the brutal battle at Fort Mifflin, Martin remembered sardonically:

While we lay here there was a Continental Thanksgiving ordered by Congress . . . We had nothing to eat for two or three days previous . . . But we must now have what Congress said, a sumptuous Thanksgiving to close the year of high living we had now nearly seen brought to a close. Well, to add something extraordinary to our present stock of provisions, our country, ever mindful of its suffering army, opened her sympathizing heart so wide, upon this occasion, as to give us something to make the world stare. And what do you think it was, reader? Guess. You cannot guess, be you as much of a Yankee as you will. I will tell you; it gave each and every man *half a gill* of rice and a *tablespoonful* of vinegar!

An army chaplain chose to commemorate the occasion with a sermon drawn from the biblical text "And the soldiers said unto him, 'And what shall we do?' And he said unto them, 'Do violence to no man, nor accuse anyone falsely.'" Martin and his fellow soldiers knew the Bible and knew that the chaplain had left off the last sentence, " 'And be content with your wages,'" as "it would be too apropos. However, he heard it as soon as the service was over, it was shouted from a hundred tongues."[15]

How did Martin persevere so heroically for a country and people he thought had abandoned or exploited him? Throughout the remainder of the war, he and his fellow soldiers adapted an ethic from the "moral economy" of small eighteenth-century New England communities. The system demanded support for those in need and fair prices in exchange for goods and services. When local people denied Martin and his fellow soldiers food or supplies, they exerted their "right" to take them through deceit or theft. At the same time, people who supplied the army with all they had sometimes received protection from the soldiers. When a Pennsylvania woman traded some vegetables for a soldier's shirt, Martin and his fellow soldiers resented that she gave so little though "she seemed to have a plenty of *all* things." They waited until she was asleep, took the shirt back and a "little good cider," and "marched off early in the morning before the people of the house were stirring," and "consequently did not know to see the woman's chagrin at having been overreached by the soldiers." At Redding, Connecticut, in 1779, Martin remembered that soldiers stole tools from local inhabitants to build their huts, but he commented, "Do not blame them too much, gentle reader . . . remember, they were in distress, and you know when a man is in that condition he will not be over scrupulous how he obtains relief, so he does obtain it."[16]

As supply problems increased in 1779 and 1780, Martin and his fellow soldiers grew resentful toward their officers and government. Martin increasingly found that many of his officers fell short of their obligations to their men and their rank. He thought most Pennsylvania officers were "gentlemen" but considered Pennsylvania Colonel Richard Butler, who commanded his light infantry unit, "a fiery austere hothead." Martin adamantly defended Washington—"the general well knew what he was about; he was not deficient in either courage or conduct, and that was well known to all the Revolutionary army." Yet he resented lower-level officers who claimed the best lodging and food when their men were hungry. As the Continental Army approached winter quarters in Redding in 1778, Martin complained that "we were conducted into our bedroom, a large wood, by our landlords, the officers, and left to our repose, while the officers stowed themselves away snugly in the houses of the village, about half a mile distant." The worst officers conspired to steal from their own men, like the "Brigade Major" who tried to get the boots off an executed soldier's body by hiring a "ragamuffin fellow" to pull them off the corpse hanging from the gallows. Martin and his fellow soldiers set the matter right by pelting the thief with stones until he gave up.[17]

When no other method for gaining material relief or officers' support seemed to work, Martin and his fellow members of the Connecticut Line tried to get supplies through mutiny. During the Seven Years' War, mutiny had become a semi-acceptable method for soldiers recruited in the colonies to enforce their enlistment and supply contracts with the British regular army, but these earlier mutinies generally included both officers and men and simply consisted of refusing orders and marching home. Martin's mutinies were different in that enlisted men attacked their officers, and rather than going home to save themselves, they tried to contribute to solutions by negotiating with legislators. At Danbury Camp in 1779, after days with no food, the soldiers decided, "We were now in our own state and were determined that if our officers would not see some of our grievances redressed, the state should." They began to march, but their officers convinced them instead to send a series of petitions to the Connecticut General Assembly.[18]

A year later, in May 1780, Martin and the First Brigade of the Connecticut Line revolted again, and this time a small skirmish ensued and several officers were wounded. Through the winter of 1779–80 the Continental Army encamped at Morristown, New Jersey, suffered severe ration shortages compounded by one of the coldest winters in memory. Martin remembered this as a severe period of starvation:

> We were absolutely, literally starved. I do solemnly declare that I did not put a single morsel of victuals into my mouth for four days and as many nights, except a little black birch bark which I gnawed off a stick of wood, if that can be called victuals. I saw several of the men roast their old shoes and eat them,

and I was afterwards informed by one of the officers' waiters, that some of the officers killed and ate a favorite little dog that belonged to one of them. If this was not "suffering" I request to be informed what can pass under that name. If "suffering" like this did not "try men's souls," I confess that I do not know what could.

By the last week of May conditions had barely improved; General Nathanael Greene wrote from Morristown, "We have been starving for three weeks past, and have but poor prospects before us at this time." The Connecticut Line mutiny began after Martin and his fellow soldiers returned from a particularly dangerous forward zone duty in Elizabethtown, New Jersey.

> For several days after we rejoined the army, we got a little musty bread and a little beef, about every other day, but this lasted only a short time and then we got nothing at all. The men were now exasperated beyond endurance; they could not stand it any longer. They saw no other alternative but to starve to death, or break up the army, give up all and go home. This was a hard matter for the soldiers to think upon. They were truly patriotic, they loved their country, and they had already suffered everything short of death in its cause; and now, after such extreme hardships to give up all was too much, but to starve to death was too much also. What was to be done? Here was the army starved and naked, and there their country sitting still and expecting the army to do notable things while fainting from sheer starvation.

This second mutiny was directionless and confused; the soldiers could not form a plan that resolved both their patriotism and their starvation. The officers kept the rebellion from spreading by stationing a camp guard over the remaining supply of arms. Surrounded and partially disarmed, the Connecticut Line ended their mutiny. But the mutiny revealed the depth of desperation and frustration that Martin and his fellow soldiers felt, as well as their expectation that their sacrifices deserved a fair level of material support from the population.[19]

◆

In the final years of the war, Martin experienced yet another "material change in my circumstances." In 1780 French engineers introduced new methods of military engineering to the Continental Army. Martin had a steady drafting hand and was recruited into the Sappers and Miners, who were to oversee the construction of fortifications designed by the engineers. He received a promotion to sergeant, the highest noncommissioned-officer rank in the army, which gave him close access to the commander of his new unit, Captain David Bushnell. At the climactic Battle of Yorktown, Martin served as foreman in the construction of siege lines and remembered proudly that his unit was designated to break through British fortifications with ten-pound axes and thus became the first inside British lines. Martin took obvious pride in his unit and paraphrased Washington's orders forming the unit and calling it an "honorable" corps.[20]

Finally having found a home within the army at the very end of the war, Martin was surprised that news of the peace treaty in 1783 left him more unsettled than happy: "My anticipation of the happiness I should experience upon such a day as this was not realized." Martin had found in his Sappers unit a kind of surrogate family and in Bushnell a father figure. Martin remembered that tensions between officers and men continued in the Sappers, but they were not the open rebellions of previous years. He and his fellow Sappers called Captain Bushnell "the old man." In turn, Bushnell treated his men like an extended family of dependents. He ruled them with small rewards for good behavior and kept punishments for small crimes outside the army's court-martial system, sometimes by using his rattan, or rod, a typical punishment for children. As for his fellow enlisted men, Martin remembered that "we had lived together as a family of brothers for several years, setting aside some little family squabbles, like most other families, had shared with each other the hardships, dangers and sufferings incident to a soldier's life; had sympathized with each other in trouble and sickness; had assisted in bearing each other's burdens or strove to make them lighter by council and advice"; and now "we were to be, the greater part of us, parted forever; as unconditionally separated as though the grave lay between us." Ironically, after all Martin's suffering in the army, he was relieved of his duty only after his fellow soldiers had become his family and the army his home.[21]

As the war ended, Martin and his "brothers" turned their attention toward the lands promised in their enlistment contracts. By a 1776 Act of Congress, soldiers like Martin who enlisted for the duration of the war were guaranteed one hundred acres of land in unspecified territory. By the end of the war, most northern soldiers like Martin expected to receive lands either in the new Ohio territory or in western New York on land recently taken from the Iroquois Indians. In the spring of 1783, after Martin received his discharge from the Sappers and Miners, a friend persuaded him to serve the remainder of a Massachusetts soldier's term, "telling me that at the expiration of our service we would go together into the western parts of the state of New York, where there was a plenty of good land to be had as cheap as the Irishman's potatoes . . . and there we would get us farms and live like heroes." Having secured American national independence, it was time to find some of the rewards of cheap land and recognition that recruiters had promised since the start of the war.[22]

Yet at the end of the war Martin did not receive such rewards. As he put it, bitterly yet eloquently:

> When the country had drained the last drop of service it could screw out of the poor soldiers, they were turned adrift like old worn-out horses, and nothing said about land to pasture them on. Congress did, indeed, appropriate lands under the denomination of "Soldier's lands," in Ohio state, or some state, or future state, but no care was taken that the soldiers should get them. No agents were appointed to see that the poor fellows ever got possession of their lands; no one ever took the least care about it, except a pack of speculators, who were driving about the country like so many evil spirits, endeavoring to pluck the last feather from the soldiers.[23]

The truth was even more cruel. In the late 1780s, as soldiers looked to recover their bounty lands, Congress prohibited settlement on tracts of less than four thousand acres, larger than the bounty grant even for a major general. Congress assigned veterans individual bounty land grants in the 1790s, but by then, like most other soldiers, Martin had settled elsewhere and assigned his land to a speculator.[24] Martin's disappointment at the wartime settlement illuminates the theme he chose for the title page of his 1830 *Narrative:* "Long sleepless nights in heavy arms I've stood; and spent laborious days in dust and blood." He quoted "The Anger of Achilles," the central poem in Homer's epic *The Iliad,* in which the warrior Achilles scorns his king for denying him the spoils of war. Achilles' anger resonated with Martin because he understood his suffering not as historically specific to the American Revolution but as part of a timeless struggle between soldiers and their governments.[25]

After the war Martin faced another kind of fight: this time over land rights on the northern American frontier. In 1784 he went to Maine, another place where land was supposed to be available for the taking. Without title to the land, he built a cabin on Cape Jellison, a three-mile spit that juts into the Penobscot River near the Atlantic coast at a town called Frankfort (present-day Stockton Springs), a lumbering and fishing village. A decade later, at thirty-three, he married Lucy Clewley, the daughter of Isaac Clewley, a shipbuilder with good connections to local landowners. But by the first decade of the nineteenth century, Martin's family had lost most of the land and property for which they had worked.

The land where Martin had settled, known as the Waldo Patent, became hotly contested between speculators with legal titles and settlers like him, who claimed rights to the land based on the improvements they had made with their labor. In 1786 former Continental Army major general Henry Knox, by virtue of his influence with the Massachusetts legislature, secured title to most of the Waldo Patent, and what he did not own, he secretly bought up. Martin and his fellow veterans insisted on a "moral economy" where labor had a fair value, just as they had insisted on a fair level of support for their military service. Martin would have agreed with his neighbor Jeremy Black, who petitioned the Massachusetts legislature in 1797, asking "who made these lands more valuable than when in the state of nature? Was it not the settler?"[26]

Instead of showing benevolence, Knox insisted that settlers pay for legal title or get off his land. For ten years a legal and shooting war went on between Knox and secret societies of settlers calling themselves White Indians. When the land magnate sent surveyors to mark out his land, he found farmers and laborers waiting for them with guns. By 1797 arbitrators appointed by the Massachusetts legislature had negotiated a settlement between Knox and many settlers. Commissioners determined that Martin had to pay $170 by December 1800 for legal title to his hundred acres. When the deadline came, Martin's sickly wife, his severely disabled son, and his own war wounds left him unable to pay. He wrote to the general pleading for an extension to "save a poor family from distress." Knox promised some relief, but by 1811 Martin's estate had shrunk to fifty acres, and by 1820 he had lost it all. By offering help, Knox acknowledged the conventions of a "moral economy," yet his policies drove Martin into poverty.[27]

Like many citizens frustrated by the outcome of the Revolution, Martin turned to politics. In 1812, running as a Jeffersonian Republican, he was elected Prospect's representative to the Massachusetts legislature. The Jeffersonian party was a minority in New England but a majority in frontier Maine, where its antielitist rhetoric struck chords among Knox's old opponents. Martin served two terms, but in the Federalist-dominated legislature, he met with more frustration; he never held a single committee appointment or succeeded in forwarding any petitions. By 1818 he turned away from state politics, serving instead as a justice of the peace and town clerk. He also helped found a Congregational church in Eastern Prospect (present-day Sandy Point, Maine), returning perhaps to his minister father's religious commitments.[28]

The federal pension law for Revolutionary War veterans passed in 1818 brought Martin some long-overdue compensation, but only at the expense of his humiliation. The initial act allowed $8 a month to Continental Army veterans of more than nine months' service and who were in "reduced circumstances." When more than sixteen thousand veterans successfully applied, however, the high cost of the bill threatened to bankrupt the federal treasury. An 1820 amendment required soldiers to prove need by including a "schedule" of their goods before a court. Approximately 20 percent of the original pension recipients did not submit to this public scrutiny, but Martin's needs exceeded his pride. "I have no real nor personal estate," he testified in 1820, "nor any income whatever, my necessary bedding and wearing apparel excepted, except two cows, six sheep, one pig." For the rest of his life, Martin received a military pension of $96 a year but faced scorn from, as he put it, the "heardhearted [*sic*] wretches" who were "vile enough to say that [the soldiers] never deserved such favor from the country."[29]

It was during this controversy over pensions in the 1820s that Martin seems to have written his memoir. He may have been prompted to write by Maine's congressman William D. Williamson. In his 1832 *History of Maine,* Williamson praised Martin as a "man of great worth and intelligence" and thanked him for the research materials he had provided in 1824 while serving as Prospect's town clerk. Shortly after this correspondence, Williamson's publisher, Glazier, Masters, and Company of Hallowell, Maine, agreed to publish Martin's book. Martin said he wrote solely from memory, but he testified in 1820s pension depositions that he had personal notes dating back at least to the early 1790s, and the chronological rhythm and accuracy of his memoir strongly suggest that he had kept a wartime diary.[30]

In his epilogue Martin argued that veterans deserved pensions because of the many broken promises he had described in his narrative:

> Had I been paid as I was promised to be at my engaging in the service, I needed not to have suffered as I did, nor would I have done it; there was enough in the country and money would have procured it if I had had it. It is provoking to think of it. The country was rigorous in exacting my compliance to *my* engagements to a punctilio, but equally careless in performing her contracts with me, and why so? One reason was because she had all the power in her own hands and I had none. Such things ought not to be.

Martin's feelings of betrayal—by Congress, by Knox, and by his Federalist colleagues in the Massachusetts legislature—sharpened his anger at his treatment during the war, making his account more than a vivid soldier's narrative. In his epilogue Martin channeled his anger into a powerful statement of democratic political principles that great inequalities of power "ought not to be."[31]

If Martin hoped for any direct financial benefit from the publication of his book, it never came. In all likelihood, Glazier and Masters issued fewer than four hundred copies, a small run probably with a local circulation. His book fit neither the Jeffersonian narrative of the war, which condemned standing armies as wasteful and dangerous, nor the Federalist narrative, in which enlisted men entered the scene to express awe of generals. For Martin, the Revolution was not a story of coordinated effort and patriotic consensus. It was a cautionary tale about the dangers of irresponsible authority and the continuing need for vigilance against the growth and corruption of power, even in a republic. If Martin's biting narrative had a moral, it was that resistance to authority protected freedom. By writing his narrative, he tried to embed that message in the original moment of American independence.[32]

In the last decade of his life, Martin finally received land for his war service. In 1835 the Maine legislature granted one hundred acres to Revolutionary War veterans who had served in the Massachusetts Line, lived in Maine, and had never received a land grant. In 1841, after the legislature altered the law to include Connecticut Line veterans like Martin, he at long last received a land grant of two hundred acres in Aroostook County. Martin's land may have improved his fortunes, but for the rest of his life his children shared responsibility for paying his taxes.[33]

Martin died on May 2, 1850, in the care of his family after a three-hundred-day struggle with "old age," as a local census put it. Joseph Williamson, nephew of Congressman William D., wrote Martin's obituary, which was published in the *Republican Journal*. Williamson praised Martin as "the last link" to the Revolution "whose valor and blood procured for us our goodly inheritance." He acknowledged the "lively view" the book gave of the "privations and sufferings" of a Revolutionary soldier, but he had to note that "one could wish that he had submitted this book to some competent, judicious friend for revisal, before it was sent to the press." Williamson doubtless wanted the book edited to diverge less from the consensus narratives of the war that had become so politically useful. But Martin had insisted on getting the story right as he saw it. The story he had to tell, and the warnings he had to give, were too hard won for anything less.[34]

Years later, members of Martin's church raised a small granite obelisk over his grave at Sandy Point Cemetery in Stockton Springs with a simple but powerful epitaph: "Joseph P. Martin, Revolutionary Soldier." Republished in 1962, his memoir has now been reprinted more than five times, and a shortened edition has been published for young readers. Valley Forge National Park has named its main bike path through the old encampment lines "The Joseph Plumb Martin Trail." Martin's narrative has been used to represent the voice of the ordinary Revolutionary soldier in military histories, movies, and documentaries. Measured by quotations in books and documentaries, Martin vies for importance with many of the "great men" that he thought always got "great praise."

In a sense, the current popularity of Martin's narrative points to the radicalism of his revolution. In his own time he may have measured himself against his father's gentility or suffered the disappointment of repeated financial misfortunes. His frank account may have left contemporary readers angry or silent. But in the twentieth and twenty-first centuries, Martin's defense of the place of common soldiers has resonated deeply with Americans' egalitarian ideals. To the extent that Martin hoped for recognition, he succeeded remarkably.

FOR FURTHER READING

For Martin's narrative, I relied most heavily on the following edition: *Private Yankee Doodle, Being a Narrative of Some of the Adventures, Dangers and Sufferings of a Revolutionary Soldier,* ed. George Scheer (Boston, 1962; rpt., [U.S.,] 1988). Other accessible editions are *A Narrative of a Revolutionary Soldier,* ed. Thomas Fleming (New York, 2001), and *Ordinary Courage: The Revolutionary War Adventures of Private Joseph Plumb Martin,* ed. James Kirby Martin (St. James, N.Y., 2003). The original edition of the book is *A Narrative of Some of the Adventures, Dangers and Sufferings of a Revolutionary Soldier; Interspersed with Anecdotes of Incidents That Occurred Within His Own Observation. Written by Himself* (Hallowell, Me., 1830). This essay draws from my larger study of autobiographical writings by enlisted Revolutionary War soldiers, " 'Melancholy Landscapes': Personal Autobiography in the Continental Army, 1775–1830" (Ph.D. diss., Harvard University, 2010). A brief narrative of the life of Ebenezer Martin, Joseph P. Martin's father, can be found in Franklin B. Dexter, *Biographical Sketches of the Graduates of Yale College with Annals of the College History,* 6 vols. (New York, 1885–1912), 2:421–22. For an alternative interpretation of Martin's memoir that emphasizes the novelistic conventions of his narrative, see Catherine Kaplan, "Theft and Counter-Theft: Joseph Plumb Martin's Revolutionary War (Narrative of Some of the Adventures Dangers and Sufferings of a Revolutionary Soldier)," *Early American Literature* 41, no. 3 (2006): 515–34.

For the culture and attitudes of Continental soldiers, Charles Royster, *A Revolutionary People at War: The Continental Army and the American Character* (Chapel Hill, N.C., 1981), remains fundamental. For more focused studies, see Caroline Cox, *A Proper Sense of Honor: Service and Sacrifice in George Washington's Army* (Chapel Hill, N.C., 2004), and Gregory Knouff, *Pennsylvanians in Arms and the Forging of Early American Identity* (University Park, Pa., 2004). For more on Revolutionary War veterans, see John Resch, *Suffering Soldiers: Revolutionary War Vet-*

erans, Moral Sentiment, and Political Culture in the Early Republic (Amherst, Mass., 1999). For more on the culture in Martin's part of Down East Maine, see Alan Taylor, *Liberty Men and Great Proprietors: The Revolutionary Settlement on the Maine Frontier, 1760–1820* (Chapel Hill, N.C., 1990).

Other surviving soldier narratives from the Revolutionary War, which provide context and points of comparison with Martin, are listed in J. Todd White and Charles H. Lesser, *Fighters for Independence: A Guide to Sources of Biographical Information on Soldiers and Sailors of the American Revolution* (Chicago, 1977), still the best bibliography on the subject. The massive collection of Revolutionary War Pension Files at the United States National Archives (National Archives and Records Administration Series: M805) include more than eighteen thousand depositions from relatives and their families and can be accessed on microfilm at any National Archives branch. They are also available online at Footnote.com and at HeritageQuest.com, where they are searchable by soldier's name and by the state line in which he/she served. Martin's file is under his wife Lucy Clewley's name and is number W1629. Selections from these files are published in John C. Dann, *The Revolution Remembered: Eyewitness Accounts of the War for Independence* (Chicago, 1980).

CHAPTER EIGHT

"The Spirit of Levelling": James Cleveland, Edward Wright, and the Militiamen's Struggle for Equality in Revolutionary Virginia

Michael A. McDonnell

In early 1776, five months before the American colonies declared their independence from Britain, Virginians almost went to war with one another. On February 12 some six hundred angry men descended upon Leesburg, the county capital of Loudoun, one of the largest and most populous counties in Virginia. Local militia officers, keen to drum up new recruits for the Continental Army, had summoned them to a muster. But the men of Loudoun used the muster to share complaints and drum up support for their own cause. They were angry about new measures taken by patriot leaders to fight the war against Britain, which they thought were eminently unfair to poorer and tenant farmers and their families. While the new rules shifted the burden of the war onto the shoulders of those who could least afford it, wealthy landlords in the region continued to demand rents from their tenants. With no markets for their crops and new demands for them to serve in the army, protesters in Loudoun had had enough.

First, they forcibly closed the county court before it could hear any new debt cases. Then they broke up the militia muster. There was, according to one observer, only "great confusion" that day. Another witness predicted worse to come. "The first battle we have in this part of the country," he warned, would be against the protesters. As patriot leaders prepared to fight for the liberty of the colonies, ordinary white Virginians mobilized in the name of equality.[1]

Though unlikely to have been the only leader, local officials singled out one man from the crowd that day as the main antagonist—James Cleveland. Lund Washington, who was managing his famous cousin's plantation at Mount Vernon, told General Washington that Cleveland had "turn'd Politician" and was "setg all Loudon to gether by the Ears." Cleveland was a rough-lettered tenant farmer with a volatile temperament. Like up to a third of his neighbors in Loudoun County, he was a tenant farmer struggling to make ends meet on mostly short-term leases and not particularly good land rented from wealthier planters in the region. He likely grew a little wheat and made flour to sell when he could. But Lund Washington hadn't picked Cleveland out from the crowd randomly. There was already bad blood between the Washingtons and Cleveland. Unable to raise enough cash to buy property of his own, Cleveland had labored as an overseer of slaves for George Washington at Mount Vernon. At the time of the Loudoun uprising, Cleveland and Washington were at loggerheads over the settlement of his contract.[2]

~e

The Loudoun uprising and Cleveland's participation in it reveals a story of early Virginia that seems unfamiliar. In the first place, few people think of colonial Virginia as home to white tenant farmers who did not own their own land. But there were as many as three hundred tenant farmers in Loudoun County alone. As many as a third of the farmers in Loudoun and numerous other counties were in a similar situation to Cleveland. Some tenants were on long-term leases (up to seven years) that gave them the right to vote. An increasing number, however, were on short-term leases that gave them little economic security, and they had no right to vote. In total, nearly three-quarters of the white population in Loudoun was landless, and a half overall in the rest of Virginia.

Perhaps this should not be so surprising. Though we often think of Virginia as a slave society, divided by white masters and black slaves, late-eighteenth-century Virginia was, in effect, a society with slaves. Most people were not slave owners. Moreover, those who did own slaves commonly engaged only one or two at most. Indeed, enslaved Virginians formed only the bottom of a hierarchical edifice that included male and female convicts and indentured servants (laborers from Britain who were bound for a certain term of labor as punishment or to pay their passage), apprentices, free wage-laborers and overseers, tenant farmers and nonslaveholding smallholders, poorer slaveholders and substantial landholders, and finally local and cosmopolitan elites, some of whom owned dozens of slaves, and others of whom held hundreds of Africans in bondage and owned thousands of acres of land throughout the colony. Even within some of these apparently monolithic social blocs, many sometimes overlapping layers of differences complicated social relations within and between different classes of Virginians. Ultimately, as any self-respecting gentleman, tenant farmer, or enslaved Virginian would know, this was a deeply divided and carefully defined hierarchical society in which social and economic inequalities were on conspicuous display.

In this context, the imperial crisis and the outbreak of war with Britain posed as many challenges for the patriot leadership as it provided opportunities for others. Men such as Cleveland might have joined the ranks of the patriots in hopes of a better and more secure future. Enticing rumors of boundless Indian lands beyond the mountains were dampened only by the knowledge that Britain had prohibited further settlement there. Small farmers too may have been anxious to rid themselves of the Scottish merchants who seemed to monopolize the trade in goods to Britain. Some might have dreamed of a more radical outcome: one wealthy planter worried that the only definition of independence he had heard among his neighbors was that "it was expected to be a form of Government, that by being independent of the rich men eve[r]y man would then be able to do as he pleased."[3]

Patriot leaders in Virginia—most of whom were drawn from the ranks of those "rich men"—were keen to harness the support of their neighbors in the contest against Britain even while they worked hard to control it. They celebrated popular participation in protests against unfair taxes, and they encouraged their neighbors to join the volunteer companies of militia that formed in early 1775 in a show of defiance. When war broke out in April 1775, volunteer companies composed of rich and poor joined General Washington in Massachusetts when he was appointed commander of the newly formed Continental Army.

By the end of the year, however, this mutual enthusiasm ran headlong into the revolutionary aspirations of another group of Virginians—enslaved African Americans. When war broke out, thousands of slaves began to make their way to British lines in the belief that they would find freedom. British officers, including the royal governor and commander of the British Army in Virginia, Lord Dunmore, were keen to encourage them. By November 1775 so many slaves had joined Dunmore that he felt bold enough to issue a proclamation declaring that any enslaved or indentured Virginians who belonged to patriot masters could have their freedom if they joined him to fight the rebels. The gloves were off. While in the long run the actions of enslaved Virginians and Dunmore's response helped convince many patriot leaders of the need to push for independence, in the short run, they were terrified.

To stop Dunmore and his newfound allies, slave-owning patriot leaders stopped relying on volunteers and immediately created a large regular army of paid professional soldiers. In doing so, they drove a wedge between themselves and popular support for the conflict. The new army would be enormously costly to ordinary farmers who paid regressive poll taxes (paid equally by everyone, regardless of how much property they owned). It would also inevitably prolong the war, as traditional means of eighteenth-century warfare would prevail over the successful hit-and-run tactics of the volunteer companies. At the same time, cash-strapped landlords in Virginia—many of whom were prominent patriot leaders—continued to demand rents from their cash-strapped tenants.

⁓

By early 1776 men like Cleveland had had enough. Keen to support the patriot cause, they also wanted everyone to shoulder their fair share of the war effort. For Cleveland, the last straw came when the most famous patriot of all, Washington, refused to pay him as much as he had promised. In early 1775, when Cleveland realized he would not be able to sell his surplus crops because the economic boycotts would prevent him, he took on a dangerous and arduous mission for Washington to raise some extra cash. For before he took command of the newly raised Continental Army, Washington undertook to protect his title to two tracts of land he had purchased in the Ohio Valley as a speculative venture. Virginia's colonial land grant law required land grant recipients to make "improvements" on their land within three years or forfeit the patent. So in January 1775 he hired James Cleveland, who had served him as an overseer since the early 1760s, to lead a crew of slaves and servants hundreds of miles over the mountains to the Ohio country to plant corn and build cabins on the land.

Cleveland risked a great deal to travel so far for so long. Moreover, the expedition was plagued with problems. Many of the white servants Washington had sent with him deserted. Cleveland had barely managed to improve the tracts when Shawnee warriors forced him homeward after they began attacking colonists on the Ohio. At least he could expect some reward for his efforts. After all, he had contracted with Washington to be paid in hard money—gold or silver, or its equivalent. But when a tired Cleveland presented his bill to Washington's cousin Lund, he was paid only in paper money that was already depreciating.

Cleveland thus had good reason to be among the angry crowd. He had spent the growing season working for Washington in the Ohio country helping him make money speculating on land, yet Washington did not pay him as much as he promised. At the same time, Cleveland was pressed to pay the rents he owed. If he had any crops to sell, he could no longer export them through Alexandria because of the nonexportation agreement. Yet landlords like Washington now wanted their rents, and some of them demanded hard currency. As patriot leaders—many of whom were landlords—mobilized for what looked like a long and expensive war with the British, Cleveland was caught between a rock and a hard place.

So were most of his tenant neighbors, who, like Cleveland, thought they should not have to pay their rents if they could not sell their crops or they were away fighting the war. Not only in Loudoun but throughout Virginia tenants and small farmers complained in petitions that they were "poor men with families that are Incapable of Supporting themselves without Labour." It was therefore "extreamly hard & no ways equatable or Just that we should be obliged to leave our Families in such a Situation that if ever we shou'd return again [from militia service, we] Woud find our Wives & Children dispers'd up & down the Country abeging and aStarving."[4]

Hardship was only part of the issue. They were also incensed at the inequities built into the new army, which would be modeled along traditional British lines. Officers, who were usually drawn from the ranks of the patriot elite, were to receive up to *sixty* times the pay of regular soldiers. So the protesters demanded fairer pay for equal work: the "pay of the officers and Soldier should be the same."[5]

Just as galling, while poor farmers were forced to leave their homes, plantation owners received special treatment: one overseer for every four enslaved Virginians was exempt from military service, leading one group of petitioners to complain that many wealthy planters had "become Overseers that Otherways would not, on purpose to Screen themselves from Fighting in defence of their Country as well as their own Property."[6] Though patriot leaders had created a large regular army of paid professional soldiers, they also claimed they needed to stay at home to keep their enslaved laborers from running off with the British. The exemption of overseers meant that many of those who could most afford to serve in the army—slave-owning planters whose laborers could work while they were away—evaded military service.

Even paying for the war was inequitable. Because most taxes in 1775–76 were poll taxes, poorer Virginians ended up paying a disproportionate amount of the taxes to support the war. That's why some of the protesters even demanded that *no one* should get paid in the new army—neither officers nor soldiers. They wanted to keep costs down.

In recognizing the inequalities inherent in the new military establishment, farmers across Virginia were conscious of one of the seemingly timeless truths about wars—the main burden of conflict would fall disproportionately on the poor. It was inevitable, as farmers knew, that while richer members of the community found ways to avoid military service, the poorer, younger members of society, those with the least to defend, would end up fighting, and paying, the most.

This time, though, because patriot leaders needed their support against Britain, less wealthy Virginians sensed they could fight back. Tenants refused to pay their rents, while tenants and small farmers alike used the militia musters to close the courts so they could not be prosecuted for nonpayment of debts. Together they acted to challenge the patriot leadership's control over the Revolutionary situation. It was in this context that James Cleveland assumed leadership sometime around February 1776 and announced that for farmers like himself, the new military measures were intolerable. There was "no inducement for a poor Man to Fight," he declared, "for he has nothing to defend." Instead, he said, "let us go and Fight the Battle at once, and not be Shilly Shally, in this way, until all the Poor, people are ruined."[7]

The Leesburg uprising demonstrates that in Virginia the Revolution was not the product of just a small class of men such as Washington, Jefferson, and James Madison. Nor was it a simple story of Americans versus British, or patriots versus Tories. While it has now been amply shown that the Revolution was also a battle between masters and slaves over the meaning of "liberty" and "independence," so too must we recognize that *white* Virginians themselves were divided over the meaning of equality. As patriot leaders in Virginia—mostly large landholding and slave-owning tobacco planters—initially fought for equality within the British Empire, less wealthy white Virginians fought to define equality in a way that would better their own lives. The struggle over home rule, then, like almost everywhere in the colonies, was equally a contest over who should rule at home. In Loudoun County, as elsewhere in Virginia, these struggles culminated in a heated confrontation pitting local patriot gentlemen against their less wealthy but no less patriotic neighbors.

Wealthy Virginians felt the threat. In northern Virginia, Lund Washington told his cousin George that he would go out and collect the rents owed to them "if I thought Mt. Vernon wou'd stand where it does, when I returned"—though he was worried about a possible slave rebellion, he was mostly concerned about the damage protesting tenants might inflict. Within weeks the Revolutionary government in Williamsburg, the Committee of Safety, began to take measures to send troops to northern Virginia to quell

The Alternative of Williamsburg, attributed to Philip Dawe and dated February 16, 1775. In 1774 legislators in Virginia passed a resolution urging people to sign the Continental Association—a series of measures drawn up in response to the Intolerable Acts. One of these was to support a boycott on exports from the colony. The print shows what might happen if planters refused to sign: barrels of tar and feathers hang ominously on the gallows behind the table. Though a satire by a London artist, this image reminded genteel readers that when in rebellion, men of property could be subject to challenges from below. The artist suggests that the lower sort helped push the colonies toward revolution, an idea that we have too often and too easily dismissed.

the disturbances. Lund Washington believed that there would be an outright battle between these troops and "General Cleveland." Thus, even while patriot leaders focused on attaining "liberty" from their imperial yoke, they were taking measures to suppress small farmers and tenants who sought greater equality. Invoking the language of the English civil wars, one worried observer asked a colleague in Loudoun County, "How goes on the Spirit of Levelling?"[8]

As it turned out, the protests in Loudoun County never boiled over into armed conflict, contrary to Lund Washington's prediction, nor was anyone prosecuted for taking part in the uprising. In part, this was because people like James Cleveland *supported* the patriot cause; throughout the crisis Cleveland continued to assert his loyalty and challenged his critics to give him a proper hearing so he could prove that. In part, it was also because patriot leaders needed all the help they could get against the might of the British Army and navy.

Perhaps most important, though, with the powerful words of Thomas Paine echoing up and down the eastern seaboard in the early months of 1776, ordinary Virginians began to expect, and demand, a new government, and new laws, in which they had a greater voice in return for their support of the patriot cause. Small farmers and tenants like Cleveland, then, channeled their anger into changing the political landscape of the colony.

Indeed, though many patriot leaders in Virginia were slow to take notice of Paine's *Common Sense,* ordinary white Virginians were quick to embrace its principles. One observer noted that in Loudoun in particular the pamphlet made "a great noise" and soon "nothing but Independence talked of." But Paine didn't just make a case for independence. He also equated independence with republicanism. And the central thesis of *Common Sense* was the guiding principle of many ordinary Virginians who had struggled with the patriot leadership over the past year: that the common people possessed enough sense to govern themselves. Years later Edmund Randolph noted that the pamphlet was "pregnant with . . . proud republican theories, which flattered human nature." Landon Carter believed his neighbors wanted a government in which "no Gentleman should have the least share."[9]

At the very least, most ordinary Virginians believed that independence would give them a greater role in the affairs of state: a new government would have to be better than the old one. While *Common Sense* may have been an original articulation of the desire of many for independence and a more inclusive, responsive government, what made Paine's pamphlet so compelling was that it simply expressed what people were already thinking. Virginia in 1775 and early 1776 was fertile soil for a pamphlet that urged not just independence from Britain but also the creation of a new form of government based on far different principles from the old.

Thus, when Virginians went to the polls in April 1776 to send delegates to a new convention to decide on the question of independence and a new government, many voted for new candidates who would do their bidding. At least one delegate was elected because he had opposed the new militia laws; another who had been accused of provoking a mutiny in the militia was elected. Landon Carter was disgusted to hear that someone else was elected to the new convention after he had publicly complained that the new militia laws were unfair "because a poor man was made to pay for keeping a rich mans Slaves in order." There was a noticeable change in the ensuing assembly: one man thought the delegates were "not quite so well dressed, nor so politely Educated, nor so highly born," but rather were "plain" and "full as honest, less intriguing, more sincere . . . They are the People's men (and the People in general are right)."[10]

Ironically, though, people like Cleveland pushed many wealthy and many conservative Virginians into supporting independence—precisely to stop what some called this incipient "Levelling." As John Page, a friend of Jefferson's, argued, independence would allow patriot leaders to restore the rapidly diminishing authority of government. If they moved quickly enough, they could create a new constitution "as nearly resembling the old one as Circumstances . . . will admit of" to "prevent Disorders in each Colony." "For God's sake declare the Colonies independant at once," Page pleaded with Thomas Jefferson, "and save us from ruin."[11]

Pro-independence leaders also used the "disorders" and the prevailing mood of the people to convince their more conservative colleagues that they had no choice but to move for independence. When congressional delegate Francis Lightfoot Lee received a letter from Landon Carter complaining about the "licentiousness" in Virginia, Lee told Carter the only way to put an end to it was declare independence and restore formal government. Without independence and a new government, he warned, the situation would be even worse: "Anarchy must be the consequence."[12]

Thus, while they fueled the drive for independence, the actions and expectations of ordinary Virginians ran headlong into the reactions and worries of conservatives in the patriot movement. This collision ensured that the struggle for equality, at least between white Virginians, would continue in an independent Virginia as fiercely as the war itself. That struggle would initially involve clashes between patriotic leaders and the very lowest classes of white Virginians. Gradually, under the demands of war, the conflict would become general once again.

～℮

The new battle began in the convention that declared independence and created a new constitution. Many conservative patriots wanted as little change as possible, including the president of the convention, Edmund Pendleton, who preferred the "true English Constitution, which consists of a proper combination of honor, virtue and fear." Carter Braxton offered the most conservative proposal, calling for triennial elections of representatives, who would elect an upper house, or Council of State, who would in turn elect a governor and executive committee. He wanted to keep the government out of the hands of the people as far as possible. The upper house, governor, and council would not be elected by popular vote and, significantly, would be elected for *life.* Though Braxton's plan was ridiculed by some, he still had a great deal of support in the convention. And few wealthy Virginians were keen to deviate far from it. Even Richard Henry Lee's plan, which was popular among most outspoken patriot leaders, differed from Braxton's only in that the tenure of the governor, council, and upper house would not be for life. (They would be appointed for seven-year terms instead.)[13]

But the agitation of ordinary Virginians over the previous year had an effect in the assembly. For in the end, though modern historians have generally missed it, the Virginia Constitution was remarkably—and surprisingly—democratic. It was also more democratic than any of the extant written proposals. Elections for the lower house were to be held annually, and there were no extra property qualifications for representatives. And though almost all extant written proposals called for an indirectly elected upper house with senators serving long terms—or even for life—to balance the popularly elected lower house, the final constitution stipulated that senators too would be directly elected for only six-year terms. In New England, John Adams scratched his head and wondered at the result. He had believed his plan in *Thoughts on Government* would be too radical for the conservative gentry who dominated politics in the South. Afterward he noted that the Virginia Constitution was "remarkably popular, more so than I could ever have imagined, even more popular than Thoughts on Government." The people "out of doors"—men like Cleveland who had little direct influence in the formal corridors of power—had made an impact.[14]

Still, the new constitution was clearly intended to shore up support among propertied freeholders—those who owned land—in Virginia at the expense of poorer white Virginians. Indeed, the turmoil of the previous year also had the effect of ensuring that reform would be limited. The right to vote, for example, was only to "remain as exercised at present." This meant that only white Virginian males over the age of twenty-one who owned at least twenty-five acres of land could vote (including long-lease tenants)—or about 60 percent of white males over twenty-one. The convention failed to extend any more concessions to lower-class white Virginians. Jefferson's proposal to give fifty acres of land (and thus the vote) to every landless adult white male, for example, was struck from the final constitution. The new form of government and the laws proposed by the new convention attempted to steer a middle way between "Levelling" and "liberty."[15]

The convention followed a similar path with respect to the makeup of the army. On the one hand, it removed the exemptions from military service of overseers, but simultaneously, to appease propertied voters, it turned to the lowest classes of white Virginians to shoulder the burdens of the war. Enlarging the regular army, it targeted the unemployed, wage-laborers, and the landless poor in its search for new recruits. The convention even authorized the impressment of "rogues and vagabonds"—defining vagabonds so broadly as to include anyone who neglected or refused to pay their public county and parish levies and who had no visible estate (that is, those who were not eligible to vote).

As predicted by the protesters in Loudoun County, fighting the British on their terms, with a traditional army, helped prolong the war. As the war dragged on, the appropriation of labor for military service continued to dominate politics and social relations in the new state. Patriotic leaders' desire to make the poor and vulnerable fight for the defense and security of the country, for example, became more explicit. As early as 1777, as enthusiasm for the war waned considerably, legislators came under pressure from Continental officers—including George Washington—to draft soldiers for Virginia's contingent of the Continental Army. Washington believed that they needed to fill the army with the "lower class of people." Washington particularly wanted lower-class recruits whom he believed they could discipline properly (with corporal punishment, etc.) to fight the British on their terms. A disciplined, paid professional army of the lower sort would do the bidding of patriot leaders. The Virginia Assembly, specifically targeting the vulnerable, told senior officers in the militia and senior magistrates in the counties to "fix upon and draught" men who in their eyes could be "best spared, and will be most serviceable."[16]

If legislators hoped to avoid involving their propertied middle-class constituents, they nevertheless provoked angry resistance from many white Virginians—as they did once more in Loudoun. In August 1777 at least eight men from the county were charged with resisting the government and raising "tumults and disorders in this state." Among the men charged with endeavoring to excite the people of the county to "resist the government" was James Cleveland, who was again singled out as the ringleader.[17]

Yet community sentiment protected Cleveland. The local magistrates handed down sentences that were light for what effectively was treason—Cleveland was hit hardest with a £50 fine and five days in jail. Then, when Cleveland apologized, the jail term and fine were suspended on his future good behavior. All across Virginia, many local officials agreed with people like Cleveland that the law was "unjust" and "striking bad policy," and refused to enforce it. In the end, outright opposition or the quiet evasion of such laws stalled recruiting and forced legislators to abandon conscription in 1778. Instead, they turned to high bounties to attract young men into the army in return for financial gain. What lower-class white Virginians could not gain in the new constitution and assembly, they achieved via collective opposition and evasion.[18]

ဆ

Opposition from below between about 1776 and 1780 crippled mobilization and had a ripple effect. Poor recruiting, for example, forced Washington to wage a defensive campaign and again prolonged the war. Unable to compel enough men to join the regular army, legislators also had to turn increasingly to the rest of the militia to defend the state and lend aid to the Continental Army during emergencies. Most militiamen were willing to do their bit and contribute what they could. But as the demands on the militia increased, so too did complaints from the militiamen about the equity of those demands. While nonslaveholding farmers especially could scarcely afford the time away from their farms to do military service, they often made the sacrifice. But what was particularly galling was the belief that wealthier Virginians were not shouldering their fair share of the burdens of war.

Again, real and substantive equality was the key issue. For men like Edward Wright of Richmond County, a small farmer with a large family, it was a matter not of patriotism but of fairness. Throughout the war he and his neighbors had paid high and increasing taxes. They had suffered through numerous requisitions for food, horses, carts, and other supplies for which they were given only worthless promissory notes. They had pooled money to raise recruits for the Continental Army, and many had already done months and even years of service in either the militia or the regular army themselves. They were willing to do more. But they were appalled that the laws were not equitable, and they were especially chagrined to see their wealthy neighbors—most often slaveholders who helped make the rules, planters who could most afford to contribute to the war effort—escape military service and often even evade paying a share of the costs of war, let alone a fair share. For men like Edward Wright, it seemed an all-too-familiar story: "the Rich wanted the Poor to fight for them, to defend there property, whilst they refused to fight for themselves."[19]

Once again wealthy Virginians who had secured exemptions from such service were the target of many of the complaints. In May 1780, for example, petitioners from one county told the legislature that they had so far supported the government and had contributed their "just proportion of the expence" of the war as well as "personal service when required." In doing so, the poor among them "who scarce obtain a precarious subsistence by the sweat of their brow are call'd upon as often and bound to perform equal Military duty in defence of their little as the great & oppulent in defence of their abundance." Worse yet, the "great and oppulent" they claimed, "who contribute very little personal labour in support of their families [because they had slaves to labour for them], often find means to screen themselves altogether from those military services which the poor and indigent are on all occasions taken from their homes to perform in person." Poorer Virginians were on the verge of "Compleat Ruin," noted another group of petitioners in the fall of 1780, and in early 1781 petitioners from across Virginia warned that the unequal demands placed on them tended to "create great Uneasiness and heart burning amongst our people."[20]

These growing complaints about the equity of military service came to a head in 1781, at the very moment when the British invaded Virginia. The first blow came at the hands of the infamous Benedict Arnold in January. British advances culminated in a strike in April against Charlottesville, where the General Assembly had reconvened after fleeing Richmond. They came within an hour of capturing the sitting governor, Thomas Jefferson, who was forced to flee his hilltop home, Monticello. At the same time, the British raided plantations along the Potomac and Rappahannock rivers, encouraging enslaved Virginians to seek freedom. Mount Vernon, George Washington's home, was raided, and sixteen enslaved Virginians fled, including some of Washington's most trusted house servants and artisans.

If ever white Virginians needed to band together to defend themselves, this was the time. Some did. Militia turned out in good numbers against Arnold, albeit too slowly to be of much use. Many southern militia served willingly to oppose British general Lord Cornwallis as he advanced through North Carolina toward Virginia with a sizable army in February 1781. And many militiamen did long periods of service as the British focused their efforts on Virginia itself from mid-April onward. Among them was James Cleveland, who had slowly risen over the course of the war to become a captain of a company of Loudoun militia in early 1780. Having complained about the erection of a permanent regular army and later resisted the draft, Cleveland had proved his loyalty through long service as an officer in the militia, serving at minimum pay for local defense.

Many other white Virginians, however, including Edward Wright, were tired of the onerous—and unequal—impositions on them. According to a local magistrate, Wright was a "hard-working" if "illiterate" man, who "regularly did duty" in the militia when he lived in a nearby county earlier in the war. Yet now, in 1781, Wright was having trouble making ends meet under the pressure of heavy and repeated taxes and frequent interruptions to the running of his farm because of militia call-outs. His health was also failing. Under such pressure, Wright approached a lieutenant colonel of the militia, William Bernard, to seek advice as to how to do what he had seen many of his wealthier neighbors do over the course of the war, which was to "get clear from Militia Duty as an infirm Man."[21]

Wright didn't make such a claim lightly. He was clearly troubled by the existing injustice inherent in the mobilization laws. He had threatened neighbors who tried to capture deserters from the army in lieu of serving themselves. He had also grown angry over the years about the exemptions from military service enjoyed by many of his wealthier neighbors. Only three months before, there was a public outcry among Wright's neighbors when the county lieutenant, Leroy Peachey, revealed that at least sixty men—or 15 percent of the militia—had been exempted from militia duty. There was an even bigger uproar when the militia found out Peachey had classed himself as an invalid. Peachey noted that in doing so he had the support of all of his genteel colleagues: "the whole of the Gentlemen were of Opinion that I was not an able Body'd Man." But as fellow petitioners from Cumberland County complained, the most galling aspect of the draft laws was that invalids and exempts were often "the most wealthy part of the Yeomanry" whose property would be "equally protected in common with other Citizens" who were subject to a draft "without an alternative."[22]

Moreover, prominent planters from all across the state were putting their property ahead of their principles and fleeing their plantations with their slaves in tow. Thomas Jefferson, Richard Henry Lee, Edmund Pendleton, and George Mason were among the most prominent Virginians who had their slaves pack up their houses and flee their homes when the British came calling. Even Thomas Nelson, soon to be governor and head of the Virginia militia in the field, took the time in the face of Cornwallis's advance to return to his Hanover County plantation to pack up some of his property and his family and send them to safety. Edward Wright and his neighbors did not have this option. Under the circumstances, they concluded that the Revolution had become just another rich man's war, and a poor man's fight.[23]

Wright was no Tory. Even when he threatened to evade militia duty if he could not get an exemption, Wright told Bernard that he "never would fight against his Country." Nor was he trying to evade doing his fair share. He simply needed a respite because of his health and economic worries. Wright told another witness that if he could only get but six barrels of corn for his family, "he was willing and ready to turn out to serve his Country." As the possibility of being called to serve in the militia increased with the arrival of the British in the area, Wright tried to think of ways out of his dilemma. By reducing his stock, he thought, he might free up food stores for his family's use and reduce his workload on the farm. At the same time, Wright told another neighbor that he had been unwell, "but that he was getting stout [healthier] and would turn out in the next division."

The exigencies of the war, however, would not allow him to wait. When the Richmond militia were called out once again in early June 1781, Wright faced a difficult decision. With not enough bread on the table, his health failing, and his fears of British plunder mounting, Wright might have to serve in the militia or come under censure and perhaps be condemned to serve for eight months in the regular army for disobeying orders—the standard punishment by that point in the war. His neighbors faced ruin too. Lacking alternatives, pushed to the edge, Wright fought back. He and several other men set afoot what local officials called a "conspiracy" to try to disrupt the callout and "Oppose the Measures of Government."

Wright and another leader of the so-called conspiracy, Fauntleroy Dye, called a meeting of neighbors and friends to plan action. They decided to hold a "barbecue" at Daniel Wilson's house on the same day the militia was supposed to turn out. They sent runners throughout the county to "warn in" all the men of the militia, mimicking the mechanism for calling militia musters. They wanted to test the strength of feeling among their neighbors but apparently "expected in a little time they should be able to get a sufficient Number to Oppose sufficiently the Militia's going out."

This time, however, given the acute crisis in Virginia, the government moved quickly and forcefully against the alleged conspirators. Labeled "a party of Torys" by the patriot leadership, Dye and Wright quickly found they had overplayed their hand. Local officials appealed to the state government for help, and Colonel William Nelson sent a detachment of trained professional troops along with a party of mounted volunteers under Major Beesly Edgar Joel into the county to root them out. They found a party of men at Dye's house with a number of their supporters and called on them to surrender. The men at first refused and called out to Joel, "Come on, we will have life for life by God—We have arms plenty." Joel then ordered his men to set fire to the house, upon which the party "call'd for quarter and gave up." In the confusion, Dye and Wright escaped, but Joel subsequently rounded up Wright and others he believed were involved. A few days later he found Dye, hiding in a thick wood.

The main offenders were brought to a military court-martial—presided over by Continental Army officers—where they faced punishment by death. Dye was charged with aiding and assisting the enemy, encouraging desertion, and dissuading the militia from opposing the enemy. Wright was only charged with discouraging the militia from opposing the enemy and encouraging desertion from the army. But despite numerous assertions by patriot leaders that both men, along with the men they rallied, were Tories who were keen to join the British Army and promote sedition, neither man was found guilty of treason or sedition. The court-martial sentenced both to imprisonment for the duration of the war, and they were sent to Richmond.

The court-martial singled out Dye and Wright mainly because it could not afford to seize too many of the disaffected. They needed men for the war effort. But even Dye and Wright were not the determined disaffected ringleaders that patriot leaders claimed they were. Wright in particular emerges from a careful reading of the evidence as a desperate man confronting the politics of war and the politics of subsistence. For him, the two were intimately related. Behind Wright's allegedly "boasting," violent demeanor lay a man deeply troubled by the demands placed on him, yet committed to the principles of equality that he believed constituted the fruits of the Revolution.

Wright and his neighbors were not alone. The troubles in Richmond County in the summer of 1781 were typical of dozens of other uprisings. As the British began their incursions into the heart of the state, thousands of militia from all across Virginia rose up in revolt against onerous impositions on them for their taxes, food supplies, and military services. From the western borders of the state to the counties on the eastern shore, angry Virginians confronted their field officers and local magistrates demanding "equal justice." Riots involving hundreds of men broke out in dozens of counties. Elsewhere, local officials bowed to popular pressure and ignored executive calls to raise the militia. Many were forced to resign, opening the way for more compliant replacements. Consequently, the critical prewar links between local and provincial elites were broken, and several counties assumed considerable autonomy from the demands of the state and congressional governments. The politics of war had significant repercussions.[24]

Though some wealthy planters and local officials questioned the loyalty of the protesters, those opposing the laws often frustrated efforts to label them by reiterating their commitment to the Revolution and their own interpretation of its principles. Protesting militiamen in one county told an official they were "cheerfully willing to Spend their hearts blood in Defence of the Cuntery," but they felt "Imposed upon" by the unjust laws. As another group put it, they were more than willing to sacrifice their lives and property for the cause, but only when such sacrifices were "Equally proportioned with our fellow Citizens who have they're all Equally at Stake." Among many ordinary Virginians, the "Spirit of Levelling" was still an animating force in their support of the ongoing Revolution in 1781, just as it had been in 1776.[25]

⌇

These claims for equality in the midst of the Revolutionary War had important results. For one thing, ordinary white Virginians, through their collective actions, were able to manipulate the recruitment laws, even to the point of crippling mobilization in Virginia. When unjust draft laws were introduced, Virginians protested sufficiently to get them dropped or changed. When they were unsuccessful in getting such changes, they resisted or evaded the laws, often without punishment. Wealthy planters' efforts to compel Virginians to fight on their behalf were constantly frustrated. At the same time, many ordinary Virginians were able to wrest concessions at important moments from the planter-dominated legislature in return for their allegiance to the new state and their promises of service. Religious dissenters such as the Baptists, for example, put the state on the road to the free exercise of religion. Middling Virginians insisted on more equitable tax laws to pay for the war effort—and eventually got them.

Of course, such claims to equality and the means used to advance them frustrated the war effort more generally, prolonging the conflict and making it far more divisive, bloody, messy, and complicated than it might have been—certainly more than many patriot leaders had initially envisioned. In effect, ordinary white Virginians turned the conflict from one of a simple contest between colony and metropole to one between Virginians. In doing so, the claims of ordinary white Virginians also provoked reactions from frustrated wealthy planters that were equally important in shaping the result of the Revolutionary War.

In 1776 many patriot leaders believed the appropriate response to explicit challenges to their authority and this "Spirit of Levelling" was to declare independence, restore government, and put an end to "rising disorders" by resuming the reins of government. In 1781, faced with continued challenges to their authority from within *and* with external threats from the British, some patriot leaders began to think about new ways of organizing government and compelling their fellow Virginians to do their bidding. Indeed, the patriot leadership was shaken enough to demand and debate the creation of a "dictatorship" in the state. Concealing their deliberations in the assembly, a motion was made to establish "a Dictator . . . in this Commonwealth who should have the power of disposing of the lives and fortunes of the Citizens thereof without being subject to account."[26]

Ordinary white Virginians were less convinced of the necessity of such measures. Their proposed solutions to the crisis in 1781 were far more democratic and in keeping with their push for greater equality throughout the war. Rockbridge County militiamen proposed shorter terms of militia service so that no one man would have to face ruin from serving too long. Another group proposed that those who served ought to be compensated out of the public purse for the loss of their crops and the relief of their families while away. One man even proposed that Virginia formalize an already informal practice of allowing enslaved Virginians to enlist in the army in return for their freedom. He believed the plan would succeed because enslaved soldiers would make good recruits and "the men will be equal to any."[27]

The planter-dominated legislature chose to put property ahead of principles. While making some concessions to ordinary Virginians by shortening tours of militia duty, legislators strengthened the executive powers. While not appointing a "dictator" per se, the assembly did give the newly elected governor, Thomas Nelson, more extensive powers than ever before, including the authority to order out all the militia if necessary and to send them wherever he chose. He was authorized to impress supplies, imprison suspected Tories, and create special courts to try them. The assembly also passed a special act establishing martial law within twenty miles of the American army. Anyone who opposed a call of men into the field would be declared civilly dead (and thus would forfeit their property, etc.), while anyone caught deserting could be sentenced to death.

In the end, within months of the introduction of these measures, a fortuitous coincidence of events that included a mistake by Cornwallis and the intervention of the French put a quick end to the conflict in Virginia at Yorktown, where the British were trapped. And while George Washington famously arrived from the north with the remnants of the Continental Army in time to help seal the fate of Cornwallis, very few Virginia militiamen—wealthy or poor—participated. Indeed, ironically, even tragically, there may have been more formerly enslaved Virginians at Yorktown seeking freedom with Cornwallis than white Virginians alongside Washington. While many white Virginians stayed at home to protect their freedom, many black Virginians died defending theirs. The American Revolution, dedicated to the proposition that all men were created equal and endowed with inalienable rights to life, liberty, and the pursuit of happiness—all predicated on the consent of the governed—came to an ignominious end in Virginia.

The wartime conflicts in Virginia helped lay the groundwork for heated contests a few years later over the efforts of nationalists to strengthen the powers of Congress and write a new federal constitution. In 1787 debt-ridden farmers in Virginia formed associations, flooded the state legislature with petitions, and finally stormed courthouses in several locations, much as James Cleveland and his Loudoun County neighbors had done back in 1776. Conservatives reacted against what they called an "excess of democracy"— or what many other Americans would call the fruits of the Revolution. We have come to think of the popular unrest that preceded the Constitution as unique to its time, but it wasn't. Throughout the Revolutionary War ordinary Americans claimed the right to govern themselves and challenged their leaders by demanding more equitable laws and fairer legislation for paying back debts and taxes. Virginians like James Cleveland and Edward Wright, by standing up for their own definition of equality, provoked some conservative-minded nationalists—many of whom had served in the Continental Congress or Army and had been frustrated by their protests—into taking measures that would ultimately create a stronger, more centralized, and in some ways more "effective" government than most had envisioned in 1776. But it was also a far less democratic government than Cleveland and Wright would have wanted.

Though they might not have gotten everything they wanted, the remarkable thing about this revolutionary resistance is that it continued through the most trying times, even as dissent became more hopeless and as patriot leaders moved to crush any signs of it. By resisting patriot leaders, Wright and Cleveland were forging and upholding the principles that would eventually become the bedrock of the Revolutionary legacy. As George Mason, author of the Virginia Declaration of Rights, was forced to concede in the face of massive resistance to unjust laws during the war: "The People in this Part of Virginia are well disposed to do everything in their Power to support the war, but the same Principles which attach them to the American Cause will incline them to resist Injustice or Oppression."[28]

Democracy and equality were not, then, free gifts bestowed upon the people by patriot leaders when they declared independence. Indeed, many patriot leaders were strongly opposed to democracy and equality of any kind. These were principles that many ordinary Virginians fought for, and continued to fight for, often in the face of great opposition. From the turbulence of a war that forced patriot leaders to rely upon an army of ordinary men arose a new world in which men of all ranks believed it was their right both to express forcefully their ideas about governance and social relations—and to act to ensure that those ideas were taken seriously.

FOR FURTHER READING

The Revolution in Virginia and the internal challenges posed by war are treated in Michael A. McDonnell, *The Politics of War: Race, Class, and Conflict in Revolutionary Virginia* (Chapel Hill, N.C., 2007), and " 'Class War': Class Struggles During the American Revolution in Virginia," *William and Mary Quarterly*, 3rd ser., 63 (2006): 305–44. For other kinds of challenges over a longer period, see especially Rhys Isaac, *The Transformation of Virginia, 1740–1790* (Chapel Hill, N.C., 1982), and Woody Holton, *Forced Founders: Indians, Debtors, Slaves, and the Making of the American Revolution in Virginia* (Chapel Hill, N.C., 1999). While details of Cleveland and Wright are scarce, see Holton and McDonnell, "Patriot vs. Patriot: Social Conflict in Virginia and the Origins of the American Revolution," *Journal of American Studies* 34, no. 2 (2000): 231–56. Thomas J. Humphrey puts tenancy during the Revolution into broader perspective in "Conflicting Independence: Land Tenancy and the American Revolution," *Journal of the Early Republic* 28, no. 2 (2008): 159–82. More specifically for Cleveland, see Nicholas Cresswell, *Journal of Nicholas Cresswell, 1774–1778* (London, 1925), and the letters of Lund and George Washington in *The Papers of George Washington,* ed. W. W. Abbot et al. (Charlottesville, Va., 1976–). For Wright and the court-martial transcript, see Proceedings of a General Court Martial held at Leeds Town, June 18–19, 1781, Executive Papers, at the Library of Virginia. The Library of Virginia also holds an extensive collection of Virginia Legislative Petitions from the Revolutionary War period that can be searched at http://www.lva.virginia.gov/public/guides/petitions/. Some of them have been printed in the valuable seven-volume collection *Revolutionary Virginia: The Road to Independence,* ed. Robert L. Scribner et al. (Charlottesville, Va., 1973–83).

CHAPTER NINE

Mary Perth, Harry Washington, and Moses Wilkinson: Black Methodists Who Escaped from Slavery and Founded a Nation

Cassandra Pybus

During the summer of 1772, when the moon provided just enough light, Young Mary would strap her baby to her back and slip out of the house of merchant-planter John Willoughby in Norfolk, Virginia. Cautiously making her way out of the sleeping town, Mary would walk about ten miles to the edge of the Great Dismal Swamp to meet with other enslaved people hidden in the woods, and here exhort her fellow sufferers to open their hearts to salvation so that their spirits could be freed from bondage. She knew the book of Exodus, with its promise to deliver the enslaved from bondage, and could read St. Paul's advice to the Galatians: "Stand fast therefore in the liberty wherewith Christ has made us free and be not entangled again with the yoke of bondage." When the meeting was over, she would trek back to the Willoughby house just in time to start her morning labor.

Many years later, when Mary was far away from Virginia, she told an English clergyman of her experiences as a slave preacher. By this time she was known as the widow Mary Perth and was the prosperous owner of a boardinghouse and produce store in Sierra Leone. This unusual British colony on the west coast of Africa had been created by abolitionists as a home for emancipated slaves residing in England or evacuated from North America at the end of the American Revolution. The company-appointed chaplain was very impressed with Mary's piety, and he wrote about her experiences as a slave preacher in the *Evangelical Magazine* of 1796. According to his account, Mary kept at her spiritual labors among the enslaved in Virginia until "they were formed into a body, so considerable as to invite a minister to settle amongst them."[1]

In making her nocturnal journey, Mary was returning to familiar haunts. She had not always been the property of John Willoughby. By the time she was sold to him in 1768, Mary had been in her late twenties, had one infant child, and was possibly pregnant again. Given that her children were later identified with the surname Savilles—miswritten as Cevils in the records—it is highly likely that one of a family named Savilles, who lived ten miles southwest of Norfolk in the New Mill Creek region, was the previous owner of Mary, or owned the father of her children.

At some stage Mary learned to read and write. Judging from the biblically inspired names of her children, it seems that she was a professing Christian by the time she was sold to John Willoughby. Her conversion to John Wesley's radical ideology came later. In all probability, she came to Methodism through the preaching of a self-funded Wesleyan itinerant called Robert Williams, who arrived at Norfolk en route from Ireland to New York in the summer of 1769. Barely a soul noticed this fierce proselytizer on his brief stopover. Williams's return, however, in February 1772 was a highly memorable event. Standing on the steps of the Norfolk County courthouse, Williams loudly burst into song, thereby drawing a curious crowd, including many of the town's enslaved workers. Williams then launched into an impassioned discourse on sin and salvation, to the astonishment of his audience, who had never witnessed such an uninhibited evocation of God's mercy. Most of the audience was inclined to dismiss Williams as a lunatic; however, the mayor detected the sinister ramifications of Williams's message and was heard to observe: "If we permit such a fellow as this to come here we shall have an insurrection of the Negroes."[2]

If Mary did not hear Williams preach at Norfolk on that day, she had numerous opportunities in the weeks that followed. Although Williams was unwelcome in Norfolk, the preacher was invited to stay with a prominent merchant in nearby Portsmouth. Here he preached openly at large biracial meetings held in a converted warehouse. He also traveled around Norfolk County, spreading the word about God's infinite capacity for redemption. With a raw, unrestrained, and emotional style, Williams declaimed a doctrine of spiritual autonomy, which permitted any individual to freely choose salvation and to be accountable only to God. The concept of being born again in God's grace, enabling the untrammeled spirit to soar free even as the physical body was compelled to labor for others, hit a responsive chord among people defined as property.

By the time Williams left Virginia in the spring of 1772, he had created the core of a Methodist meeting in Portsmouth, and he had formed several "classes"—or prayer groups—along the edge of the Great Dismal Swamp in the area between Great Bridge and New Mill Creek. Three months later another preacher, Joseph Pilmore, arrived in Portsmouth. He was delighted to find a Methodist meeting "about five miles into the woods from Portsmouth," as well as at New Mill Creek and Great Bridge.[3] Pilmore worked tirelessly to consolidate these biracial Methodist strongholds until the fall of 1772. At that time Williams returned, soon establishing an itinerant circuit from Portsmouth to the North Carolina border.

Two years later Williams settled down to live among his converts, marrying a local woman and establishing a smallholding beside the road from Portsmouth to Suffolk in the region of New Mill Creek. Suffolk was a thriving mercantile town on the Nansemond County side of the Dismal Swamp, where Mills Wilkinson was an influential merchant. His father, Willis Wilkinson, was a significant slave owner from Pigs Point on the Nansemond River, and he had bequeathed his son several of the family slaves. Among these inherited slaves was a charismatic man in his thirties called Moses. When Williams died in September 1775, it was Moses who took on the role of preacher for the enslaved population around the Great Dismal Swamp. Although Moses was illiterate, he could hold his clandestine congregation spellbound with his highly emotional renditions of the story of Exodus. His ecstatic visions revealed God's plan that the enslaved would be led out of bondage and across the water into the promised land.

Williams's death came at an extremely turbulent time in Virginia. Anger against the British had rapidly escalated into armed rebellion, and in September the royal governor of Virginia, Lord Dunmore, was forced to flee his mansion in Williamsburg. Taking refuge on a British warship in the James River, on November 14, 1775, he published a proclamation that offered to free any slaves and indentured servants willing to bear arms for the king. It had an electrifying effect on the enslaved population around Norfolk. By the end of the month Dunmore was able to report to England that he had received between two and three hundred runaway slaves, whom he intended to form into a military unit he called the Ethiopian Regiment. The preacher Moses was one of several of Mills Wilkinson's enslaved workers who ran away to join Dunmore.

These slave runaways were given basic training in the use of weapons and then set to work building fortifications at the strategic area of Great Bridge. Rumor had it that they wore a uniform bearing the provocative inscription "Liberty to Slaves," but in reality Dunmore spent months desperately begging army headquarters to send any sort of clothing for them. Moses was part of the "ragged crew" that engaged the Virginia militia at Great Bridge on December 9, 1775, which ended in a complete rout of the ragtag British forces.[4] More than one hundred men, including a large number of the black recruits, were killed or taken captive. Moses was among several hundred who retreated back to the safety of the British fleet.

After the military victory at Great Bridge, white Virginians channeled their fears about slave defections into ridicule of the British efforts to create a regiment of black recruits. At Mount Vernon, the plantation of George Washington on the Potomac River, his manager cousin expressed scorn at the seemingly absurd notion that slaves could be soldiers. But Lund Washington could not avoid the realization that enslaved and indentured workers were driven to Dunmore's side by their passion for liberty—the very same passion that animated his illustrious cousin. Speaking of the indentured and enslaved workforce, Lund acknowledged that "there is not a man of them, but would leave us, if they believe'd they could . . . Liberty is sweet."[5]

Harry, the enslaved stable hand at Mount Vernon, was one man who knew that liberty was sweet. Harry was a "saltwater slave" imported from Africa, whom Washington had purchased in 1763 as part of his contribution to the workforce of the Great Dismal Swamp Company formed to drain the swamp. For two terrible years Harry labored amid clouds of mosquitoes in a futile attempt to cut a drainage canal. He was then moved to Washington's home plantation at Mount Vernon, where he had responsibility for the care of the colonel's horses. In this role, Harry had close contact with Washington and his neighbors. No doubt he listened with more than idle interest when Washington discussed ideas about tyranny and the inviolable concept of liberty. Harry fully understood the concept of liberty; he had previously attempted to seize it for himself by running away from Mount Vernon in 1773. He was captured within a matter of weeks after Washington posted a reward for his return. That experience might have taught him that his own attachment to liberty had no place in the Revolutionary fervor that so animated his master. If Harry was to obtain freedom, he would have to entrust his aspirations for liberty to the tyrant king and cast his lot with his master's enemy. However, when Lord Dunmore made his offer to free slaves who would fight for the king, he was in Lower Chesapeake Bay, too far away to make a successful escape. Harry was forced to bide his time.

Closer to Norfolk, enslaved people were prepared to risk everything to join Lord Dunmore. As the defections of enslaved people intensified, so too did the backlash against suspected Loyalists. The town of Norfolk was widely believed to be a hotbed of Loyalist intrigue, and John Willoughby, the most illustrious planter-merchant in the region and a friend of the deposed governor, was a particular target. On New Year's Day 1776 the Virginia militia burned British-occupied Norfolk to the ground. For safety, Willoughby moved his family and household slaves to his plantation at Willoughby Point in Princess Ann County, but even at this distance he was still regarded with suspicion. In April 1776 the Virginia Committee of Safety demanded that he move at least thirty miles away from the coast, and to ensure that he did so they ordered his slaves be taken by the militia. Willoughby was still a powerful man in Norfolk. He refused to comply with the Committee of Safety's decree and within a month his entire enslaved workforce of sixteen men, twenty-one women, and fifty children—including Young Mary—was settled in the camp established by Lord Dunmore at Tucker's Point. Soon after that Willoughby died at his plantation.

Two years later Willoughby's son petitioned for compensation from the Virginia legislature for the mass defection of his late father's entire slave property. He claimed that the punitive action of the Committee of Safety had caused his father's slaves to run away to the British on April 10, 1776. This quixotic petition was probably a strategy to dispel any suggestion of the family's collusion with the British as well as a ruse to help John Willoughby Jr. recover from financial disaster. However, the minutes from the meeting of the Committee of Safety and the reports in *The Virginia Gazette* show that the defection of Willoughby's slaves actually occurred in May, on a day when a ship from Dunmore's fleet was in the vicinity of Willoughby Point. This evidence suggests that Willoughby's slaves did not escape of their own accord. Rather than this large group of people taking it upon themselves to make a dangerous and difficult escape across miles of country to the British camp near Portsmouth, it seems that Willoughby took all his slaves to the British ship in his own boat. After a day or so, Willoughby himself returned to his plantation at Willoughby Point, probably because of the epidemic of smallpox raging among Dunmore's forces. Here he died, having hastily made his will, in which he declared that he was financially ruined. He bequeathed the plantation to his son John Willoughby Jr., but there was no mention of slave property.

At Dunmore's camp, where Mary was now liberated in body as well as in spirit, she and her four children faced an uncertain future. In the confined and unhealthy conditions at Tucker's Point they were exposed to greater danger than ever before. True, they had protection, food, and shelter, but disease and misery were their daily companions. A virulent outbreak of smallpox crippled the camp. While the British soldiers and sailors were largely immune, the local recruits were highly vulnerable to its hideous ravages. They died in great numbers. In order to isolate the sick and inoculate the healthy, the naval surgeons persuaded Dunmore to move his base farther into Chesapeake Bay to Gwynn's Island, opposite the mouth of the Rappahannock River. Even here Dunmore continued to draw fresh recruits of runaway slaves at the rate of six to eight each day, most of whom succumbed to the disease soon after they arrived. Those who recovered from inoculation then fell victim to an outbreak of typhoid fever. The combined ravages of these diseases cost Dunmore more than two-thirds of his Ethiopian Regiment. Eyewitness accounts suggest the death toll at Tucker's Point and Gwynn's Island was near to eight hundred souls. Among the people from the Willoughby plantation, only a dozen or so survived, including Mary and her daughters Patience, aged twelve, Hannah, aged eight, and Zilpha, aged four. The preacher Moses fell victim to the disease, but he too survived, although it left him blind and unable to walk unaided.

In this dreadfully weakened condition, Dunmore's forces were easily driven from Virginia. On July 19, 1776, just before leaving Chesapeake Bay, a small fleet of eight British vessels made a foray up the Potomac to get fresh water. News that the British ships had entered the Potomac probably reached Washington's home plantation on the same day. It appears that the stable hand Harry, along with two indentured servants, soon made a bolt for the British vessels in a stolen boat. Cautiously avoiding the armed militia patrolling the riverbanks, these three fugitives made their way down the Potomac. On July 24 they took advantage of a skirmish between the British and the patriot militia to draw alongside the British flagship HMS *Roebuck*. In the logbook for that day, the *Roebuck*'s captain noted his satisfaction at having recruited "three of General Washington's servants."[6]

Two months later Mary, Moses, and Harry were all part of the massive British force that invaded and seized New York. By October, Harry, Moses, and Mary, along with many other surviving recruits of Dunmore's, were employed by the Royal Artillery Department and housed in barracks created out of four rowhouses in Lower Manhattan. They found themselves part of a community of some two thousand black refugees behind the British lines in occupied New York. Drawn from different colonies and various life experiences, these black refugees were bound together by the shared experience of work, exile, and hope for the future.

A number of black preachers occupied a prominent place in this newly constituted black community, which was yearning for spiritual guidance and comfort. Most influential was the prophetically named blind preacher who had run away from Mills Wilkinson in 1775 and was now known to his many followers as Daddy Moses. His right-hand man was another influential

Methodist preacher from Virginia named Luke Jordan. He was part of a large group of about five hundred escaped Virginia slaves from plantations in three separate counties whom Admiral Collier carried back from his raid on Portsmouth. They were closely connected through ties of kinship, and almost everyone in this group had a connection to someone who had fled with Dunmore three years earlier. Most, if not all, professed to be Methodists. More than thirty people in the group, including Luke Jordan's wife, Rachel, and son Joshua, had been enslaved on the plantations of Willis Wilkinson and his son. Another member of this group was Caesar Perth, who was enslaved to a builder whose house was located close to the Willoughby house where young Mary lived. Given the relatively close proximity of Mary and Caesar's households in Virginia, their subsequent formal marriage in New York may have been the first official record of what was probably a long-standing relationship.

Love and marriage, stories and prayers: these mitigated the separation from kinfolk in Virginia and softened the challenging business of staying alive in New York. The tentative sense of security that the black community developed over five years with the British was shattered late in 1781 when they heard the news from Yorktown that Cornwallis had lost the campaign for the South. Now they had no hope that they would be reunited with the family members they had left behind in Virginia; if they were to try, they would face the awful punishments meted out to fugitive slaves. In December 1782 more terrible news arrived: the provisional peace treaty signed in Paris included a last-minute clause that prohibited "carrying away any Negroes or other property of the American Inhabitants."[7]

Rumors swept through Manhattan that the British were obliged to abandon the thousands of black refugees who had sought their protection. Having experienced years of freedom, these black refugees were horrified at the prospect of being turned over to their former masters. Day and night they urged the British authorities to make good on their promises of freedom and to remove them from the reach of their vengeful masters. Fortunately, the British commander in chief, Sir Guy Carleton, was receptive to their pleas and—defying the tentative peace treaty—gave instructions that all runaways who had been with the British for a year or more were to be issued certificates of freedom by Brigadier General Birch. They would then be free to go wherever they wished.

Until they were able to leave, the black refugees faced an anxious time as slave owners came freely into the city to reclaim their former property. As one of the black refugees later recalled, they were in paroxysms of fear at "our old masters coming from Virginia, North Carolina, and other parts, and seizing upon their slaves in the streets of New York, or even dragging them out of their beds."[8] Without warning, runaways could find themselves knocked on the head, bound hand and foot, and taken back to the place they had fled. Tensions had reached a fever pitch by the time John Willoughby Jr. arrived in New York to recover Mary Perth, her children, and the other people he regarded as his inheritance. Willoughby complained to Carleton that he had been put to the expense of a disagreeable journey from Virginia only to discover that his property had been guaranteed free transport to Nova Scotia, which would permit them to slip out of his grasp forever. He insisted that the embarkation to Nova Scotia be aborted. If these chattel were permitted to leave, he told Carleton, he and his neighbors would be financially ruined. Carleton did not even bother to reply to Willoughby's argument. Willoughby returned empty-handed to Virginia, where he bombarded Congress with outraged complaints. As a result, General George Washington was directed to confront Carleton with this flagrant violation of the treaty.

At his meeting with the defeated British commander on May 6, 1783, Washington was nonplussed to hear Carleton, instead of acknowledging his treaty obligations, provide a lecture on moral obligations. The British government would never accept the dishonor of "violating their faith to the Negroes," the British commander forcefully insisted.[9] As a sole concession to the treaty, Carleton agreed that the Americans might inspect the embarkations of the ships leaving New York and that they could recover any person they could prove was not free. British inspectors were directed to compile a list of all the black émigrés to serve as a record in case compensation was necessary. Two American commissioners were appointed to inspect British embarkations. One of these was the army contractor Daniel Parker, the very man Washington had instructed to recapture those of his own property who had run off from Mount Vernon.

Parker proved powerless to prevent Washington's property from sailing away. Under Parker's impotent gaze, Harry embarked upon the *L'Abondance,* bound for Nova Scotia, in July 1783. The inspectors recorded his name as Henry Washington. He was noted to be forty-three years of age and claimed to have run away from General Washington seven years earlier. The inspectors of the *L'Abondance* also included on their list of passengers Moses Wilkinson, the blind and crippled preacher; Caesar Perth; his wife, Mary; and their baby daughter, Susan. Mary's daughters Zilpah and Hannah were also on the list, as was the eldest, Patience, whose husband, Thomas Freeman, was to follow in another ship a few months later.

When they arrived in Nova Scotia, the majority of the black émigrés settled in a large community near Shelburne, which they named Birchtown after the signer of their freedom certificates, General Birch. Here a life of freedom proved to be a constant struggle. There were interminable delays in the allocation of the promised land grants, and some people were still waiting for their land allocation three years after arrival. Once the grants were allocated, the land proved to be poor and rocky, unsuitable for sustainable agriculture. In this place of bitter cold and unremitting hardship, the only thing to be found in abundance was a vibrant spiritual life. A licensed Methodist preacher who visited Birchtown was astonished to find fourteen Methodist groups meeting nightly. This wondrous circumstance, he explained to his superiors, was due entirely to the self-appointed preacher, Daddy Moses, whom he described as "a poor negro who can neither see, walk nor stand."[10]

In 1791 Daddy Moses played host to John Clarkson, brother of the abolitionist Thomas Clarkson, who was in Nova Scotia as the emissary of the Sierra Leone Company. Addressing the hundreds of people who packed the Methodist meetinghouse, Clarkson outlined the company's offer of free land grants in Sierra Leone: twenty acres for every man, ten for every woman, and five for every child who would relocate to their colony in West Africa. He further assured his rapt listeners that in Sierra Leone there would be no discrimination between black and white settlers. Within three days the congre-

Rose Fortune was about ten years old when her family joined thousands of African Americans leaving America with the British in 1783. Her family settled on the western side of Nova Scotia in the port of Annapolis Royal, where she later became a baggage handler, delivery woman, and colorful character well known to everybody. She died at the age of ninety in 1864. The drawing is from a watercolor by an unknown artist, presumably done at Annapolis, Port Royal, Nova Scotia.

gation of Daddy Moses had decided to emigrate en masse, even though this meant the abandonment of their freehold land grants. The first names on the list of emigrants were those of Caesar Perth and his wife, Mary. Harry Washington was also listed, with his wife, Jenny. He took with him an ax, a saw, a pickax, three hoes, two muskets, and several items of furniture. In leaving Nova Scotia he was abandoning his house, two town lots, and forty acres.

The English abolitionists who set up the Sierra Leone Company liked to think of their new settlers as Africans, but the settlers from Nova Scotia conceived of themselves in a very different way. In their eyes, they were God's chosen people, just like the children of Israel. In undertaking the exodus to Sierra Leone, they were not Africans returning home but rather a new people, reborn through conversion, participating in a divinely ordained project to leave their Egyptian bondage, travel through the wilderness, and enter the promised land of Canaan.

After long weeks at sea, the fleet entered the mouth of the Sierra Leone River on February 28, 1792. The settlers were led ashore by their preachers, singing the Wesleyan hymn:

> Wake! Every heart and every tongue
> To praise the Savior's name.
> The day of Jubilee is come!
> Return ye, ransomed sinners, home.[11]

It soon became apparent that the day of Jubilee, which would see an end to slavery, an abolition of debt, and an equitable redistribution of land, was a long way off in this remote wilderness.

First the settlers had to hack through a jungle of thorny bush and sharp-edged elephant grass; then they had to clear a site for their settlement, which they called Freetown. Early in the morning of April 2, 1792, a monsoon arrived, a tremendous storm that tore through their makeshift huts. Inadequate shelter and the constant rain meant that nearly everyone came down with malarial fever. The provisions brought from England were completely spoiled, and the steaming monsoonal air soon carried the nauseating stench of rotting food.

The settlers struggled to adjust to the strange and sometimes terrible environment of Africa, but they had less inclination to adjust to the changed conditions that governed their new home. None of the Sierra Leone Company had ever been to West Africa. The concept of Jubilee was alien to the English directors, who envisaged vast profits from plantation crops. These directors sought to recoup their shareholders' initial investment by charging an annual ground rent of two shillings an acre on the settlers' land grants. Nor did they understand that the rugged terrain meant that there was not enough arable land to provide the large grants as promised. The secular leader of the community, Thomas Peters, was bitterly disappointed that yet again promises were broken. Peters had been elected by the black refugees in Nova Scotia to go to England in order to petition the government on their behalf. In England, Peters had garnered the support of the British government for the emigration to Sierra Leone. Upon arrival in Sierra Leone, he was shocked to find that Clarkson was appointed governor, while he—Peters—was denied any role in the administration of the new settlement. Clarkson took the view that as company-appointed governor, he alone was in charge, and he saw Peters's opposition to his autocratic rule as self-serving jealousy. He decided that Peters was responsible for the "irritability of temper and peevish disposition" the settlers had begun to display.[12] In mid-April 1792 Clarkson engineered a confrontation with his imagined rival under a massive cotton tree, and here he threatened that either Peters or himself would be hanged from that tree before the matter was settled. By that time Peters was already ill with fever. He died on June 26, 1792, a sorely disillusioned man.

Thomas Peters was just one of many victims of malarial fever. Anna Maria Falconbridge, wife of the company agent, described a desperate situation with seven hundred people "under the affliction of burning fevers," while the rest were "scarce able to crawl about." Every day handfuls of people were "buried with as little ceremony as so many dogs and cats."[13] Caesar Perth was among the very first who died. Mary Perth and her daughters survived these first traumatic months, as did Harry and Jenny Washington. Throughout the ordeal the survivors were sustained by intense commitment to the otherworldly life of the spirit, which was the lifeblood of this black community and a source of amazement to Mrs. Falconbridge. Regardless of the time of night, she could hear preaching from some quarter or another. "I never met with, heard, or read of, any set of people observing the same appearance of godliness," she wrote in her journal.[14]

While the arrival in Sierra Leone went badly, the settlers were determined to press forward with their desire to participate in their governance. As Clarkson ruefully observed in his diary, the settlers' expectation of the day of Jubilee and their belief that they were living out the story of Exodus gave them "strange notions from Thomas Peters as to their civil rights."[15] Soon after they arrived, he received a barely literate petition from the congregation of Daddy Moses to say that they willingly agreed to be governed by the laws of England, but that they must have a role in government. They would not accept a white-only government "with out haven aney of our own culler in it," they told him.[16] Reminding Clarkson that he had promised that in Sierra Leone they would be free and equal, they argued their right to choose the men who would govern them.

After six months with no response, the settlers were in a fever pitch of indignation. They had no representation in the government of the new colony, and they possessed only the huts they had built on small town lots carved out of the jungle in Freetown. The survey for the promised farm lots had not even begun. The only basis for their subsistence was working two days per week for the company, for which they were paid in credit at the company store—a form of labor exchange they believed was akin to bondage. Clarkson did what he could to allay the fears of the settlers, but the company summarily dismissed him when he took leave to visit England at the end of 1792. Throughout the next five years clashes between the disillusioned settlers and the high-handed new governor, Zachary Macaulay, were the norm. As the preachers Daddy Moses and Luke Jordan wrote to Clarkson, "We once did call it Free Town, but since your absence we have a reason to call it a town of slavery."[17]

Yet for all the persistent conflict of these years, Freetown began to prosper. By the end of the century it was the largest town on the west coast of Africa. About four hundred timber and shingle houses were neatly laid out along nine streets, and an assortment of livestock cropped the grass-covered paths. The waterfront was a site of frenetic activity where at any given time there would be one or two visiting slave ships, as well as several trading vessels of the Sierra Leone Company and the canoes of hundreds of Africans who brought produce to trade each day. The settlers had finally gotten land grants of farm lots in the surrounding hills, but few wished to become farmers. Harry Washington was one of the few settlers devoted to farming, and he grew subsistence crops for his large family. Much as the settlers valued ownership of land, the idea of agricultural labor appealed to very few, as so many had formerly been plantation slaves. In their eyes, deliverance from bondage meant that they were free to work as they pleased, and they pointedly refused to bend to the company's demands that they grow cash crops like sugar and coffee.

Rather than farm, the settlers preferred to engage in fishing and small-time trading. Some worked as porters loading visiting ships at the wharves. Even if their work was sometimes tainted with the odium of the slave trade, they were at liberty to choose their employment and to negotiate the terms under which they would work. Others chose to engage in entrepreneurial activities. The widow Mary Perth ran a boardinghouse and shop near Freetown's waterfront; she was kept very busy as a shopkeeper and landlady. In addition, she worked as housekeeper for Governor Macaulay, who entrusted her with the care of a group of African children living at his house. Such was the exacting workload of this indefatigable widow that the company chaplain thought she was about seventy when in truth she was only fifty-five. Mary was among the most successful of Sierra Leone's entrepreneurs, and she ran her lucrative waterfront businesses until her death in 1813.

Disputation over the ground rent and the company's denial of settler representation in the management of the colony continued to pose a running conflict. Governor Macaulay blamed the Methodists, whose self-validating religious experience and refusal to defer to ordained clergy fed resistance to company rule. "Their government is pure democracy," he noted with distaste, "without subordination to anyone."[18] He was furious to hear one of the Methodist preachers compare the governor to Pharaoh and tell his flock, "God in his own good time would deliver Israel."[19] As an arrogant young man whose previous work experience had been as a supervisor on a slave plantation in the West Indies, Macaulay failed to understand that when Daddy Moses preached about the delivery out of oppression and over the mighty waters into the land of Canaan, his congregation of self-emancipated slaves had a very firm idea of what that meant in their own lives.

Macaulay had nothing but scorn for the "mad Methodists," who were the overwhelming majority of the settlers in Sierra Leone. He did make one exception for the widow Mary Perth. Even though Mary was a staunch Methodist, Macaulay felt that her piety set her apart from the rest of that despised sect. In his letters to his fiancée, Selena Mills, in England, Macaulay spoke of "the good old woman" who was the only one of the settlers with the judgment to relish the religious tracts Selena sent.[20] For her part, Mary sent gifts of her own to Miss Mills and laid plans to go to England as supervisor for the African children Macaulay was taking to be educated as Christian missionaries. She sent to the company chairman the large sum of £155 to be invested in order to pay for her trip. In 1799, when Macaulay left the colony, Mary Perth went with him, not to return until December 1801.

Monumental changes that happened in Mary's absence ruptured the settler community and severely weakened the authority of the Methodists. In 1800 a rebellion led by Methodist settlers challenged the company's right to rule in Sierra Leone; the company ruthlessly suppressed it. After a hasty court-martial, two members of the Methodist congregation were executed and another forty settlers, most of them Methodists, were sent into exile at other places along the African coast. Harry Washington was one of the exiled rebel leaders. He died within a year or so, before he could return to Sierra

Leone. The abolitionist directors of the Sierra Leone Company were un-apologetic about their draconian response to those who challenged their authoritarian paternalism. The colony was much better off without men like Harry Washington, they insisted, and they expected to hear no more radical notions about individual rights. Runaway slaves from America had made "the worst possible subjects," director William Wilberforce complained, "as thorough Jacobins as if they had been trained and educated in Paris."[21]

Wilberforce and his fellow directors would learn to their cost that these radical notions were tenacious among the settlers in Sierra Leone; people who radically remade themselves in the American Revolution and who believed they were actors in a divinely inspired project could never be brought to heel.

FOR FURTHER READING

This essay is based on material described at length in my book *Epic Journeys of Freedom Runaway Slaves of the American Revolution and Their Global Quest for Liberty* (Boston, 2006). The best accounts of African-American participation in the Revolution are Benjamin Quarles, *The Negro in the American Revolution* (Chapel Hill, N.C., 1961), and Gary B. Nash, *The Forgotten Fifth: African Americans in the Age of Revolution* (Cambridge, Mass., 2006). Also of interest on the subject of the black Loyalists who left America after the Revolution is Simon Schama, *Rough Crossings: Britain, the Slaves and the American Revolution* (New York, 2006). For a calculation of the number of enslaved people who defected to the British, see my essay "Thomas Jefferson's Faulty Math: The Question of Slave Defections in the American Revolution," *William and Mary Quarterly,* 3rd ser., 62 (2005): 244-64. The full story of the Black Loyalists who went to Sierra Leone can be found in Ellen Gibson Wilson, *The Loyal Blacks* (New York, 1976), while the most thorough account of the origins of the colony of Sierra Leone is Stephen Braidwood, *Black Poor and White Philanthropists: London's Blacks and the Foundations of the Sierra Leone Settlement, 1786-1791* (Liverpool, U.K., 1994). Christopher Brown examines the moral climate that facilitated the British willingness to emancipate slaves and how this fed into the rise of radical abolitionism in *Moral Capital: Foundations of British Abolitionism* (Chapel Hill, N.C., 2006).

CHAPTER TEN

James Ireland, John Leland, John "Swearing Jack" Waller, and the Baptist Campaign for Religious Freedom in Revolutionary Virginia

Jon Butler

James Ireland, John Leland, and John Waller, Baptists all, knew the dangers of pursuing freedom of religion and became major figures in the drive for the Revolutionary achievement of religious freedom in Virginia. They fought for two revolutions in Virginia, one for political freedom and one for religious freedom. They demonstrated how colonists of modest background led sophisticated discussions of fundamental political and religious principles; how the Revolution itself challenged all Virginia religious groups, including Baptists, in unexpected ways; and how a small, determined movement could profoundly change the long-vexed relationship between religion and government in Europe and America. They remind us how common men and women could shape society as profoundly as the well known and wealthy.

As with many little-known participants in the Revolution, no contemporary likenesses of Ireland, Leland, or Waller have survived or ever existed, although a portrait of John Leland, probably made a half century later when he was in his seventies, still conveys a certain righteous sense. But the action and principles they articulated resonate without portraits, even to the point of upending some stereotypes about Baptists. Baptists had, and still have, a reputation for plain speaking and an almost ostentatiously unlettered style. Yet Ireland published an affecting autobiography shortly before his death in 1819, and Leland published many sermons and tracts throughout his lifetime. In contrast, Waller appeared on page after page of Robert Semple's early *History of the Rise and Progress of the Baptists in Virginia,* published in 1810. Semple knew Waller, and no matter Waller's lack of educational sophistication, Semple understood how he commanded much of the Baptist campaign in Virginia.

What did it mean to be a Baptist in Virginia? Baptists were Protestant Christians who uniquely reserved the rite of baptism for adults who could testify to their Christian knowledge and commitment, rather than administer it to infants as a sign of their entrance into the Christian faith after birth. At the same time, Baptists often disagreed about what was required of adults who sought baptism. Virginia's "Regular Baptists" offered baptism to adults who accepted John Calvin's theology of predestination, outlined for English Baptists in the 1689 "London Confession of Faith" and the 1742 "Philadelphia Confession of Faith," and who expressed their commitment to a Christian life. "Separate Baptists" did not so much reject Calvinism, or predestination, as they emphasized revivalism and required a vivid "born-again" experience in the believer who desired baptism, an experience usually associated with an outpouring of emotion focusing on a previously sinful life and joy at the prospect of salvation.

Virginia's Baptists worried about religious freedom because, as in most southern colonies, the Church of England—the Anglican Church—was Virginia's exclusive, legally established church, and non-Anglican "dissenters" worshipped only through government sufferance. Since the seventeenth century Virginia law had presumed all Virginians to be members of the Church of England. Residents were required to pay taxes to support it, and no one could preach in the colony without a license, a regulation reinforced in 1747 by the Virginia governor and council who demanded restraints on "all Itinerant Preachers." This meant that Virginia licensed only ministers it approved; could refuse to license dissenting preachers, such as Baptist and Presbyterian itinerant preachers who upset parish stability; and did not respect freedom of conscience, as did Pennsylvania.[1]

Organized religion was scant in Virginia from 1607 until the 1680s, and questions of religious freedom were muted by early Anglican disorganization and spiritual indifference among early Virginia colonists. Church of England parish life lagged, ministers were few, and only Quakers offered competition, though in small numbers that attracted little negative attention. Between 1680 and the 1760s, however, Virginia developed a powerful Church of England establishment strongly inflected by wealth and social class. By the 1750s Anglican parishes in Virginia were renowned for large, beautiful church structures and generally well-paid ministers. Sunday worshippers drawn from the local planter aristocracy strengthened the authority of the Church of England and their own local and colony-wide prestige. After 1755 Baptists aggressively challenged this religious authority and personal prestige.

Baptists were not Virginia's original religious dissenters. Quaker "Public Friends," itinerant nonordained preachers, had irritated Virginia authorities in the 1660s. But George Fox preached in Virginia in 1672 without incident, and Public Friends who visited Virginia later usually sought converts discreetly, so Virginia Quakers remained small in number. Presbyterians appeared in Virginia in the 1690s but seriously challenged the Church of England only in the 1740s. Well organized and generally well educated, their congregations grew slowly, and most Presbyterian ministers ultimately acknowledged Virginia's laws on establishment and applied for preaching permits, although this produced not inconsiderable wrangling.

Baptists, however, presented a more powerful challenge to Virginia's eighteenth-century Anglican order. The careers of James Ireland, John Leland, and John Waller illustrate how and why ordinary Baptists took dissent to a new level in Virginia.

Born in 1741, the young John Waller scarcely bore religious promise, although his early feistiness later became a hallmark of his Baptist commitment. Literate though not formally educated, with what the early Virginia Baptist historian Robert Semple called a "satirical wit," by his own account the young Waller was a drunken, obnoxious lout who enjoyed tormenting Baptist preachers for sport. This won him the nickname "Swearing Jack." Waller's service on a grand jury, however, turned his life around. When it indicted a Baptist named Lewis Craig for preaching without a license, Craig's fearless court performance led Waller to reconsider his own life and initiated a powerful conversion experience. As Waller would remember his encounter, he "saw and felt himself a sinner . . . [and] now, for the first time, except in blaspheming, began to call upon the name of the Lord."[2]

James Ireland's Baptist story was different. A Scot raised in Edinburgh by a Presbyterian lawyer father and a mother "of taste and fashion," Ireland shared a Latin-school education with "noblemen['s] and gentlemen's sons and others," some of whom were "wild youths" whose habits he sometimes adopted. Hoping to obtain a naval commission, his father helped him secure a "coasting voyage" to London "to discover how the sea would agree with my constitution." But "an act of juvenile indiscretion"—its nature unknown— plus "the rigor of the penal laws" got Ireland banished to America.[3]

Landing in Virginia, Ireland edged toward respectable society. He joined a fraternal society (probably the Freemasons) and enjoyed the "recreations, pleasures, and pastimes" of the colony's many young people. He was, he admitted, "a most complete dancer." But he struggled with religious doubt, fueled by his own anxieties and the vigorous arguments about religion he encountered there. Yet when Ireland accepted baptism from two revivalist Baptist preachers, he turned almost immediately to preaching, buoyed by a dream he had had even before his baptism—that he had been captured by a man on a red horse and given a sword to do battle with the world, the kind of events he believed were "spoken of in Revelation 6:4."[4]

Ireland soon battled for his right to preach. He defended another Baptist minister from one of several "dissipated men" who "seized [the minister] by the throat, and choked him till he was black in the face." Culpeper County officials warned Ireland not to preach, but he preached anyway, then "heard a rustling noise in the woods, and . . . was seized by the collar by two men whilst standing on the table." When challenged on who authorized his preaching, Ireland replied, "He that was the Author of the gospel." But the officials rejected Ireland's Baptist "credentials" as "not being sanctioned and commissioned by the Bishop." Ireland recounted how Culpeper County magistrates "brow-beat me, maltreated me," and demanded that they "hear no more of my vile, pernicious, abhorrible, detestable, abominable, [and] diabolical doctrines, for they were nauseous to the whole court." Thrown in jail, where "sticks and stones" were thrown at him "the whole night," Ireland charged that his jailors "plotted to blow me up with powder, . . . smoke me with brimstone and Indian pepper," and finally poison him.[5]

This kind of governmental repression of religious activity had occurred earlier in other American colonies. Puritans had banished Anne Hutchinson and her followers in 1638, hung Quakers in the 1660s, and executed accused witches in scattered trials from the 1660s through the infamous 1692 Salem trials. In 1707 New York authorities arrested the Presbyterian minister Francis Makemie for preaching without a license, although a jury found Makemie innocent based on the 1689 Act of Toleration. Closer to home, Virginia Presbyterians struggled over preaching licenses with the Virginia Council off and on from the 1730s into the 1760s, in most cases winning licenses.

But the attacks on Ireland typified a physical repression of Baptist preaching in Virginia not equaled in any other eighteenth-century British mainland colony. More than 160 attacks on Virginia's Baptist preachers in the 1760s and 1770s graphically describe the persecution. John Afferman of Middlesex County: "cruelly beaten—incapacitated for work." Joseph Anthony of Chesterfield County: "jailed for preaching. 'Three months.' " Elijah Baker of Accomac County: "pelted with apples and stones, banishment attempted." David Barrow of Nansemond County: "ducked and nearly drowned by 20 men." Rene Chastain of Chesterfield County: "ordered to leave the county, or go to jail."[6]

As difficult as it was to endure, John Waller's success depended partly on his persecution. By the time of the Revolution, Robert Semple proudly wrote, Waller had "lain in four different jails, for the space of one hundred and thirteen days, in all; besides buffetings, stripes, reproaches, etc." True, "as a preacher, his talents in the pulpit were not above mediocrity." But Waller's "talents for art and intrigue, were equaled by few." This ordinary and unlearned but feisty and resolute preacher baptized more than two thousand persons before his death in 1802, helped ordain no fewer than twenty-seven ministers, worked to form at least eighteen Virginia Baptist congregations, and served as clerk to several Virginia Baptist associations that engineered critically important petitions that laid issues of religion and freedom directly before the Virginia legislature.[7]

The movement created by Virginia's Baptist preachers challenged the very notion of religious hierarchy. When William Fristoe published his early history of the Ketocton Baptist Association in 1808, he turned contemporary ridicule of Baptist social class against Baptist critics: "The cant word was, [we] are an ignorant illiterate set . . . of the poor and contemptible class of the people." But as Fristoe noted, "It was not the rulers that believed when Jesus Christ preached his own gospel—it was the poor the gospel proved effectual to, . . . the common people heard him gladly," while those who claimed to be "wise and prudent were left to judicial blindness."[8]

Fristoe was not so wrong, at least about his fellow Baptists. They were indeed typically poorer than their neighbors, mostly farmers tilling few acres, growing some crops for their own consumption, and hoping to sell any excess for precious cash. If many Baptists were poor, others owned a bit more land, sometimes owned slaves, served on grand juries, oversaw roads, and acted as guardians for orphans and widows. Although Fristoe acknowledged the epithet about the Baptists' illiteracy, the many careful signatures on Baptist petitions suggest that the vast majority could sign their name and, probably, could read. But few wealthy Virginians would leave seats in the colony's substantial Anglican churches to sit in crude, unfinished meetinghouses or even outdoors with much poorer Baptists.

In an eighteenth-century society where hierarchy determined even how residents greeted each other, the Baptists' modesty, combined with their blunt assertiveness and claims of religious independence and spiritual vision, may be what most offended so many officials. Anglican authorities believed that the Baptists' modest social status simply gave them no right to ignore the established church, to preach without licenses, or as Fristoe put it, "to abundantly enrich their minds with spiritual ideas" outside the guidance of Church of England ministers. These very modest Baptists nonetheless shaped effective, dynamic communities outside the colony's established hierarchical religious and social order. And Baptists accomplished their goals by preaching in people's homes and the open air, beyond the church buildings Anglicans had worked so hard to construct in the previous half century. The Baptist success provoked Anglican officials to consider jailing them, but in the end they ridiculed them as "ignorant enthusiasts," "a Babel of religion," and "a general delusion."[9]

Baptists thus challenged the restrictions on itinerant preaching and confronted their lack of religious freedom through their own organization, persistence, daring, and ingenuity as much because of their ordinary background as in spite of it. If Baptists often indeed dressed in severe, plain clothes, then the historian Rhys Isaac rightly argues that we must "look into the rich offerings beneath this somber exterior." Baptists valued close relations among members. They sought one another's company in worship and singing. They aimed, as John Leland put it, for "a congregation of faithful persons, called out of the world by divine grace, who mutually agree to live together, and execute gospel discipline among them." Thus they saw their persecution in Virginia as "resembl[ing] primitive times, when the gospel was preached in the land of Judea," very much by ordinary people to ordinary people.[10]

The frustration of Virginia county officials in failing to break the back of Baptist itinerancy and cohesion can be felt in John Williams's description of John Waller's whipping while preaching in Caroline County in 1771: "While [Brother Waller] was singing[,] the parson of the parish would keep running the end of his horsewhip in his [Waller's] mouth, laying his whip across the hymn book, &c. When done singing [Waller] proceeded to prayer. In it he was violently jerked off the stage, [they] caught him by the back part of his neck[,] beat his head against the ground, some times up[,] sometimes down, they carried him through a gate . . . where [the sheriff] give him . . . Twenty Lashes with his Horse Whip."[11]

Virginia's ordinary Baptists also created institutions that solidified communities, fostered leadership, adjudicated congregational issues, and ultimately challenged Virginia's laws restricting preaching and worship more directly than any other group. The Philadelphia Baptist Association, formed in 1707, sponsored four itinerant Baptists who preached successfully in Virginia in the 1750s. Not surprisingly, Virginia's Baptists formed their own "associations" of ministers and "messengers" that quickly defended Baptists against Anglican persecution and campaigned for full religious freedom.

As Baptist proselytizing escalated, Baptist congregations and associations petitioned local officials and the Virginia House of Burgesses, or legislature, demanding freedom to preach. In 1770 Baptists petitioned the burgesses against compelling preachers "to bear arms and to attend musters" because they could not then preach. In September 1771 Middlesex County Baptists told the county court that "God could not Consent" to the court's demand forbidding Baptist ministers to "preach or teach in the County for six months." Instead, the Baptists demanded that the magistrates seek legislative changes to "Redress the Grievances of Dissenters." In 1772 Baptists from five Virginia counties petitioned to demand "the benefits of the [1689 English] Toleration Act . . . [and] be treated with the same indulgence, in religious matters, as Quakers, Presbyterians and other Protestant dissenters enjoy." When the burgesses instituted a ban on night meetings, Baptists petitioned again to insist that Baptists and other dissenters be treated "with the deference shown to the Church of England," if without its financial support.[12]

The petitions to county officials and members of the House of Burgesses reveal how persistently Virginia Baptists proved more demanding and even radical than Virginia's Quakers and Presbyterians in pursuing religious freedom rather than a more modest toleration. They were not always satisfied merely to accept the limitations of the English 1689 Act of Toleration, which applied only to Protestants. Instead, they frequently argued that freedom to preach and form congregations were God-given rights that superseded Virginia law or even the English 1689 Act of Toleration.

At the same time, many of the local officials confronted by Baptists would be involved in protests against Parliament and, finally, against the Crown that produced the Revolution in Virginia. This included many Church of England worshippers whose formal ceremonial style and social life epitomized behavior censored by the most vigorous Baptist preachers, to say nothing of Church of England clergy who bore the brunt of Baptist opprobrium.

Thus, if Baptists positioned themselves as opposing the entire structure of Virginia society, they also ran the risk of marginalizing themselves as anti-British protest swept across the colony, from the Stamp Act protests in 1765–66 to protests against the Intolerable Acts in 1774. After all, in Virginia, as in many colonies, anti-British protest succeeded in part because local officials supported and, indeed, often led opposition to British regulations. Thus many Virginia county officials offended by Baptists also were offended by Parliament's efforts to tax and regulate colonists.

Between 1770 and 1776 Virginia Baptists found ways to intensify their protests and demands while aligning themselves with political protests against British incursions against colonial rights and privileges. They accomplished this in three ways. First, they joined Presbyterians to support legislation applying the 1689 Act of Toleration to most Protestant dissenters in ways that stressed their common cause. A May 1774 petition on toleration came from "persons of the community of Christians called Baptists and other Protestant dissenters," as did a similar petition in June 1775. Another petition from "all the Presbyterians in Virginia in particular and all Protestant dissenters in general" made clear how Presbyterians had gathered signatures from a variety of Virginia's Protestant dissenters.[13]

Second, the Baptists' (and Presbyterians') argument for broader freedoms took advantage of their own increasing numbers to make clear how restrictions against them were both unsuccessful yet increasingly problematic for the colony as a whole. Baptist petitions reminded the burgesses, for example, that Baptists were "loyal and quiet Subjects" (not always believable, of course) and that requiring preaching licenses was a burden to government administration. Yet the increasing frequency of the petitions, the multiplication of Baptist congregations in the colony, and the failure of arresting and jailing Baptist preachers made it clear that the Baptist dissenters could not be stopped. Baptists made their ultimate argument that they were not only "loyal and quiet Subjects" but subjects "whose Tenets in no wise affect the State."[14]

Third, by 1775 Baptist petitions linked their movement to the defense of the colony by its leading protesters against British actions. In August 1775 John Waller forwarded a letter as "clerk" of the Virginia Baptist Association to the Virginia Convention, which essentially governed the colony after Lord Dunmore dissolved the House of Burgesses in 1774, praising convention members as "Guardians of the Rights of Your Constituents[,] pointing out to them the Road to Freedom." The Baptist petition pointedly approved "a Military resistance against Great Britain, in regard to their unjust Invasion, and tyrannical Oppression." Then the Baptists petitioned the convention to give four Baptist preachers "free Liberty to preach to the Troops at convenient Times without molestation or abuse." This deftly coupled vigorous support for colonial resistance to British tyranny with an approval of Baptist preaching that would overturn two decades of Virginia resistance to the Baptist cause.[15]

Finally, the Baptists' resistance to persecution and their petitioning campaigns raised public awareness of their plight, specifically with the young James Madison. In January 1774 Madison wrote his former Princeton college friend William Bradford to condemn religious persecution in Virginia. "There are at this time in the adjacent county not less than 5 or 6 well meaning men in close Goal [jail] for publishing their religious sentiments which in the main are very orthodox," referring to Culpeper County's jailing of Baptists, possibly of James Ireland. As Madison wrote Bradford again in April 1774, "Petitions I hear are already forming among the persecuted Baptists and I fancy it is in the thoughts of Presbyterians also to intercede for greater liberty in matters of religion." Madison clearly recognized the Virginia Baptists' leadership in 1774 and would employ it again a decade and more later.

Virginia Baptists' petitioning and persistent preaching in the face of often-violent persecution had moved both them and their rhetoric far toward an emphasis on broad freedom for religion rather than a mere toleration under the law. Virginia Baptists still argued that they qualified for inclusion within the 1689 Act of Toleration. But increasingly they also argued that their preaching—including preaching that excoriated the worship and religion of many other Virginians—was privileged by God and not a proper subject for human legislation.

Virginia Baptists pressed for toleration because they believed they qualified for it, yet also denied the right of government to regulate religion. They were resilient in the face of arrest, jailing, public derision, and mob violence. Despite differences with Presbyterians, they joined Presbyterians to protest Virginia's restrictions on religion and embraced colonial protest against parliamentary legislation when protesters included local figures—magistrates and sheriffs—who had arrested Baptists. They placed the issue not merely of toleration but of religious freedom squarely on the agenda of the Virginia Convention.

The Virginia Baptist campaigns for what, in modern times, we call religious freedom laid a critical public foundation for two major legislative changes that transformed the legal ground for religious activity in Virginia. The first of these achievements, Virginia's Declaration of Rights, drafted by George Mason and passed in June 1776, employed political language that Thomas Jefferson would refine a month later in the Declaration of Independence—that "all men are by nature free and independent" with "inherent rights" they cannot surrender.

But the Declaration of Rights also discussed the issue of religious freedom, which the Declaration of Independence bypassed. Mason's original draft employed the language of toleration—"that all men should enjoy the fullest toleration in the exercise of religion." But James Madison, who had reacted so passionately to news of imprisoned Baptist preachers in 1774, thoroughly redrafted the article, freeing religion from government regulation: "That religion, or the duty which we owe our Creator, and the manner of discharging it, can be directed only by reason and conviction, and not by force or violence and, therefore, all men are equally entitled to the free exercise of religion according to the dictates of conscience; and that it is the mutual duty of all to practice Christian forbearance, love and charity towards each other."[16]

Virginia's Baptists could not have agreed with Madison's cool Enlightenment-style definition of religion—that it was merely "the duty which we owe our Creator," or that it "can be directed only by reason." But they could heartily agree that religion was founded in "conviction," meaning deeply held belief based on personal experience, and certainly they were the Virginians who most personally understood that religion cannot be "directed . . . by force or violence." Without hesitation, Madison and Virginia Baptists could agree that "all men are equally entitled to the free exercise of religion according to the dictates of conscience." It was a principle Baptists had pressed for two decades in Virginia. Now it became a guiding principle for the new independent state when the legislature passed the Declaration of Rights on June 12, 1776.

One nagging, parochial religious issue remained unsettled, however: In a state now detached from the British monarchy, what should happen with the still legally established Church of England, irrespective of the Declaration of Rights? The question was narrow and practical as well as broad and philosophical. The Anglican parish was an important form of local government, and its governing vestries levied taxes to pay for many local services far beyond religion, such as support for the indigent and the substantial lands known as "glebes" that the congregations owned, as well as the construction and upkeep of church buildings. It had been Virginia's established church since 1607, epitomized traditional Virginia culture and society, and exemplified the traditional English and European notion that state-supported religion represented the foundation of civilized society. Thus supporters of the state church tradition believed that if established religion fell, so too would government and social order. But two simple facts made the Church of England anomalous in post-Revolutionary America; the king was its head, and at least half of Virginia's Church of England ministers had opposed the Revolution. Although disestablishment came piecemeal, by 1784 the Virginia legislature had incorporated the Episcopal Church as a private group, voided previous establishment acts, and transferred the secular duties of the old vestries to Virginia's counties.

Virginians renewed the debate over government, religion, and churches even before the Revolution ended. Could dissenters assume the privileges of the declining Church of England? In 1780 a Baptist association that gathered at "Waller's Meeting House," with the feisty John Waller signing as "clerk," petitioned the Virginia burgesses for the right to perform marriages on an equal basis with Anglicans. Then in 1784, only a year after the Treaty of Paris ended the Revolutionary War, the Virginia legislature moved to an even broader discussion after receiving petitions from many Protestants, but

This Baptist petition of May 19, 1776, came from Virginia's Prince William County. It tied the protests "of this colony with others" against Britain's "enslaving schemes" to the Baptists' own campaign for freedom to "maintain our own Ministers &c and no other" in Virginia and to "be married, buried, and the like" without supporting other ministers. Many names signed by the same hand may have represented Baptists who were unable to write. *Courtesy Library of Virginia, Richmond.*

not Baptists, advocating tax assessments to support all Protestant Christian denominations, including the old Church of England, now renamed the Episcopal Church. Major Presbyterian leaders supported proposals to allow assessments for "public worship" and require that "every man as a good Citizen, be obliged to declare himself attached to some religious Community." To effect these wishes, Patrick Henry drafted a "general assessment" bill to support "teachers of the Christian religion" through tax levies that also would acknowledge the post-Revolutionary abolition of "all distinctions of pre-eminence amongst the different societies or communities of Christians."

In spite of the fact that Henry's bill endorsed financial support for many kinds of Christian "teachers," Baptists, Presbyterians inclined toward strict church discipline, and most eloquently James Madison attacked it ferociously. In June 1785 Madison sent his anonymous essay, "A Memorial and Remonstrance," to the Virginia legislature. It opposed Henry's broad bill for "teachers of the Christian religion" for two main reasons. First, Madison articulated a broadly rationalist and secular argument for separating religion from government. Second, he simultaneously employed religious reasons for opposing Henry's scheme. He argued that taxing citizens was "adverse to the diffusion of the light of Christianity," that Christianity "disavows a dependence on the powers of this world," and that Henry's bill established the "Civil Magistrate [as] a competent Judge of Religious Truth," a fact every Virginia Baptist knew from bitter experience to be false. Madison further observed, "It is proper to take alarm at the first experiment on our liberties," meaning rolling back principal achievements of the 1776 Virginia Declaration of Rights.[17]

Baptists turned to petitioning again when delays pushed Henry's bill into the fall 1785 legislative session. In August 1785 the Virginia Baptist General Committee instructed counties to secure petitions opposing Henry's general assessment bill and designated one of their members, Reuben Ford, to gather and present the petitions to the legislature. They were not fooled by the threat Henry's bill posed: "should the legislature assume the right of taxing the people for the support of the gospel it will be destructive to religious liberty." The petition campaign made an enormous impact. In the October 1785 legislative session, Madison noted that "the table was loaded with petitions and remonstrances from all parts against interposition of the Legislature in matters of Religion."[18]

The public clamor raised by the Virginia Baptists' effective petitioning affected even George Washington. In a letter to George Mason, Washington confessed that he was not "one of those who are so much alarmed at the thoughts of making People pay toward the support of that which they profess." But, he told Mason, "I wish an assessment had never been agitated . . . [and] that the bill could die an easy death." If the bill passed, Washington feared, it would "rankle, and perhaps convulse the state." Washington's worry foretold the fate of Henry's bill. Presbyterians shifted ground; Quakers joined in opposition, as did Virginians who did not identify their religious inclinations; and the legislature tabled Henry's general assessment bill.[19]

Sensing that the tide had turned, Madison reintroduced Jefferson's 1779 bill for religious freedom. Jefferson was, by then, the U.S. ambassador to France, and the Virginia legislature's adoption of Jefferson's text, revised in some small details (to Madison's irritation), owed nothing to further Baptist agitation or petitioning. Nor did it need to. The Statute for Religious Freedom—one of the three achievements Jefferson asked to be inscribed on his tombstone—spoke eloquently for principles for which Baptists had campaigned for several decades. The statute prescribed that "no man shall be compelled to frequent or support any religious worship, . . . nor shall otherwise suffer on account of his religious opinions or belief." It held that "all men shall be free to profess, and by argument to maintain, their opinion in matters of religion." And it did so because, as Jefferson noted in the preface to the statute, "Almighty God hath created the mind free . . . who being Lord both of body and mind, yet chose not to propagate it by coercions on either, as it was in his Almighty power to do." Here was an acknowledgment that persecuted Baptists could share; here was a deist who appreciated the sensibilities of religion, even if he could not, and did not, share the Baptists' faith.[20]

The ratification by the states of the First Amendment to the federal Constitution was not a Baptist achievement. But the amendment's link to Virginia's 1776 bill of rights, the struggle to defeat Patrick Henry's general assessment proposal, and the passage of Jefferson's Statute for Religious Freedom both summarize the Virginia Baptists' campaigns for religious freedom in Virginia and point up the importance of another Baptist, John Leland.

Born in Massachusetts in 1754, where he experienced a religious awakening at about age twenty-one, Leland began preaching in Virginia in 1776, not returning to New England until 1791. Leland became a successful and popular preacher almost instantly, described by Robert Semple as "probably the most popular of any that ever resided in the state." And as Semple also wrote, Leland "was certainly very instrumental in effecting the just and salutary relations concerning religion, in this state."[21]

Leland's oblique entrance into politics and relations with Virginia's most important politicians, specifically Madison and Jefferson, stemmed from the state's importance to the ratification of the Constitution of 1789. Leland had been involved in Baptist opposition to Patrick Henry's general assessment bill and in promoting Jefferson's Statute for Religious Freedom. But his contact with Madison, and later Jefferson, stemmed from the importance of the Baptist vote in electing candidates to the Virginia legislature that would vote on ratification. In 1788 Madison's father, James Sr., wrote him warning that "the Baptists are now generally opposed to [the Constitution]" and suggesting Madison speak with them. Other supporters of the Constitution suggested likewise, and two suggested that he contact Leland, "the leader of the Virginia Baptists." Another expressed concern that Baptists feared that "religious liberty is not Sufficiently secur'd," meaning that it lacked a bill of rights, such as Virginia had enacted in 1776. Even more important, one of Madison's correspondents sent him a copy of a Leland letter outlining ten objections to the Constitution, including the fact that it had no bill of rights and that "Religious Liberty is not sufficiently secured."[22]

Historians have debated whether Madison and Leland actually met to discuss Leland's concerns. Claims for such a meeting were made later in Leland's life and after his death (he lived until 1841), although nothing can be confirmed by documents from 1789. But Madison asked his father to give copies of the *Federalist Papers* to two Baptist preachers, including "one to Mr. Leland," Madison's phrasing suggesting that if he did not know Leland, he knew well of Leland's importance.[23]

Two things do seem clear, however—that Virginia Baptists ultimately expressed no adamant opposition to the Constitution and that they quickly became supporters of both Madison and Jefferson. Madison made it known that he would not oppose amendments guaranteeing personal liberties like the 1776 Virginia Bill of Rights, and Baptists supported Madison's election to the U.S. Congress. Leland congratulated Madison on his victory and noted, "One thing I shall expect; that if religious Liberty is anywise threatened, that I shall receive the earliest intelligence."[24]

What Leland received, of course, was news not of a threat but of what would become the first of the amendments to the new federal Constitution. It was odd, considering that religion was a nearly absent subject in the Constitution beyond Article VI, which barred religious tests for federal office-holding. But in words that echoed the earliest Baptist complaints about their treatment in Virginia, Congress fashioned an amendment whose sixteen spare words would lead the Bill of Rights and become the measure of federal policy on religion in the infant republic: "Congress shall make no law respecting an establishment of religion, or prohibit the free exercise thereof." The amendment said what it meant and meant what it said. Congress would not establish religion, not just a church, and it would honor religious worship broadly, not merely tolerate some forms of Christian worship. For Baptists, so often criticized for their almost painful simplicity, economy of expression witnessed the amendment's truth of principle.

Leland and some Virginia Baptists would not be content simply to end direct government involvement in religion and worship. In 1785 the General Committee of Virginia Baptists pronounced "heredity slavery to be contrary to the word of God," and in 1788 Leland offered the general committee a resolution stating that "slavery is a violent deprivation of the rights of nature, and inconsistent with a republican government, and therefore recommend it to our brethren, to make use of every legal measure to extirpate this horrid evil from the land." Robert Semple's account of post-Revolutionary antislavery sentiment at the Ketocton Association well described the fate of these efforts. In 1787 the Ketocton Association "appointed a committee to bring in a plan of gradual emancipation," having "determined that hereditary slavery was a breach of the divine law." But the subject "excited considerable tumult in the churches," and the committee found itself "treading upon delicate ground." As a result, the association "resolved to take no further steps in the business." Other Virginia associations acted similarly, and post-Revolutionary Virginia Baptist antislavery failed, even if, decades later, it stood as a small beacon to nineteenth-century reformers.[25]

Unquestionably, the First Amendment enshrined the absolute impossibility of creating a national religious establishment in the new nation. In New England and the South, and especially in the middle states, unprecedented numbers of different religious groups clamored for attention. The mixed history of religious repression in the colonies, including Virginia, suggested that prohibiting religious practice was not easily accomplished, even when local officials acted viciously and were unanimous in trying.

Neither the writing nor the passage of the brief and eloquent First Amendment, especially with its establishment of "free exercise," would have been likely without the Baptist campaign for religious freedom that roiled Virginia after 1760. Virginia's Baptists, more than any other group, created that contest. Without their resilience, eloquence, skill, and patience, the state and the nation would likely have moved merely to tolerate some Christian groups and, as Patrick Henry wanted, to levy taxes to support several such groups but exclude others. These changes would have revised the European past in important ways. But Virginia's Baptists helped shape a uniquely American future where organized religion was free to practice on its own and where government was obligated to honor the spiritual independence of groups and individuals alike.

FOR FURTHER READING

Indispensable modern histories of Baptists in Virginia include Jewel L. Spangler, *Virginians Reborn: Anglican Monopoly, Evangelical Dissent, and the Rise of the Baptists in the Late Eighteenth Century* (Charlottesville, Va., 2008), and Rhys Isaac, *The Transformation of Virginia, 1740–1790* (Chapel Hill, N.C., 1982).

Early histories of Virginia Baptists include William Fristoe, *A Concise History of the Ketocton Baptist Association* (1808; rpt., Stephen City, Va., 1978), and Robert B. Semple, *A History of the Rise and Progress of the Baptists in Virginia* (Richmond, Va., 1810). Two early autobiographies appear in Keith Harper and C. Martin Jacumin, eds., *Esteemed Reproach: The Lives of Reverend James Ireland and Reverend Joseph Craig* (Macon, Ga., 2005). All make fascinating reading.

Broad perspectives on religion in colonial and Revolutionary America can be gained in Jon Butler, *Awash in a Sea of Faith: Christianizing the American People* (Cambridge, Mass., 1990), and Nathan O. Hatch, *The Democratization of American Christianity* (New Haven, Conn., 1989).

Mark S. Scarberry, "John Leland and James Madison," *Penn State Law Review* 113, no. 3 (2008–2009), provides a recent account of relations between these two important figures. Thomas E. Buckley, S.J., *Church and State in Revolutionary Virginia, 1776–1787* (Charlottesville, Va., 1977), is invaluable on legislative history regarding religion in Virginia. Two books by Edwin Gaustad provide broad guides to church and state issues in the Revolutionary Era and across the sweep of American history: *Faith of the Founders* (Waco, Tex., 2004) and *Proclaim Liberty Throughout All the Land* (New York, 2003). A more controversial account of the First Amendment can be found in Philip Hamburger, *Separation of Church and State* (Cambridge, Mass., 2002). John A. Ragosta, *Wellspring of Liberty: How Virginia's Religious Dissenters Helped Win the American Revolution and Secure Religious Liberty* (New York, 2010), offers a broad perspective on the roles various dissenting Protestants played in the struggle for religious freedom there.

CHAPTER ELEVEN

Declaring Independence and Rebuilding a Nation: Dragging Canoe and the Chickamauga Revolution

Colin G. Calloway

In May 1776 fourteen Indians painted black arrived at the Cherokee "Beloved Town" of Chota on the Little Tennessee River. They were delegates from northern nations—Shawnees, Delawares, Mohawks, Nanticokes, and Ottawas—"with a Cherokee fellow as interpreter," and they had traveled seventy days to get there. They brought with them a nine-foot-long wampum belt, painted red as a sign of war. Meeting with Cherokee chiefs and warriors in the council house, they urged them to take up arms against the Americans. The older chiefs would normally have guided the Cherokees in such critical decisions, but years of land sales had eroded their authority. A war chief named Tsi'yu-gûnsini, or Dragging Canoe, stepped forward and struck the war post with his hatchet. In symbolically accepting the invitation to war, he declared independence from his father's generation of Cherokee leadership and charted a path that would lead to rebuilding a Cherokee nation in the West—the Chickamaugas.

Dragging Canoe was head warrior of Malaquo, or Great Island, one of the Overhill Cherokee Towns that were located on the Little Tennessee and Tellico rivers. (The Middle and Valley Towns were in the Blue Ridge region; the Lower Towns, in South Carolina.) He was born sometime in the 1730s and apparently earned his name—*tsi'yu,* "canoe," and *gûnsi'ni,* "he is dragging it"—as a boy. When his father refused to let him join a war party he was leading against the Shawnees, so the story goes, the boy slipped away through the woods, got ahead of the warriors, and waited for them at a portage, hiding under a dugout canoe. When the war party found him there, his father told him he could come along, provided he was able to carry the canoe over the portage. Not strong enough to lift the canoe, the boy picked it up by one end and began dragging it, thus acquiring the name he would proudly use for the remainder of his life. His father was Ada-gal'kala or Attakullakulla, known to whites as Little Carpenter because of his diplomatic ability to fashion agreements. In his youth, in 1730, Attakullakulla had visited King George II in London; he was now recognized as the "Second Man" of the Cherokee Nation. (Attakullakulla may in fact have been Dragging Canoe's uncle rather than his father; in matrilineal Cherokee society the most important male figure in a boy's life was usually the mother's brother.)

Tension between young war chiefs and older civil or peace chiefs was nothing new. The red path of war and the white path of peace existed as alternative strategies and philosophies that Cherokees often struggled to keep in balance. Southwestern territorial governor William Blount attributed such tensions to "the nature of Indian government, or, more properly, the total want of it . . . There is ever among them, young warriors, wishing to rise into consequence, and nothing so like to effect it as complaining against chiefs for having sold their hunting grounds. This, at once, pulls down the chiefs, makes way for themselves, and gives them popularity with the young and rising part of the nation."[1] Nevertheless, the showdown between Dragging Canoe and Attakullakulla at Chota in 1776 was a momentous incident and had far-reaching repercussions. The American Revolution marked an emphatic divergence between the Cherokees and their colonial neighbors as the warriors in both societies "took control of the path."[2] It also produced two new societies that were in headlong collision: the Americans asserted their independence and built a new nation by expanding onto Indian land; the Chickamaugas asserted their independence and rebuilt a nation by defending Indian land.

Cherokees experienced revolutionary changes long before the American Revolution. Hernando de Soto had brought Spanish soldiers to Cherokee country in 1540 and left destruction and disruption in his wake as he raped and pillaged his way across the Indian Southeast. After the English established Charles Town, South Carolina, in 1670, traders funneled new goods, new values, and alcohol into Cherokee communities, and Cherokee hunters furnished thousands of deerskins for insatiable European markets. Traditional hunting practices that involved observing important rituals to establish and preserve reciprocal obligations between hunters and prey became strained under the pressure of new economic forces. Subsistence practices and settlement patterns began to change as Cherokees adopted English styles of farming and domesticated animals. English colonial governments insisted that the various Cherokee towns function as a single tribe, and as a consequence, Cherokee political structure became more unified. Colonial traders recognized the importance of marrying Cherokee wives if they were to do business in Cherokee country, but colonial governments often ignored the traditional influence of Cherokee women as they focused attention on the men's spheres of hunting and warfare.

Their new connections exposed the Cherokees to Old World germs and viruses. Smallpox cut their population almost by half in 1738. Dragging Canoe appears to have been afflicted, but he was one of the lucky ones. He survived and was therefore immune to further bouts of smallpox, but he bore the scars for life. The dread disease returned in 1759. By the time of the American Revolution, war and disease had drastically reduced the Cherokees to perhaps twelve thousand people.

Their location on the western frontiers of the English colonies placed the Cherokees in a strategic position in the struggle for North America waged between Britain and France at midcentury. Cherokee warriors served with the British during General John Forbes's campaign against Fort Duquesne (the site of the future Pittsburgh) in 1758, and Forbes referred to the Cherokee warriors and the Highland Scots soldiers in his command as "cousins." But the allies were soon at war. Escalating tensions exploded in open conflict, and British armies invaded Cherokee country in 1760 and 1761. After Highland regiments burned Cherokee villages and cornfields, Cherokee leaders sued for peace.

Dragging Canoe grew to manhood at a time when the very foundations of Cherokee manhood were being compromised. Prowess in war and hunting gave young men status in Cherokee society and demonstrated their ability to protect, feed, and provide for a family. Now military defeats and recurrent losses of hunting territory threatened to undermine Cherokee masculinity, and it seemed to some young men that their chiefs bore part of the blame for what was happening.

The Cherokees ceded land throughout the eighteenth century, but the pace of land loss increased dramatically in the decade before the Revolution. At the Treaty of Fort Stanwix in 1768 with British Superintendent of Indian Affairs in the North, Sir William Johnson, the Iroquois agreed to shift westward the boundary to British settlement established at the Appalachian Mountains by the royal proclamation five years earlier. The Iroquois deftly diverted pressure away from their own country by ceding lands south of the Ohio River, opening Shawnee and Cherokee hunting lands to invasion by colonial hunters and settlers. The Treaty of Hard Labor, the same year, fixed the Cherokee boundaries with North and South Carolina, but two years later the Cherokees agreed to new limits and lost nearly six million acres of trea-

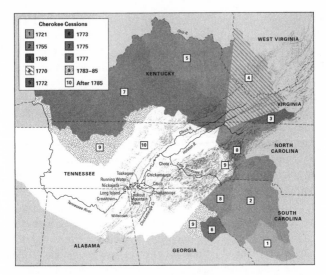

Cherokee land losses and the Chickamauga towns. Dragging Canoe's break with the older chiefs in the council at Chota in 1776 reflected the frustration of Cherokee warriors at the steady erosion of their homeland by treaty. Dragging Canoe and his followers moved west and built new towns, first on Chickamauga Creek and then lower down the Tennessee River.

sured land at the Treaty of Lochaber. Two years after that, Virginia demanded another cession of everything east of the Kentucky River, a further seven million acres. No matter how much land Cherokees gave up, the colonists kept coming; Cherokees said they could "see the smoke of the Virginians from their doors."[3]

Then in March 1775, at the Treaty of Sycamore Shoals in Tennessee, Judge Richard Henderson and a group of North Carolina land speculators known as the Transylvania Land Company induced Attakullakulla, principal headman Oconostota, and the Raven of Chota to sell twenty-seven thousand square miles of land between the Kentucky and Cumberland rivers—most of modern Kentucky and a slice of today's northern Tennessee—in exchange for a cabin full of trade goods. The treaty was in clear defiance of the royal proclamation, and the chiefs later claimed that Henderson had deceived them as to what they were signing. Dragging Canoe reputedly stormed from the treaty council in disgust, vowing to make the ceded lands "dark and bloody." He told the British "that he had no hand in making these Bargains but blamed some of their Old Men who he said were too old to hunt and who by their poverty had been induced to sell their land but that for his part he had a great many young fellows that would support him and that they were determined to have their land."[4] In agreeing to land sales, the older chiefs were perhaps trying to create a buffer zone of ceded territory while at the same time keeping trade contacts open. They may also have hoped to ensure a measure of security by maintaining reciprocal obligations with the colonists.

John Stuart, the British Superintendent of Indian Affairs in the South, explained to Secretary of State Lord George Germain that loss of land was the root cause of Cherokee discontent:

> Amazing great settlements beyond the established boundaries in the hunting grounds of the Cherokees have been made upon tracts held under titles obtained from individuals, by taking advantage of their wants and poverty, or by forgeries and frauds of different sorts in which the nation never acquiesced; for they are tenants in common and allow no person, however so great, to cede their lands without the consent of the nation obtained in general council.[5]

Recurrent sacrifices of Cherokee homeland infuriated younger men who had not had their fathers' opportunities to achieve standing through war and hunting. They were especially enraged by squatters in the Watauga and upper Holston valleys in northeastern Tennessee. John Stuart's brother and deputy, Henry, had a hard time "restraining their young people from falling on them too rashly."[6]

The outbreak of the American Revolution gave Cherokee warriors an opportunity to drive the trespassers off their land. But the Revolution severed trade routes with Charles Town, and they needed British supplies and ammunition. They also needed to gain the upper hand in the councils of the Cherokee Nation where the older chiefs held sway.

Contrary to colonial rumor and propaganda, the British did not want to turn the Cherokees loose on the frontiers—at least not until they could coordinate Cherokee attacks with British troop movements. John Stuart sent Henry Stuart to supply the Cherokees in anticipation of war but with orders to keep them at peace for the time being. Dragging Canoe met him en route at Mobile "to inquire into the cause of the present quarrel and disorders in the colonies and the reason why their supplies of ammunition and goods were stopped." Angrily denouncing the older chiefs for selling land, Dragging Canoe said that the Cherokees "were almost surrounded by the White

People, that they had but a small spot of ground left for them to stand upon, and that it seemed to be the Intention of the White People to destroy them from being a people." Stuart feared Dragging Canoe was "firmly bent on doing mischief."[7]

Stuart headed for Cherokee country with a pack train of thirty horses loaded with supplies and ammunition. Dragging Canoe and eighty warriors escorted him up the Tennessee River to Chota. When he arrived in late April 1776, Stuart called together the headmen, distributed his supplies, and urged the Cherokees to refrain from going to war. They should listen to their agent, Alexander Cameron, he said. Like many Scottish traders and agents, Cameron had a Cherokee family and had lived with the Cherokees so long that "he had almost become one of themselves."[8] He was also Dragging Canoe's adopted brother. With the consent of the older chiefs, Cameron and Stuart sent letters urging the settlers to leave the Watauga Valley, but colonial propaganda twisted their words into an ultimatum threatening destruction. Meanwhile, newly armed Cherokee warriors were growing impatient to expel the intruders.

At this critical moment the Indian delegates from the North made their dramatic entry into Chota. Stuart recorded what happened. They told of traveling from Fort Pitt through country that was once Indian hunting grounds but was now "thickly inhabited and the people all in arms." The northern nations had joined the king's troops, they said; if the Cherokees attacked the Americans in the South, victory was assured. Stuart, Cameron, and the principal chiefs argued against war, but "every young Fellow's face in the Overhill Towns appeared Blackened, and nothing was now talked of but War."[9]

Representatives from the different parts of the Cherokee Nation gathered at Chota. On the day appointed for the northern delegates to deliver their talks, Cherokee warriors erected the war standard and painted the posts of the town house black and red. Many of the assembled warriors had blackened their faces. The Mohawk speaker urged united Indian resistance and handed Dragging Canoe a purple and white wampum belt. The Shawnee deputy recounted the grievances of his people at the hands of the Virginians and reminded his listeners how the Indians had been reduced from a great people to a handful in just a few years. "Better to die like men than diminish away by inches," he declared. He offered "a War Belt about 9 feet long and six inches wide of purple Whampum strewed over with vermilion." Dragging Canoe stepped forward and took hold of the belt. He struck the war post and sang the war song. Doublehead, Young Tassel (aka Kunokeski, or John Watts), Bloody Fellow, and other warriors followed. Attakullakulla,

Oconostota, and the older chiefs "who were averse to the measure and remembered the calamities brought on their nation by the last war, instead of opposing the rashness of the young people with spirit, sat down dejected and silent." With the Cherokees committed to war, said Stuart, "it was in vain to talk any more of peace." Traders made hasty preparations to leave the Cherokee towns, although Cameron stayed with his Cherokee family.[10]

In their own way, the events in the council house at Chota in May 1776 were as dramatic as those that occurred in Philadelphia's statehouse in July. Seizing the opportunity presented by the arrival of the northern delegates, Dragging Canoe committed the Cherokees to war and issued a resounding renunciation of Attakullakulla's policies. Chiefs who had pursued policies of appeasement and had built trade networks with the colonists were unsure how to act now that the colonists were divided. For younger warriors, the course was clear. Dragging Canoe and his followers would rebuild an independent Cherokee nation based on militant defense of their land and sovereignty rather than accommodation to colonial pressures.

The war went badly for the Cherokees from the start. The Cherokee Women's Council opposed the war. Dragging Canoe's cousin or sister Nanye'hi, known to whites as Nancy Ward, sent warning to the settlements of the impending storm. Formerly a war woman, Nanye'hi was now a *ghighau,* or beloved woman. Though her acts earned her heroine status in some American history books, they represented an allegiance to a philosophy of peace and her obligations as a beloved woman rather than a betrayal of her warrior relative.[11] Dragging Canoe and his brother Little Owl were both severely wounded in an unsuccessful attack in July 1776 on Eaton's Station, a fort on the Holston River. In the summer and fall militia armies from Virginia, North and South Carolina, and Georgia swept through Cherokee country. "Make smooth work as you go," William Henry Drayton, chief justice of South Carolina, instructed the troops; "cut up every Indian corn field and burn every Indian town." Every Indian they captured would be "the slave and property of the taker." The goal of the campaign was clear and simple: that "the nation be extirpated, and the lands become the property of the public." As far as Drayton was concerned, "I shall never give my voice for peace with the Cherokee Nation upon any other terms than their removal beyond the mountains." Thomas Jefferson wanted more: "I hope the Cherokees will now be driven beyond the Mississippi," he wrote. The soldiers dutifully destroyed crops, burned towns, and drove the inhabitants into the woods.[12]

Faced with massive destruction, the older chiefs reasserted their influence and sued for peace. They blamed Dragging Canoe and young warriors they could not control for starting the war, which was both a statement of fact and "a traditional tactic to promote a peaceful frame of mind by assigning responsibility for misdeeds to third parties."[13] The Americans demanded that the Cherokees hand over Alexander Cameron and Dragging Canoe. Much to Dragging Canoe's disgust, Oconostota reputedly attempted to do so. He assured the Americans that the chiefs were back in control: "the beloved men are now talking, & the boys on both sides sitting listening." Old Tassel promised to carry words of peace to Dragging Canoe and said the young warriors would listen to him. But Dragging Canoe remained steadfast in his loyalty to his adopted brother and in his allegiance to Britain: "My thoughts and my heart are for war as long as King George has one enemy in this country," he assured Cameron.[14]

In the spring of 1777 Attakullakulla, Oconostota, and a delegation of thirty Cherokees traveled to Williamsburg for peace talks. It was one of Attakullakulla's final acts. The Lower Cherokees made peace with South Carolina and Georgia at DeWitt's Corner in May; Overhill Cherokees made peace with Virginia and North Carolina at Long Island on the Holston in July. The two treaties cost the Cherokees more than five million acres as the price of peace, bringing their total losses over the last decade to almost thirty-seven million acres. Dragging Canoe, "that daring & enterprising Chief," stayed away from the treaty talks.[15] He and Cameron moved south and west and continued to fight.

Many Cherokees "being thus burnt out of their towns, and by these treaties very much curtailed in their hunting grounds to the eastward and northward," followed them. They built new towns, lower down the Tennessee River, on its steep banks near the base of Lookout Mountain. "The most bold and active part," said William Blount, "settled on a creek called Chickamauga."[16] Dragging Canoe soon had four or five hundred men, "notwithstanding the Remonstrance made against those Imigrations [*sic*] by the old Warriors, most of whom have expressed great wrath and Bitterness against the headstrong & Lawless part of their Nation." Patrick Henry said they were "separated from the rest of the nation with sentiments of determined hostility to the United States."[17] Dragging Canoe and his followers were not just impetuous young warriors driven by blind hatred; the new towns they built gave Cherokees a place to reassemble and resist American efforts "to destroy them from being a people." But like many nationalist resistance movements, the Chickamaugas were frequently denounced as renegades and terrorists.

So were those who allied with them. The Chickamaugas had access to British goods via John Stuart's deputy and commissary, John McDonald, who operated a trading post at the base of Lookout Mountain and obtained supplies from St. Augustine. McDonald spoke fluent Cherokee and lived for forty years with the Cherokees. Like Stuart, Cameron, and other Scots Loyalists who made common cause with their Cherokee relatives, McDonald was hated by the Americans and had a price on his head.

In April 1779 Colonel Evan Shelby led a large Virginian force down the Tennessee and attacked the Chickamauga towns while Dragging Canoe and McDonald were away attacking frontier settlements in Georgia and South Carolina. The women and children escaped into the woods, but Shelby burned eleven towns, destroyed some twenty thousand bushels of corn, and looted McDonald's home. The Virginians hoped that Shelby's expedition would stem the flow of recruits to Dragging Canoe's cause, but younger Cherokees continued to make their way to the Chickamauga towns. Sometime after the attack Dragging Canoe and his followers moved around the base of Lookout Mountain and rebuilt their towns farther down the Tennessee River, where it courses through southern Tennessee and northern Alabama. Dragging Canoe's towns at Running Water, Nickajack, Long Island, Lookout Mountain, and Crow Town became known as the Five Lower Towns, although other villages such as Will's Town were built in the area. The move downriver made sense as a defensive measure, although William Blount said Dragging Canoe's people abandoned Chickamauga Creek in 1782, "believing it was infested with witches." Whatever their origins, Blount reported, the Five Lower Towns attracted "the young and active, more or less from every town in the nation, and have now become the most formidable part of it, not only from their disposition to commit injuries on the citizens of the United States, but from their ability to perform it."[18] Born fighting, the Chickamauga towns existed on a war footing.

The Chickamauga secession split the Cherokee Nation. Dragging Canoe and his followers claimed for themselves the name Ani-Yunwiya, "the Real People," and derided those who did not join them as "Virginians," a term of the utmost contempt. Chickamaugas raided the American frontier and retreated to their strongholds; Americans in the Revolution often drew little distinction between Indian enemies and Indian neutrals, and they now retaliated against the towns of Cherokees who were attempting to live at peace, rather than march far to the south and confront Dragging Canoe and his Chickamauga freedom fighters. Jefferson, now governor of Virginia, sent troops under Arthur Campbell and John Sevier into Overhill Cherokee country late in 1780. The Raven of Chota said the Virginians "dyed their hands in the Blood of many of our Woman [*sic*] and Children, burnt 17 towns, destroyed all our provisions by which we & our families were almost destroyed by famine."[19] The next spring Sevier burned fifteen Middle Cherokee towns. Oconostota and other older chiefs worked for peace, and Nanye'hi and the women's council acted "as diplomatic mothers in order to urge peace in the face of warfare conducted by young men on both sides."[20] Nevertheless, the American assaults drove more warriors from the previously peaceful towns into the Chickamauga ranks.

While the Cherokee Nation fractured, Dragging Canoe reached out to other tribes to widen the Indian war for independence. Speaking to a delegate from the northern tribes in July 1779, he reminded them of their obligations to assist in the fight:

> We cannot forget the talk you brought to us some years ago into this Nation, which was to take up the hatchet against the Virginians. We heard it and listened to it with great attention, and before the time that was appointed to lift it we took it up & struck the Virginians. Our Nation was alone and surrounded by them. They were numerous and their hatchets were sharp; and after we had lost some of our best warriors, we were forced to leave our towns and corn to be burnt by them, and now we live in the grass as you see us. But we are not yet conquered, and to convince you that we have not thrown away your talk here are four strands of whampums we received from you when you came before as a messenger to our Nation.[21]

In token of their renewed pledge of mutual support, some Chickamaugas moved north to live and fight with the Shawnees, and about one hundred Shawnees joined the Chickamaugas, many of them taking up residence with Dragging Canoe at Running Water Town. Chickamaugas continued their fight for independence in the West after the Americans had won their fight in the East. They fended off an expedition from North Carolina in September 1782. The following January, Dragging Canoe and a deputation of some twelve hundred Cherokees, Shawnees, Delawares, Ottawas, and Iroquois met at St. Augustine to form a multitribal confederation united in opposition to the Americans. In April 1783 Britain and the new United States made peace in Paris, but little changed in Cherokee country. The Treaty of Hopewell with the United States in 1785 ostensibly secured Cherokee boundaries, but Dragging Canoe did not attend, and many frontier settlers— and John Sevier's new "state" of Franklin—ignored its terms. "Your people settle much Faster on our Lands after a Treaty than Before," Old Tassel reflected bitterly.[22]

Cherokees who wanted peace distanced themselves from the "Roages at Chuckemogo" and tried to restore economic connections with the Americans.[23] Chickamaugas who wanted to restore Cherokee autonomy distanced themselves from the Americans and sought trade connections elsewhere. John McDonald continued to live and fight alongside his Cherokee friends and relatives, but with British agents and traders withdrawing from the territories ceded to the United States, the Chickamaugas needed new sources of supply. Chickamauga delegates solicited aid from the British at Detroit, and Dragging Canoe traveled to Pensacola to open trade talks with the Spanish governor Estevan Miró. Chickamaugas traded for arms and ammunition with the Spaniards in Pensacola, and with both Spanish and French merchants in New Orleans. While their eastern relatives tried to rebuild the nation on accommodation and economic ties with the Americans, Chickamaugas "sought autonomy in international trade."[24]

Americans continued assaulting Cherokee towns and invading Cherokee lands; Chickamaugas continued to strike back. Old Tassel told the governor of Virginia that he "formerly Loved War, and Lived at Chicamogga," but he now lived in "the Middle Ground between Chota and Chickamogga" and worked for peace. "I stand up like a wall between Bad people and my Brothers, the Virginians," he said. "Both Creeks and Chickamoggans has been turned back from doing mischief by me."[25] But in May 1788 a Cherokee named Slim Tom killed the family of John Kirk, who were squatting on Cherokee land. When James Sevier called for volunteers to go against the Cherokee towns on the Little Tennessee in June, Kirk enlisted in Major James Hubbard's militia company. Calling Old Tassel and several other neutralist chiefs together for peace talks in a cabin, Hubbard posted guards at the door, handed Kirk a tomahawk, and told him to take his revenge.

Old Tassel's murder under a flag of truce propelled another round of recruits to the Chickamauga cause. Dragging Canoe worked to maintain ties with the Shawnees in the North and extend ties with the Creeks in the South. With the addition of Shawnees and Creeks, as well as new Cherokee recruits, Chickamauga towns became increasingly multicultural. While the Shawnee and their allies battled to defend Indian country in Ohio, the Chickamaugas and their allies fought to preserve Tennessee. Chickamauga warriors terrorized settlers on the Cumberland, stole horses, and repulsed another American invasion at the Battle of Lookout Mountain in August 1788. Little Owl and sixty Chickamaugas participated in the Northwest Indian Confederacy's massive victory over General Arthur St. Clair's army in November 1791, near modern-day Fort Wayne, Indiana. It was, however, the high-water mark of Indian resistance.

Dragging Canoe died at Running Water Town in March 1792, shortly after returning from a diplomatic mission to try and bring the Chickasaws into his confederacy and reputedly from the exertion of participating in an all-night victory dance. Little Owl was killed in an attack on Buchanan's station in September. Secretary of War Henry Knox hoped that with Dragging Canoe gone, the majority of Cherokees would seek peace, but the Chickamaugas were more than a band of freedom fighters united around a charismatic leader. Historians often exaggerate the importance of individual chiefs in societies where power tended to be diffused rather than centralized. Tennessee historian John Brown called him the "Savage Napoleon," but Dragging Canoe was one of a number of prominent leaders. His nephew Black Fox said simply: "Dragging Canoe has left the world. He was a man of consequence in his country."[26] William Blount said that as a warrior Dragging Canoe "stood second to none in the nation, except John Watts." Watts, also known as Kunokeski or Young Tassel, was a nephew of the murdered Old Tassel. Knox described him as "a bold, sensible, and friendly half breed," but Watts assumed leadership of the Chickamauga resistance movement, and the Chickamauga-Shawnee-Creek alliance continued to block American expansion. Knox reckoned the five Chickamauga towns contained between three and five hundred warriors, "aided by a number of banditti of the Upper Creeks, chiefly young men."[27]

In the summer of 1794, however, General Anthony Wayne defeated the Northwest Indian Confederacy at the Battle of Fallen Timbers in Ohio, and an expedition of more than five hundred men from Nashville penetrated the Chickamauga stronghold, burned Running Water and Nickajack, and killed fifty people. Watts and the Chickamaugas made peace with William Blount at the Treaty of Tellico Blockhouse in November. The Northwest Confederacy made peace with Wayne, and ceded most of Ohio at the Treaty of Greenville the following August. The Indian wars of independence that continued for a dozen years after the American War of Independence were coming to a close.

Both the United States and the Chickamauga Cherokees were born out of revolution and a long war for independence. At a time when the bulk of the Cherokees in the East sought peace, neutrality, and survival by accommodating to American demands, the Chickamaugas fought to restore a Cherokee nation that was separate and autonomous from the Americans. They frustrated, at last for the time being, Thomas Jefferson's expressed desire to see the Cherokees driven west of the Mississippi. The Chickamauga cause survived Dragging Canoe's death. Chickamaugas continued to put space between themselves and the Americans. Duwali, or Bowl, who came to prominence as a chief at Running Water Town after Dragging Canoe's death and attacked the Muscle Shoals settlement along the Tennessee River in

1794, led one group down the Tennessee River and across the Mississippi in 1810. He went first to Arkansas and later to Texas, where he died fighting Texan troops in 1839. When John Norton, a Cherokee-Scot and also an adopted Mohawk, visited one of the Chickamauga Lower Towns in 1816, he found that many of the inhabitants had "already crossed the Mississippi and the remnant are preparing to follow them."[28] United States Indian policy soon dictated the removal of all Cherokees, and the nation again divided over whether accommodation or resistance offered the best strategy for survival. In the 1780s and 1790s, Scots trader John McDonald had joined the Chickamaugas in their fight for independence; his grandson, Principal Chief John Ross, took the Chickamauga path in his defense of Cherokee lands, albeit by political rather than military means. Even after Ross led his people into forced exile along the Trail of Tears in 1838, the Cherokee Nation did not perish. What Cherokee scholar Daniel Heath Justice calls "the Chickamauga consciousness" of defiance survived, alongside negotiation and accommodation, as an enduring cultural tradition and a defining characteristic of Cherokee nationhood.[29]

FOR FURTHER READING

A handful of studies focus on Dragging Canoe: Brent Alan "Yanusdi" Cox, *Heart of the Eagle: Dragging Canoe and the Emergence of the Chickamauga Confederacy* (Milan, Tenn., 1999); E. Raymond Evans, "Notable Persons in Cherokee History: Dragging Canoe," *Journal of Cherokee Studies* 2, no. 2 (1977): 176–89; and Jon W. Parmenter, "Dragging Canoe (*Tsi'yu-gûnsi'ni*) Chickamauga Cherokee Patriot," in *The Human Tradition in the American Revolution,* ed. Nancy L. Rhoden and Ian K. Steele (Wilmington, Del., 2000), 117–37. John P. Brown, *Old Frontiers: The Story of the Cherokee Indians from Earliest Times to the Date of Their Removal to the West, 1838* (Kingsport, Tenn., 1938), contains a substantial section on Dragging Canoe, and Cherokee novelist Robert J. Conley includes a biography of Dragging Canoe in his "Real People" series of historical fiction in *Cherokee Dragon* (Norman, Okla., 2000). Daniel Heath Justice portrays Dragging Canoe and Nancy Ward as exemplifying the complementary paths of war and resistance, peace and accommodation, and traces the "Chickamauga consciousness" in contemporary Cherokee culture in *Our Fire Survives the Storm: A Cherokee Literary History* (Minneapolis, 2006).

Henry Stuart's report of his mission to Chota is reprinted in *Documents of the American Revolution, 1770–1783,* ed. K. G. Davies, 21 vols. (Shannon, Ire., 1972–78), 12:191–208. Nathaniel Shiedley explains the connection between "Hunting and the Politics of Masculinity in Cherokee Treaty-Making, 1763–1775," in *Empire and Others: British Encounters with Indigenous Peoples, 1600–1850,* ed. Martin Daunton and Rick Halpern (Philadelphia, 1999), 167–85. Frederick O. Gearing provides the most stark portrayal of the Chickamauga secession as a generational split disruptive of Cherokee government in "Priest and Warriors: Social Structures for Cherokee Politics in the 18th Century," *Memoirs of the American Anthropological Association* 93 (1962). His interpretation is qualified by Cynthia Cumfer in *Separate Peoples, One Land: The Minds of Cherokees, Blacks, and Whites on the Tennessee Frontier* (Chapel Hill, N.C., 2007), chaps. 1–2.

Cherokee experiences in the Revolutionary Era are covered in James H. O'Donnell, *Southern Indians in the American Revolution* (Knoxville, Tenn., 1973); Tom Hatley, *The Dividing Paths: Cherokees and South Carolinians Through the Era of the Revolution* (New York, 1993); and Colin G. Calloway, *The American Revolution in Indian Country* (New York, 1995), chap. 7. Gregory Evans Dowd, *A Spirited Resistance: The North American Indian Struggle for Unity, 1745–1815* (Baltimore, 1992), places Chickamauga resistance in a broader context of intertribal alliances.

CHAPTER TWELVE

Forgotten Heroes of the Revolution: Han Yerry and Tyona Doxtader of the Oneida Indian Nation

James Kirby Martin

No one can say for sure when the great Oneida warrior chief Han Yerry Doxtader was born. Some sources place his birth in the 1720s, others in the 1730s. His father was a young German settler bearing the name Dockstader (sometimes rendered Dachstättor), and his mother was a Mohawk. Han grew up in New York's Mohawk Valley region, raised by his mother in the vicinity of the native village Canajoharie. This community was one of two principal Mohawk settlements located along the Mohawk River. Canajoharie was close to Oneida territory, which helps to explain why Han Yerry, sometime before the Seven Years' War (1756–63), came to be identified as a member of the Oneida Nation. His mother may have found it more convenient to nurture her son in a nearby Oneida community, or she may have married into an Oneida clan. Whatever the explanation, and extant sources are silent, Han likely learned to hunt and train for possible combat during his teenage years under the tutelage of adult Oneida males. The Oneidas would call him Han Yerry Tewahangarahken, or "He Who Takes Up the Snowshoe." Why he obtained this name is not known.[1]

More generally, Han was a member of the powerful Six Nations Confederacy of Iroquois-speaking Indians. Back before the voyages of Christopher Columbus, the Mohawks, Oneidas, Onondagas, Cayugas, and Senecas established a league to foster peace and amity among themselves. Their territory, called Iroquoia, encompassed most of modern upstate New York, running west from Albany all the way to Buffalo. Over time the league evolved into a mighty confederacy, a kind of political-military alliance among these five nations; later the Tuscaroras, migrating north from the Carolinas during the 1720s, joined, to form the Iroquois Confederacy of Six Nations. They employed their combined strength to sustain their collective interests in reckoning not only with various Indian enemies beyond Iroquoia but also with the floodtide of European adventurers, traders, and settlers sweeping westward into the Americas.

Until the American Revolution, the confederacy was largely successful in playing off competing European interests, especially the French to the north and the British to the east and south. Over and over again during the eighteenth century, these European rivals tried to lure Six Nations warriors into supporting their side in various imperial wars. By and large the confederacy held tight to the course of neutrality prescribed by its ranking chiefs, who met whenever necessary around a perpetual flame in Great Council gatherings at the village of Onondaga. Almost everyone understood that to openly support either of these European combatants might well cost them control of their ancient tribal lands, where the spirits of their ancestors resided, if they happened to ally with the wrong side.

On rare occasions, confederacy members did openly align with one or the other side. In 1759 during the Seven Years' War, the famous British Northern Department Indian Superintendent, Sir William Johnson, convinced Mohawk and Oneida warriors to join him in a campaign to seize French-controlled Fort Niagara, on the Lake Ontario shoreline in western New York. Han Yerry, described as an "ordinary sized" person and very much "a gentleman in his demeanor," would attain quite a reputation for his fighting skills during this expedition.[2] Like his fellow Iroquois warriors, however, Han refused to engage in battle against any of his Seneca cousins, a few of whom were standing with the fort's French defenders. A strength of the confederacy was that its members, even if temporarily aligned against each other, as at the siege of Fort Niagara, would avoid, if at all possible, making war against each other. Should that happen, the confederacy would start to lose its unity of purpose and become susceptible to being picked apart in piecemeal fashion by the ever-growing number of European Americans migrating across New England and up the Hudson River with an eye toward settling on the Mohawk River valley's fertile lands.

A few years before Han Yerry joined Johnson's campaign, he had taken a wife. Her name was Tyonajanegen, roughly translated to mean "Two Kettles Together." Tyona quickly bore him three children: Cornelius (born about 1754), Jacob (about 1755), and Dorothea (about 1756).[3] During the mid-1760s Han Yerry and his family joined a few others in founding the settlement of Oriska, about eight miles southeast of Fort Stanwix, an imposing edifice that the British had constructed during the Seven Years' War. Both

Oriska and Fort Stanwix sat astride the Oneida Carrying Place, a major portage trail between the Mohawk River and waterways leading to Lake Ontario.

Travelers and traders regularly passed through Oriska, a village consisting of a few modest cabins and a small population, probably fewer than one hundred inhabitants, about half of whom were Oneidas. The village leader was Han Yerry, who sometime during this period became a chief warrior of the Wolf clan. In addition, he prospered as a farmer and trader. By the time of the Revolution, Han, Tyona, and their children lived in a frame house with a barn nearby. They owned several horses and a variety of farm animals. When guests visited them, Tyona could serve them meals on pewter plates, and she cooked with brass and copper kettles. Their way of living no longer resembled that of their ancestors, known as the Haudenosaunee, or the "People of the Long House." Han and his family had adapted to European ways, but in their hearts they were still Oneidas who, above all else, wanted to protect and defend their homeland from hostile intruders.

Those hostile intruders included aggrandizing white settlers, who by the 1760s had overrun major portions of the Mohawk Nation and were settling not that far east of Oriska. Generally, Han and Tyona got along with those European Americans with whom they came into contact. On the other hand, they lost their affection for Sir William Johnson, once he negotiated the Fort Stanwix Treaty of 1768. Back in 1763 the Crown had drawn a north-to-south Proclamation Line to the west of the colonial settlements, beyond which European Americans were not to take up residence. Territory to the west of that line was to be reserved forever for the Indian nations. When Johnson finally sat down in 1768 to parley with representatives of various Indian nations and establish the exact location of that boundary in the New York colony and surrounding regions, he browbeat Oneida delegates into ceding an eastern section of their homeland to the Crown. This territory included both Oriska and Fort Stanwix. From Han and Tyona's point of view, Johnson had simply stolen valued territory not only from them but from the Oneida Nation more generally.

As the imperial crisis deepened and pointed toward open rebellion, Han, Tyona, and their Iroquois brethren had to consider their allegiance options: neutrality, loyalty to the Crown, or assisting the patriot cause. Various factors caused Han and Tyona to lean in their personal preferences toward the American rebels. Besides their good relations with local European Americans and their disgust with Sir William Johnson (he died in July 1774, but his heirs carried on his policies), Han and Tyona felt great affection for the Presbyterian missionary Samuel Kirkland. Kirkland did much more than preach his "New Birth" message once he launched his Christian witness among the Oneidas in 1766. He lived among them, learned their Iroquoian dialect, translated portions of the Bible into their language, and performed everyday acts of kindness and benevolence. Just as warriors like Han Yerry did when they returned from food-hunting expeditions, Kirkland shared what few material goods and foodstuffs he had when various Oneidas needed assistance. In time he also shared the patriots' message about liberty seeking to overcome imperial tyranny, just as he had so often taught them about Christians being able to overcome evil in the world by virtue of the liberty they had gained through Christ to be of great service to others.

When Han, Tyona, and all the other Oneida peoples learned about the bloody combat that took place at Lexington and Concord on April 19, 1775, they gathered together in a council at the principal village of Kanonwalohale. Considering all their alternatives, they agreed overwhelmingly to hold fast to the proven course of neutrality. Then in July, Kirkland, who had become an agent of the Continental Congress, carried a message from Philadelphia to all the Iroquois peoples asking them to stay out of the "family quarrel" with England and "to remain at home, and not to join on either side, but keep the hatchet buried deep."[4] At virtually the same time, Kirkland encouraged Han

This painting, drawn by master artist Geoffrey Harding of New York in 2005, portrays an Oneida warrior overlooking the Mohawk River valley around the time of the Revolutionary War. Harding conducted careful research to depict how warriors such as Han Yerry Doxtader dressed while on the trail during warmer weather. By the time of the Revolution, bows and arrows were in less common use than muskets when warriors hunted for game or prepared for combat, such as the bloody fighting that occurred at the Battle of Oriskany in August 1777.

and other Oneida warriors "friendly to the Americans in their struggle for liberty" to scout and report back information concerning the actions of other Iroquois warriors, especially the Mohawks, who were aligning with the British to snuff out the rebellion in the Mohawk Valley region.[5]

Even though the Oneida Nation was officially neutral, Han was active in scouting missions. In his mind, there was no inconsistency in helping the rebels, so long as he was not engaging in actual combat. Like all Oneidas, he had the right to act according to his own convictions, even if not fully in alignment with his nation's declared policies. Further, he recognized the hypocrisy of his fellow Iroquois, especially among Mohawk and Seneca warriors, whose nations also professed neutrality while they engaged in bloody raids against European American settlers in the valley. Burning homes and crops and killing animals and people clearly defined the strong pro-British leanings of Han Yerry's Iroquois cousins, as led by the likes of the great Mohawk warrior chief Joseph Brant (Thayendanegea).

Thayen, as we will call him, had close ties with Guy Johnson, who became the British Northern Department Indian superintendent when his uncle Sir William died in 1774. Late in 1775 Thayen traveled to England with Guy and gained an audience with George III. The king promised to restore the Mohawks to their homeland if they actively supported His Majesty's redcoats in crushing the rebellion. Once back in America, Thayen worked tirelessly on behalf of the British war effort. In doing so, he would soon find himself on a collision course with Han Yerry, a course with devastating consequences for the once happily united Iroquois Six Nations Confederacy.

As winter weather gave way to warmer spring temperatures in 1777, the British laid plans for a massive invasion of the colonies from Canada. The goal was to send a force of eight thousand redcoats, Loyalist soldiers, and Indians under the command of John Burgoyne south through the Lake Champlain region to Albany. There Burgoyne's army would link up with British units coming up the Hudson River from New York City. Gaining control of the Hudson-Champlain water corridor would have the effect of cutting off the rest of the colonies from New England, the initial center of the rebellion. In time the British could then reconquer that troublesome region and bring an end to the patriot insurrection against imperial authority.

As part of this strategy, British planners decided to send a diversionary force under Colonel Barry St. Leger westward to Lake Ontario, where elements would assemble at Fort Oswego. Then this force would move southeast across Oneida Lake and right into the heart of Oneida territory. St. Leger would first have to knock out Fort Stanwix (called Fort Schuyler during the war) and then proceed eastward, causing havoc throughout the

Mohawk Valley, before meeting up with Burgoyne's minions at Albany. Besides ravaging local rebels, the purpose was to divide the rebel resisters facing Burgoyne, making it easier for his force to push aside his opponents in reaching Albany.

At Oswego, St. Leger brought together about 750 redcoats, Hessians, and Loyalists, the latter known as the Royal Green battalion, under Sir John Johnson, another son and a direct heir of the late Sir William. In addition, an estimated eight hundred to one thousand Indians joined St. Leger's force, including many warriors from the Six Nations. Thayen was among them, reminding his Iroquois cousins that they had a much greater chance to retain their territory if the British defeated the land-hungry rebel insurgents.

Before the end of July, St. Leger's army was on the move and headed directly into Oneida territory. Han Yerry and other nation leaders knew they were coming. They had received a threatening message from Canada's royal governor, Guy Carleton, admonishing them for their scouting missions on behalf of the rebels. "To take up arms against their King," stated Carleton, "is death." Fortunately, the king was merciful and had "spared the shedding of their blood" with the objective of restoring "them to a proper sense of duty and obedience."[6] As such, Carleton indicated, the Oneidas could regain King George's favor by not in any way resisting St. Leger's force as it passed through their territory, subdued Fort Schuyler, and proceeded through the valley to Albany.

The issue was now one of territorial sovereignty. None of the Six Nations considered themselves subservient to British authority. They were independent nations organized into a confederacy for mutual protection. As much as possible, they respected each other's territorial rights, but now the Oneidas' own cousins—Mohawks, Senecas, Cayugas, and Onondagas—would be moving through their homeland, without their permission. Some Oneidas spoke in favor of letting the British-Indian column proceed without opposition. Others, prominent among them Han Yerry and Tyona, argued that the only acceptable alternative, if Oneida territorial sovereignty meant anything, was to resist the invading force. They had to do so out of respect for the spirits of their ancestors, which resided in their homeland. The king's threats aside, they believed the time had come to engage more directly in the "family quarrel" by linking arms with the American rebels at such places as Fort Schuyler, where patriot soldiers were preparing to challenge St. Leger's advance into the valley.

For Han and Tyona, much more than maintaining the sanctity of Oneida territory was at stake. Already predisposed toward the rebel cause by the opinions of the Reverend Kirkland, their distrust of manipulating British officials as embodied in Sir William Johnson, and their friendships with rebel-minded settlers, they helped carry the argument that to stand up against the invading minions of St. Leger, even including their Iroquois cousins, was the most honorable course to take, regardless of the consequences for the once-united confederacy.

On August 2 St. Leger's force began moving into position to put Fort Schuyler under siege. Inside the fortress were about 750 Continental defenders and a few Oneidas ready to stand with them. Meanwhile, Tyona, an expert horsewoman, was on her way to Fort Dayton, some thirty miles downriver, to advise the local militia commander, Nicholas Herkimer, that St. Leger's army was surrounding Fort Schuyler. Herkimer was already gathering local farmers and laborers based on earlier reports of the British-Indian advance. Once alerted by Tyona, he ordered a forced march upriver to relieve the fort. By the evening of August 5, he and his militiamen had reached the vicinity of Oriska. There Chief Warrior Han Yerry and about sixty Oneidas joined the patriot column, ready to assist in driving off St. Leger's army.

Sometime during that evening Han Yerry and others parleyed with Herkimer. They offered to scout ahead, looking for any signs of enemy resistance or potential entrapment. Herkimer consulted with his junior officers, who dismissed this proposal as senseless folly. How could he trust a bunch of savages, they asked, who were probably already in league with St. Leger's Indians, to do anything but guide them into a deadly ambush? They asked Herkimer about his Loyalist brother Jost, who had joined St. Leger's column. They wanted to know if Herkimer himself was somehow deceiving them by secretly harboring pro-Tory sentiments.

The next morning, August 6, was already hot and muggy with thunderstorms looming when the patriot militia lurched forward with no pickets scouting the woods around them. They entered a swale and passed over Oriskany Creek. With no pickets probing ahead, what they did not know was that hundreds of Iroquois warriors, among them Thayen, along with Sir John Johnson's Royal Greens and a few redcoats, had hidden among the dense forest on both sides of the trail they were following. As Herkimer, riding at the head of the column, started up a hill, about six miles from Fort Schuyler, musket balls and arrows rained down on him and his whole column. The Battle of Oriskany, one of the bloodiest engagements of the whole Revolutionary War, had begun. The fighting raged for hours; a powerful thunderstorm intruded on the engagement before the battle finally came to an end because of the surviving combatants' sheer exhaustion and so much carnage on both sides. Overall, the casualties were staggering, with more than a thousand persons killed, wounded, captured, or missing from both sides.

As the battle progressed, Han and Tyona, along with their son Cornelius, were in the thick of the fighting. Han, at first mounted on a horse, wore a sword, signifying his chief warrior status. He and Cornelius kept loading and firing their muskets, while Tyona did the same with two pistols. At one point a musket ball tore into Han's wrist, immobilizing his hand. Tyona took over loading his musket. Before the battle ended, Han fought with more than one opponent in hand-to-hand combat, brandishing his tomahawk and sword. Contemporary accounts credit him with dispatching as many as nine enemy combatants, and apparently Cornelius killed two more. Even though a family friend later referred to Han as "too old for the service" during the Revolutionary War, he still went "fearlessly into the fights," as clearly demonstrated by his martial performance at Oriskany.[7]

Individual battlefield prowess aside, Oriskany represented the beginning of a civil war within the Six Nations, growing out of another civil war, that between the British and their rebellious American colonists. The ancient confederacy pact that discouraged combat among the brethren of the Six Nations had lost its meaning. As proof, more than thirty Seneca warriors lay dead, as did several Oneidas, on the Oriskany battlefield, sure evidence that unity of purpose no longer characterized confederacy actions.

Within another two weeks, St. Leger would find himself forced to lift the siege and retreat. With their losses, his Iroquois allies had already endured enough and wanted to go home. When word reached them that a huge relief force under the command of Major General Benedict Arnold was coming up the valley and about to fall on them, they broke camp and retreated back toward Lake Ontario. St. Leger had little choice but to follow, now having lost a substantial portion of his force. Even as some of the Indians fell back in panic, at least one sizable party, furious with the Oneidas, swung back through the woods and attacked a defenseless Oriska. As described by one British observer, this party "burned their houses, destroyed their fields, crops, etc. [and] killed and carried away their cattle."[8] Han and Tyona found their home and barn in ashes. They had lost their horses and farm animals and virtually all their material possessions, an immense personal price to pay for having stood and fought alongside the American rebels even as they defended their homeland from St. Leger's invading army.

Once fully committed to the patriot side, Han, Tyona, and most Oneidas kept finding ways to assist their rebel friends and allies. When attending a conference in Albany called by General Philip Schuyler in September 1777, they received intelligence about General Horatio Gates's efforts to block the main British advance force under Burgoyne's command. Han may have been present at a supper with Schuyler on the evening of September 19 when word reached them of a great but indecisive battle at a place called Freeman's

Farm that day. Gates was hoping to obtain reinforcements. The Oneidas, along with a few Tuscaroras, heeded that call. Within twenty-four hours, some 150 of them, including Han, Tyona, and possibly their sons Cornelius and Jacob, made the thirty-mile trek north from Albany to Gates's Saratoga headquarters.

Since most of Burgoyne's native allies, bothered if not bored by the slow pace of the British southward advance, were returning to their villages in Canada, the patriot force now had the advantage in the tactics of harassment. Harass the Oneidas did, with Han serving as the head warrior. Burgoyne's troops were no longer safe when venturing outside British lines. In one instance, the Oneidas led three enemy soldiers they had captured into the American lines with ropes tied securely around their necks. In another, they used war paint to color the faces of two British regulars. Playing on perceptions and fears of these captives about Indian savagery, they easily gained intelligence about the deteriorating conditions facing Burgoyne and any possible attempts to break through rebel lines.

The only point of friction between the Oneidas and the rebel commanders was over scalping. When a warrior scalped a British regular, Gates formulated an agreement with the Oneidas that would "not deprive them of trophies of war like achievements."[9] The Oneidas agreed to accept a cash bounty for each British soldier they captured, but there would be no cash payments for scalps. Eventually, the Oneidas asked to have three Iroquois captives, probably Senecas and Mohawks then being held in Albany, turned over to them as an additional payment for the British soldiers they had captured. They intended to free these warriors to return to their respective nations. Han and others hoped this act would be received as a symbolic gesture reflecting their desire to resolve their differences with their Iroquois brethren, despite the internecine bloodshed at Oriskany. This action had no positive effect. Confederacy unity was in shambles, as graphically symbolized by the extinguishing of the eternal confederacy flame at Onondaga in January 1779.

Han and Tyona likely regretted what was happening to the confederacy, but they also reveled in the recognition they received for their pro-rebel actions. In time Han received a captain's commission in the Continental army. More immediately in recognition for Tyona's services at Saratoga, which involved carrying messages back and forth among the patriot commanders, she accepted "three gallons of rum, for a winter's supply for her family."[10] Tyona and Han needed all the supplies they could get. Still, they were not without housing because Han, in retaliation for the destruction of Oriska, had earlier joined a rebel raiding party that attacked and sacked Mohawk-controlled Canajoharie, likely his early childhood home that now functioned as a Tory base of operations. Han and Tyona took over the dwelling of Molly Brant, Thayen's sister and the longtime common-law wife of Sir William Johnson. Molly had continually informed her brother about rebel activities in the valley, including getting Thayen early word regarding Herkimer's ill-fated march to relieve Fort Schuyler. To Han, driving off Molly was fully justified, given the wreckage of Oriska, even though he certainly knew that these kinds of retributive acts reduced the likelihood of ever reestablishing some semblance of unity among the Six Nations Confederacy.

Early in 1778 Han Yerry and other Oneida leaders received word that George Washington, ensconced at Valley Forge with some ten thousand suffering troops, hoped to have up to two hundred native warriors join his force by no later than mid-May. Wrote Washington to Schuyler, "The Oneidas have manifested the strongest attachment to us throughout this dispute."[11] The commander in chief thought the Oneidas could help the Continentals better control the hinterland around Philadelphia, which the British had captured the previous September. Functioning as scouts and raiders, the Indians could harass enemy foraging parties and capture soldiers who might reveal British plans for the upcoming campaign season; and they could serve as pickets to keep an eye on possible enemy troop movements toward Valley Forge.

Schuyler appreciated that the Oneida chiefs, including Han, would be reluctant to travel so far from their homeland. The reason was self-evident: if the bulk of Oneida warriors journeyed to Valley Forge, their villages, along with the elderly and women and children, would be wide open to attack from their enemies, now especially including their Iroquois brethren. Negotiations followed. The Oneidas would allow a portion of their warriors to make the 250-mile trek to Valley Forge, so long as Schuyler provided additional forms of defense, including building a fort at their most exposed settlement, the village of Kanonwalohale.

Some forty-seven warriors, including a few Tuscaroras, began their southward journey through the mountains on April 25, 1778. Han Yerry was their designated leader. Twenty days later they arrived at Valley Forge, where they regarded thousands of Continentals, mostly bedraggled in appearance but getting ready for the new campaign season. Each warrior considered it a special honor to meet the rebels' "Great Chief Warrior" Washington, and as an act of diplomacy, the commander hosted Han at supper that first evening. Three days later Han would learn that his party was to join the Marquis de Lafayette and twenty-two hundred Continentals and militiamen in a reconnaissance-in-force mission. Lafayette's column was to move closer to Philadelphia to see what could be learned about British plans and possible movements. His units crossed over the Schuylkill River and settled in at the small hamlet of Barren Hill on May 19. No more than two miles away were British outposts.

The Oneidas moved into their assigned position ahead of the main force along a road that ran northwest from Philadelphia close to the Schuylkill. The British, for their part, had spies tracking Lafayette's movements, and they prepared for an attack in massive numbers from several directions, which they launched early on the morning of May 20. Realizing the exposed position of his force, Lafayette engineered a successful retreat back across the Schuylkill, even as Han and the Oneidas fought off British cavalry at their advanced position.

A Frenchman, nearly killed in this action, credited the Oneidas with saving his life. The war cries of the Indians, he stated, had momentarily stunned the British cavalry charging toward them, as had their marksmanship in firing at the horsemen. The Oneidas then retreated from tree to tree, doing whatever was possible with their limited numbers to delay the British force moving toward them, even as Lafayette was guiding the bulk of his soldiers to safer ground back across the Schuylkill. The price the Oneidas paid for this valiant performance was six of their own number killed as they slowly retreated, thereby helping so many others in Lafayette's force to avoid the same fate.

Within the next few weeks, Washington received intelligence reports that the British troops in Philadelphia had no intention of attacking his army. Rather, their plan was to retreat across New Jersey to the main British base of operations in New York City. As such, the commander saw no need for "that kind of service in which the Indians are capable of being useful."[12] Keeping them in camp "could answer no valuable purpose" and would "be productive of needless expense." Washington thanked the Oneidas kindly for their service before they departed for home, beginning in mid-June.

Han Yerry's record of service begins to fade from the record after 1778. In 1779 he decided not to become involved in General John Sullivan's punitive raiding expedition, primarily directed against the Cayugas and Senecas. Han still held out hope for reconciliation among all the confederacy nations, but one result of Sullivan's scorched-earth campaign was to deepen further the breach among the Iroquois. Thayen proved that point in 1780 when he led a retaliatory strike against Kanonwalohale and leveled that village. Many Oneidas, already fearful of such attacks, had migrated to the area of Schenectady, where they suffered from food and clothing shortages, as well as deplorable housing conditions. Still, Han and other warriors did some scouting, but they could offer little else to the cause of American liberty.

What they did receive were grandly worded pronouncements in regard to their service to the rebels. In December 1777 the Continental Congress offered them praise for their actions at Oriskany and Saratoga. "We have experienced your love, strong as the oak, and your fidelity," declared the delegates. "While the sun and moon continue to give light to the world, we shall love and respect you. As our trusty friends, we shall protect you; and shall at all times consider your welfare as our own."[13] General Schuyler joined this chorus of fulsome praise in thanking Han and the other Oneida warriors for going to Valley Forge. He acknowledged their "friendly care and attention to the interest of the United States." Then he elaborated with these haunting words: "I have often told you that the conduct which you have held would always entitle you to our love and esteem, yet, I repeat it with pleasure and sooner should a fond mother forget her only son than we shall forget you."[14]

In the end, none of the Six Nations fared well at the close of the Revolutionary War. The British, for their part, abandoned their erstwhile Indian allies in the Peace of Paris that gave their former colonists their independence. In back-to-back conferences among the Six Nations, the state of New York, and the Continental Congress, held at Fort Stanwix during the late summer and early fall of 1784, the Mohawks, Onondagas, Cayugas, and Senecas had to make land cessions along Lake Ontario as punishment for having supported the losing side. New York governor George Clinton, in turn, conveyed his "gratitude" to the Oneidas, noting that they "have often in the hour of danger given indubitable proofs of your inviolable attachment to us and of your determination of living and dying with us." Rumors aside, Clinton stressed that New York had "no claim on your lands; its just extent will ever remain secured to you."[15] However, the governor urged the Oneidas to trace their boundaries and share that information to ensure that no one violated the territorial integrity of their homeland.

At the proceedings between the Six Nations and the Confederation Congress, leaders expressed the same sentiments. They rebuked those who had sided with the British and praised the Oneidas. The Marquis de Lafayette was in attendance. When invited to make a formal speech, he gladly did so, reminding everyone present that "the cause of the Americans was a just one." He pointed out that "meddling with the quarrels of whites" was going to cost some of the Six Nations dearly, but apparently not the Oneidas. In closing, he wished them all good "health, fortunate huntings, peace and plenty, and the fulfilling of such of your dreams as foretell good luck."[16]

Lafayette, on at least one point, was prescient. Meddling in the "family quarrel" had subverted the Six Nations long-standing unity of purpose: their ability to stand together and fight as one against any and all external enemies who threatened Iroquoia. At the time Lafayette did not realize that his prophecy also included the Oneidas. Repeatedly promised, as an expression of unbounded patriot gratitude, that their homeland would forever be held sacred, Han, Tyona, and all Oneidas would soon learn otherwise. In June 1785 Governor Clinton called representatives of the nation to a council meeting and initiated the process of demanding large land grants for relatively small sums of money.

Once under way, the grabbing of Oneida lands continued at a frenetic pace. In 1792 Good Peter, a highly respected chief, expressed the sense of betrayal the Oneidas felt in regard to their former patriot allies when he stated: "We Indians are unwise, and our want of wisdom is owing to our want of knowledge of the ways of white people. . . . We verily thought our white brothers meant good to us; and hence we have been deceived in respect to our lands."[17] Chief Warrior Han Yerry witnessed the beginnings of the disintegration of his homeland before he passed away sometime prior to 1794. Tyona lived on for another three decades. In her final years she was blind and could not see for herself what was happening as her people dispersed to northern Wisconsin and Ontario Province in Canada. A few Oneidas stayed on in New York, watching as their homeland all but ceased to exist, despite all those high-sounding phrases about allies standing together forever, even as the sun and the moon continued to provide light for the world.

FOR FURTHER READING

For a complete history of the Oneidas in Revolutionary America, see Joseph T. Glatthaar and James Kirby Martin, *Forgotten Allies: The Oneida Indians and the American Revolution* (New York, 2006). Another recent study with additional findings is David J. Norton, *Rebellious Younger Brother: Oneida Leadership and Diplomacy, 1750–1800* (DeKalb, Ill., 2009). Thayen, more commonly known as Joseph Brant, has garnered the most historical attention among Six Nations Indians. A comprehensive study of his life is Isabel Thompson Kelsey, *Joseph Brant, 1743–1807: Man of Two Worlds* (Syracuse, N.Y., 1984). For the Six Nations more generally, Barbara Graymont, *The Iroquois in the American Revolution* (Syracuse, N.Y., 1972), remains a standard work, which may be supplemented by Alan Taylor, *The Divided Ground: Indians, Settlers and the Northern Borderland of the American Revolution* (New York, 2006). For cultural interactions between European settlers and Iroquois peoples, see David L. Preston, *The Texture of Contact: European and Indian Settler Communities on the Frontiers of Iroquoia, 1667–1783* (Lincoln, Neb., 2009).

PART III

{stylized ornament}

THE PROMISE OF THE REVOLUTION

CHAPTER THIRTEEN

"Satan, Smith, Shattuck, and Shays": The People's Leaders in the Massachusetts Regulation of 1786

Gregory Nobles

There's a crude-looking woodcut from a 1787 Boston almanac that, over two hundred years later, has become a staple illustration in many American history textbooks for the section on what is commonly but incorrectly called Shays's Rebellion. It depicts Daniel Shays (1747–1825), a Revolutionary War veteran who allegedly led a rural insurrection against the government of Massachusetts in 1786–87, standing next to Job Shattuck (1736–1819), another veteran of the Revolution who likewise gained a good deal of notoriety in that period of post-Revolutionary unrest. The picture is not only cartoonish in its artistic technique but sarcastically comic in its political intent. The figures of Shays and Shattuck are short and distorted, stiffly holding swords and a furled flag in the foreground, with a cannon in the background reinforcing their martial appearance. Surprisingly

The cartoonish caricatures of Daniel Shays, left, and Job Shattuck, right, first appeared in *Bickerstaff's Boston Almanack for 1787*, a pro-government publication. Since then this woodcut image has become all but emblematic of the insurrection, frequently reproduced—typically without explanatory comment or analysis—in standard U.S. history textbooks.

well dressed and well armed for agrarian rebels, the two are also assigned impressive-seeming military titles in the picture's caption, Shays as "Gen." and Shattuck as "Col.," supposedly as officers in an organized army. The text that accompanies the image further connects them in a couplet:

> Thro' drifted Storms let SHAYS the Court assail,
> And SHATTUCK rise, illustrious from the Jail.[1]

Another bit of contemporary doggerel, written in the form of a child's alphabet lesson, also puts the two together, this time in a foursome filled out by a fellow insurgent named Nathan Smith and a more famous biblical figure who frequently gets blamed for unpopular political activity:

> R stands for Rebels who mobs dare to raise,
> S stands for Satan, Smith, Shattuck, and Shays.[2]

The picture and the poems accomplished something on the printed page that apparently never happened in life: they brought Shattuck and Shays together, side by side in one place, as partners at the head of a political insurrection. In fact, there's no direct evidence that the two men ever met, much less collaborated or otherwise conspired as co-leaders of the protest that rocked post-Revolutionary Massachusetts in 1786–87. It's possible that they encountered each other a decade earlier, in the first months of the American Revolution: they both served as militiamen in the Battle of Bunker Hill in June 1775, and later, in 1777, they took part in the campaigns at Ticonderoga and Saratoga. Both men rose to the rank of captain in their respective militia units, Shays in the Fifth Massachusetts Regiment and Shattuck in the Sixth, and both apparently performed their duties with some distinction.[3] If they overlapped in service at Saratoga, however, their paths apparently parted, and they lived considerably different lives for the duration of the war.

After Saratoga, Job Shattuck came home to Groton, a town about thirty miles northwest of Boston, where he assumed a position as leader of the local militia until the end of the war. He had a good reputation as a fighting man, having first gone to war as a nineteen-year-old in the French and Indian War; now in his forties, he was known locally as being "skilful in the use of the broadsword . . . and utterly insensible to fear." He also had a good reputation as a political leader, serving as town selectman in the 1780s and, perhaps more important in light of later events, a leader in local protest against outside authorities. In 1781, after the Massachusetts legislature imposed a requirement that the town taxes be paid in silver, Shattuck led a group of sixteen other Groton men in threatening the two town constables responsible for collecting the tax; for his involvement in the so-called Groton riots, he had to appear in court, where he pleaded guilty and paid a fine plus court costs. His protests against the state's tax policies did not stem from personal poverty, however: he had inherited an extensive holding of family land, making him one of the largest landowners in town. Indeed, as a local historian later explained, "his position and means, his remarkable bodily vigor, his good war record, and his undoubted honesty gave him great influence . . . he was uneducated and obstinate, with the broadest ideas of personal rights."[4] Those "ideas of personal rights" would be called into play again soon enough, when the situation in postwar Massachusetts came to a crisis not only in his hometown but in communities all across the state.

Compared to Shattuck, Shays was younger, less prosperous, less prominent in his community, and less probable to emerge as a leader of a Massachusetts-wide movement. He had remained a captain in the Revolutionary army until 1780, at which point he resigned his military commission and settled in Pelham, a hardscrabble Scots-Irish community in the hills above the Connecticut River, about seventy miles west of Boston. Pelham had a comparatively short history as a town (it was established only in 1739), but by the time Daniel Shays came to live there, his new neighbors already knew quite a bit about how to make themselves a presence in the regional political scene. In 1762, for instance, a group of Pelham men and women surrounded a Hampshire County deputy sheriff who came to town to serve a warrant, greeting him "with Axes, Clubs, sticks, hot water and hot soap in a riotous and tumultuous manner" and making it necessary for him to retreat with his warrant still in his pocket. A few years later, in early 1775, Pelham people went on a "tour of education" to a couple of neighboring towns, threatening some of the most prominent suspected Tories there with physical abuse and extracting confessions of political error from them. A perplexed Protestant minister in one of those towns looked on in shock, writing, "They act like mad people, tho' well for a Mob."[5]

Shays may have known something of the reputation of Pelham before he arrived in 1780, but he came to town too late to have taken part in any of the raucous political activity of the earlier Revolutionary Era. Instead, he lived the relatively quiet life of a small farmer for a few years, holding minor town office on a few occasions but mostly trying just to feed his family and stay out of debt. In that latter regard, he didn't always succeed: like a good number of his neighbors in Pelham and elsewhere, he wound up in court on a few occasions, hauled in by his creditors for unpaid debts—but not, as was the case with Job Shattuck, charged with acts of political defiance. In 1786, when the people of Pelham did begin to express their distress about the political and economic conditions that would soon result in insurrection, Shays was undoubtedly a participant in the community's conversation. He was not, however, one of the men initially chosen to represent Pelham in the county conventions, where people from the surrounding region came together to address common concerns and hammer out petitions to the state government. Other local leaders, who had lived in Pelham longer and had a larger circle of friends and family, apparently took the early lead in speaking for the town and instigating countywide action.[6]

In general, given their differences in location, age, wealth, political experience, and perhaps even force of personality, Job Shattuck and Daniel Shays seem an unlikely pair of insurgent leaders to be operating in concert on a statewide basis, especially with Shays the "general," as the old woodcut put it, and Shattuck his military inferior as mere "colonel." It makes more sense, in fact, to see them as participants in parallel protest movements that arose at the same time, shared the same concerns, and contributed to a statewide, even national, sense of crisis in a still-unsettled society in the immediate aftermath of the American Revolution. They began to appear on the same pages of history only when the pens of their enemies put them there.

One of those pen-wielding opponents took quite a few pages to do so, in fact. George Richards Minot, the author of a decidedly unsympathetic *History of the Insurrections in Massachusetts* (1788), didn't mention Shattuck or Shays until more than forty pages into his book. Instead, he started with a long lesson about the troubled political economy of the post-Revolutionary era, and his survey of the situation offers a still-credible summary of the run-up to unrest. Minot, a Harvard-educated lawyer and well-connected member of the Massachusetts political establishment, considered himself a "Friend of Government" during the unrest and certainly no advocate for ordinary people, much less a sympathizer with agrarian insurrection. Still, he was not altogether uncritical of his colleagues in state government, nor of their role in creating the conditions that caused the crisis. It didn't take much to see the basis of the people's grievances.[7]

Once the war had ended, Minot pointed out, Massachusetts fell under a heavy burden of debt, both public and private. The state had to find some way to pay for the late war effort and restore credit, and to do that the legislature imposed new taxes on the people, the vast majority of whom were suffering from their own financial distresses. Many people had little capacity to pay, especially since they now had to do so in specie, hard currency that had become hard to come by. Within the legislature, political leaders debated the cause of the crisis; rural representatives accused their urban, more commercial counterparts of various vices, including political indifference and personal "luxury," the latter a fondness among the wealthy "to exceed each other in the full display of their riches." In the face of such self-indulgence, Minot admitted, the poor patriots who had fought the war "could not realize that they had shed their blood in the field, to be worn out by burdensome taxes at home; or that they had contended, to secure to their creditors, a right to drag them into courts and prisons." Small wonder, then, that people in many rural communities had become mistrustful of the men who dominated the political and legal systems—the lawyers who prosecuted them, the judges who passed sentence on them, and the elected officials who refused to address their grievances or provide relief. Summing up the list of economic and political ills—decreased trade and manufacture, imported luxuries, widespread debt, inadequate credit, a scarcity of money, and a punitive-seeming legal system—Minot made no attempt to minimize the menace that they posed to rural people. The "evils" of the postwar period, he concluded, "leave us under no necessity of searching further for the insurrections that took place."[8]

By the time Minot's narrative turned its attention to those insurrections, which began in the late summer and early fall of 1786, Job Shattuck and Daniel Shays seemed comparative latecomers to a process of protest already well under way. But their appearances at that point give us an opportunity to see how both men emerged from within the insurgency to assume roles as leaders of an already aroused people.

Shattuck first appears paired with Nathan Smith. They are the two most visible figures among a mass of men and boys, perhaps three hundred in all, crowded into the town square of Concord, Massachusetts, on Tuesday, September 12, 1786. The Middlesex County court was scheduled to meet, and Shattuck, Smith, and hundreds of others from surrounding communities had come to town to make sure it wouldn't. If ordinary people couldn't quickly rectify the many economic and political ills that they felt the state's leaders had visited upon them in recent years, they could still try to stop the most immediate source of legal authority, the county courts, from imposing punishment on debtors and other victims of the system. The best way to close the court was to keep it from opening, and for that the crowd got to town a day early. After spending a rainy and miserable Monday night huddled into whatever shelter they could find, they awoke to more rain Tuesday morning but still managed to arrange themselves in a semblance of military order, posting armed guards around the town square and waiting for the justices to come into view.[9]

Around nine Nathan Smith began to address the crowd in a loud voice, insisting that the court would have four hours to agree to the terms of the protesters or face being driven out of town. No one could ignore Nathan Smith. A good soldier in the Revolution, he didn't confine his combativeness to the war; he took manly pride in his pugnacious personality and got into frequent fights, one of which had cost him an eye. Minot dismissed him as "exceedingly outrageous" and said that the "profanity of his language" staggered even some of his allies. A nineteenth-century account of the events of September 12 described how Smith—a man who was "quarrelsome, coarse in speech, and given to drink"—fortified himself with rum, got a drum, and rallied his recruits by declaring, "As Christ laid down his life to save the world, so will I lay down my life to suppress the government from all tirannical oppression." Anyone who didn't join him, he continued, would suffer the consequences of God's wrath—and certainly Smith's own.[10]

The boisterous Smith provides a narrative foil to Job Shattuck, who played a comparatively moderate role in the day's proceedings. Shattuck initially sent a message to the justices of the court saying that the "voice of the people" called upon them not to enter the courthouse and not to take any sort of judicial action "until such time as the people shall have a redress to a number of grievances they labor under." A little later in the day Shattuck represented a "Pacific Committee" of local communities that offered a compromise arrangement whereby the court could sit one day on the condition that it adjourn the next. As the justices of the court were dawdling inside the tavern where they had taken refuge, a group of mounted men and a hundred or so men on foot arrayed themselves in front of the tavern and "faced the house in a stern and menacing manner." That display of purpose convinced the justices that the time to leave town had indeed come, and they "called for their horses and rode away in time to escape a second visit." Thus the confrontation ended with no one hurt, Nathan Smith still agitated, the justices humiliated, and the assembled protesters vindicated. In the various accounts of the day, Job Shattuck emerges as a forceful figure, a respected man of resolve, but a man of reason as well.[11]

Two weeks later, about ninety miles to the west, a similar drama played out in Springfield, where the Hampshire County Superior Court was scheduled to sit for its September session. To stop it from doing so, more than a thousand protesters came from all over the county, "headed by one Daniel Shays" (who thus makes his first appearance in Minot's account of the insurrections).[12] This time, though, the Massachusetts authorities had ordered some six hundred militiamen to Springfield to counter the protesters and protect the court—and, perhaps even more important, to protect the federal arsenal that had been established in Springfield during the Revolution. The commander of the government troops, Major General William Shepard of the Hampshire County militia, must have known that many of his men had misgivings about going to battle against people from their own region and that he therefore couldn't be too aggressive against the protesters. At the same time, Shays no doubt understood that the men on his side had far too little military skill to take on a better-armed if not altogether better-disciplined force, and he too sought to exercise restraint. "At one point," Minot writes, the insurgents "marched down upon the militia with loaded muskets, and every preparation was made for an engagement; but they were dissuaded from an attack, as it was said, by their commander," Daniel Shays. Indeed, Shays later explained that "the sole motive with me in taking the command at Springfield, was to prevent the shedding of blood, which would absolutely have been the case, if I had not."[13] Instead of fighting, then, the two sides fell into a stalemate for three days, making camp about a mile apart; each came out occasionally to try to impress the other by going through the motions of military maneuvers. The justices of the court couldn't conduct any business in such a situation, and after three frustrating days of doing nothing, they gave up and adjourned.[14]

As soon as the court called it quits, all the armed men in town got ready to break camp and head home, but not without a final military display. Before departing, both sides put on a ceremonial parade that caught the attention of a local clergyman, the Reverend Justus Forward. Taking sketchy notes, he recorded that committees from the two forces met and reached an agreement that the Hampshire militia should "march to the Laboratory Hill & there disband," leaving Springfield open so that Daniel Shays and his men "might march thro' the town" and then likewise disband. In both cases the men threw off the unofficial insignia they had worn in their hats to distinguish one side from the other—"a white paper in ye Militia Hats, Green Bush in ye Mobb." Then they could "go Home friendly," or at least unbloodied.[15] They had truly dodged a bullet.

The close of this showdown in Springfield was a remarkable moment in a tumultuous time, a surprisingly peaceful conclusion to a potentially deadly encounter between two armed but unprofessional forces suddenly thrown together in a tight space. This last exercise in soldiery—the two sides parading in sequence, exchanging center stage in Springfield, and then breaking up and marching away—may seem rather anticlimactic. Still, it made a point at the time, and it makes one now. If the two sides could not really "go Home friendly," they could both depart the scene with some of their political legitimacy intact. General Shepard and his militiamen could take comfort in having done their duty by protecting the justices and keeping both the court and the arsenal out of the hands of the protesters. Daniel Shays and his fellow insurgents could likewise take satisfaction in having made a forthright stand against the state, defying its arms and authority in the defense of their rights and interests. Like Job Shattuck, Daniel Shays stands out less as a dangerous firebrand than as a moderating but effective figure who kept order, prevented violence, and ultimately prevailed in stopping the court from doing its work—all told, a successful start for someone rather suddenly risen to a position of leadership.

So it went in Middlesex County and Hampshire County, and so it went in other Massachusetts counties in September 1786, from Bristol County in the east to Berkshire County at the western end of the state. Crowds of people numbering in the hundreds surrounded the county courts that month; all of them called for redress of the same basic grievances, especially legal proceedings against debtors, and all of them took up what arms they could find—guns and bayonets but sometimes just staves and clubs—to show their resolve in the face of the state.

In their petitions they never identified themselves by the name of their leaders—Smith, Shattuck, Shays, or anyone else—but instead referred to themselves simply as "the people" or some variation thereon, "the body of the people," or "the people assembled in arms." In some cases local groups called themselves "Regulators," taking up a term that had originated in seventeenth-century England and had more recently entered the political lexicon of Revolutionary America. The notion of "regulation" implied an attempt to exert popular control over government in response to abuse and corruption, restoring the political and economic system to its proper order and making it responsive to the needs of the people. It was an old idea in a new context, but one that seemed to have sudden currency in post-Revolutionary Massachusetts.[16]

The absence of a single name for the movement offers a clue to its decentralized nature. While an anxious observer might have thought this widespread unrest was a well-organized uprising, craftily coordinated by a cabal of co-conspirators, that would have been wrong. Instead, these first court closings seem to have been mostly local actions, each one energized, if not directly organized, by people coming together in town meetings and county conventions, discussing their grievances, and reaching the mutual conclusion that they had to take direct action in their immediate region. When Minot wrote of the "insurrections," plural, in Massachusetts in 1786, he got that part right.

Still, how did these insurrectionary actions get organized? That question speaks to a larger issue of political mobilization that runs throughout the

Revolutionary Era and from Massachusetts to other places as well. For all the work of the most prolific pamphleteers, the most articulate radicals, or the most active committees of correspondence, the protest of the era remained a remarkably decentralized process. Ordinary people organized at the local level to take action—or not, as the case may have been.

For the most part, rural unrest had its deepest roots and broadest reach in the western part of the state, where specie remained especially scarce for the payment of debts and taxes, and where struggling farmers thus felt themselves the victims of unfair financial policies in the postwar period. Some of the smaller rural communities in western Massachusetts had long been distant, politically as well as physically, from the government in Boston; in many cases these struggling towns could not afford to send delegates to the legislature, and when they did, they often grumbled that their representatives were outnumbered and overwhelmed by the political influence of the more commercially integrated towns in the east.

And yet as the actions of Job Shattuck and his neighbors in Groton and several other eastern Massachusetts towns made clear at the closing of the Middlesex County court, debtors in several rural communities closer to Boston also felt the economic and political system worked against them, and some comparatively prosperous men—again, Job Shattuck, for instance—joined and even led the challenges to government. On the whole, the pattern of protest of 1786–87 does not lend itself to neat east-west, creditor-debtor divides. Additional explanations for participation in the insurrections include close social connections, the ties of community, church, and family that became reflected in local loyalty, common concerns, and mutual reinforcement in a time of increasing crisis. Put simply, the insurrections that arose in Massachusetts seem to have stemmed not only from individual deprivation and deeply felt economic grievances, which were serious indeed, but also from pre-existing standards of communal sentiment and solidarity, which played out differently from one town to the next.[17]

Yet when we look at those communities and the people who *did* participate in the court closings and subsequent protests in the fall of 1786, one point becomes apparent: no one needed instructions from some central command to know what to do. Instead, local insurgents followed the patterns of protest that had been common in the recent past, both before and after the Revolution.

The sort of political pageantry that marked the various events of September 1786 had taken place before, and people seemed to know their parts. In September 1774, for instance, thousands of people from communities all across Massachusetts had converged on their respective county courts and, with quick victories, forced the justices to give up their commissions from the British Crown. The pride of successful collective action became apparent in Hampshire County, for instance, where the people closed the courts and then organized themselves into a quasi-military formation of the various communities, in which "separate companies marched with stave & musick . . . trumpets sounding, drums beating, fifes playing, and Colours flying."[18] The parade before the Hampshire County court in 1774 provided a precursor, perhaps a model, for the ritual march that Shays and his allies made in 1786.

Sandwiched between those major events in 1774 and 1786 were lesser eruptions of protest in the immediate postwar period that brought people back into action. In one of the more striking events of the era, a sizable mob from the surrounding towns converged on the Hampshire County court in April 1782, where an itinerant minister named Samuel Ely urged the protesters to "go to the wood pile and get clubs enough, and knock their grey wigs off." When the county authorities later had Ely locked up in the jail in Springfield, over a hundred men marched on that town to set him free, and Ely soon escaped.[19] There's no indication that Daniel Shays, still a relative newcomer to the county, took part in that protest, but no matter. The people of the region clearly knew how to mobilize themselves quickly and in considerable numbers, playing the role of minutemen in taking care of political affairs in their immediate neighborhood. An eloquent exhorter might energize them with fiery speeches, and a military veteran might organize them into marching order; but no single leader could claim the responsibility, much less the ability, to get them going in the first place.

Shays actually admitted as much, insisting that he bore no responsibility for organizing the movement that later came to bear his name: at the height of the insurrection in early 1787, he told a state official, "I never had half so much to do in the matter as you think." He portrayed himself as a reluctant rebel at best, a man propelled forward by the force of events, perhaps even by the force of his fellow insurgents. And despite the subsequent emphasis on Shays as the "generalissimo" of the movement, his disclaimer made an implicit, even inadvertent point about the nature of political leadership— that the insurgents selected Shays, not that he incited them.

One might argue, in fact, that Job Shattuck actually had a longer and more robust record of political leadership, and given his strong personality and physical prowess, he seemed a much more likely figure to emerge as the head of a statewide protest. But his political visibility led to his vulnerability. In late November 1786, ten weeks after he had played so prominent a role in the court closing in Concord, the Massachusetts authorities issued a warrant for his arrest, along with that of Nathan Smith and three other men from Middlesex County, on the grounds that they had become "dangerous to the said Commonwealth, its peace and safety." Shattuck got wind of his impending arrest and tried to hide out in a friend's house, but his pursuers, a mounted troop of some three hundred horsemen, caught up with him, and in the process of arresting him, one of the state officials slashed Shattuck across the leg with a sword. Subdued and wounded, Job Shattuck spent the rest of the insurrection closely confined in a Boston jail, incommunicado and unable to influence events elsewhere in the state.[20]

With Job Shattuck out of the picture, Daniel Shays would become the main focus of Massachusetts authorities—and of subsequent historians. To his credit, Shays proved to be a resourceful and courageous commander of his men, but still only one of several regional leaders in western Massachusetts and hardly the "generalissimo" of the whole Massachusetts movement. In fact, the most dramatic event in which he figured, the attack on the federal arsenal at Springfield on January 25, 1787, would underscore the underorganized and localized nature of the insurrection's leadership.

Soon after the beginning of the new year, Shays had apparently begun to speak openly of raising the stakes, brazenly saying that he and his men planned to march on Boston and take action against the government officials who had been enacting laws so detrimental to the lives of common farmers. But first they would have to march on Springfield again, not to close the courts, as had been the goal in September, but to take possession of the arsenal and the stores of weapons there. The insurgents needed either to acquire the arms—some seven thousand muskets and bayonets were stored there, along with a substantial supply of powder and shot—or at least to neutralize the government's control of such a large stockpile of firepower.[21] Everyone knew the arsenal was a logical target, and by late January 1787 Springfield had become a powder keg.

Once again, as he had in the earlier confrontation in September 1786, General William Shepard of the Hampshire County militia commanded the pro-government force. This time he had no illusions about escaping an armed confrontation with a respectful exchange of ceremonial parades that would allow everyone to feel good and "go Home friendly." On January 24 he nervously wrote to the overall commander of the Massachusetts militia, General Benjamin Lincoln, that he and just over one thousand militiamen were surrounded by a force almost twice their size and cut off from supplies and reinforcements. For the past several days, columns of county insurgents had been converging on Springfield, one from Berkshire County to the west, another one from Worcester and Middlesex to the east, and the largest one

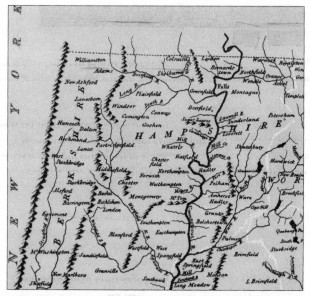

This 1795 map of western Massachusetts shows some of the main sites of Regulator activity, including Springfield (or "East Springfield" as indicated here), the location of the government armory, on the Connecticut River just above the southern border of Massachusetts; Pelham, the home of Daniel Shays, upriver and in the hills to the east; and Petersham, the scene of the regulation's last significant military engagement, above the *E* in "Hampshire."

from Shepard's own Hampshire County, commanded by Daniel Shays and another county leader, Luke Day of West Springfield. "Shays and Day with their forces have stopped every avenue by which supplies and recruits can be brought to this post," Shepard warned Lincoln. "Before tomorrow morning I expect the trial will be made to force me from this post . . . *That mans party* is increasing fast."[22]

"*That man*" was Daniel Shays, but it would be Luke Day who made the most decisive move—or non-move, as it turned out—that inadvertently let Shepard win the day. Shays and Day and the other insurgent leaders had divided their troops, planning a three-pronged attack for January 25, just as Shepard feared. But presuming to speak for "the body of the people assembled in arms," and without telling his allies in advance, Day sent Shepard an ultimatum that morning, giving him twenty-four hours to surrender and dissolve his force or otherwise face a fight of no quarter. A copy of Day's ultimatum never reached Shays and the others, however, and they never knew about the twenty-four-hour delay in the anticipated attack. Instead, while Day and his men waited to see what Shepard would do, Shays went ahead as planned, and he and his men marched on the arsenal in the fading daylight of January 25.[23]

Shepard was ready for them. He sent two of his aides out on horseback to warn the advancing insurgents to turn back lest they be fired on with muskets and cannons. By that time Shays had apparently warmed to the task of command, brushing aside the warning and telling his men the arsenal would soon be theirs: "March, God Damn you, march!" And so they marched—straight into the arsenal's artillery. At first Shepard ordered his artillerymen to fire over the heads of the Regulators to scare them into retreat, but when that didn't work, the gunners sent several rounds of grapeshot directly into the insurgent force. Four men fell dead, and several more staggered away wounded.[24] By sunset the second Shays-Shepard showdown was over, and this time the bloodstained scene gave a very different cast to the outcome.

Shays's failure at Springfield had exposed flaws in the fundamental nature of the insurgent movement as an organized force; its strength, the localized mobilization of armed farmers in a county-based coalition led by commanders chosen by their men, proved also to be its weakness. In January 1787 no less than in September 1786, there was no coherent central command, and Luke Day's decision to act on his own without calling a council of war left his fellow insurgents in the lurch. The loss of a message from Day to Shays meant there would be no coordinated assault on the arsenal, no overwhelming victory over the militia, and certainly no subsequent plundering of Boston or any direct regulation of the lawmakers there. Instead, a handful of defeated and demoralized local units would scatter to neighboring towns in retreat, suddenly on the defensive and wondering what sort of military force General Benjamin Lincoln might be about to bring against them. They would find out soon enough.

In the aftermath of the Springfield defeat, Shays and Day regrouped their men and headed northward toward Pelham, the familiar hill town where Shays felt relatively safe. From there Shays sent two proposals for a truce and general pardons to Lincoln, who had camped his militia force in the nearby town of Hadley. But Lincoln offered to pardon only the common soldiers of the insurrection, not the leaders, and certainly not Shays. On February 3, figuring that Lincoln was about to make a move, Shays marched his men a dozen or so miles eastward to Petersham, where they found refuge in the homes of sympathetic inhabitants. Lincoln put his men in motion too, and after a nightlong forced march in blowing snow, they arrived at Petersham on the morning of February 4, with two cannons in tow. The surprise of their unexpected arrival threw the insurgents into panic, and over a hundred surrendered while the rest fled farther into the countryside.

Shays, Day, and some two thousand of their allies eventually made their way to Vermont, and others crossed into New Hampshire or New York. Back in Massachusetts, small bands of insurgents still carried out sporadic attacks against unpopular merchants, lawyers, and government officials, but such hit-and-run tactics did not constitute a widespread insurrection. By June 1787 the unrest in Massachusetts had sputtered to a halt.[25]

Even while those last guerrilla attacks continued, the Massachusetts government set about taking action against those men who had taken up arms against the state. Some of the individuals identified as leaders, Shays and Shattuck most prominent among them, were indicted for treason and condemned to hang. An angry Samuel Adams argued that taking up arms against a monarchy may have been legitimate in the Revolution, "but the man who dares to rebel against the laws of a republic ought to suffer death." For most of the rank-and-file insurgents who did rebel, however, the punishment was comparatively lenient. In February 1787 the state passed a Disqualifying Act that stripped them of their citizenship—particularly the right to vote, hold office, and serve on juries—but also provided a path to pardon for those who would lay down their arms, sign an oath of loyalty, and pay a small fine. Within three years insurgents could be citizens again.

Almost immediately the issue of punishment became entangled in electoral politics. Not all friends of government were friends of the governor, James Bowdoin, and his political opponents accused him and his legislative allies of disenfranchising insurgents in order to skew the electorate in his favor. Instead of imposing penalties on the surrendering rebels, they called for a more generous policy of reconciliation to restore peace to the troubled state. Motivated by that hope for closure, the vast majority of Massachusetts voters turned against Bowdoin and most of his supporters in the General Court, effecting a political housecleaning in the May elections and bringing John Hancock back to the governor's chair. Hancock had had the good fortune, perhaps even good sense, to resign the governorship in 1785, just as the level of unrest was rising, and now, in 1787, he seemed to offer a refreshing return to some form of normalcy.[26]

Hancock also had the good sense to listen to those who called for clemency. In Daniel Shays's own hometown of Pelham, a young man named Henry McCullough stood condemned to death for his alleged role in the local unrest, but a justice of the peace from a neighboring town, Ebenezer

Mattoon, urged Hancock to spare him. Mattoon made the politically astute point that the "tempers of the people" had grown more moderate in the aftermath of the recent election, and a show of gubernatorial mercy would "conciliate the town of Pelham to the government, and be attended with very happy consequences." Hancock did so, and some months later he also extended pardon to an even more notable Pelhamite, Daniel Shays, and his putative partner in the rebel leadership, Job Shattuck.[27]

"Satan, Smith, Shattuck, and Shays"—if only it had been that simple for the opponents of the Massachusetts insurrection. The state's officials might capture, condemn to death, and essentially demonize a few leaders, fingering them as the ringleaders of a movement of foolish and "deluded" people.[28] But the sentiment for regulation of government ran deep and wide throughout the state and, indeed, other parts of the nation. Ebenezer Mattoon's wise advice to John Hancock stemmed from his recognition that the proper response to recent unrest must be reconciliation with the aggrieved people, not the execution of a handful of individuals. To be sure, Smith, Shattuck, and Shays—not to mention Luke Day, Eli Parsons, Adam Wheeler, and a handful of others—had assumed positions of leadership in the Massachusetts movement, but they had not created the unrest in the first place. At best, they directed it, providing some measure of military organization to ordinary people who were already rising up in arms. When Daniel Shays said, "I never had half so much to do in the matter as you think," we should take him seriously.

We should also take seriously the impact of the Massachusetts Regulation on the subsequent post-Revolutionary settlement in the new nation. The fifty-five men who assembled in Philadelphia in May 1787 to hammer out a new framework of government for the United States began their work with the recent insurrection fresh in their minds. The struggle in Massachusetts had come to an uneasy conclusion, but other states in the still-fragile confederation might share the same fate. Throughout their deliberations the framers remained mindful, even fearful, of the "tempers of the people," particularly what they termed the "people out of doors," who could still be a source of political unrest. Thus in Article 1, Section 8, of the Constitution they created, they made sure that the federal government would be empowered "to provide for calling forth the Militia to execute the Laws of the Union, suppress Insurrections, and repel Invasions." Indeed, there would soon be other insurrections to suppress.

But in addition to focusing on the suppression of insurrection, we should seek to understand the justification of such unrest in the post-Revolutionary era. People felt a serious threat to their basic rights, even from their own elected governments, and they felt they had good reason to rise up to defend them. Those rights and those reasons are what we still need to search for. Above all, if we look beyond the common caricature of Daniel Shays and an event too easily labeled "Shays's Rebellion," we may look more deeply and perhaps differently at the nation-building narrative in standard textbooks, giving us a better grasp of history as it was lived by people at the time. One of those people, Daniel Shays, would no doubt be grateful.

FOR FURTHER READING

The best brief overview of the issues at the heart of this essay is Ronald Formisano, "Teaching Shays/The Regulation: Historiographical Problems as Tools for Learning," *Uncommon Sense* 106 (Winter 1998): 24–35. Formisano underscores the political and intellectual importance of referring to the uprising of 1786–87 as the "Massachusetts Regulation" rather than "Shays's Rebellion," not only to challenge the long-standing historical overemphasis on Daniel Shays as the central ringleader but, more important, to locate the Massachusetts movement within a larger pattern of populist protests that arose elsewhere in the Revolutionary Era.

The first book-length treatment of the events discussed here is George Richards Minot, *The History of the Insurrections in Massachusetts in the Year Seventeen Hundred and Eighty-six, and the Rebellion Consequent Thereon* (Worcester, Mass., 1788). Although Minot was by no means sympathetic to the armed resistance of the Massachusetts farmers, he did include in his book verbatim versions of their petitions and grievances, and for that reason it serves a useful documentary, if not explanatory, function. In the latter part of the nineteenth century, New England experienced an effusion of town and county histories that dealt with the Revolutionary Era, some of which include the text of documents related to the regulation. Among the most useful are Samuel Adams Drake, *History of Middlesex County, Massachusetts . . .* (Boston, 1880); James Russell Trumbull, *History of Northampton Massachusetts from Its Settlement in 1654* (Northampton, Mass., 1898); and C. O. Parmenter, *History of Pelham, Mass., from 1738 to 1898 . . .* (Amherst, Mass., 1898). The most significant repositories for primary source material dealing with the Massachusetts Regulation are the Massachusetts Historical Society and the American Antiquarian Society.

In the 1950s the Massachusetts Regulation received scholarly (and generally sympathetic) treatment in Robert J. Taylor, *Western Massachusetts in the Revolution* (Providence, R.I., 1954), and Robert A. Feer, "Shays's Rebellion" (Ph.D. diss., Harvard University, 1958; rpt., 1989). Feer's work remained the standard book-length study for over twenty years until the appearance of David Szatmary, *Shays' Rebellion: The Making of an Agrarian Insurrection* (Amherst, Mass., 1980), which emphasizes the "chain of debt" that pitted small farmers against mercantile elites;

and Leonard Richards, *Shays's Rebellion: The American Revolution's Final Battle* (Philadelphia, 2002), which takes account of the growing economic crisis and political corruption but also looks more closely at local leadership and family ties in the "banner towns" that played a major part in the insurgent movement. Coming in between these two books was a collection of essays dealing extensively with economic, political, and even religious issues: Robert A. Gross, ed., *In Debt to Shays: The Bicentennial of an Agrarian Rebellion* (Charlottesville, Va., 1993). Books that give a broader historical context for two counties at the center of the insurrection are Gregory H. Nobles, *Divisions Throughout the Whole: Politics and Society in Hampshire County, Massachusetts, 1740–1775* (New York, 1983), and John Brooke, *The Heart of the Commonwealth: Society and Culture in Worcester County, Massachusetts, 1713–1861* (New York, 1989). Ray Raphael, *First American Revolution: Before Lexington and Concord* (New York, 2002), also provides the pre-Revolutionary political background for the post-Revolutionary patterns of protest discussed in this essay. Recent works that discuss the connection between the deliberations at the Constitutional Convention in 1787 and the rural protest movements of the 1780s, including the Massachusetts Regulation, are Woody Holton, *Unruly Americans and the Origins of the Constitution* (New York, 2007), and Richard Beeman, *Plain, Honest Men: The Making of the American Constitution* (New York, 2009).

CHAPTER FOURTEEN

William Findley, David Bradford, and the Pennsylvania Regulation of 1794

Terry Bouton

On August 1, 1794, two men faced off at a political crossroads. Physically they stood at different points, separated by thirty miles. But in terms of life crossroads—and a crossroads for the new nation—they had arrived at the same place, at the same moment. Each wrestled with a question about democracy: In a republic, how far could ordinary people go to oppose government policies they saw as oppressive? The answers they gave would help define the kind of democracy that emerged from the American Revolution.

The first man, a lawyer named David Bradford, sat atop his horse beneath the hot August sun on a road near the frontier town of Pittsburgh, watching lines of militia march by. Men clogged the road. They had flooded in from every direction, all heading to nearby Braddock's Field. Grouped by battalions, they formed a parade that one observer said stretched "upward of two and one half miles long." Bradford squinted in the glare, his brown eyes narrowing, and guessed at the numbers. Some said that by "the space of ground they took up there might be between 5 & 6 thousand." Others said 7,000 or 8,000 or even more. The best estimate may have come from the *Pittsburgh Gazette,* which placed the number at around 9,000 men: 5,400 marching at that moment, another 1,500 that arrived later in the day, and an additional 2,000 that marched halfway to Pittsburgh, only to return home when they received a muddled order suggesting the meeting had been called off. None of these figures included the many women who had accompanied their fathers, husbands, sons, and brothers on the march. Whatever the actual number, it was an astounding assembly.

It was also a broad cross-section of western society. There were landless farmers and laborers, sturdy landowning yeomen, and members of the region's gentry. As one observer noted, it was not "an inconsiderable mob" of the poor and ignorant; rather, "they are a respectable & powerful combination" composed of "some of the most respectable people in the country."

All of these people marched to protest the new federal government that they believed was acting against the ideals of the American Revolution. They were convinced that the federal government was undermining democracy through policies that benefited "moneyed men" at the expense of ordinary, hardworking Americans like themselves. They were especially angry about the financial policies put in place by Treasury Secretary Alexander Hamilton. They saw Hamilton as rewarding bankers and war debt speculators and punishing ordinary people by limiting currency and credit and enacting new taxes, including an excise tax on distilled spirits. The marchers wanted Hamilton's entire program rolled back and new policies put in place that limited speculation, taxed the wealthy, and made it easier for ordinary people to acquire the money and credit they needed to run their farms and businesses. These new policies, they said, would protect democracy and restore the Revolution.

Although Bradford shared these goals, he also hoped this march would pave the way for western secession and independence. He had become convinced that the existing political system—either in Pennsylvania or in the United States—was so corrupt and the deck so stacked in favor of "aristocracy" that there was no alternative but to break away. Consequently, he had helped organize this march of "brave sons of war," hoping to set the stage for a new independent government that would be more responsive to the wishes of "the people." This goal helps explain the choice of Braddock's Field for the meeting: it was near the federal armory at Fort Pitt, which Bradford thought could be raided for the arms needed to counter any federal force that might be sent against them.

The prospect of western secession—and the march itself—terrified the second man at this political crossroads: a politician named William Findley. Findley, who lived near Greensburgh, Pennsylvania, about thirty miles east of Pittsburgh, had been a representative in the state assembly for the past decade and now served as a congressman from western Pennsylvania. He shared Bradford's concern about the lack of democracy and policies favoring the wealthy. For the last decade he had fought against the growing concentration of wealth and power on the floor of the assembly and in Congress. Unlike Bradford, however, Findley still had faith that change could happen through the existing political system.

Moreover, he thought this armed march was imperiling the cause of democracy. Findley had seen this showdown coming for months—and even years. He had long cautioned against rising to take the bait that he believed Alexander Hamilton and his Federalist allies had thrown out to prompt just such an armed protest. Findley believed this was a setup. He was convinced that, by marching with guns and clubs, westerners were undercutting their cause. Rather than saving democracy, they were playing right into Hamilton's attempts to further scale it back.

Instead of marching, Findley urged westerners—and all ordinary people in the new United States—to mobilize at the ballot box to wrest power from the Federalists. Organizing to win elections was the key to saving democracy, he believed. Ordinary people needed to work within the political system to reform it, rather than trying to rail against it or break away from it. Federalist politicians needed jettisoning, he believed, not the whole federal system.

These were the choices for Bradford and Findley: Was democracy primarily about voting? Or did citizens have broader rights of protest and even rebellion? If both strategies were permissible, which was more effective for getting change, mass protest or electoral politics?

Years earlier neither Findley nor Bradford had viewed such questions as either/or propositions. Both men had once believed that ordinary people needed to combine voting and protest to be effective. If anything, it was Findley rather than Bradford who had been the greater champion of "the people" and of expanding the bounds of popular democracy.

Of the two, Findley certainly looked more ordinary. By 1794 he was in his mid-fifties. He had a long-weathered face, small sad eyes, and thick bushy eyebrows. His shoulder-length brown hair was graying, unruly, and thinning slightly on top, receding enough to reveal a brow creased with furrows. His clothes were decent but not the garments of a gentleman.

By comparison, Bradford projected genteel airs. In his mid-thirties, he cut something less than a dashing figure. His face was wide, and his unusually broad forehead was framed by dark, receding hair and punctuated by thick lips and a long, sharp nose. His clothes were not flashy but were made from expensive material, and they were well tailored. Not especially attractive, he at least dressed the part of the local gentry.

The two men had also started out life on different ends of the social spectrum. Findley's average looks mirrored his humble origins. Born in the north of Ireland, he was trained as a weaver. He had arrived in Pennsylvania at the end of the French and Indian War and plied his trade successfully enough to buy some land to farm on the side. When war with Britain broke out, Findley joined the Cumberland County militia, entering as a private and rising to the rank of captain by war's end. In 1784 he was elected to the Pennsylvania General Assembly as a representative from the new western county of Westmoreland. In the assembly Findley displayed skill as a political tactician: steering reform bills through the legislature; mobilizing floor fights against laws he opposed; working the boardinghouse backrooms, tavern counters, and coffeehouses where political deals were cut; and trying to steer public opinion by writing newspaper editorials and pamphlets. That success led his constituents to elect him in 1791 to the U.S. Congress, where he emerged as a strong critic of Federalist policies.

In the assembly and in Congress, Findley was a tireless advocate for rights and interests of "the people" and of small farmers in particular. Findley liked to say that democracy belonged to people like him—ordinary men of little fortune. The Revolution, he said, was about equality and uplifting ordinary folk, not about advancing the "principles of united avarice" or allowing the affluent to "engross all the wealth, power, and influence of the state." "No man has a greater claim of special privilege for his £100,000," he declared once on the assembly floor, "than I have for my £5."[1]

Findley's biggest worry was that the economic inequality that Revolutionary leaders were creating was a threat to the democratic republic. The American Revolution had been forged by people—elite and ordinary alike—who viewed concentrations of economic power as a threat to liberty as great as concentrations of political power. Drawing on history, such Revolutionaries feared that wealthy men might use their affluence to buy power and subvert the republic—just as they had done to Greek and Roman republics. Findley worried that Revolutionary leaders were repeating this pattern by working to promote the interests of "congregated wealth." Such wealth, he declared, "like a snowball perpetually rolled . . . must continually increase its dimensions and influence." In the end, he predicted, "democracy must fall before it."[2]

While Findley was making a name for himself as a defender of democracy, David Bradford had been building his legal career. Born in Maryland, Bradford had taken to the law and eventually set up practice in a backcountry area claimed by both Virginia and Pennsylvania. He quickly earned both wealth and respect. While under the jurisdiction of Virginia, he served in its colonial assembly. When a border resolution made his land part of Pennsylvania, he became a deputy attorney general of his new state's southwestern corner. His prosperous practice allowed him to build an elegant two-story stone house in the town of Washington. He outfitted it with the trappings of gentility, including a grand mahogany staircase and finely crafted wood paneling.

Politically, the biggest difference between the two was over ratification of the federal Constitution. Findley had led the fight against ratification in Pennsylvania, viewing the Constitution as an antidemocratic, aristocratic document that would promote the interests of moneyed men at the expense of ordinary folk. This wasn't paranoia: the Constitution's architects had indeed envisioned the new national government as creating what Virginian Edmund Randolph called a "stronger barrier against democracy." As Alexander Hamilton put it, this less democratic government would protect the interests of "the rich and well born" against "the mass of the people." However much Bradford feared the Constitution's antidemocratic provisions, he was more swayed by promises that it would help the region by opening trade down the Mississippi River and defeating Indians in the Ohio Valley. Prior to the 1794 march on Pittsburgh, Bradford was probably best known in the region as the leading advocate of opening the Mississippi. He had made it a central plank of a "Patriot Convention" he helped organize in 1787. Since he believed that a stronger national government was the key to the Mississippi, his support for the Constitution makes sense.[3]

No matter why Bradford supported ratification, he later joined Findley in believing that the powers of government at both the national and the state levels were being used to undermine democracy. At the state level, Bradford and Findley had seen leading politicians enact policy after policy that seemed to punish ordinary people to bolster the power of the elite. During the 1780s state leaders had eliminated paper money, which was the primary medium of exchange, especially in the backcountry, where gold and silver coins were always scarce. They had killed a government loan office that had offered long-term low-cost credit to small farmers and craftsmen—and replaced it with a private bank that offered loans only to merchants and land speculators. The state government had adopted a plan to repay the Revolutionary War debt that taxed the soldiers and farmers who had fought and supplied the war effort so that wealthy men who had speculated in once-worthless war bonds and IOUs could make a financial killing. Those new taxes were often to be paid in gold and silver. All of these policies stripped the countryside of cash and left thousands of farmers unable to pay debts, mortgages, or taxes. The result was waves of sheriff's auctions that swept the state, a floodtide of misery that, in Findley's home county, foreclosed about 40 percent of the taxable population.

At the same time that ordinary Pennsylvanians were losing cows, tools, and farmland at auction, state leaders were making it increasingly hard for them or their children to acquire new land. Officials at the land office gave preferential treatment to big speculators (including themselves). Revenue officials refused to prosecute large speculators who had not paid their taxes at the same time that they pushed to foreclose ordinary taxpayers. Judges ruled in favor of wealthy speculators over settlers in nearly every land conflict. In 1792 the state supreme court turned a clear anti-land-speculation law into a pro-speculator one. The law had put caps on the amount of land anyone could purchase to limit speculation. Defying the law's stated objectives, however, the supreme court ruled that the limits applied only to small farmers and that wealthy speculators could buy as much land as they could afford (which, in practice, meant a great deal of land, since state officials permitted speculators to skirt payment rules and buy vast tracts by putting down only a small fraction of the purchase price).

Both Findley and Bradford saw this same pattern of pro-speculator, pro-affluent policies repeating at the federal level. Their biggest concern was the implementation of Alexander Hamilton's financial plans, which magnified the problems inherent in state policies. From their perspective, Hamiltonian finance promised to exacerbate the profound scarcity of money and credit. It offered no new paper money and no new government loans for small farmers. Instead, Hamilton created a new private national bank that looked as if it would only concentrate wealth and power even more. Hamilton's program also rewarded war debt speculators by paying full face value for IOUs they had bought at pennies on the dollar, and like the state plans, it funded that expenditure with new taxes.

Then there was the tax on distilled spirits, which westerners found particularly insulting. In the countryside, where coins were especially scarce, whiskey (which was easier and cheaper to transport than corn or grain) had become a form of money. To westerners, whiskey barter was already a potent reminder of failed economic policies. Now national leaders were deepening the insult and injury by taxing the only form of money they had left.

Findley and Bradford were united in their belief that ordinary people needed to stand against the attempts of state and national leaders to undermine the kind of economic equality that they believed was needed to sustain democracy. As Findley put it, the time had come for ordinary Americans to compel their leaders to make government and society more "democratical." They needed to change things so that "every man feels his own importance and asserts his privileges" in creating "a well regulated republican government." Findley believed that "the body of the people" working to "regulate" government was the only way to "secure the native dignity and equal rights of the citizens and provide for their happiness."[4]

This language of "regulation" had become part of the lexicon of the Revolution, used by those who felt that "the people" had the right to "regulate" unresponsive governments. The term had been used by insurgent farmers in

North Carolina in a 1768–71 uprising to redress similar ills: a cash scarcity, heavy specie taxes, a flurry of lawsuits for unpaid debts and taxes, courts favoring large land speculators, and rampant government "corruption" benefiting the wealthy and powerful. That regulation had ended with armed confrontation and bloodshed; the Regulators had gone down in defeat. More recently, in 1786, "regulation" had been used by Massachusetts farmers who were facing nearly identical problems as postwar Pennsylvanians. These Massachusetts Regulators, as some called themselves (they were dubbed dismissively as "Shays's Rebels" by their opponents), had petitioned, lobbied, voted, and organized against policies that they thought bankrupted "the people" to reward the affluent. When state leaders stymied those electoral efforts, Massachusetts Regulators turned to physical protests, which ended, once again, with arms and bloodshed. By invoking the term "regulation," Findley was tying resistance in Pennsylvania (and across the new nation) to this long-standing tradition of popular opposition.

Yet Findley was also clear that the real potential of regulation lay in electoral politics, not protests or armed conflict that, he believed, were doomed to fail. Findley remained convinced that the most powerful tool of the new democracy—voting—was the only real way to obtain meaningful change. Thus, when he cited the Massachusetts example, Findley downplayed the physical protest and focused instead on electoral organization, like the Massachusetts tradition of frequent and open town meetings, which encouraged participation in electoral politics. For him, the true legacy of "regulation" was building political institutions and mobilizing the masses to vote.

Findley's faith was based on a seeming paradox of the Revolution: although the Revolution had expanded voting rights, few people actually went to the polls. For example, in Pennsylvania—where, as a result of the Revolution, more than 90 percent of adult men could vote—turnout was usually only 20 to 30 percent of eligible voters, and even lower in national elections. Findley believed that if the majority of Americans who opposed Federalist policies were organized to vote, then they could eventually get whatever change they wanted.

Furthermore, by doing so—by protecting the interests of ordinary people against powerful "moneyed men"—they would save democracy. As Findley put it, the public needed to wake up and do its "duty to watch over the administration" by voting. "Unless people exercise this constitutional watchfulness" and exert themselves at the polls, he said, their rights would continue to be "be a dead letter." The "monied interest" would continue to use "the influence of over-grown wealth at our elections" to win power and enact "a change of politics favourable to aristocracy and monarchy."[5]

Findley wasn't alone in believing that the time had come to organize to take political power. Throughout western Pennsylvania and in various places across the new nation, many ordinary people began forming new democratic societies in a similar attempt to regulate their government. Those societies went by many names. In western Pennsylvania alone, there was the Association, the Society of United Freemen, the Republican Society of the Yough (a reference to the Youghiogheny River that runs through southwestern Pennsylvania), the General Committee, and numerous Patriotic Societies. Bradford had helped organize both a regional Patriotic Convention and the Democratic Society of Washington County, for which he served as vice president. Many of these societies drafted formal constitutions calling on members to regulate the "audacious and corrupt administrations" and to reverse the current situation where "the people" were "but the shadow of a name" in "their own governments." Those pronouncements led one observer to say that they were "more democratic" than any institution he had ever seen.[6]

Although most of these societies in western Pennsylvania were formed independently, in the early 1790s, they began to link their efforts. Their constitutions spoke of forming a "cordial union of the people west of the Allegheny Mountains" and overcoming the "intestine divisions among our citizens here." They called for the creation of "committees of correspondence" to "form a speedy communication between ourselves" and to ensure that resistance was "carried out with regularity and concert." If needed, they wanted to be able to instantly "call together either [a] general meeting of the people in their respective counties or [a] conference of the several committees."

More than this, the societies were intent on spreading their model of organization and recruiting a nationwide network of "the people." Westerners used their committees of correspondence to try to connect their efforts with the rest of Pennsylvania and with people "in other parts of the United States." That effort gained momentum when democratic societies began forming in other states starting in 1793. Indeed, on the eve of the militia march, western Pennsylvanians were corresponding with democratic societies in western Maryland, Virginia, and Kentucky—a remarkable feat given organizing problems of the past.[7]

Although this was exactly the kind of organizing Findley advocated, he was worried, because voting was only part of what many of the new democratic societies were about. While democratic societies in eastern towns and cities focused on electoral reform, most of the inland and frontier societies also organized resistance efforts. Findley feared that such protest, especially violence, would cause Federalists to crack down on political organization of any kind—even peaceful efforts focused on voting.

This was the biggest difference between Findley and Bradford: as Findley moved further away from direct action protest, Bradford moved to embrace it. The two men identified the same problems facing the nation and shared the same ideas about a solution. But they disagreed sharply over how to get there. Put differently, Findley and Bradford shared a commitment to regulation, but they were divided over exactly how "the people" should regulate their government. Findley wanted to work through the existing system. Bradford, who eventually grew frustrated at the constant political losses and the slow pace of reform, shifted his focus from voting to direct action protest.

Indeed, by 1794, Bradford had amassed an impressive résumé of resistance. For example, the Patriotic Convention that Bradford had organized in 1787 had endorsed protest along with policy changes. It issued the familiar calls to solve the cash and credit scarcity by insisting that the government issue paper money, offer low-cost loans, and limit the payout to war debt speculators. But the convention also called for a boycott to highlight the cash scarcity, urging farmers to refuse trading with Fort Pitt until the army paid farmers in gold and silver, rather than store credit at the fort's commissary.

With the passage of Hamiltonian finance—and the failure of Federalists to open the Mississippi River to trade—Bradford's organizing intensified. Perhaps feeling betrayed after giving his support to ratification, he seemed less willing to compromise and more intent on taking action. He wasn't alone: all the meetings and organizations he was involved with adopted a similar stance. For example, the 1791 multicounty meeting that Bradford had helped to organize called for citizens to take every "legal measure that may obstruct the operation of the law." Although the meeting specified only shunning excise tax collectors "with the contempt they deserve" (like the Stamp Act collectors in 1765), its words no doubt helped inspire the waves of extralegal protest that followed.[8]

Follow they did, with a sharp increase in violent attacks on public officials tasked with upholding the law. Tax collectors, constables, judges, jail keepers, and surveyors working for land speculators all came in for their share of abuse. Federal excise collectors were assaulted by people in disguises or with blackened faces, and sometimes by undisguised crowds as large as 150 strong. Most crowds offered collectors the chance to avoid punishment by resigning their commissions. If they refused, pain followed. One group tarred and feathered an excise collector, cut off his hair, and took his horse; when local authorities sent a constable to make arrests, a crowd whipped the constable, then tarred and feathered him, tied him up blindfolded, and left him in the woods for five hours. Another crowd pulled a collector from his bed, marched him several miles, stripped him naked, and burned his clothes; then they tarred and feathered him and tied him to a tree. A different

This drawing of the imagined execution of an excise collector, thought to have been done by a participant in the 1794 uprising, reveals the emphasis placed on physical protest by many ordinary westerners. The excise man is chased by farmers who want to tar and feather him, and later is killed by an "evil genius" who hooks him through the nose and hangs him from a tree. "The people" then blow up the corpse by exploding a cask of whiskey beneath the gallows.

crowd did the same thing to a collector, except, rather than tie him to a tree, they branded him with a hot fireplace poker. One crowd burned a collector's barn; another torched a collector's house.

There were also less violent protests, like closing area roads to halt property foreclosures. To prevent sheriffs and constables from holding foreclosure auctions or hauling away debtors' property, people across Pennsylvania began shutting down roadways. In some places people built six-foot-high fences that stretched fifty feet across the highway. Others felled trees across roads or hauled timber into log piles that sometimes measured thirty feet wide and forty feet long. Sometimes they dug eight-foot-wide and five-foot-deep ditches in the road, imposing enough to halt any wagon or coach. One group in the southeastern county of Chester shoveled enough dirt out of the main highway to Philadelphia to create an impassable crater measuring fifty feet in circumference and seven feet deep. People in two other eastern counties flooded roads by carving out canals that redirected streams and rivers to flow across the highway. Along a narrow passage that cut through the western frontier, people dug into a hillside, causing an avalanche of earth and rocks. In the central county of Cumberland, farmers dumped fifteen wagon-loads of manure on a highway, creating a four-foot-high wall of stink.

Although this tradition of closing roads predated the enactment of Hamilton's financial program, the protests often overlapped with organizing against Hamiltonian measures. For example, several of the delegates to the 1791 and 1792 multicounty conferences against Hamilton's program participated in those road closings—including David Bradford, who was arrested for creating a barricade of heavy stones, decaying logs, and scrub brush on a main route in Washington County. Bradford also protested by refusing to do his job as county road supervisor to clear roadways when ordered. For his resistance, Bradford was hauled into court in 1791 and fined along with every other road supervisor in the county.

For Findley, these kinds of protests were too much—particularly the ones involving violence. He knew that Federalists would connect them to the democratic societies, which they would try to discredit or outlaw. Many Federalists in the Washington administration, alarmed by the French Revolution, considered any political organizing in opposition to their policies to be a threat. Those fears deepened when officers in the democratic societies, like David Bradford, sometimes adopted the practice of French revolutionaries and signed correspondence with the title "Citizen." Some Federalists, like Alexander Hamilton, worried about a French-style revolution in America and, consequently, viewed opposition of nearly any kind to be sedition or treason.

Findley worried, in particular, that Federalists would target western Pennsylvania for retribution. In 1792 he started hearing rumors that Hamilton "wishes to make us examples" and enforce tax collection in western Pennsylvania by any means necessary. "The scene of operation will be Washington County," he declared, where Hamilton would work "either to subdue Washington County or else to provoke them to such conduct as will destroy their character in the public opinion." Now, more than ever, Findley wanted his constituents to avoid anything inflammatory so they could evade Hamilton's trap. Instead, they were about to march right into it.[9]

∿

That march on August 1, where as many as nine thousand men assembled on Braddock's Field, had been triggered by exactly the chain of events that Findley feared. In July 1794, as a part of Hamilton's crackdown on Washington County, a federal marshal arrived to deliver a mass of warrants that ordered distillers who had not paid their excise taxes to appear in a Philadelphia courtroom. On July 16 a militia company associated with a democratic society in Washington County had retaliated by marching to the home of an excise collector to demand that he renounce his commission—just as patriots before the Revolutionary War had once demanded the resignations of British tax collectors.

That collector, John Neville, was one of the wealthiest men in the western counties, who, in the last few years, had become one of the most reviled. A former politician who had once denounced Hamilton's policies, Neville had made a political about-face when Hamilton had offered him the position of excise collector. Neville used his influence to effectively monopolize the western whiskey trade and grew so prosperous that he built a new luxurious estate he called Bower Hill, which he filled with imported finery from Europe. Neville lived here in frontier elegance with eighteen slaves waiting on him. Reclining in one of his many Windsor chairs, he stopped talking as he once had about the virtues of "the people." Now he spoke only of his neighbors as "the rabble."

Neville's newfound unpopularity no doubt helped fuel the conflict. At Bower Hill the militiamen shouted for Neville to come out. He yelled back that the militia should stand off. Moments later Neville fired his gun into the crowd. Soon afterward his slaves "fired out of their cabins upon our backs, and shot several," as one militiaman recalled. By the time the shooting ended, one of the militiamen lay dead.[10]

The following day between five hundred and seven hundred militiamen— led by officers, justices of the peace, and, as one witness put it, the "most respectable characters in the county"—returned to demand Neville's resignation. Despite the death the previous day, the militiamen were restrained. They promised Neville that "no harm should be done to his person or property" if he resigned peacefully. They even stopped in midmarch to debate the wording of the resignation. Some of them worried that the statement on taxes made it seem like they opposed all taxation. Wanting to make sure their intentions were clear, they started a formal debate—in the middle of the road. After considerable back-and-forth, they voted to add the phrase "the people did not refuse to pay a proportional part of the revenue" to make it clear that they did not want to throw off the war debt altogether; they just did not want to pay a regressive tax that would go to funding an enormous windfall for speculators. The matter settled, the men re-formed their ranks and continued the march, no doubt fully expecting Neville to resign his commission peacefully

Neville, however, had no intention of surrendering. He had enlisted eleven soldiers from nearby Fort Pitt to defend his home. The two sides negotiated, and when they could not reach an agreement, the shooting started. They traded volleys for the better part of an hour, when suddenly the soldiers in the house stopped shooting. The militia captain ordered his men to silence their weapons. A voice called out from inside the house. Thinking it was a call for a cease-fire to surrender, the militia captain stepped out from behind a tree to negotiate. A shot rang out from inside the house. The militia captain dropped, perhaps dead before he hit the ground. Outraged, the militiamen opened up on the house. Other men began setting fire to Bower Hill, aiming to torch the whole estate, sparing only a few buildings that the collector's slaves had begged them to leave alone. The battle ended with the soldiers surrendering and being allowed to return unharmed to Fort Pitt. They left amid curses from the militiamen for refusing to surrender when so badly outnumbered.[11]

The following weeks saw a flurry of organization and increasing talk about independence. Secession was not a new goal in the region. Since the formation of the western counties, there had been plans for independence. Most recently, in the early 1780s, Bradford had joined neighbors in calling for the western counties to be considered a separate state. Those calls had largely been made peacefully, usually through petitions, and they had subsided when westerners tried to work through the Pennsylvania government to solve their problems.

These new calls for secession appeared far more ambitious and serious. Statehood was the least of the objectives, as many people, like Bradford, hinted that they wanted to break from the new nation altogether. Moreover, Bradford and others sought independence through the threat of armed resistance. Having lost faith in the state and national governments, they believed petitions and legislative appeals were a waste of time. A show of force would get the federal government to back down, or it would lead westerners to go it alone.

Secession was clearly on the mind of many of those who marched to Braddock's Field. That goal was reflected in a new flag they carried, with six stripes that represented potential breakaway counties from western Pennsylvania and northwestern Virginia. To bolster the cause, Bradford's plans initially included a raid on the federal armory at Fort Pitt. But he scrapped the idea when he learned that the weapons were intended for fighting Indians in the Ohio Valley. Instead, the march served primarily as a display of popular discontent and set the stage for more regionwide meetings about secession.

The drama of those meetings heightened significantly when President Washington issued a proclamation on August 7, calling for militia to mobilize against the western insurgency. When westerners elected delegates to represent them at the first of those meetings on August 14, they were no longer just deciding on secession. When those delegates (260 of them) met at Parkinson's Ferry, about twenty miles southeast of Pittsburgh, it would be a vote for war or peace.

The debate at Parkinson's Ferry centered on all the ways that westerners believed the Revolution had been betrayed. Of course, delegates cited the excise tax. But their concerns were much larger. They explained that the underlying issue was how the new governments denied "industrious men of a middle and low class an equal privilege with those of the rich." They condemned policies that promoted the "engrossing of large quantities of land in the state by individuals." They blasted the judges for constantly ruling in favor of land companies over settlers. They called for replacing the excise with a "direct tax on real property" (by which they meant speculative land-holdings) that would keep "men of wealth from engrossing lands profusely." They complained about "the use of [state-appointed] judges in courts" rather than elected justices of the peace—an antidemocratic change made by the Federalist-drafted Pennsylvania Constitution of 1790 (which had replaced the far more democratic 1776 state constitution). They also denounced "the high salaries of officers both in the general and state governments." Some delegates reported that "the people" were "outrageous to do something" about problems like "the costs on the suits before justices" and "court expense" from all the cases for unpaid debts and taxes. These people believed their governments were working against the kind of economic equality that "ought to be the true object of a republican government."[12]

The decision for war or peace remained in doubt at Parkinson's Ferry. Bradford urged westerners to stand their ground and fight for independence. In what one observer called "a violent speech," he made the case "for open resistance, stating the practicability of it." Bradford declared that western forces could "easily defeat" this small army, which he said would have no stomach for battle.[13]

Meanwhile, Findley attended the meeting to urge submission. Findley's call against violence was echoed by other prominent westerners. Among them was Herman Husband, a leader of the North Carolina Regulation, who had fled to Pennsylvania after a violent showdown that eventually led to the hanging of several of his compatriots.

When neither side carried the day, another meeting was set for August 28, with a committee of sixty appointed to decide the matter. The tensions at that meeting would be particularly acute: federal negotiators were demanding a unanimous 60–0 vote for submission to halt the federal army. Ultimately, the prospect of actual fighting, and the cautioning of men like Findley and Husband, won the majority of votes. Twenty-three delegates voted for war and thirty-four to submit, the rest abstaining. But since the vote was not unanimous, the army would march anyway.

Even with an army approaching, many westerners continued to resist. Some defiant communities raised liberty poles to greet the soldiers. Some townships refused to sign submission pledges. In other places people signed the pledge but changed the wording to make it clear they were not surrendering their right to protest or speak their minds.

There were shows of support from counties farther east as well. Some Pennsylvanians in every county refused to muster for the militias called out to march against westerners. In several central Pennsylvania counties, whole communities raised liberty poles for what they saw as a shared defense of democracy. For example, in Franklin County, five hundred men paraded alongside a wagon filled with timber in a militia battalion of equals, saying "they had not officers they were all as one" and would "set up the pole if the Devil stood at the door."

At the town of Derrs in Northumberland County, a crowd of between two and three hundred people (including the county sheriff) made sure that their defense of democracy was democratic by voting on *everything*: whether to raise a pole, what the flag attached to the pole should say (they agreed on "Liberty, Equality of Rights, a Change of Ministry, and no Excise"), who should go to the woodland to cut down a tree, and who would stay and dig so they could plant the pole. They voted on who would go door to door to get people to sign a petition and who would ride to neighboring townships to get the "support of the people." When a county judge came out to read them the riot act (literally), the men proclaimed that they were an orderly assembly following the rule of law. One man shouted that they were not in opposition to the government and that they were raising a pole to support "*Liberty and Government*" for "the people" against the "land jobbers." As soon as he finished speaking, "immediately the whole company huzzaed for *Liberty and Government*." In their minds, they were not rebels; they saw themselves as the defenders of democracy, order, and good government.

Despite those shared ideals, these like-minded Pennsylvanians remained fragmented. Westerners divided between submission and resistance, cooling the push for war and independence. While a handful of settlements in the central counties offered pledges of support for western insurgents, no one actually marched west. Most of the resistance in the east remained localized and pacifist. People refused to muster, crafted petitions against the march, hoisted liberty poles, and gave hard stares to the federal army that eventually marched through their neighborhoods. There was no armed resistance. Nor was there any concerted attempt to organize county or statewide resistance.

When it became clear that the opposition was fractured, Bradford fled. The Washington administration had exempted him from the general amnesty for westerners. Facing arrest for treason and a possible hanging, he escaped down the Ohio River, floated down the Mississippi, and landed in Spanish Louisiana. Bradford was not alone in fleeing in the face of defeat. As many as two thousand westerners also headed west and south, in search of a new start on lands that would become the states of Ohio and Kentucky.

In exile in Louisiana, Bradford remained somewhat unrepentant, but he was a changed man. In particular, his broad notions of democracy narrowed. Once a founding member of the Washington County antislavery society, he bought a cotton plantation in Louisiana and became a large slaveholder. His 1794 fight to defend democracy against "moneyed men" by negating federal laws and possibly seceding from the state or union slowly transformed into a push for "states' rights" and a call to nullify federal laws that threatened the institution of slavery. Bradford's descendants completed the transformation. One of his sons would marry the sister of Jefferson Davis, the future president of the Confederacy. His children and grandchildren would consider themselves "Southern Patriots," and long after the Civil War, they would continue to espouse the genteel white supremacy of the Lost Cause.[14]

Defeat transformed Findley as well. He remained in Congress and eventually earned the honorary title of "Father of the House" for being its longest-serving member. He was a loyal Jeffersonian and continued to support popular causes, especially those that pitted the interests of "the people" against those of "the moneyed men." But Findley was a different politician than before.

In particular, he now denounced resistance as a political strategy. Angered that mass protest had destroyed a promising political movement (and had led Federalists to accuse him of being an accomplice of treason), he became one of its most vocal opponents. "Forcible opposition," he wrote in 1796, never moved "those who administer government . . . to change their measures." It only hardened positions and led to "hostility and bloodshed." Direct action was only for those rare moments when it was "morally right"— "such as the opposition of the colonies to the stamp and tea acts." To Findley, 1794 was not one of those moments, no matter how much it might embody the spirit of 1776.

Findley went even further, though: he wrote a book about the "Insurrection" that denied any connection between resistance efforts and the kind of reform he was tying to achieve. As he framed it, the 1794 protest was only about a whiskey tax, which had offended the cultural sensibilities and drinking habits of Scots-Irish backwoodsmen. It was not about ideology or the threats that Federalist policies posed to democracy and equality. He even said it was not about the funding system, aside from the excise tax. Instead, Findley declared that the protest was little more than "an unbridled gust of passion" on the part of the "uninformed."[15]

Of course, this was a far cry from what had really happened. From start to finish, the protesters had said that they were protecting the Revolution's democratic inheritance. They had blasted the government's "unjust and oppressive" redistribution of wealth from ordinary citizens to the affluent. They had condemned the "insulting" provisions to enrich war debt speculators by taxing the "laborious and poorer class," whose only form of money was the whiskey they distilled. They had denounced the "evil" of creating the Bank of the United States and turning over financial authority to a few wealthy private men. All these policies, they had said, would "bring immediate distress and ruin" to a countryside populated with indebted farmers still suffering from the "scarcity of a circulating medium." Moreover, they said the excise and all these policies undermined democracy and liberty by further concentrating wealth and power. In short, their arguments were exactly the same ones Findley had made.[16]

Seen broadly, Findley's self-serving rewrite of the protest's history is not so unusual. He was hardly the first or last reformer to change his or her story when a resistance movement blew up. Findley joins a long list of those who, when things went bad, pointed fingers at former colleagues and recast themselves as the voice of reason in a stark morality tale about tactical choices. That list is a testament to the tensions within any social movement: between electoral strategies and protest, between working within the system and working against it from outside, and all the other inevitable conflicts between like-minded reformers over the best way to attain their shared vision of change.

In the end, Findley ensured that the events of 1794 would be remembered as Alexander Hamilton intended when he coined the term "whiskey insurrection." Hamilton used the dismissive title "Whiskey" to convince Americans that what had driven western Pennsylvanians to rise up had nothing to do with the discontent with the narrowing of democracy or policies that favored the affluent. Findley's book did that and more. He divorced the 1794 uprising from the larger story of the Revolution and the era's popular regulations, thereby making it seem like a peculiar, isolated tragedy. In short, it may have been Hamilton's title, but Findley provided the story. As a result, we are left with an odd historical memory of 1794: the distortions of "history as written by the winners" compounded by history written by one member of the losing side.

Perhaps if Findley had waited longer before writing his account, America's public memory of the 1794 uprising might be different. Free from accusations of treason and the heat of battle, Findley might have offered a more sober memoir. He might also have tempered his critique of mass protest. After all, although the protest failed in its immediate objectives, its suppression by federal troops exposed the kind of heavy-handed approach to governing that began to turn public opinion against the Federalists. Ironically, as

Federalists did exactly what Findley feared by cracking down on democratic societies and trying to outlaw dissent through measures like the Alien and Sedition Acts, they helped to spur political organization rather than stifle it.

Indeed, the death knell of Federalist power in Pennsylvania was the suppression of another armed popular uprising: a regulation movement in 1798-99 in the state's eastern counties that Federalists would dub "Fries Rebellion." Popular anger following a second march of federal troops into Pennsylvania produced a surge in voter turnout that transformed many once-reliable Federalist counties into supporters of Thomas Jefferson in the election of 1800. With that election, Pennsylvanians finally started voting in large numbers for political leaders who openly espoused the cause of reform and championing "the people" instead of "the moneyed men." Findley and his Jeffersonian colleagues didn't deliver on all (or even many) of their promises. Nevertheless, the popular reforms they actually achieved owed at least something to the protests that Findley had once reviled.

That said, something was lost by the defeat of this regulation. The defeat helped confine democracy to forms of political self-expression that did not overtly threaten elite interests. The Revolution had convinced many ordinary Pennsylvanians—and common folk across the colonies—that they had a right to monitor government, to shape policy, and to regulate government if they believed their leaders were not responding to the popular will. For these people, politics was not just about casting ballots—indeed politics was not even primarily about voting. To them, regulating government to act on behalf of the governed happened mostly outside one's polling place. And "the people" expected to participate, not just on election day but 365 days a year. Indeed, many Pennsylvanians believed they had a sacred right to regulate their government and that it was their duty to exercise that right whenever they saw fit to preserve democracy. That idea of regulation, while certainly not obliterated, took a hard hit as "the people" were pushed to channel their hopes and frustrations through an electoral system replete with barriers against democracy. From then until now, those barriers have continued to frustrate the kind of major reforms that so many of these "regulators"—and their ideological descendants—thought was essential for their democracy to remain healthy.

FOR FURTHER READING

The first histories of the 1794 uprising were accounts written by participants and their descendants, largely to defend personal or family honor. These were often dueling histories, where one was published to refute claims made in another. The two most important are Hugh Henry Brackenridge, *Incidents of the Insurrection in the Western Parts of Pennsylvania, in the Year 1794* (Philadelphia, 1795), and the response by William Findley, *A History of the Insurrection in the Four Western Counties of Pennsylvania* (Philadelphia, 1796). Brackenridge's work is particularly valuable for the inclusion of appendices reprinting depositions and testimony from those involved. These works remain the main source for information on David Bradford, for whom documentary evidence is thin.

Aside from the participant accounts, most of the published primary sources on the 1794 insurgency reflect the perspectives of the Washington administration. The documents collected in volume 4 in the second series of *Pennsylvania Archives,* ed. Charles F. Hoban (Harrisburg, Pa., 1857–1935), are mostly official records of the events that followed the march on Braddock's Field. Within the administration, *The Papers of Alexander Hamilton,* ed. Harold C. Syrett et al., 27 vols. (New York, 1961–87), offers the most informative window into western grievances, popular opposition, and the attempts to suppress the uprising.

Modern histories tend to follow the interpretations of Brackenridge and Findley, who both were attempting to downplay the threat the insurgency posed. The most important of these works are Leland Baldwin, *Whiskey Rebels: The Story of a Frontier Uprising* (Pittsburgh, 1939), which is mostly a descriptive narrative of events; and Thomas P. Slaughter, *The Whiskey Rebellion: Frontier Epilogue to the American Revolution* (New York, 1986), which follows Findley's interpretation in portraying the uprising as a response to conditions specific to the frontier. For a good overview of this historiography, see *The Whiskey Rebellion: Past and Present Perspectives,* ed. Steven R. Boyd (Westport, Conn., 1985).

Other scholars have questioned the interpretations of Brackenridge and Findley and have searched for new evidence and explanations. In an important unpublished 1981 dissertation, "From Rebelliousness to Insurrection: A Social History of the Whiskey Rebellion, 1765–1802," Dorothy Elaine Fennell probed more closely the occupations and landownership of known insurgents, viewing their actions as a response to increasing economic inequality brought about primarily by the region's economic development. Terry Bouton connected the insurgent's ideals, grievances, and actions to a long-standing struggle over democracy and economic equality at the core of the Revolution: *Taming Democracy: "The People," The Founders, and the Troubled Ending of the American Revolution* (New York, 2007) and "A Road Closed: Rural Insurgency in Post-Independence Pennsylvania," *Journal of American History* 87, no. 3 (2000): 855–87. For a recent popular history retelling the basic story, with attention to the contexts illuminated by Fennell and Bouton, see William Hogeland, *The Whiskey Rebellion: George Washington, Alexander Hamilton, and the Frontier Rebels Who Challenged America's Newfound Sovereignty* (New York, 2006).

CHAPTER FIFTEEN

The New Jerusalem: Herman Husband's Egalitarian Alternative to the United States Constitution

Wythe Holt

Imagine the following proposal for the reform of American society: All representatives of the people would be popularly elected in political districts so small each voter would know the character of every candidate. Legislatures would be peopled overwhelmingly by workers, farmers, and craftsmen. The owner of every large factory would "take every workman into partnership." Each such worker would "receive a proportionate share of the profits equivalent to his labor." Every farmer would be entitled to a minimum of one hundred acres of land, but no farm family could ever have more than two thousand acres. Such a proposal was made, not by a nineteenth-century European utopian socialist, but in the eighteenth-century United States by a deeply religious farmer and lay preacher, Herman Husband, who "wish[ed] well to Liberty and Equallity."[1]

Husband called this vision the New Jerusalem, after the book of Ezekiel, a place where, according to the book of Revelation, Jesus would come and rule for a thousand years. He laid out his vision in four published pamphlets between 1782 and 1790, and in a pamphlet of sermons that remained unpublished at his death in 1795. Of the many millennialists in America in his day, Herman Husband was the most political and the most radical. And he was the only one who (on the basis of a vision sent by god) developed a full-scale egalitarian utopia.

He believed that ordinary people would predominate in any fair government because of their vast numerical superiority. Moreover, Husband thought that Jesus's Second Coming would be ushered in through the assumption of political power by those who produced society's wealth.

Farmers cultivated the land, laborers toiled productively, and artisans made useful articles. The wealthy in contrast "rob[bed]" such people of the surplus they produced, and "live[d] upon their labour . . . in idleness. . . . To depend on the labour of other people for a living . . . especially in luxury and waste is the . . . [sin] most provoking to God." However, god was about to set matters right. "In the last days, the labouring, industrious people, the militia of freemen, shall prevail over the standing armies of kings and tyrants."[2]

Husband praised and supported the American Revolution, imagining that its popular democratic tendencies were the embodiment of god's progress. He thought that the Revolution heralded an even greater, millennial revolution. But developments in the 1780s, particularly the Constitutional Convention, "introduc[ed] Tyranny" and, in moving power from the people to elites, betrayed what to him were the principles of the Revolution. Husband sadly concluded that it "is the Case more or less in Every Revolution, where the People at Large are Called on to assist & Promised true Liberty[,] but when the forreign Oppressor is thrown off[,] as [popish] Rome over England and as England over these States[,] then our own Learned and designing men Emediately Aim to take their Places."[3]

⟡

Born in 1724 in Maryland into a prosperous Anglican slave-owning gentry family, Herman Husband was marked from childhood as intelligent, stubbornly independent, and resourceful. Puncturing his adolescent frivolity, a December 1739 sermon by the itinerant dissenting Protestant preacher George Whitefield deeply impressed him. The first Great Awakening was sweeping through English North America with the message that each human could know god from his or her own inner light, "the voice of God in his own conscience." Each sinful human could have a New Birth, enabling that person "to deny and be master of his passions, . . . bring[ing] them subject to his reason."[4] And some revivalist preachers stressed that the millennium of Jesus was nigh.

Husband experienced his New Birth about a year after standing among the hundreds in Whitefield's audience. His piety deepened throughout the rest of his life, and he joyously awaited the Second Coming. His repeated condemnation of "riot[ous living] glutteny luxery waste and costly superfluity" came from a Calvinist austerity he took to heart.[5]

The inner light doctrine was revolutionary. Arrogant gentry-born ministers of the official Anglican Church in Maryland told people what to believe, upholding the authority of the state and a society openly based upon class as ordained by god. Popular criticism of this official doctrine was forbidden.

But dissenting Protestants, commencing with the English Revolution in the 1640s, overthrew these hierarchical constraints with a vengeance. All ordinary people could—and must, for the sake of their souls—come personally to know and speak with god. Now people could determine their own religious principles, preach, and even become prophets.

Many common people transformed such antiestablishment religious egalitarianism into antigentry political egalitarianism and democratic beliefs, as did Husband. Since each person was capable, mistakes made by "the learned and wealthy" were often shown "to be false by unlearned mechanics and laboring men." With experience gained through governing his family, followed by an apprenticeship in local government, Husband believed, "a Man, who will make a good Mechanick, or good Farmer[,]" will "make a good Assembly-man to rule the State."[6] Husband went much farther toward a belief in egalitarian participatory democracy than his contemporaries. These views would anchor the New Jerusalem.

౨

In Maryland in the 1740s and 1750s, Husband sought that dissenting Protestant group "which most closely resembled the apostolic church," as his biographer Mark Haddon Jones has noted. He became first a Presbyterian, then a Quaker—but he still had to pay the tithe, a tax to support the official church. He was "threatned with damages to a thousand pounds for treason against the Church for calling . . . the tythe, a yoke of bondage." Frustrated, in 1762 Husband moved to the Piedmont country of North Carolina, where a variety of dissenters had congregated in large numbers on rich farmland. This was the outermost edge of the American frontier at the time; it had none of the slave plantations of the seaboard. He continued as a successful farmer, owning large tracts of land. He hoped to find there "a new government of liberty," but was soon disappointed.[7]

Small freeholders were being cheated mercilessly by land speculators, lawyers, court functionaries, and sheriffs. Their poverty deepened by a lack of circulating money, debt-ridden farmers lost valuable animals through distraint or worked off debts on elite farms while their crops went unharvested. When they made complaint, Governor William Tryon treated them as ignorant serfs, incapable of moral judgment. Ordinary farmers were a lower class to be ruled.

Outrages, culminating in a sheriff's seizure of a mare for taxes while its owner was riding it, brought an explosion of farmers' meetings and protests, and some violence. Calling themselves Regulators, reformers of a government gone astray (a term with English roots, in use in nearby South Carolina), the farmers were joined by Husband as their "Patron"—that is, agitator and pamphleteer. Though he personally renounced killing and violence, Husband understood that only the threat of violence would enable ordinary folk to be heard by their governors, so he praised the "militia of freemen." Husband insisted that the common people claim their ancient English "natural rights and privileges," thundering that "God give all men a . . . true zeal to maintain [such privileges]" and that Regulators acted out God's will in a "Spirit of Enthusiasm . . . to redeem their Country."[8]

Summing up his role, Marjoleine Kars, historian of the North Carolina Regulation, concludes that Husband "quickly emerged as a spokesperson, arbitrator, and chief political thinker among the Regulators."[9] He was expelled from his elected seat in the legislature and twice jailed, targeted by Tryon, who considered him the backbone of the disturbances.

Facing trial in September 1768, and told that he would surely hang, Husband wanted to flee to save his neck. However, his resolve was steadied by ordinary Regulators, who in grim humor said if he absconded they "would let the Governor do as he pleased,"[10] and by the extraordinary devotion of hundreds of men, women, and children who twice marched to free him from prison. Thereafter Husband never blinked at personal harm or death. His faith held true: a petit jury acquitted him in 1768 and a grand jury refused to indict him in 1771.

Husband's Regulator writings began to develop his theme of popular smallholder political and economic democracy. A Regulator petition that Husband penned demanded the secret ballot, progressive taxation, a small claims court, a steady paper currency backed by realty, justice for squatters, and the termination of illegal land grants by the governor to his noncultivating favorites. These "extraordinary" demands, as Kars writes, represented a "wide-ranging, radical, and concrete vision of agrarian reform" favoring ordinary farmers.[11]

Husband's fiery pamphlets were in the same vein. He excoriated tax-paid ministers, greedy lawyers, and land speculators who robbed "Thousands of poor families." Hardworking small producers contributed the most to the community and should be favored. Most crucially, he urged that the people personally monitor and instruct their government, since "the nature of an Officer is a servant to the Publick," and all citizens needed to know their representatives and to learn how their tax money was used. This popular democracy needed to be put into fundamental law. Husband wrote that "when a Reformation can be brought about in our Constitution . . . then will commence that Thousand Years Reign with Christ."[12]

Tryon stonewalled, suspicious that farmers "assum[ed] to themselves

Power and Authorities (unknown to the Constitution) of calling Publick Officers to a Settlement." The Regulators turned to the violence that Husband feared the elites "Endeavored to Drive the Populace to."[13] The governor's militia with its artillery easily put down two thousand disorganized Regulators at the Alamance River on May 19, 1771.

With a price on his head, Husband slipped out of North Carolina disguised as a minister, using the pseudonym Tuscape Death. His wife, Emy, pregnant, met him in Maryland in 1772, and they moved to western Pennsylvania, where they built a prosperous new farm life. He could not stay quiet, however. For the next quarter century he would be drawn into political controversy.

~℃

Herman Husband was enthusiastic about the changes brought by the Revolution from 1775 to 1785. Democratic constitutional reforms accelerated. The Revolution presented a fine model, organized as it was by "honest and undesigning . . . Committee-men [elected] in each Neighborhood, who met at the County Towns, and there chose a standing Committee for the County." Pennsylvania's constitution of 1776 extended the vote to all taxpayers, with annual elections to a unicameral legislature. Fondly calling it "our revolution," he believed that the "revolutionary struggle was what he intended at the time of the Regulation." He said excitedly in 1778 that Americans were "contend[ing] for permanent Freedom" under a popular government "which will have for its Object not the Emolument of one Man or Class of Men only, but the Safety, Liberty and Happiness of every Individual in the Community."[14]

Elected to the Pennsylvania General Assembly in 1777, he praised the state's new constitution, especially its adoption of the rights of free speech and freedom of religion ("Union without the Least force or Conformity in Opinion"). Its monumental changes had "been Preparing and forming in the Minds of the Workmen" for a century.[15] By the time the session ended, however, Husband had realized that reliance on free speech and "Annuall Ellections" was not enough. Despite having a majority of radical democrats, the legislature contained a full share of the "same sort of wicked Men . . . possessed of Wealth" who served their own interests that he had encountered before. The problem was the huge size of electoral districts. Most voters could only know their near neighbors and were forced to vote blindly on the recommendation of the powerful, or for wealthy "unsuitable" people they did know, "Tavern-keepers, Merchants, . . . Lawyers," officials, and the like.[16] Husband hated the class castigated in the Bible as "the rich," who cannot be saved. Only the poor would be saved.

"According to Herman Husband's own account," as his biographer Mark Jones recounts, "in June 1779, while walking through the mountains near Pittsburgh, he underwent a remarkable religious experience." He saw what he later described as a detailed vision of the New Jerusalem in the distance to the west.[17] In the context of the importance contemporaries put on the inner light, and a widespread belief that biblical passages referred to their own time, dissenting religious people firmly believed in the reality of visions, prophecies, and dreams. The vision showed Husband how and where the common people would undertake and perfect their governance.

Interpreting what he saw in the light cast by biblical prophets, since "both the old and new testament was on the subject of Outward Civill Government," he believed that the trans-Appalachian "western country" would become "the glorious land of New Jerusalem." It would be "fifteen hundred miles square," its eastern "wall" would be the Appalachian Mountains, and other great mountain ranges would square off this huge area (see Diagram 1, drawn by Husband). Farmers, artisans, and laborers would "at last produce an everlasting Peace on Earth," modeling further democratic change in the rest of the United States. He plucked a leaf from the Tree of Life and "felt its healing Virtue to remove the Curse and Calamities of Mankind in this World."[18]

Husband spent the remainder of his life proclaiming this good news to all. He wrote short items in almanacs, a favorite of common people. He wrote for newspapers and published an astonishing number of pamphlets, probably more than any other agrarian leader in the Revolutionary Era. In addition to five pamphlets expounding on New Jerusalem, Husband wrote the two Regulator pamphlets, an early treatise on his experience with established and dissenting religion, a plan to shift the burdens of the depreciation of paper money from ordinary people to the wealthy, and a short plea to purchase needed land from the Indians.

The first of the New Jerusalem pamphlets, "Proposals to Amend and Perfect the Policy of the Government of the United States of America" (1782), introduced the vision at the end, as "an American riddle," after setting forth at length many of his democratic proposals, as though the two were unconnected. New Jerusalem seemed to be only the location of Jesus's Second Coming, and Husband was still hopeful about the possibilities of expanding American democracy. By 1788, however, after the secretive Constitutional Convention revealed its product and the states were close to ratification, he had become deeply alarmed.

The great defect of Pennsylvania's constitution had been worsened. The new federal Constitution had made national electoral districts even larger,

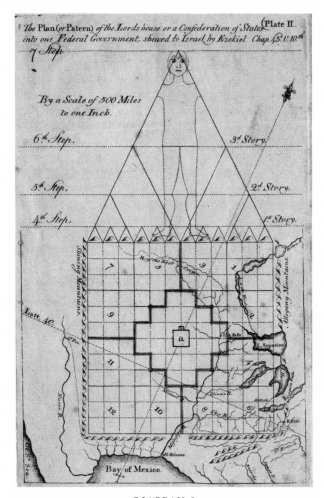

The Plan (or Patern) of the Lords house or a Confederation of States (Plate II. into one Federal Government, shewed to Israel by Ezekiel Chap.48. V.10.th

By a Scale of 500 Miles to one Inch.

DIAGRAM 1

New Jerusalem is shown somewhat awkwardly inserted into the middle of the United States, with the Rockies (or "Shining Mountains") placed along the western edge and fancied mountain ranges in the north above the "origins" of the "river of the west" and along the southern edge (punctuated by the effluent of the Mississippi River into the "Bay of Mexico" at New Orleans). The "Allegany" Mountains erroneously run northwesterly from Lake Superior; below them, the Great Lakes are turned on edge. Santa Fe is placed beyond the Shining Mountains. The empires are numbered from 1 to 12. No locations for the meetings of empire or quarter councils are shown, but the huge metropolis of New Jerusalem is located at "a," in the center.

"put[ting] it out of the hands of the people to have any choice at all" in their representatives.[19] He published a series of pamphlets linking democratic reform with god's promised land across the Appalachians, and he always carried copies of his pamphlets with him. The most notable of them was "XIV Sermons on the Characters of Jacob's Fourteen Sons" (1789). A lengthy untitled pamphlet of sermons remained unpublished at his death.

The most important way for Husband to spread the idea of New Jerusalem to the nonreaders who frequently formed his principal audience in the sparsely populated wilderness was word of mouth. Like many mechanic preachers during the radical Protestant outburst in England a century earlier, this millennial prophet preached barefoot with unkempt hair and in homespun (like his auditors) in churches and wherever farmers and itinerant farm laborers gathered. After all, Jesus wore homespun. Husband regaled visitors of all classes about the New Jerusalem.

The highly educated could not hear his message. Pittsburgh lawyer and Princeton graduate Hugh Henry Brackenridge visited Husband's farm in 1780 and contemptuously concluded that his church must be "composed, like many others, of the ignorant and the dissembling." The German naturalist and traveler Dr. Johann David Schoepf in 1783 was "astonish[ed]" at the homegrown expertise Husband displayed in several scientific fields, but was only bemused by his expostulation of the New Jerusalem. Albert Gallatin, Swiss educated, an entrepreneur and Pennsylvania assemblyman, later secretary of the treasury under Jefferson and Madison, called him "the crazy man of Bedford." Congressman Robert Smilie chuckled on the witness stand at Husband's 1795 sedition trial that he had "written some foolish things about the New Jerusalem."[20] The gentry would have no important place in New Jerusalem and did not want to believe their eyes and ears.

Husband's ordinary neighbors in Bedford County, noting that he did not always make sense, did not find him a "crazy man." Without mocking him, plain farmer James Wilson stated matter-of-factly under oath at the 1795 trial that Husband was "employed in writing upon prophets, & making riddles" and—as though everyone must know what he was talking about—had "found the situation of New Jerusalem [to be] at Kentucky."[21] Other neighbors testified that he was the most respected person in the county, being chosen chair of local meetings. They elected him to the Pennsylvania legislature twice, to the 1790 state constitutional convention, and as constable, township tax assessor, auditor of road-maintenance accounts, and county commissioner. Court records in Bedford County show no attempt by any fellow citizen to discipline him for poor service in such positions, though it was not uncommon for officials to be so reprimanded. His neighbors marveled at his lack of pretension, his honesty, his frugality and industriousness, and his business acumen. They had no difficulty understanding the New Jerusalem, because it was what they needed and longed for. Husband was giving "the Lower Classes," in his words, "the same Knowledge" as the upper classes, to ensure reform and their salvation.[22]

⟅

"The populist and militant thrust" of Husband's New Jerusalem pamphlets, in the judgment of Ruth Bloch, historian of early American millennialism, offered an "intriguing vision of an autonomous western paradise." He envisioned a new society and government which he superimposed on a map of the United States as it was then known (see Diagram 1). Immediately west of the Alleghenies were the Great Lakes, and the Ohio, Illinois, and "Meshura" rivers, which flowed into the Mississippi down to the "Bay of Mexico."[23] The western boundary was the "Shining Mountains."

Inside the huge "city" of mountain walls, Husband's New Jerusalem was an intricately plotted agrarian utopia patterned directly upon biblical passages relevant to his vision, with most of its features diametrically opposed to those of the new Constitution. His chief concern was the common people, those he called "the lower classes." Social, economic, and legal structures had to be put in place to guarantee their continued political equality, achieving what he called proper "balance." The resulting body politic, "made up of different members and classes of officers united into one general interest," was designed to produce "universal peace and distribution of justice, judgment, and mercy throughout its extensive divisions," since "all should have the same care one for another, as the different [parts] of the body natural have for each other."[24]

The best security Husband could devise for the people was a multilayered, interconnected government that they could control. The fundamental political unit was the township. About ten miles square, so that all residents would know each other, each township would elect its own legislature to coordinate local affairs. There would be nearly 21,000 townships, 144 of them in each of 144 states.

Townships would be combined into districts, while districts would be joined into counties and counties into states (see Diagram 2). Each district, county, and state would also have its own legislature. After the township, the most powerful unit was to be the state, "capable of exercising all the powers of government within itself."[25]

States would be combined into "empires," empires in turn joining into "quarters" (see Diagram 1). Each empire and quarter would have a council,

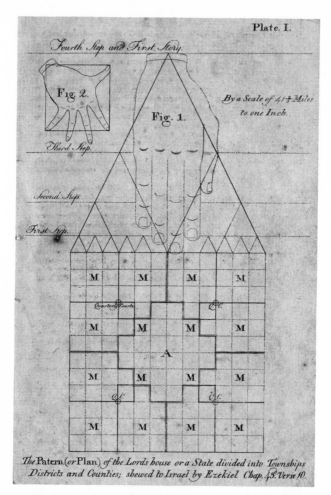

The Patern *(or* Plan*) of the Lords house or a State divided into Townships Districts and Counties; shewed to Israel by Ezekiel Chap. 48. Verse 10.*

DIAGRAM 2

The diagrams Husband drew of New Jerusalem in "XIV Sermons," repeated in "Dialogue," demonstrate how the physical structure of his utopia followed these biblical prophecies. A township (see Figure 1), the smallest political unit, represents the initial joint of a finger, a district (9–11 townships) the first and middle joints of a finger, a county (3 districts) the entire finger, a state (5 counties) the whole hand (see Figure 2), or foot, an empire (9–11 states) the lower arm or leg, a quarter (3 empires) the entire arm or leg, and the Supreme Council of New Jerusalem (5 quarters) the entire body. Each is additionally labeled "the Lord's house," and the whole is strongly symmetrical and thus supposedly sturdy. At central locations marked "M" district legislatures would be held monthly. County quarterly "courts" would meet at even more central places marked "QC." The annual state legislatures would meet in the center of the whole, marked "A."

while the five quarters together would be governed by a Supreme Council. The levels of government above states were primarily to provide protection for the people, checks against abuses by the states and by executive officers.

The plan envisioned ordinary people as the rulers. Husband thought that "God sett up the true Republican form of Right Government . . . in which the body of the People will have Supream Power to choose their [governors], and their will [shall] be the Supream Law of the land."[26] The legislatures, the most powerful part of the government, and the councils (except the Supreme Council) would be staffed by members of the township legislatures, elected by and from among their own members in increasingly smaller groups to serve at the next level upward. Since most members of the township legislatures would likely be farmers, artisans, and laborers, the great defects in both the Pennsylvania and new national constitutions were solved.

Since people could become eligible for a higher level only after serving a term in a lower legislature or council, Husband's proposal would be "a school to train up and learn [mechanicks and farmers] of the best Sense and Principles the Nature of all publick Business." It would give them practice at delivering a public address or engaging in debate. Natural ability needed education, but well apprenticed, the people could rule, "the Goverment of a Famaly and that of a State being the same in nature." To keep legislators or councilors from venality, they would receive no pay, only their "bare maintenance." High salaries for lawmakers meant the end of liberty and the distribution of offices "to the hands of a few wealthy men."[27]

Accountability of officeholders to those who put them into office was crucial. Government, Husband believed, was a trust (not, as it is thought today, a top-down, dictatorial business), all officials being "the trustees and servants of the people, . . . at all times accountable unto them." Men chosen under his plan would initially be "the most likely and best qualified to act," but even good men get drunk with power, "turn[ing] the outward letter of the law to answer their own private purposes." The people must be ready to "venture life and property" to make their democratic government work. Normally, the remedy against abuse of their trust by officials would be complaints, petitions, and eventually voting them out.[28]

The Supreme Council would consist of twenty-four men, elected by joint sessions of the quarter councils. Aged between fifty and sixty when elected, each would serve a single term of ten years and would receive no salary but only living expenses. Four (initially chosen by lot) would rotate off each year. Councilors would live apart from everyone else (in the ten-mile-square area marked "b" in Diagram 1), would (like a church board) hold whatever property they had in common, could not marry during their term, and must remain celibate (unless a wife was past childbearing), since without the care of a family they could devote themselves fully to government.

The former rebel wanted to eliminate the causes of rebellion. By majority vote, the Supreme Council would appoint and set pay for the Supreme Court, divide overpopulated governmental units, and appoint a commander in chief of the militias to "quell insurrections"—but only after he inquired "into the causes of the grievances" and treated them with the "lenity and forgiveness [of a father] when he finds them misguided." (Husband was disappointed that George Washington did not really act as the understanding and forgiving father of his country.) Offensive war, peace, alliances, and the appointment of ambassadors would lie with the quarter councils sitting together—that is, with the uppermost level of persons originally elected by the people in the townships. The Supreme Council's chief functions would be to rent or sell vacant lands after purchase from the Indians, to listen to popular petitions and complaints about official abuse, and "to redress their grievances."[29]

With legislation primarily being made at the state level, the people would be flooded with publicity about legislative debates. Upon passage, each law would be read out loud in township meetings for three months. The vote of a majority of townships would decide the law's continuing validity. Empires, quarters, and the Supreme Council might also veto any law. Reenactment then depended upon six months' broad public deliberation on the veto and a two-thirds vote in the state legislature. Husband provided for no executive veto.

Members of the executive at each level would be chosen by that level's legislature. Thus county assemblies would appoint jurors, county surveyors, officers in charge of roads and strays, and the like. Executive officers would be merely ministerial, having no hand in the making of laws. They would receive pay, in order to get people to take the jobs. This would make them exactly like servants, who did someone else's bidding—in this instance, the people's.

Husband's judiciary proposals were similarly simple and easy to understand. He admitted that "obtain[ing] impartial judges of the law" was difficult and that partial judges often "poisoned" juries. Even good judges were "surrounded" with venal clerks and lawyers, "whom our Lord called vipers." Husband viewed the judiciary "as an umpire" to settle controversies and to attend to the "ballancing" of governmental power. He trusted the Supreme Council to choose wise and impartial "elderly men" for the task, but he proposed that judges would attend a school where state, empire, and quarter legislation would be kept, along with journals they would make of cases they heard.[30]

States needed to have approximately equal population, "so they may be as equal in Strength to one another as possible."[31] The western country would be founded upon such equality, and when two thousand families petitioned for admittance, a new state would be formed. To maintain equality, the Supreme Council could divide them if they grew too large. The existing states in the east violated this principle, but Husband—who sometimes hinted that New Jerusalem would be independent from the United States—usually thought that the wealth and moral power of the nation would quickly flow to the west, rendering eastern states increasingly less important, and eventually they would re-form themselves.

New Jerusalem also was sensitive to the political implications of economic inequality. Because amassing land in one family led to a "nobility and lords to be over tenants—not freemen," Husband restricted the ownership of land. Each person (including women) would be entitled to land, but a nuclear family was limited to two thousand acres. The minimum plot would be one hundred acres, guaranteed to each family in perpetuity. Only by redistributing holdings in excess of two thousand acres, or lands not cultivated years after purchase, could government ever interfere with landownership. Husband could not imagine overpopulating the vast agricultural plains of central North America. Not an advocate of "development," and a farmer himself, he never expected cities and business to predominate over farmers and farms.[32]

There was a place for industry too. Husband located a large "metropolis city" in the center of New Jerusalem (marked "a" in Diagram 1). Here would be "all sorts of manufactories, tavern-keepers, merchants, soldiers, &c." Husband's piercing eye caught the essence of capitalism. He hated the "carrying on [of] large works, by a wretched set of discontented laborers, kept in no better condition than slaves, and subsisting on pecuniary and scanty wages, from one haughty tyrant, living in luxury and waste, yet equally under the same misery, torment, and vexation of mind, how to cheat these workmen, and get their labor at as low a rate as possible." He advocated what would later be called cooperatives, in which the owner of a factory with "a great number of hands . . . takes every workman into partnership, . . . to receive a proportionate share of the profits, equivalent to his labor, and stock put in." For each workman to have "an interest in the whole, it will excite industry and care through the whole."[33]

As for state funding, Husband understood that the people disliked "Taxation more than any other Thing belonging to a free Government." Taxes on workers destroyed "that Fountain out of which [Prosperity] rises." He suggested as revenue sources the sale and renting of lands, plus "an easy [annual] Quitrent" on lands sold. Public monopolies such as "saltworks, ferries, canals, &c." would produce duties. And he suggested excise taxes on alcohol and other "Superfluities of life"[34] but dropped his earlier idea of progressive taxation. Taxes *always* fueled rebellions.

His most ingenious proposal was to tax the depreciation of paper currency. Unusual for his time, he perceived that depreciation of assets was normal. Paper money had depreciated wildly during the Revolution, causing many Americans to demand a return to hard money, but he recognized that gross swings in value could be regulated by an activist government. Husband liked the wide availability of paper money (as have most farmers) and argued that freeing money from the value of metal would allow the government to seize and stabilize its depreciation. A scheduled gentle, regular drop in value would be printed on the face of a fresh issue of bills. This would solve the cash-strapped situation that ordinary people found themselves in. Husband's proposed forced exchange of war bonds for the new money would also get rid of much of the war debt that plagued ordinary folks through onerous taxes directed to pay off the bonds. Since most surplus value produced by workers found its way into the pockets of landlords, merchants, tavern owners, bankers, lawyers, and fee-taking officials, Husband thought the difficulties of war debt repayment and the fluctuation in value of money would now be visited upon elites, who would mostly pay the depreciation tax. He advocated a government that was active in aiding the people who were the vast majority of its citizens, that ran the economy through careful regulation rather than allowing merchants to control it via laissez-faire policies. Such economic policy proposals went to the heart of the difficulties his ordinary neighbors endured and would have provided solutions they applauded.

Husband was opposed to oppression and exploitation of all kinds. He defined "oppression" as one man living off the labor of a hundred. He was also opposed to luxury, grandeur, and waste. Working people did not wear costly clothes nor waste much in eating and drinking. He believed that such evils were those of elites, who spent their time scheming to exploit the people. In "Times of Distress," taxes on the rich should return the wealth to those who had originally produced it.[35]

༄

Radically democratic for its day, New Jerusalem was also seriously flawed. Most important, the lands of the New Jerusalem west of the Appalachians were not vacant. They were owned by Native Americans, who had lived there for thousands of years. Husband was more pacific than the bloodthirsty white folk around him, who successfully advocated the unilateral seizing of native lands and aggressive warfare against them. Husband wanted to purchase Indian land at something approaching a fair price. Further, whites would purchase only what was needed incrementally, in a controlled westward movement. However, he believed that "the uncultivated lands of this continent . . . is a prise worth all the kingdoms in Europe," and that the Indians, "savage" and "ignoran[t]," needed to "become civilized subjects to our form of government." In return, the tribes nearest the boundary line of white cultivation would "protect [the whites] in peace from distant tribes and their own bad people."[36] It was only a kinder, gentler form of the racist imperialism that has infected most white North Americans for three centuries.

Red people were more favored than black people, because they at least had a chance to become civilized. Husband opposed slavery because it took jobs and fertile land away from "poor labouring white" farmers and laborers—who could use the wages otherwise tied up in slave purchases to become freeholders "and thereby become able to employ more poor." As men, enslaved blacks would naturally desire freedom, so Husband also condemned slavery because it gave whites "discontent, and uneasiness" in fear of insurrection. Despite this concession, he never allowed that blacks—"more forreign by one half" than Indians—would join his white civilization.[37]

He was much tenderer toward white women, yet remained fundamentally patriarchal. Husband thought women could not run a family (or therefore a government): "though a wiked Man does often Abuse this Supream Power Given to him [by god] over a Private famaly, yet a wiked Wooman Would Abuse it far Worse."[38] The extraordinarily egalitarian Husband did not extend his benevolent views of human worth to women or persons of color— consistent with the dominant white prejudices of his time.

In other ways he did not go as far as some liberated by radical Protestant thought. During the English Revolution in the 1640s and 1650s, there was a proliferation of mechanic preachers who, as historian Christopher Hill shows, entertained "communist theories" of the mutual ownership of land and goods. That period's great theorist and pamphleteer of the common people, Gerrard Winstanley, leader and preacher of the communalist Diggers, put forward a program that was in many ways like that of Husband. He proclaimed that a few should not rule over the many; that working for another, either for wages or to pay quitrent, was wrong; and that there should be universal religious toleration. But Winstanley also believed in the "free enjoyment of the earth," the communal cultivation of the land by the starving poor to feed themselves, which he too took from reading scripture and listening to his inner light. The buying and selling of land would cease as well as the buying and selling of human labor. There would be full communal ownership of land, and there would be no need for government, prisons, nobility, lawyers, or priests. Unlike Husband, Winstanley saw the dangers of private property itself.[39]

Although for Husband human society had "no other aim but the common happiness of every individual," and the only social tie was "the common interest," neither happiness nor interest itself was communal. Government was necessary, Husband thought, to "secur[e] to every one the property he should acquire by . . . labor and industry" and to defend it "from the rest of the savage world."[40] Husband was a remarkably thoughtful, ingenious, and very democratic advocate of smallholders, but at heart he remained an individualist, an owner of land, and a devotee of private property, not a socialist.

꿏

After 1789, as the Washington administration enacted policies implementing the Constitution, it was clear to Husband that both were the very opposite of the ideals of New Jerusalem. The new Senate especially was "calculated for actually creating a nobility." Husband was disgusted with "this stinking carcass of filthy lucre," the extravagant salaries awarded to the president and other executive officers, as demonstrated by their fine clothes and carriages. Men whose object was personal gain he thought unfit for office. He was upset that Washington, a hero to him during the Revolution, was now revealed as an elitist, showing more concern for his officers than for "the people (who were all half ruined in their estates by the war)."[41]

Hamilton's policy of using public debt to draw wealthy investors into support for the new government was "the curse of all curses," ensuring that all American children would "be born with a [tax] burden on their backs," and giving in turn "a show of justice to an unjust or unmerciful set of speculators," a handful of wealthy merchants who had purchased the United States' Revolutionary War debt for a pittance and were to be paid back by Hamilton with huge windfall profits. The people must use great exertions, "equal to [but not including] an insurrection," to regain their proper dominance.[42] New Jerusalem was designed to accomplish exactly that.

The message of New Jerusalem was, as historian Dorothy Fennell puts it, "explosive." The corrupt, wasteful, people-robbing tyrants Husband talked about ceaselessly were encountered daily by his "westerner" Appalachian neighbors in their own communities—"millers who overcharged, . . . land jobbers who bought up improvements, court officers who defended them, merchants who cornered the market," politicians who bought votes with whiskey and cash gifts. The promise of democracy for all was being taken from them by designing men, and it was up to ordinary citizens to reclaim their own. Since god had explicitly "chosen westerners to complete the promise of the American Revolution," it was their duty to contact their representatives, meet together, petition, remonstrate, and if necessary march, to "overthrow tyranny."[43] People's grievances with the Hamiltonian policies of the new American government came to a head in the Whiskey Rebellion of 1794, misnamed by Hamilton, who called it so in order to denigrate it; it was indeed a rebellion against all that he stood for.

On August 1, 1794, the rebels assembled in their militia units on Braddock's Field. Frightened observers estimated them to be between five thousand and nine thousand strong. Raising liberty poles (which had proclaimed American separation from England during the Revolution) and newly fashioned six-striped flags of independence, they marched in orderly ranks on Pittsburgh. Its forewarned residents gave them a meal and persuaded them not to burn the town.

During July and August the rebels held public meetings in various open-air locations to decide their course of action. The most important conclave, consisting of about 240 elected delegates from the Pennsylvania and Virginia townships west of the Appalachians, gathered on August 14 and 15 in a large field on a riverside bluff at Parkinson's Ferry, south of Pittsburgh. The delegates debated whether to defy or to give in to the Washington administration, which was threatening to send an army westward. Perhaps an equal number of ill-clad farmers and others stood near or rode around the outskirts of the meeting, suspicious that the slightly better-off, better-educated delegates might abandon the rebellion in the face of the news from the east.

Husband was one of the two Parkinson's Ferry delegates chosen from Bedford County. He was elected by the other delegates, along with moderates Albert Gallatin and Hugh Henry Brackenridge and firebrand David Bradford, to a committee to get their resolutions into shape. The two elite moderates disdained him. Gallatin thought Husband "out of his senses"; Brackenridge smirkingly asked him about "his New Jerusalem reveries," then moved hastily to the resolutions when Husband took a pamphlet from his pocket.[44]

The delegates also elected Husband to a committee of sixty to steer activity between meetings, as well as to a conference committee of twelve to meet with the representatives of Washington's government on August 28–29 (where Husband urged submission). He was thus repeatedly trusted by ordinary people to act for them in their crisis. If urbane observers like Brackenridge and Gallatin "viewed Husband as a backwoods eccentric, it is doubtful," historian Ruth Bloch argues convincingly, "that the people who continued to elect him to positions of leadership and to listen to his preaching would have concurred." Dorothy Fennell reports that the now-lost depositions of two persons caught up in the rebellion testified to the widespread influence of Husband in the western countryside. The testimony given by farmer James Wilson at Husband's 1795 trial, quoted earlier, is a good example. Fennell and William Hogeland, historians of the rebellion, and his biographer Jones are all persuaded of Husband's importance.[45]

Husband's urgent message, spread through the countryside for fifteen years, was meant for ordinary people. It praised peoples' militias, it condemned the very businessmen and officials who were oppressing them, and it assured them that their eternal salvation lay in erecting a democratic government. Moreover, as Bloch further notes, "given the militant separatist tendencies within the Whiskey Rebellion it is certainly plausible if not provable that Husband's exalted vision of the region as the New Jerusalem enhanced his leadership role."[46]

ॐ

The Washington administration was well aware of Husband, if not of the details of his message. He was excluded by name from its proclamation of amnesty to the rebels, and he was singled out as a prime target for arrest as the administration moved quickly to crush the rebellion with overwhelming force. Hamilton had expected that his fiscal program, redistributing the people's wealth upward, would provoke deep opposition. A militia army of more than thirteen thousand was mustered and sent slogging westward. One of its first acts was to capture Husband at his Bedford County farm on October 20. After a swift hearing, federal district judge Richard Peters, traveling with the army, ordered his detention until trial. Commander in Chief George Washington was elated: he had identified "Harmon Husband" as one of the three rebel leaders he most wanted captured, and he tracked the progress of "Husbands" to a small jail cell in Philadelphia. The prophet wrote to his wife wryly that "[a] prison seems the safest place for one of my age and profession."[47]

In early June, after more than seven months in prison, Husband went on trial for his life once more, for speaking on behalf of ordinary people. He and another Bedford farmer, Robert Philson, were indicted by the Philadelphia grand jury for sedition (legally, "speech inciting rebellion"), both at the Parkinson's Ferry meeting and when they returned home to report on it. Remarkably, Husband had more witnesses to testify for him than the government amassed to testify against him, even though his witnesses had to be contacted by someone friendly, to travel from the Pittsburgh area to Philadelphia, to incur large costs awaiting a trial of uncertain date in an expensive city, and to risk possible government retaliation for their courage.

Not a single witness could state that either man had said anything seditious at Parkinson's Ferry. Defense witnesses testified that the people of Bedford County had explicitly instructed the two to promote peace and constitutional measures only, and that both believed deeply in following the instructions of the people. Several witnesses concurred that, upon their return, Husband and Philson were happy that the result of Parkinson's Ferry would be peace, not war. Noting that Husband was honored by chairing the countywide meeting, they said that both men spoke vigorously in opposition to the policies of the Washington administration. But they also testified that Husband opposed war, the burning of houses, and tar-and-feathering. Both defendants had repeatedly emphasized peaceful and constitutional opposition, such as further petitioning and a second constitutional convention. Without much ado, the petit jury—all easterners—found them innocent.

Even during a rebellion, and even when voiced by a person sneered at by their "betters," these jurors did not share the opinion of their rulers that peaceful verbal opposition to the government was seditious. Husband's faith in ordinary people had once again proved wise. It was, however, his last triumph. As the prophet made his way home, he fell ill in a tavern outside Philadelphia. After a long bout with fever, in the loving care of Emy and his son John, he passed away, probably on June 18, 1795. He had reached threescore years and ten.

✑

Herman Husband deserves to be remembered in the first rank of the heroes of American democracy. He was the only radical of the Revolutionary Era to articulate a fully developed utopian vision as a democratic alternative to the Constitution. Long depicted chiefly as a belligerent leader of violent backcountry rebellions in North Carolina and Pennsylvania, in reality the deeply religious Husband persistently advocated peaceful means of seeking redress of grievances. He exhorted ordinary people to stand up for the democracy they deserved and needed, while he praised and demanded genuinely open debate. He knew that people could live in harmony, safety, and prosperity in an egalitarian government if ruled from the bottom up. To work, such a government needed upper limits on the amount of property each family might have, and to provide the people with multiple avenues for the pursuit of grievances. Toward such ends he elaborated the New Jerusalem.

FOR FURTHER READING

This essay has been adapted from my larger manuscript, "The Federal Whiskey Rebellion Cases of 1795 and the Rise of the National Security State," a study of the federal trials of the so-called Whiskey Rebels. My conclusions are based in large part upon research in the records of the Pennsylvania federal courts at the National Archives Federal Records Center in Philadelphia; the William Paterson Papers at the Askew Library of William Paterson University; the Rawle Family Papers at the Historical Society of Pennsylvania; and the Albert Gallatin Papers at the New-York Historical Society. Contemporary newspapers; *The Documentary History of the United States Supreme Court,* ed. Maeva Marcus et al., 8 vols. (New York, 1985–2007); and the published papers of Alexander Hamilton were helpful. Herman Husband's pamphlets and other published items are cited in the endnotes. Most are available in microform and are indexed in Charles Evans, *Early American Imprints.* His unpublished manuscript sermons are in the John Irwin Scull Collection at the Historical Society of Western Pennsylvania. His comprehensive personal journal has unfortunately been mislaid.

Mark Haddon Jones, "Herman Husband: Millenarian, Carolina Regulator, and Whiskey Rebel" (Ph.D. diss., Northern Illinois University, 1983), provides the full account of Husband's life and is especially good on the religious context of the New Jerusalem. See also Jones's entry on Husband in the *American National Biography.* A study of the North Carolina Regulation that deftly emphasizes both religion and economics is Marjoleine Kars, *Breaking Loose Together: The Regulator Rebellion in Pre-Revolutionary North Carolina* (Chapel Hill, N.C., 2002). For an overview of the conflicts of the era in Pennsylvania, see Terry Bouton, *Taming Democracy: "The People," the Founders, and the Troubled Ending of the American Revolution* (New York, 2007). Dorothy E. Fennell, "From Rebelliousness to Insurrection" (Ph.D. diss., University of Pittsburgh, 1981), analyzes well the people and the economics involved in the Whiskey Rebellion, while its most recent student, William Hogeland, *The Whiskey Rebellion* (New York, 2006), writes in a comprehensive if folksy style, foregrounding many important details. On the early federal courts, see William R. Casto, *The Supreme Court in the Early Republic* (Columbia, S.C., 1995). For the outpouring of Protestant radicalism during the English Revolution, see Christopher Hill, *The World Turned Upside Down* (New York, 1972). For millennial thought, see Ruth H. Bloch, *Visionary Republic: Millennial Themes in American Thought, 1756–1800* (New York, 1985). Alfred Young takes up "English Plebeian Culture and Eighteenth-Century American Radicalism" in his book of essays, *Liberty Tree: Ordinary People and the American Revolution* (New York, 2006).

CHAPTER SIXTEEN

The Battle Against Patriarchy That Abigail Adams Won

Woody Holton

On an unusually warm morning in the middle of January 1816, seventy-one-year-old Abigail Adams, racked with pain and convinced she was dying, sat down to write her will. For Adams, scratching out this four-page document was actually an act of rebellion—for the simple reason that her husband, John, the former president, was still alive. Throughout Abigail's lifetime (which, despite her apprehensions that January morning, would continue into the fall of 1818), every wife in America was a *feme covert*—a woman covered by her husband. The most tangible manifestation of coverture was, as Adams complained to her husband in 1782, that married women's property was "subject to the controul and disposal of our partners, to whom the Laws have given a soverign Authority." Husbands assumed complete authority over their wives' real estate (land and buildings). And if a married woman brought to her marriage, or later acquired, personal property (which consisted of everything except real estate, be it cash or cattle), those possessions, along with the income generated by her real estate, went to her husband, to dispose of as he pleased. Thousands of spinsters and widows left wills distributing their belongings, but married women were not permitted to distribute their real estate—it was divided equally among their children—and they had no reason to express their wishes regarding their personal property, for they had none to give.

In defiance of these prohibitions, Adams drew up her will. "I Abigail Adams," she wrote, "wife to the Hon[ora]ble John Adams of Quincy in the County of Norfolk, by and with his consent, do dispose of the following property." *By and with his consent.* Although the document did not bear the signature of John Adams, Abigail insisted that she had persuaded her spouse

Abigail Adams at around fifty-five, ca. 1800. Painting by Jane Stuart, based on the portrait by her cousin Gilbert Stuart. *Courtesy Adams National Historical Park.*

to go along with her challenge to coverture. Over the course of their long life-times, the Adamses had worked together on a host of important projects that have earned them great renown, but this previously unreported collaboration—in which Abigail, not John, took the initiative—may have been the most extraordinary of all.[1] What prompted the wife of the second president to defy hundreds of years of statutes and legal precedents by writing a will? Given that married women of her era were not supposed to own personal property, how did she manage to acquire so much of it? John would have been well within his rights, upon discovering this document among his deceased wife's papers, in throwing it in the fire, and that raises an additional question: What made her so sure he would carry out her wishes? Abigail herself was never able to answer another question posed by her will, namely: Did John in fact comply with her instructions? But we can.

Giving only brief consideration to Abigail Adams's well-known proto-feminist statements, this essay focuses instead on her little-known effort to banish coverture from her own household. This quest had its roots in her struggle to shield her family from the financial destruction that accompanied the Revolutionary War, in the course of which she became an import mer-chant and then a speculator in depreciated government securities and Ver-mont land titles. As she repeatedly reinvested her profits, she increasingly thought of the money she earned as her own, a process that culminated in her almost unheard-of decision to write a will.

~e

There is an important difference between Adams's two most famous statements on women's rights—her March 1776 injunction to her husband and his colleagues in the Continental Congress to "Remember the Ladies" when drawing up their "new Code of Laws" and her June 1782 reflections on "patriotism in the female Sex." Adams made numerous demands in 1776 but none in 1782. She implored her countrymen to recognize women's "patriotick virtue," but she did not ask them to reward it.[2] One reason for the difference was that by the summer of 1782 Adams knew that while male patriots had succeeded in their bid to secure their natural rights, her own dream of a revolution in the status of women had come to naught. That is not to say, however, that she gave up the fight. She spent the rest of her life advocating for women, especially in the area of education, and she also did something that has never been revealed. Having failed to reform coverture, she set about driving it from her own household.

Adams had in fact begun this effort years earlier, without actually recognizing the implications of what she did. She was not thinking about coverture in 1778, when she and her husband first confronted a seemingly mundane problem: How would John, who had sailed to France as an American envoy, remit a portion of his salary home to his wife in Braintree, Massachusetts? The solution John proposed was conventional: Abigail should periodically draw a bill of exchange—similar to a modern bank check—on him. By the time Adams sent his wife this directive, she had already found her own source of funds: she would become a merchant. "I have thought of this which I wish you to assent to," she wrote her husband in mid-July, "to order some saleable articles which I will mention to be sent to the care of my unkle"—Isaac Smith Sr., a Boston businessman—"a small trunk at a time, containing ten or 15 pounds Sterling" worth of merchandise. From these trunks Abigail would extract the few items her family needed, then give the rest to her cousin Cotton Tufts Jr., "who has lately come into Trade, and would sell them for me." As excited as Adams was about the idea, she was also all too aware of its brashness, so she framed it as her response to having to "pay extravagant prices" for basic necessities. And she claimed that an import business would simply put her "more upon an eaquel footing with my Neighbours," though it would actually give her an advantage over them.[3]

If John was astonished by his wife's proposal to go into trade, he did not show it, and he immediately shipped her several small cargoes. But when he learned that at least two of the vessels carrying freight to Abigail had been captured by the British, he began to have second thoughts. "I have been so unlucky, that I feel averse to meddling in this Way," he wrote her in early November. Abigail was not so easily discouraged. "There is no remittances you can make me which will turn to a better account than Goods," she told her husband. True, it was a "risk to send me any thing across the water" during wartime. But for that very reason, the New England shopkeepers' shelves were nearly empty, and the few importers whose merchandise managed to run the blockade could name their own price. An importation business could remain profitable even if two-thirds of its cargoes ended up in the holds of enemy privateers (government-sanctioned pirates) and frigates or on the ocean floor. "If one in 3 arrives I should be a gainer," she wrote. Abigail would have run another sort of risk if she had imported European goods and then retailed them herself. There were numerous female shopkeepers in eastern Massachusetts, but it would have been undignified for the wife of a congressman to open a store. So Adams consigned the merchandise she received from John to a male cousin. But he apparently worked on commission, which meant that the risks and the rewards were hers.[4]

In his letter accompanying a 1780 shipment to his wife, conveyed from Bilbao on the Spanish coast on a privateer called the *Phoenix*, John was careful to emphasize that he was only sending her "some necessaries for the family." The envoy's description of this merchandise, along with other, similar statements by both Adamses, have led historians to underestimate the extent of the couple's commercial operations. In the eighteenth century, when frigates and privateers seized enemy merchantmen and their cargoes, they often allowed officers, crewmen, and passengers to retain their "private articles." The truth was that 84 percent of the goods that John shipped in the *Phoenix* were linens and handkerchiefs intended for sale. For a brief time in 1780, the word *family* became, in John's letters to his wife, a euphemism for its opposite: "family" goods were precisely those he expected her to sell. In June, when he promised to "send you Things in the family Way which will defray your Expences," he meant that Abigail would be able to pay her bills using the money arising from the sale of the merchandise.[5]

In the spring of 1780 John further refined his effort to keep his wife's trade goods from being captured at sea. Henceforth he would stop sending conspicuous barrels and cases, as he had from Bilbao. Instead, he would disperse his cargoes among multiple couriers. Writing from Paris, he announced that "every Gentleman who goes from here" to New England would be asked "to take a small present" to Abigail. Most of these gifts would actually be trade goods. The first man to serve as Adams's courier was the Marquis de Lafayette, who left Paris in March.[6]

Meanwhile, the *Phoenix* had successfully run the Atlantic gauntlet, putting into the port of Beverly, Massachusetts, in March 1780. The ship could not have arrived at a more opportune time, for two of Abigail's greatest financial challenges—inflation and taxation—had both spiraled to new heights. Yet she anticipated earning enough on the 216 handkerchiefs and 7 pieces of "Holland linen" received from John not only to meet her necessary expenses but to proceed with a purchase that had been a source of friction in her household. For two years the couple had been debating whether to buy a new chaise. During John's first trip to France, when Abigail opened negotiations with Boston carriage maker Thomas Bumstead, she came away discouraged by the astronomical price he demanded.[7] But the arrival of the *Phoenix* revived her hopes of obtaining a new chaise. She reported to John that the handkerchiefs he had sent her would, by themselves, fetch enough money to buy the vehicle. In the end she decided to retain some of her earnings for a possible real estate purchase. But she did put up $200 of the $300 needed to purchase the chaise, so she only had to call on John for $100. Abigail reported her acquisition of the chaise and the rosy prospects for the sale of the *Phoenix* shipment in the same April 15, 1780, letter to her husband.

Abigail's confidence in her commercial abilities rose in tandem with the success of her business, as evidenced by a letter she wrote her husband in July 1780. While thanking him for the trade goods he had sent her in Lafayette's trunk, she objected to his new strategy of dispersing his shipments among multiple couriers. John's system required him to stop buying merchandise wholesale and instead pay the much higher price retailers charged, dramatically reducing the family's profits. She nonetheless reconciled herself to the new arrangement, and in fact it occurred to her that many of the small items she ordered could be "contained in a Letter," which meant that they would travel freight free, since American diplomats' correspondence paid no postage.[8] By the time Abigail had accustomed herself to John's preference for dispersed shipments, he had concluded that her method was superior. Although he continued to ask travelers to slip a "present" or two for Abigail into their trunks, for as long as the couple remained in business, she would receive the bulk of her merchandise directly from wholesalers.

In the fall of 1780 Adams expanded her operations, consigning merchandise not only to Cotton Tufts Jr. in Boston but to her friend Mercy Otis Warren in Plymouth. Like Adams, Warren did not actually retail the goods herself (her teenaged son George handled that part of the business), but she was in charge of negotiations with Adams. These got off to a rocky start, since Warren believed the prices Adams set were too high. In December she reported to her principal that she had "not sold a single Article." For John, dealing with the merchants of Spain, France, and the Netherlands was intensely frustrating. After dispatching two pieces of chintz (printed calico) to his partner in the spring of 1780, he lamented having to pay a "horrid" price for them. But if I do your procurement for you, he added, "you must expect to be cheated. I never bought any Thing in my Life, but at double Price." Adams was, in a sense, proud of his failure as a buyer, since it highlighted his unfamiliarity with the corrupt world of commerce. Abigail wrote back offering reassurance. Do not focus on the price you pay for an item but on the difference between that figure and what the merchandise fetches in Massachusetts, she told him. By that measure, the chintz was "not dear as you Imagined," she wrote. Still, John continued to doubt his procurement skills, and he eventually suggested that Abigail send her orders directly to the European trading houses. From that point on he financed his wife's purchases but otherwise stayed out of the business—to the evident relief of both of them.[9]

❧

Sometime in the fall of 1781, Abigail decided to turn some of the income from her import business into productive capital. As she later reported to John, she placed £100 (sterling) "in the hands of a Friend" (undoubtedly her uncle Cotton Tufts Sr., a Weymouth, Massachusetts, physician) to invest for her. In this pre-banking era, a person who had saved up money could set it aside—and earn interest on it—by lending it to a relative or close associate.[10] It may seem strange that Adams decided to put her mercantile profits out at interest rather than plowing them back into the business. She could have easily sent some or all of this money to her husband to be used for the purchase of more merchandise. No doubt her primary motive for lending it out instead was to diversify her portfolio, placing some of her savings beyond the hazards of the enemy and the ocean.

John was nonetheless skittish about his wife's decision to lend out her money, for he had seen wartime inflation devastate his pre-Revolutionary savings. Even the Massachusetts legislature's January 1781 decree prohibiting debtors from foisting paper currency on their creditors did not entirely reassure him, and he may have also been somewhat alarmed that his wife had placed the money with a "Friend" about whom she provided no identifying information. So he reacted to his wife's announcement with a curt instruction: "dont trust Money to any Body."[11] Abigail could have easily implemented her husband's directive by calling in the loan, but she chose not to do so. And over time, her little savings account would, by a process so gradual that even she did not seem to notice it, metamorphose into something extraordinary: a challenge to the age-old assumption that married women could not own personal property.

૮ઓ

By the winter of 1782 Adams had her sights on a new commercial venture. She set about purchasing a 1,650-acre tract in the projected town of Salem, Vermont, near the Canadian border. This purchase would be a highly speculative investment, for the sellers had a less-than-perfect right to the land, New York and New Hampshire having denied Vermont's right to exist and laid claim to all its territory. As Abigail struggled with her decision, she "recollected the old adage Nothing venture nothing have," and she went ahead with the purchase.[12] The town charter prohibited anyone from buying more than 330 acres, but Adams was able to obtain one grant for her husband and one each in the name of four straw men, who then deeded their tracts to the Adams children. The only member of the family who received no parcel was Abigail herself, since as a married woman she was not allowed to purchase real estate in her own name.

Apparently John did not share his wife's belief in the adage "Nothing ventured nothing have," for he told her in no uncertain terms, "Dont meddle any more with Vermont."[13] But the matter was far from closed.

૮ઓ

With the conclusion of the Revolutionary War, most American soldiers and statesmen returned to their homes and resumed control of their families' finances. But Abigail continued to play an important role in managing her husband's affairs, and she strengthened her conviction that some of the property that legally belonged to John was actually hers. The preliminary peace treaty that John signed in Paris in November 1782 included a cessation of hostilities, which put an end to the astronomical profits that merchants like his wife had earned during the war. Abigail had already begun wrapping up her business, and she completed the process in 1783. It was only a matter of time before the preliminary articles were superseded by a definitive treaty, which John figured would be his last task in Europe. In preparation for his return to Braintree, Adams instructed his wife to begin buying up parcels of farmland near their cottage at the foot of Penn's Hill, and Abigail enthusiastically complied, picking up several tracts. In December 1783, while John was still in Paris, she informed him that their neighbors William and Sarah Veasey had put their farm on the market. It was a tempting proposition, but it would also be much costlier than anything she had yet undertaken. How could she possibly pay for it?

Abigail had an answer to that question. "If my dear Friend you will promise to come home, take the Farm into your own hands and improve it, let me turn dairy woman, and assist you in getting our living this way; instead of running away to foreign courts and leaving me half my Life to mourn in widowhood," she told John on December 27, "then I will run you in debt for this Farm."[14] Adams's proposal that her husband borrow money in order to purchase the Veasey place was so contrary to the couple's shared aversion to debt that it has caught the attention of nearly all of her biographers. Yet scholars have failed to identify the person from whom she wanted John to obtain the money: it was Abigail herself.

"I have a hundred pounds sterling which I could command" if you want to come home and develop the Veasey farm, she wrote. But only on that condition. If John decided to stay in Europe, Abigail's £100 was "a deposit I do not chuse to touch." Since the doctrine of coverture prohibited Abigail from possessing cash or other personal property, Abigail was, in the eyes of the law, offering to bribe John with his own money.[15] In doing so, she demonstrated that she was not content merely to register verbal objections to married women's legal disabilities. She was determined to ban coverture from her own household.

Less than a week later Abigail wrote John another letter displaying a different kind of independence. She was beginning to have second thoughts about the couple's real estate buying spree. "There is a method of laying out money to more advantage than by the purchase of land's," she told him on January 3, 1784, namely "State Notes."[16] Ever since 1777 Abigail had been investing John's money in government bonds. An excellent hedge against inflation, these securities constantly depreciated, but at a much slower rate than state and Continental paper money. But now Abigail was proposing something new: buying bonds not from the government but on the open market. Back in 1781 the Massachusetts legislature had redeemed an earlier series of state government bonds by giving each of the owners a new security called the Consolidated Note. During the winter of 1783–84, these state bonds were trading at about one-third of their face value. But the government paid 6 percent interest on their face value, not what had been paid for them, so investors earned a lofty 18 percent interest on their bonds every year. Abigail now proposed that the £100 that she had stashed away two years earlier be spent not on the Veasey farm but on Consolidated Notes.

Given that Consolidated Notes were so profitable, why did so few people purchase them? As the postwar shortage of gold and silver coin grew ever more acute, few owners of Consolidated Notes were willing to part with them for anything else. Abigail's access to cash—not only from John's government salary but from her own mercantile profits—gave her a tremendous advantage over her neighbors.

∽℮

John probably assumed his wife had dropped her effort to acquire Vermont land titles in response to his peremptory admonition, but if so he was mistaken. Abigail's mother, Elizabeth, who died in 1775, had owned (or possibly co-owned) several hundred acres of land in "Northburry," which may have been either Northborough, Massachusetts, or Northbury (now Plymouth), Connecticut. During her long marriage, authority over this real estate had passed to her husband, and even after she died, he continued to control it for the rest of his life. But upon William Smith's death in September 1783, his wife's land went to her heirs, including Abigail, who reported to John that she had received "a Right in about [2?] hundred acers of land some where in Northburry." Adams apparently did not think this land had much potential—except as a bargaining chip. She knew John would want to sell it in order to buy more land closer to home. But because it belonged to his wife, he could not dispose of it without her permission. Abigail now offered to relinquish her right to the "Northburry" tract in return for John's agreement to let her expand her Vermont investment. "I will exchange with you," she wrote.[17] John does not appear to have replied to Abigail's offer, but the mere fact that she had made it showed just how far she had diverged from the ideal of the submissive wife.

Many of these questions—including whether to buy the Veasey farm and whether to expand the family's holdings in Vermont—remained unresolved in the summer of 1784, when Abigail sailed across the Atlantic to join her husband, whom Congress had decided to leave in Europe even after the signing of the peace treaty. In August the couple and their daughter Abigail Junior, known within the family as Nabby, moved into a rented house in the little village of Auteuil, four miles west of Paris. On September 5 John wrote Dr. Cotton Tufts, his wife's uncle, who had replaced Abigail as her husband's agent in Massachusetts, instructing him to buy two parcels of Braintree farmland, the Veasey place and another tract belonging to James Verchild. Adams had only £300 (sterling) to spare, but if both plots could be had at a reasonable price, he was willing to exceed that limit. Abigail wrote Tufts three days later. She had no objection to his purchasing from Verchild. On the other hand, "Veseys place is poverty," she wrote, "and I think we have enough of that already." Tufts sided with his niece, not John, and did not make the purchase. Abigail may or may not have told John she had countermanded his instruction, but on April 24, 1785, John started a letter to

Tufts by repeating his earlier directive to buy the Veasey farm. Later in the same letter, however, John wrote, "Shewing what I had written to Madam she has made me sick of purchasing Veseys Place. Instead of that therefore" Tufts was to purchase £200 worth of "such Notes as you judge most for my Interest."[18]

The "Notes" that Abigail had convinced John to purchase in lieu of the Veasey farm were, of course, depreciated government securities of the sort she had been accumulating for nearly eight years, and Tufts wasted no time making the purchase. Astonishingly enough, Abigail's redirection of her husband's investment in the midst of his letter to Tufts was not the most extraordinary financial move she made in the spring of 1785. Two weeks after persuading John to amend his instructions to her uncle, she sent Tufts a letter of her own. Her son John Quincy was headed home to Massachusetts to prepare for the Harvard entrance examination, and he was going to bring along his mother's letter—and also £50 worth of Massachusetts currency. "With this money which I call mine," she told her uncle, "I wish you to purchase the most advantageous Bills and keep them by themselves."[19]

Money which I call mine—an extraordinary phrase. Abigail knew better than anyone that coverture prevented married women like herself from owning personal property. In the fall of 1781 she had nonetheless salted away £100 (sterling), and these were the funds that she later used to try to lure her husband home from Europe. Adams was by no means the only married woman of her era who acted as though she owned personal property despite being prohibited from doing so. But it was quite rare for a wife to insist upon her ownership rights. The use to which Abigail now put these funds was also unusual, for she wanted to speculate in depreciated government securities. Tufts bought the bonds, and he carried out his niece's instruction to "keep them by themselves." In reporting the purchase to her, he used language that was vague enough—I "have followed your Directions [by?] your Son John," he wrote—to permit her, if she so desired, to conceal the purchase from her husband.[20]

In the ensuing years Abigail bought additional securities on her own account, and over time she strengthened her hold on these assets. During this same period, her brother-in-law Richard Cranch was, by contrast, experiencing increasing financial difficulty. He and his wife had numerous creditors, including Abigail. In 1789, after John Adams became vice president, Mary Cranch wrote her sister a letter intimating that John could rescue Richard by finding him a lucrative position with the government. Abigail apparently worried that Richard would prove no more adept at government work than he had at private business, and she searched for a gentle way to deflect her sister's request. Finally she found one: she would ease the Cranches' money problems herself by forgiving their debt to her. She instructed her sister to sit down with her husband, calculate the net amount they owed the Adamses, then transmit this figure to Abigail. As soon as I know the figure, she told Mary, "I will send you a Receit in full." Despite being under legal coverture, Adams believed she was "at full liberty" to write off this debt without obtaining her husband's permission, since "the little sum Lent you was my own pocket money."[21] It came from the personal funds that Abigail had been socking away for nearly ten years.

Even though Abigail believed she had full authority over these funds, she decided not to tell her husband what she had done. Keeping him in the dark would not be easy, since John had an annoying habit of opening her mail. So she instructed Mary to enclose her letter in one addressed to Nabby. "It will then fall into no hands but my own," she explained.[22]

ꞏ⸰ꞏ

With the ratification of the U.S. Constitution in 1788, the federal government finally acquired, for the first time, the authority to levy direct taxes, which meant that it could now redeem the war bonds issued by the Continental Congress. Alexander Hamilton, who became secretary of the treasury on September 11, 1789, proposed that the federal government buy up all outstanding state-issued securities (such as the Massachusetts Consolidated Notes that Abigail Adams had purchased) as well. Although most members of Congress agreed that the federal bonds needed to be redeemed, many congressmen, especially southerners like James Madison, opposed federal assumption of the state debts. Madison and others also thought the current holders of federal securities should be forced to share the government's bounty, on a fifty-fifty basis, with the original recipients of their bonds—the soldiers and farmers who had received them in exchange for labor, merchandise, or cash. The final vote on Madison's proposal was scheduled for February 22, 1790, and it was no coincidence that the vice president's wife chose this very day to ride down to Federal Hall for her first-ever visit to the gallery of the House of Representatives. It seems safe to assume that Abigail was the only person in that hall who knew that she was among the speculators who would lose half the money they felt they deserved if Madison's amendment passed. House clerk John Beckley called the roll, and the vote was thirteen for, thirty-six against.

The debt-funding legislation would not receive its final passage until August 4, but by then Abigail had already begun the process of redeeming her government securities, instructing her uncle Tufts to compile an inventory of all her bonds. She also asked him (in an August 2, 1790, letter) to find out whether he could obtain her new securities "in your own Name" in ordeal to conceal her speculation from public view. John Adams made no such effort to hide his status as a public creditor, indicating that the information that Abigail wished to hide was not that her family was profiting from the funding legislation but that she owned personal property in defiance of coverture. She advised Tufts to veil her bond ownership by claiming her federal bonds "as a trustee for an other," without naming that other person. Tufts regretfully informed his niece that he would not be able to "conceal the Name" of the actual owner of the bonds, and he signed a receipt for them as "Trustee to Mrs. Abigl. Adams."[23]

The designation of Tufts as Abigail's "trustee" gave the redemption of her bonds a significance that even she probably did not immediately discern. The only way a married woman of this era could own personal property (or control real estate) was by obtaining her husband's permission to place it in a so-called separate estate. Both of Abigail's sisters eventually established separate estates, Elizabeth because she remarried after losing her first husband and wanted to protect her children's inheritances, Mary because Richard's financial situation continued to deteriorate. There is no evidence that the Adamses ever signed such an agreement, but couples that did so typically put the money in the hands of a trustee. The financial relationship that Abigail established with her uncle back in 1781, when she had first asked him to invest money for her, had been informal. But now, a decade later, her decision to have Tufts identify himself as her trustee, though only applied to this one transaction, had moved her one step closer to asserting ownership of personal property in defiance of the doctrine of coverture. By December 1815 Abigail was telling John Quincy that "Dr Tufts has always been my trustee."[24]

In 1802 Abigail sent a portion of the funds she referred to as "my pin money" to her son Thomas, a Philadelphia lawyer whose income consistently fell short of his expenses. "I have but one injunction to make you," she told her son in the note accompanying this gift, which was that he conceal it from the prying eyes of his father. "Make no mention of it; further than to say you received my Letter safe," she wrote.[25] Most of Adams's donations came from the annual interest she earned on her investments, and she rarely touched the principal. Indeed, her normal practice was to reinvest her earnings.

Cotton Tufts died on Wednesday, December 6, 1815, and Abigail decided that now—"while my reason is sound, and my mind tranquil"—was the time to put her own affairs in order. Her greatest anxiety was for Louisa Smith, the daughter of her deceased brother William. Louisa had lived with Abigail and John nearly her entire life—ever since her alcoholic father abandoned his family in the mid-1770s. Abigail wanted to leave this foster daughter a substantial legacy. Her son John Quincy owed her $1,200 on a promissory note, and in a Christmas Eve letter to her son, she expressed her desire to give the note to Louisa. No one in the world seemed likelier than Abigail's eldest son to have both the means and the desire to disburse these funds as she directed. So placing John in Louisa's debt was the safest thing Abigail could do for her.[26]

On January 18, 1816, as noted at the start of this essay, Adams drew up her will. She began by observing that she had already given her son Thomas her half of the Medford, Massachusetts, farm that she and her sister Elizabeth had jointly inherited from their father, and that her other surviving son, John Quincy, had received "all my right and title in the Farm given me by my uncle Norton Quincy."[27] But her primary purpose in writing her will was to distribute the personal property she had been accumulating since the early 1780s. In addition to distributing her gowns and small sums of cash to pay for mourning rings, Abigail handed out more than $4,000 worth of bank stock, John Quincy's $1,200 debt instrument, and a total of seven shares of stock in the companies managing the Weymouth and Haverhill toll bridges.

She began with gifts to her granddaughters. In addition to clothing and jewelry, each received a cash payment of anywhere from $400 to $750, depending on how wealthy she was. Nabby's daughter, Caroline De Windt, and Charles Adams's daughter Susanna, who remained single in 1816, each received $750. Susanna also got a gold watch, several gowns, "the upper part of my pearl Earings," and a share in the Haverhill toll-bridge company. The smallest bequests, $400 each, went to Thomas's daughters, both of whom were still children. The cluster of granddaughters that headed off Abigail's roll call of heirs contained one anomaly: Adams included Louisa Smith in this list, even though she was actually a niece. Having never married, she had become her aunt's steadiest companion, her most faithful nurse—and her honorary granddaughter. Indeed, her inheritance was the largest of all. In addition to transferring John Quincy's $1,200 promissory note to her, Abigail gave her a share in the company managing the Haverhill toll bridge. Additional bequests went to Adams's other nieces, her sister-in-law Catherine Smith, a pair of distant cousins who were sisters, and two female servants.[28]

One aspect of the will that must have jumped out at everyone who read it—though it has not been noticed by her biographers—is the provision she made for her grandsons, nephews, and male servants. They received nothing at all. Adams listed only two male heirs: her sons John Quincy and Thomas, each of whom received, in addition to the real estate that Adams had already given them, a tankard and a share in the Weymouth toll bridge. And that was it. There is absolutely no indication that Adams had any animus against her male relatives. So why did she exclude all but two of them from her will? Having spent the previous three decades asserting control over land and ownership of personal property despite being married, Adams now bequeathed her estate to her granddaughters, nieces, daughters-in-law, and female servants in order to enable them, as far as it lay in her power, to make the same claim.[29]

To her own surprise, Abigail held on for another year and a half after writing her will. She died at about one p.m. on October 28, 1818, a few weeks shy of her seventy-fourth birthday. In her will Adams had assigned her son Thomas the responsibility of supervising the distribution of her property, and Thomas's brother and father assisted him in carrying out Abigail's wishes. On November 9, less than two weeks after her death, the former president transferred John Quincy's $1,200 promissory note over to Louisa Smith, just as Abigail had directed. John's compliance with the provisions of his wife's will transformed it into a legally valid document. In the eyes of the law, she had acted as his agent and distributed property that belonged to him. In 1819 John Quincy replaced the promissory note he had given his mother years earlier with a new one made out to Louisa herself. No one could ever challenge his cousin's legal right to recover these funds, for she had never married.

In January 1819, when Louisa Catherine Adams learned from her brother-in-law Thomas that Abigail had left her an inheritance of $150, she told him she wanted to set aside half of the bequest to be divided equally among her three sons, who seemed "to have a better title to it than I could boast." By passing this money on to her sons, Louisa may have indicated disapproval of her mother-in-law's decision to exclude all of her male descendants other than her own sons from her will.[30] Yet it seems unlikely that Abigail would have considered the younger woman's gift a defeat. After all, by deciding on her own authority to present the money to her children, Louisa acknowledged what the law of the land had always denied and what Abigail had always affirmed: that the money was Louisa's to give.

FOR FURTHER READING

For complete documentation, see Woody Holton, *Abigail Adams* (New York, 2009). Correspondence among Adams family members up through June 1795 appears in *Adams Family Correspondence,* ed. Lyman H. Butterfield et al., 11 vols. to date (Cambridge, Mass., 1963–). More than half of the extant letters written and received by the Adamses are in *Microfilms of the Adams Papers Owned by the Adams Manuscript Trust and Deposited in the Massachusetts Historical Society,* 608 reels (Boston, 1954–59). For the impact of the Revolutionary War on American commerce, see Richard Buel Jr., *In Irons: Britain's Naval Supremacy and the American Revolutionary Economy* (New Haven, Conn., 1998). Among the most insightful biographies of Abigail Adams are Lynne Withey, *Dearest Friend: A Life of Abigail Adams* (New York, 1981), and Edith B. Gelles, *Portia: The World of Abigail Adams* (Bloomington, Ind., 1992). On married women's property rights, see Joan R. Gundersen and Gwen Victor Gampel, "Married Women's Legal Status in Eighteenth-Century New York and Virginia," *William and Mary Quarterly,* 3rd ser., 39, no. 1 (January 1982): 114–34; Marylynn Salmon, *Women and the Law of Property in Early America* (Chapel Hill, N.C., 1986); Elaine Forman Crane, *Ebb Tide in New England: Women, Seaports, and Social Change, 1630–1800* (Hanover, N.H., 1998); and Mary Beth Norton, " 'Either Married or to Bee Married': Women's Legal Inequality in Early America," in *Inequality in Early America,* ed. Carla Gardina Pestana and Sharon V. Salinger (Hanover, N.H., 1999), 30.

CHAPTER SEVENTEEN

America's Mary Wollstonecraft:
Judith Sargent Murray's Case
for the Equal Rights of Women

Sheila Skemp

In 1798 Judith Sargent Murray confidently predicted that the next generation of American women would have opportunities that she and her contemporaries had been unable even to imagine for themselves. Congratulating her female readers "on the happy revolution which the few past years has made in their favour," she assured them that "in this younger world, 'the Rights of Women' begin to do justice to THE SEX." Indeed, she thought that young women were "forming a new era in female history," an era made possible most of all by the "liberal education" which so many of them were finally beginning to enjoy.[1] Murray was forty-seven when she published these words, old enough to remember the days before the American Revolution when the most privileged women had little schooling and few choices about the way they would live their lives. Now she could rejoice in the fact that she was the author of *The Gleaner*, a three-volume compilation of her own essays, poems, and plays that she hoped would earn her a modest profit as well as the literary fame for which she had hungered as long as she could remember.

Her publication of *The Gleaner* marked Murray as truly extraordinary. Granted, there were a handful of eighteenth-century American women to whom the life of letters was no stranger. Mercy Otis Warren's *Poems, Dramatic and Miscellaneous* (1790) may well have been Murray's most immediate inspiration, even though it was not nearly as ambitious as *The Gleaner* was. New Englander Hannah Adams's histories began to appear a year after

Murray's volumes first appeared. Both Elizabeth Graeme Fergusson and Sarah Wentworth Morton garnered an admiring audience for their poetry. And Susanna Rowson was an accomplished novelist and playwright. None of these women, however, used their pens to call directly and without apology for the rights of women. And none wrote, as Murray did, with the single-minded determination to prove that women were men's intellectual equals; nor did any probe the limits that eighteenth-century women faced with such systematic intensity.

Murray always said that writing *The Gleaner* was relatively easy, but selling and distributing the book required the skills of a businessman—skills that were completely foreign to virtually all women of the age. For good reason, her counterparts all relied on men to take care of the vexing details involved in publishing. Murray, however, did everything herself, inventing shrewd market strategies out of whole cloth as she went along. In the eighteenth century, authors had to fund their own efforts, securing subscribers who promised to purchase a book before anyone would agree to print it. Murray's list of subscribers—750 in all—was impressive indeed. Prospective readers included George and Martha Washington and John Adams as well as an array of generals and governors. Literary luminaries Mercy Otis Warren, Susanna Rowson, and Sarah Morton supported their fellow author. Ordinary men and women from Georgia to Maine, from the Mississippi Territory to London, all agreed to purchase *The Gleaner.* Securing these subscribers was a full-time job. Murray wrote to relatives, friends, and even to complete strangers in an effort to garner as many customers as possible. She also developed a complicated network of friends and relatives who offered subscriptions to their own acquaintances and promised to collect money when payment was due. At the same time, she was dealing with the printers at Isaiah Thomas's Boston shop, complaining about sloppy typesetting, correcting her own errors, and begging the harried workmen to proceed at a faster pace. Once the book was ready for distribution, Murray disregarded propriety, relentlessly badgering recalcitrant customers who failed to make the necessary payments for her volumes. It was an exhausting and often disappointing task.

When she first saw *The Gleaner,* Murray was pleased. She had published before, but never in book form. A book was serious business. It exuded an air of authority and permanence that essays, poems, or plays would never have. The volumes themselves were attractive, especially those special productions for patrons who were willing to pay fifty cents more for better-quality paper, gilt edges, and marbled endpapers. At least in appearance, *The Gleaner* was nothing to be ashamed of.

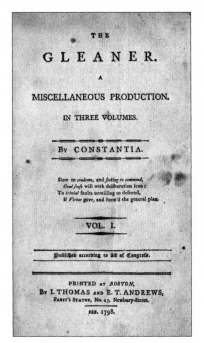

Judith Sargent Murray's *The Gleaner*, a three-volume compilation of poems, essays, and plays, appeared in 1798. Murray published her opus with an eye to making money as well as to garnering critical acclaim, goals that most genteel women of her day disdained. Its four-part "Observations on female abilities" was designed to make even future generations of women marvel at this eighteenth-century writer who was so far ahead of her time.

What about the substance? At first glance, the entire *Gleaner,* which Murray herself characterized as a "miscellany," appears to be a hodgepodge. It employs a variety of literary forms—fiction, nonfiction essays, poetry, letters, even two of her plays. It seems to jump from topic to topic. A discussion of the classics, for instance, is followed by an unrelated defense of the Federalist Party. And its popular novella, *Margaretta,* is constantly interrupted by seemingly unrelated essays. A closer examination reveals, however, that the entire book moves slowly and inexorably toward Murray's most famous essay: volume three's four-part "Observations on female abilities." Beginning with an introduction that adopts a deceptively deferential tone—Murray pretended to accept conventional notions of female inferiority and declined to attack gender prejudice head-on—the rest of the book builds a solid case for its author's contention that in virtually every aspect of human endeavor, women are men's equals. "With proper attention to their education and subsequent habits," Murray insisted, women "might easily attain that independence for which a Wollstonecraft hath so energetically contended."[2]

"Observations on female abilities" was intended to prove as its author put it, that *"The idea of the incapability* of women, is, we conceive, in this *enlightened age,* totally *inadmissible."* The "Observations" reveal as well that Murray was familiar with the most sophisticated understanding of the educational theory of her day. Drawing heavily on the tenets of both the Scottish and the English enlightenments, she argued that all humans were shaped by their environment and that, given half a chance, women were as able as men to profit from good schooling. Hence, while she conceded that women were often weak, vain, and frivolous creatures, they were "circumscribed in their education within very narrow limits." Moreover, because they had almost no opportunity to use the talents with which nature had endowed them, women saw no reason to struggle against the odds. It was nurture, not nature, that rendered women inferior beings.[3] Above all, Murray argued for the intellectual equality of the sexes, as she emphasized the human qualities that men and women shared rather than what she saw as the relatively minor gender differences that divided them. The "distinction male and female," she wrote, "does not exist in the mind." She insisted that women's inferiority was "artificial," solely the result of a "false system of education." Only despotic custom kept her counterparts from soaring to the loftiest heights.[4]

Having painted its argument in broad strokes, the "Observations" went on to compile *"a number of well attested facts,"* a long and impressive list of women who had already, despite the severe handicaps under which they operated, climbed "insurmountable barriers," achieving as much as men in virtually all areas of human endeavor. Women were brave and resourceful, patriotic and influential, loyal and steadfast. They were even capable "of supporting, with honour, the toils of government." Most important, from Murray's own perspective, women were "equally susceptible of every literary acquirement."[5] Her list of women warriors, religious leaders, queens, and authors gave irrefutable evidence of women's abilities in all areas of human endeavor. But it was also a dazzling display of Murray's own deep and wide-ranging fund of knowledge. She discussed with ease the bravery of Spartan women, the fortitude of Lady Jane Grey, the wise governance of Queen Elizabeth, and the literary achievements of Sappho and Corinna. Her knowledge of history and her familiarity with the novelists, playwrights, poets, and essayists of her own as well as bygone eras is evident on every page.

When Murray insisted that women could publish their written work without endangering their reputations for respectability, she was not alone; nor did she invite too much hostility. So long as eighteenth-century women stuck to gender-appropriate topics—motherhood, nature, charity, or morality, for example—and refused to make a profit from their endeavors, they were on fairly secure ground. To write as Murray did, however, on subjects ranging from theology to partisan politics was at least suspect. When she amassed evidence indicating that women could run governments or businesses just as successfully as men, she was venturing into still more treacherous territory.

True enough, Murray's defense of women's abilities sometimes took on a traditional cast, especially when she discussed the political rights and duties of "the sex." She never advocated suffrage, for instance. And she often pointed out that all women were connected to the nation by the same fate that tied them to the welfare of their fathers, husbands, and brothers. Women were citizens, in other words, primarily due to their relationship to the men in their lives. Still, at least on occasion, Murray claimed a more direct tie to the political world. She remarked, for instance, that she expected the new nation to produce a "female Washington" in the very near future, a notion inclined to make her contemporaries shake their heads in bewilderment. Her defense of female politicians, whose advice and judgment the country would ignore at its own peril, was similarly advanced. She confidently insisted that Abigail Adams was her husband's most "valuable auxiliary." The president, she continued, "submitted *every transaction* of his administration" to his wife before arriving at any decision. Were President Adams to die in office, she argued, many people thought that Abigail, not Vice President Jefferson as the Constitution dictated, should take Adams's place.[6] Nor, unlike most of her contemporaries, did Murray shrink from involvement in partisan politics. She was as staunch and unwavering a Federalist as any of her male relatives, and she had no qualms about expressing her views in public. *The Gleaner*'s relatively few avowedly political pieces were clearly designed with Federalist sensibilities in mind. Women, Murray proudly proclaimed, were "daughters of Columbia," and as such they were "equally concerned with men in the public weal."[7]

Murray's argument that women should be educated to assume responsibility for their own economic well-being was also unusual. As a woman of elite status who lived her adult life in a financially precarious position, she deplored a society that left women "to struggle with all the mortifications incident to artificial imbecility."[8] She rebelled against conventions that led most women to marry in order to have food, clothing, and shelter and that left far too many impoverished widows to face the indignity of relying on the charity of family or community to provide them with the barest of necessities. Education, she always maintained, whether it was formally acquired or the product of life experiences, was the path to independence.

In *The Gleaner*, Murray drew her readers' attentions to two women as proof that, given the right opportunities, women could take on tasks generally reserved to men. A widow from St. Sebastian not only ran her own thriving merchant house but educated her daughters for business as well. And a self-taught young woman in rural Massachusetts became the very successful proprietor of her own farm. The "farmeress" not only was capable of providing for her own subsistence, but acquired such a complete understanding of husbandry that she earned the "confidence of the villagers, who are accustomed to consult her on every perplexing emergency."[9] Nor was Murray's argument without broader implications. At a time when economic independence remained an indispensable prerequisite for political rights, her arguments had profoundly radical implications.

✑

Her resentment of a society that neither valued nor encouraged the talents of women, the economic obstacles she faced in her private life, and her conversion to Universalism ultimately led Judith Sargent Murray to become the new nation's most consistent and dedicated defender of the rights of women.

Murray always cherished her family's deep roots in the elite merchant community of Gloucester, Massachusetts. Indeed, it was her pride in her family name that led her to sign all of her correspondence "Judith Sargent Murray." She was fond of the name Sargent, she explained, and had no desire to relinquish it simply because she had decided to marry. Born in 1751, Judith Sargent enjoyed more intellectual opportunities than women of her mother's generation did, and she was much better off than most of her contemporaries. Bright and ambitious, she took advantage of all her privileges, but she always thought that she deserved more. She learned to read, write, and cipher. She had books, even novels, at her disposal. She had access to costly paper, pen, and ink in sufficient quantities that she could scribble away to her heart's content, even as a child.

Still, she seldom appreciated her good fortune. Rather than comparing herself to the vast majority of girls her age, who had virtually no chance to expand their intellectual horizons, she invariably contrasted her prospects with the far superior ones enjoyed by her two younger brothers, especially Winthrop. Two years her junior, Winthrop enjoyed the finest education her parents' money could buy. He attended Boston Latin School before moving on to Harvard. While he became proficient in Latin and Greek, his sister had to make do with a barely passable familiarity with French. Winthrop was no brighter or deserving than she; yet due to a mere accident of birth, he was a true scholar while she remained a "wild and untutored" child of nature.[10] What her society had offered her with one hand, due to her privileged status, it had taken away with the other. Her superiority as a Sargent ran directly up against the doors that remained closed to her because of her sex. Without her conviction that she deserved much better than she received, Murray would have had neither the desire nor the courage to enter the republic of letters.

If her youth prepared Murray to challenge gender conventions, her married life reinforced life's early lessons, leading her to question customs and laws dictating that women would depend economically and socially on men. When she married John Stevens, a well-connected Gloucester merchant, she naturally assumed that her husband would provide her with the material and cultural perquisites to which she was accustomed. Everyone else in her immediate family prospered. Winthrop became the first territorial governor of Mississippi and married well, thus acquiring a large plantation near Natchez. Her sister Esther's husband, John Ellery, was a successful merchant, as was her brother Fitz William. Unfortunately, John Stevens was both hapless and unlucky, and he endured more than his share of financial reversals. By 1786 he faced bankruptcy. Mortified by the sneers of Gloucester's finest, Judith became a virtual recluse, refusing to leave her house even to visit her parents or to attend church. In the end, John fled Massachusetts, sailing for the island of St. Eustatius, where he hoped to recoup his losses. Instead, he died there in debtors' prison, leaving his widow with no resources, no skills, and no respectable way to earn even a meager living.

Judith's second husband was scarcely more successful. An unworldly Universalist minister who trusted the Lord to provide for his modest needs, John Murray was never able to give his wife the social or material position she saw as her birthright. Even after they left Gloucester for the more prestigious Universalist congregation in Boston, the Murrays struggled financially. Thus Judith's complaint about a society that gave women no ability to provide for themselves was much more than a philosophical abstraction. As she discovered that she had no legal rights, that she could not invest money in her own name, buy or sell property, or sue those men who took advantage of her naïveté, she understood just how demeaning a dependent life could be. Her insistence that women should learn to "reverence themselves," that they "should be taught to depend on their own efforts, for the procurement of an establishment in life," was the direct result of the humiliation and fear that she suffered as a wife and a widow.[11]

Murray's resentment of her insecurity grew exponentially with the birth of her only surviving child, Julia Maria Murray, in 1791. Determined to give her daughter the extensive and expensive education that she herself had never enjoyed, and terrified that her husband—ten years her senior—would die and leave mother and child penniless, Murray became more determined than ever to find some respectable way to contribute to the family's meager coffers. Hence, despite her fear that her reputation would be damaged for doing so, she sought money as well as fame when she wrote her plays and published *The Gleaner*. In the end, her reality fell well short of her aspirations. Three years after John Murray died in 1815, Judith, her daughter, and her granddaughter moved to Mississippi. Julia Maria joined her husband, planter Adam Bingaman, at his plantation near Natchez. Murray spent her last two years living either with her daughter or with her brother in the state of dependence she had vainly resisted throughout her adult life.

Murray's conversion to the highly suspect Universalist faith in 1777 was in fact her first rebellion. If her anger at her brother's education and her own downward financial trajectory led her to see the need for economic and legal rights for all women, it was her adopted church's theology that gave her the intellectual underpinnings of her proto-feminist views. In the simplest terms, Universalism argued that all humans were tainted with original sin, but because Christ had died for the sins of all, everyone—not, as the Puritans would have it, just the predestined elect—would be saved. More important, Universalists placed particular emphasis on the notion that the spirit or mind was distinct from and superior to the body, an ephemeral and temporary shell. The eternal and genderless soul would ultimately prove its worth on judgment day. If mind or spirit was the defining characteristic of all humans, then in those areas that truly mattered, men and women were not only equal, they were the same. True, men generally had the advantage where bodily strength was concerned, but this was an irrelevant animal quality. Lions and tigers, Murray was fond of pointing out, were stronger than men, yet no one seriously suggested that the beasts of the jungle should have political rights. Because women were men's spiritual and intellectual equals, there was no reason for women to defer to any man. When, she demanded, "can we be allowed to exercise our reason, if not in matters between God, and our own consciences?"[12]

Murray's painful decision to leave the church of her birth gave her more than theological cover for her beliefs. It also provided her with practical experience in rebellion. She had not, of course, been consulted when the Continental Congress voted to sunder the bonds that tied the colonies to England. But her decision to revolt against the "despotism of tradition" that Puritanism represented was both radical and empowering.[13] Having thumbed her nose at established authority once, it became that much easier for her to do so again. If she could question received wisdom in so fundamental an arena as religion, she could attack the "shackles of superstition" in other venues as well. Because she suffered humiliation as a direct result of her chosen faith, Murray was an ardent advocate of toleration for all political or religious dissenters. Most significantly, Universalism led her to argue that while religious custom was tyrannical, so too were those gender conventions that assumed that women were naturally weak, inferior, and untrustworthy.[14]

It is surely no accident that Judith Sargent Murray first entered the list of authors in 1782 with her anonymously published *Universalist Catechism.* She had been, as she put it, a "scribbler" her entire life. Especially fond of poetry, she dashed off little verses with reckless abandon. She wrote for her own pleasure in the beginning, but she soon began sharing her work with relatives and friends. The more praise she received, the more she sought, and by the time she reached adulthood, she conceded that if she had the "choice among the various honours which the present state of existence can confer," the "literary crown" would be her most treasured possession.[15] Only her fear that she would lose her reputation for propriety, and her profound doubts about her own talent, kept her from attempting to realize her dreams. Without her conviction that she was serving her God, she would have had the desire, but not the courage, to venture into the public sphere.

If *The Gleaner* was her most important and durable contribution to the new nation's republic of letters, it was by no means Judith Sargent Murray's first or only literary venture. Two years after the publication of her *Catechism,* her "Desultory thoughts upon the utility of encouraging a degree of self-complacency, especially in female bosoms," appeared in the *Gentleman's and Lady's Town and Country Magazine.* "Desultory Thoughts," written under the pen name "Constantia," was followed in 1790 by "On the Equality of the Sexes," in the *Massachusetts Magazine.* Significantly, these essays, which outlined Murray's core beliefs concerning women's intellectual ability, reached the public eye well before Mary Wollstonecraft's famous *Vindication of the Rights of Woman* (1792) arrived in the United States. Thereafter Murray's prose and poetry appeared regularly. Her anonymous "Gleaner" essays, which formed the basis of the first volume of *The Gleaner,* entered the literary scene beginning in February 1792. In 1795 Murray broadened her scope with a short-lived career as a playwright. At a time, especially in Massachusetts, when the theater remained a suspect venue even for men, she wrote two comedies, *The Medium* (1795, later titled *Virtue Triumphant*) and *The Traveller Returned* (1796), which were performed at Boston's Federal

Street Theater, making her the first American woman to have her plays produced in the Massachusetts capital. While both efforts were conventional in form, they were replete with strong female characters whose wisdom and rationality enabled them to surmount all obstacles until they arrived at their well-deserved happy ending.

Nothing she wrote, however, gave Murray as much pride as *The Gleaner*, which she saw as the crowning achievement of her literary career. She knew that Wollstonecraft's *Vindication* had been an international triumph, and she could not help but hope that her own publication would be similarly successful, bringing her the fame she craved and the money she desperately needed. Perhaps because her aspirations were so high, she was bound to be disappointed. True, elite Federalists throughout the new nation praised her effort. George Washington, for instance, referred to Murray as "the first literary Lady as was ever seen in any country."[16] But what pleased Federalists—*The Gleaner*'s commitment to hierarchical order, its distrust of democracy, and its fulsome praise of New England's own John Adams—led Jeffersonian Republicans to dismiss it out of hand. Other readers were repelled by *The Gleaner*'s defense of Universalism, a religion that most Americans viewed with horror.

Murray was less distraught by criticism, however, than she was by indifference. As someone who valued fame even more than fortune, she admitted that her hopes had been "blighted by the icy influence of frigid neglect."[17] Her hopes for literary renown were never realized. She was, to be fair, as big a name as any of America's women writers of her day, with the probable exception of the popular novelist and playwright Susanna Rowson. But Murray's goals were lofty. If she aspired to be compared to Mary Wollstonecraft, she was surely disappointed. Her volumes earned enough money to pay off the family's mortgage on its Boston residence, but she did not even sell all of the thousand copies she had originally ordered. By the end of her life, she was reduced to giving them away. After 1798 she wrote relatively little and published even less.

In large measure, her failure to attain the heights to which she aspired was due to circumstances beyond her control. She was increasingly bogged down with domestic cares—supervising the education of Julia Maria and a stream of sojourners from Natchez, tending to John Murray who suffered a series of debilitating strokes beginning in 1809—and of course she endured the usual indignities of old age.

Murray lived and wrote, moreover, at a time when most American women—including Murray herself—did not even ask for the franchise; nor did they organize formal protest movements demanding any other rights or privileges for women. There was no women's movement to which she could belong, even if she had had the time or the inclination to do so. In that sense, her willingness to write about problems that women—as a group—faced was unique. She was not like most of her counterparts, who complained about their individual burdens without linking them to a wider, more universal perspective. Rather, Murray tended to see her own obstacles as ones that all women faced.

Still, while she was truly exceptional in some regards, Murray was conventional in others. Although she rejected most arguments implying that women and men were essentially different, for instance, she nevertheless thought that all women naturally longed to be mothers. And while she believed that women *could* lead armies when called upon to do so, she did not imagine that a military life would—or should—be a desirable career for any woman. As she explained in *The Gleaner,* "We do not wish to enlist our women as soldiers; and we request it may be remembered, that we only contend for the *capability* of the female mind to become possessed of any attainment within the reach of *masculine exertion.*"[18]

Moreover, the Revolution was not even Murray's most formative experience. True enough, she often employed the language of the Declaration of Independence, demanding for "all women" the rights that Thomas Jefferson famously granted to all men. But she did not use her pen to celebrate the sacrifices of American patriots. If anything, she tended to see the war as an obstacle to her own ambitions. Military endeavors almost invariably accentuated the differences between men and women, reminding everyone that weak women relied on men to protect them from the depredations of a heartless enemy. Worse, if women were not on the front lines in the fight for independence, then no one would insist that they deserved the political or economic fruits of victory. Thus it was only with the end of the war, when differences between men and women seemed less obvious and less invidious, that Murray was able to use her talent as a writer to challenge traditional constructions of gender and to help shape and define the character of the new nation.

~C

Unfortunately, her timing could not have been worse. Immediately after the American war against England ended, many people were at least open to a discussion of women's rights. *The Gleaner* appeared, however, at the very moment when the supporters of women's rights were beginning to encounter a "backlash" that would grow ever stronger in the decades to come.[19] The egalitarian message of the French Revolution led many of Murray's own compatriots to question all movements calling for equality of any sort. Thomas Jefferson's election to the presidency in 1800 convinced most New Englanders—including, ironically, Judith Sargent Murray—that the lower orders were taking over and anarchy was about to engulf the American landscape. Thus Murray's nuanced argument that class hierarchy was good while gender differences were to be avoided fell on increasingly deaf ears. Science, as it was understood at the end of the century, also turned against Murray's rationale—which advocated the blurring of all gender lines. In particular, a new breed of thinkers was arguing that men and women were "naturally"—both physically and mentally—complementary opposites, not intellectual equals, thus preparing the way for the definition of gender relations and identities in terms of "separate spheres."

Perhaps most important, at least in the short run, Murray published *The Gleaner* at the very moment when even Wollstonecraft's most dedicated American supporters were having second thoughts about the English feminist. The *Vindication* had been well received when it first appeared on American shores. Men and women alike had praised its basic arguments, and only a handful condemned its bold case for women's equality. Thus Murray had no reason to worry when she drew attention to the book's author in *The Gleaner.* All that changed when Wollstonecraft died in 1798 and her husband, William Godwin, published his *Memoirs,* a laudable but misguided effort to win sympathy for his wife. Godwin described Wollstonecraft as a passionate being whose three-year sexual affair with American Gilbert Imlay resulted in the birth of an illegitimate daughter, Fanny. When Imlay abandoned her for another woman, Wollstonecraft twice tried to commit suicide—not, significantly, because she repented her sin, but because she was disconsolate at the loss of her lover. After she formed a second illicit relationship, with Godwin, resulting in yet another pregnancy, the two reprobates reluctantly married. Wollstonecraft received what many Americans thought was her just punishment when she died, just a few days after Mary Godwin's birth.

Americans everywhere were horrified by the tale. Those who had condemned the *Vindication* from the beginning were only too eager to use the *Memoirs* as an object lesson in the dangers of any philosophy that espoused women's equality. The book's former supporters quickly joined in the condemnation, characterizing Wollstonecraft as an "unsex'd female," and a "whore whose vices and follies had brought about her providential end."[20] Murray herself said nothing about the scandal in public, but in private she indignantly—even courageously—defended a woman with whom she had always identified. Wollstonecraft's *Vindication,* she insisted, was filled with "many luminous truths" and was clearly the "offspring of a superior mind."[21] Convinced that the English writer was the object of malicious gossip grounded in exaggerations, even outright lies, Murray maintained that her hero's only "real *crime was her able defence of the sex.*" It was her support of women's rights, not her actual behavior, that led Wollstonecraft's enemies to attack her with such glee.[22]

If her timing was unfortunate and the very real obstacles that she faced were nearly insurmountable, the fact remains that in some ways Murray's problems were uniquely her own. They were, ironically, the product of the very elite sense of entitlement that had given her the confidence to enter the public arena and to demand rights for women. Unlike the more famous Mary Wollstonecraft, Murray clung to a social structure upon which her own identity was based. Wollstonecraft lived on the margins of respectability, never confining her criticism of social mores to gender issues, challenging what she perceived as all unjust authority as she insisted that women could not achieve equality until the entire social order underwent a fundamental transformation.

Murray, on the other hand, who had so much more to lose than her English counterpart, confined her attack to an establishment that kept talented women from rising to the top. Although she supported the colonial war for independence, she always resisted what many Americans saw as the logical consequences of that war. She was profoundly uncomfortable with the calls for social equality that arose almost as soon as the war had ended. Murray had no problem with a social structure that kept inferior men and women in their place. She asked only that women be allowed to compete with men of their own status for literary fame. She may have resented conventions that unjustly consigned women like herself to an insignificant role. But she totally rejected any system that would destroy the organic order that she cherished. Any society worthy of the name, she insisted, had to be characterized by hierarchy and due subordination, and it was incumbent upon all humans to "seek by every means to preserve legitimate distinctions." To do otherwise was to invite chaos, confusion, and anarchy. "Providence," she insisted, "hath, no doubt for wise reasons, established subordination in our World." Distinctions, which she clearly assumed were based on class rather than gender, had to be preserved.[23]

Ironically, it was the Englishwoman, not the American, who had an intuitive sense of the direction in which the Western world, especially the United States, was heading in the years after the American Revolution. Despite her clarion calls for women's equality, Judith Sargent Murray was in some ways on the wrong side of history. Even as she entered her nation's list of authors, poets, and playwrights, her own country was beginning to marginalize her beloved New England, rejecting the Federalism she and her compatriots embraced, and inching, however slowly, toward a society that was based upon truly egalitarian principles. The very sense of entitlement that had allowed Murray to believe that she deserved literary renown would soon become a defect, not an asset. Thus, while future generations of feminists might find her demands for women's equality laudable and daring for their time, reformers such as Susan B. Anthony and Lucretia Mott would be puzzled and a little bemused by the archaic intellectual apparatus upon which Murray built her case for those demands. More comfortable with an egalitarian worldview, more determined to give all women—not just the intellectual elite—concrete political and economic rights, insisting upon the vote rather than the right merely to "influence" the nation's leaders, the women who looked to Seneca Falls as their defining moment would not have been altogether anxious to claim Judith Sargent Murray as one of their own. And thus this brave and ambitious pioneer in the battle for women's rights would be temporarily forgotten along with her very real contributions to the debate over gender issues.

A product of her time, Murray valued order as much as equality. Nevertheless, she made a valiant effort to discredit what she saw as the artificial barriers that kept women from utilizing their talents in the service of themselves, their families, and the nation. She never stopped urging women to "reverence themselves," nor did she relinquish her desire to carve out a niche for women in the public sphere. She despised what she saw as artificial and outmoded customs that kept women in their place. She longed above all for a meritocracy. She hoped that one day, at least in America, "the career being open to all, we may with democratical equality, pursue the splendid prize."[24] Women, at long last, would be able to reach for the stars.

FOR FURTHER READING

The Gleaner, with an introduction by Nina Baym, was reproduced in its entirety in 1992 by New York's Union College Press. It is also available on *Early American Imprints* (Evans), first series (1639–1800), no. 34162. Judith Sargent Murray's papers, consisting of her letterbooks, poems, and essays, are in the Mississippi Archives, Jackson. My *Judith Sargent Murray: A Brief Biography with Documents* (Boston, 1998), as well as my longer and more detailed *First Lady of Letters: Judith Sargent Murray and the Struggle for Female Independence* (Philadelphia, 2009), are the first biographies of Murray based on her papers, which were discovered by

Unitarian-Universalist minister Gordon Gibson, who helped secure a home for them in the Mississippi Archives in Jackson.

Biographies of other eighteenth-century women put Murray's life in context. Especially useful in this regard are Edith Gelles, *Portia: The World of Abigail Adams* (Bloomington, Ind., 1992); Rosemarie Zagarri, *A Woman's Dilemma: Mercy Otis Warren and the American Revolution* (Wheeling, Ill., 1995); and Catherine la Courreye Blecki and Karin A. Wulf, eds., *Milcah Martha Moore's Book* (University Park, Pa., 1997). Studies of the meaning of the American Revolution for women are both deep and wide. See in particular Susan Branson, *These Fiery Frenchified Dames* (Philadelphia, 2001); Elaine Forman Crane, *Ebb Tide in New England* (Hanover, N.H., 1998); Joan R. Gundersen, "Independence, Citizenship and the American Revolution," *Signs* 13 (1987): 59–77; Linda Kerber, *Women of the Republic* (Chapel Hill, N.C., 1980); and Mary Beth Norton, *Liberty's Daughters: The Revolutionary Experience of American Women, 1750–1800* (Boston, 1980). A clear explanation of early Universalism can be found in Ann Lee Bressler, *The Universalist Movement in America, 1770–1880* (New York, 2001), while an analysis of John Murray's particular perspective on Universalism is lucidly presented in John Murray, *The Life of Rev. John Murray* (Boston, 1869). The essays in Doron Ben-Atar and Barbara B. Oberg, *Federalists Reconsidered* (Charlottesville, Va., 1998), provide an excellent overview of the Federalist culture within which Judith Sargent Murray operated. Lyndall Gordon's *Vindication: A Life of Mary Wollstonecraft* (London, 2005) is one of many excellent biographies of Murray's English counterpart.

CHAPTER EIGHTEEN

Prince Hall, Richard Allen, and Daniel Coker: Revolutionary Black Founders, Revolutionary Black Communities

Richard S. Newman

On December 29, 1799, the Reverend Richard Allen delivered a stirring abolitionist eulogy of George Washington in his Philadelphia Methodist church. A former slave himself, Allen skillfully used Washington's recent death, and news that he had left an abolitionist will, to spur emancipation nationally. "May a double portion of his zeal rest with the whole of the American people," Allen thundered. Not content merely to give an oration celebrating Washington's late conversion to abolitionism, Allen prevailed upon the editor of a Philadelphia newspaper to reprint the galvanizing speech. Editors in Baltimore and New York followed suit, making Allen perhaps the most famous black man at the start of the nineteenth century. As one editor commented, Allen's speech proved that African Americans were more than worthy of freedom.[1]

Allen was just one of many black leaders who refused to wait patiently for abolitionism and equality in the new American Republic. In New England, Phillis Wheatley, Newport Gardner, and Lemuel Haynes gave voice to African-American freedom dreams in the 1770s; in the mid-Atlantic region during the early 1800s, James Forten, William Hamilton, and Peter Spencer struggled alongside Allen for black equality; and in the early national South, Benjamin Banneker and Morris Brown attempted to put the cause of interracial democracy before white statesmen and citizens alike.

These "Black Founders," as we might call them, formed a potent counterpart to the more famous white founding generation of Adams, Franklin,

Hamilton, Jefferson, Madison, and Washington. Comprised of a rising leadership cadre, Black Founders dedicated their lives to two objectives. First, they joined a broad spectrum of African Americans to build the communal infrastructure that would guide black life beyond bondage. In Boston, Baltimore, Philadelphia, New York, Providence, and myriad other locales, African Americans started nearly from scratch, laboriously creating autonomous churches, benevolent societies, Masonic lodges, insurance groups, and literary organizations. Havens from racial oppression, these self-propelled groups allowed people of color collectively to demonstrate racial pride while simultaneously emphasizing principles of self-reliance and uplift.

Second, Black Founders sought to ignite a moral revolution against racial injustice. When most white citizens would not entertain the notion of a biracial democracy, Black Founders proclaimed life, liberty, and the pursuit of happiness as African Americans' birthright—an essential part of the empire of liberty. They did so despite nearly insurmountable odds. Though some white figures challenged slavery during the Revolutionary Era, the peculiar institution not only survived independence but thrived in the early republic. Between 1776 and 1800 the slave population rose from about five hundred thousand to nearly a million. And in the emancipating North, slavery gave way to early forms of segregation in schools, churches, and employment. Many white leaders responded to these ominous trends with silence, hoping that racial injustice—as well as people of color—would someday disappear from the white republic. Black Founders reacted by putting racial injustice squarely before the American public. In speeches, newspaper essays, petitions, pamphlets, marches, and other public events, they articulated a strikingly modern vision of racial equality.

Yet building the early freedom movement was no easy task. As the experiences of three key figures—Boston's Prince Hall, Philadelphia's Richard Allen, and Baltimore's Daniel Coker—illustrate, Black Founders confronted an array of challenging questions following the Revolution. What tactics and strategies best suited the struggle for justice? How could black leaders organize and inspire members of their own community, men and women who had only recently emerged from slavery and faced day-to-day struggles to find work, raise families, and survive? Could slavery and racism be abolished, or should people of color remove themselves altogether from the United States? The answers provided by Hall, Allen, and Coker helped free black communities survive and even thrive in the New Republic—and in no small way, shaped civil rights activism well into the Civil War era.

Prince Hall's Plan

Prince Hall's regal-sounding name was fitting. Masters often bestowed ironic names like "Caesar" or "Cato" on slaves to ridicule their lowly position. But Prince Hall surpassed the promise of his name. Born around 1735, possibly in Barbados, Hall lived in a world where African people built emerging plantation economies yet occupied the lowest rung of Atlantic society. The life expectancy of a person of color, whether in the French Caribbean or British North America, was dismally low. In colonial New England, where Hall moved with his master (a leather merchant), slavery was both a status symbol and part of the region's labor base. Though they did not produce a cash crop, northern enslaved people worked on ships and farms; served as maids, butlers, and washerwomen; and toiled in shops.

Yet for Hall, hardship inspired dreams of African redemption. Joining a Congregational church at age twenty-seven, he discovered that the Bible prophesied blacks' deliverance. "Princes shall come out of Egypt," Psalm 68 declared, and "Ethiopia shall stretch forth its hands to God." Hall took those words to heart during the Revolutionary Era. After securing a manumission agreement from his master in 1770, he married and established himself as a leather dresser and caterer in Boston. Seeking access to a social group that might enhance black uplift and undercut notions of black inferiority, Hall and fourteen other black men approached Masons in a British battalion about forming an African lodge. In 1775, with British support, Hall initiated the first black Masonic lodge in the world. Twelve years later, he received official recognition from London.

By seeking British sanction at a time of revolutionary ferment, Hall had defied town leaders who seethed under British occupation. Indeed, while he soon supported American forces (by producing leather goods for troops in Boston) and may have fought at Bunker Hill, he refused to sit quietly while Revolutionary leaders ignored racial injustice. In Masonry he saw a mechanism for organizing black Bostonians; he also found a commitment to "universal love to all mankind," the phrase he used to describe one of "the two grand pillars of Masonry." A Masonic lodge was a school, a node for political organizing, and an arena for exercising equality and fraternity—among its black members and, it was hoped, among Masons throughout the Atlantic world.

In 1777 Hall and seven other African Americans petitioned the Massachusetts legislature to gradually end slavery (the first four signers were members of the black Masonic lodge). Borrowing from a dissenting tradition in Anglo-American politics that emphasized both universal rights and egalitarianism,

Hall bristled at the notion that the American Revolution stopped at independence. We "resent the unjust endeavors of others to reduce [us] to a state of bondage and subjugation," the petition protested.[2]

Though slavery comprised roughly four thousand souls in Revolutionary Massachusetts, Hall hoped to set an abolitionist precedent. Parts of the 1777 petition, largely repeating a petition circulated four years before, highlighted the religious and political legitimacy of black equality. In a society whose founding document was the Declaration of Independence, and whose citizenry adhered to the Christian gospel, slavery was a betrayal. Until it had been banished and "the Natural Right of All Men" restored, the American Revolution would be a moral failure. "Your petitioners have long and patiently awaited the event of [abolition in] petition after petition," Hall argued. Though frustrated, he vowed to keep struggling until freedom had been secured.[3]

With his forceful and commanding presence, his deep religiosity, and his ceaseless belief in the "love and benevolence to all the whole family of mankind," Hall assumed the mantle of leadership in Boston's black community in the 1780s and 1790s. The African Lodge served as an organizational hub for a small but growing free black community that emerged in the wake of a 1783 state supreme court decision declaring slavery unconstitutional in Massachusetts. Inspired by enslaved black litigants (including Elizabeth Freeman and Quock Walker), the case ended bondage. But it did not destroy white citizens' belief that people of color were inferior. Hall and fellow black Masons had to contend with the brute fact that most whites envisioned the new United States as a white republic. While slavery had been wrong, white citizens argued that free blacks would be a drain on government and society. Black Masons like Hall sought to prove otherwise.

Though vocal and politically active, Boston's free black community remained relatively small when compared to those in New York City, Philadelphia, and Baltimore, each of which would have free populations many times larger by the early nineteenth century. By contrast, Boston's free black community numbered between only 766 in 1790 and 1,174 in 1800. Even at the time of Hall's death in 1807, it was less than 1,300.

Comprising such a small percentage of the city's population, black Bostonians saw communal activism as a vital means of survival. The African Masonic Lodge, with Prince Hall as Grand Master, assumed a key role in free black life. While it had special appeal to ambitious and entrepreneurial black men and their families, the lodge also brought together a cross-section of free blacks. By the early 1800s lodge members included shopkeepers, tradesmen, mariners, and laborers. Hall thrust the city's black Masons into the swirl of post-Revolutionary events while becoming their main spokesman. His name routinely appeared on petitions to local and state government on issues ranging from black education to ending the slave trade.

The immediate postwar years brought Hall and black Masons to the crux of their predicament. The Shays insurgency of 1786, played out mostly in western Massachusetts, offered black Bostonians a chance to prove their courage and loyalty to the city, the state, and the nation. In this way, perhaps, they could mute white hostility and gain redress of their grievances. Answering the call for volunteers to suppress the uprising, Hall wrote Governor Bowdoin that as members of the Commonwealth "we . . . are willing to help and support [the government] . . . in this time of trouble and confusion as you in your wisdom shall direct us." But the governor turned aside the offer of some seven hundred black militiamen, partly because white officers were unwilling to command them and perhaps partly out of fear of hundreds of armed black men.

A month later seventy-three blacks (with Hall the second signer and twelve members of the African Masonic Lodge involved in hammering out the document) petitioned the legislature about the "very disagreeable and disadvantageous circumstances" in which most African Americans found themselves. Discouraged that "so long as we and our children live in America" the new nation had little to offer them, they proposed to return to their African homelands, where they would unite in Christian churches led by their own ministers. Hall asked the state legislature to support the repatriation scheme, knowing that some of his brethren had long viewed West African society as a refuge from American oppression. So now he too embraced the cause. By recrossing the Atlantic, the petition stated bluntly, people of color would finally "live among our equals." When the state legislature buried the petition in committee, Hall and his colleagues enlisted emigrationist support from free black communities along the Atlantic seaboard.[4]

Spurned by the legislature and dismayed by reports in the summer of 1787 that the first wave of black settlers in (British) Sierra Leone had encountered grave difficulties, Hall remained in Boston and evinced a renewed sense of purpose. Nine months after his emigration petition, he was back with another petition on behalf of "a great number of blacks, freemen of this Commonwealth." Why did Boston impose taxes on black citizens while denying their children a "common education" in the public schools? Were black parents expected to have "offspring and [then] see them in ignorance in a land of gospel light . . . and for no other reason . . . [than] they are black"? Rebuffed again, Hall and his followers appealed to the Boston selectmen for black public schools. Spurned again, Hall and his family formed their own school, which they ran out of his leather shop, the Golden Fleece, for several years before moving it to the African Society on Beacon Hill.

The African Lodge also served as a tactical sounding board in the struggle for racial justice. Knowing that print was an important part of racial reform, black Masons contributed to the publication of Hall's best-known pamphlets, both entitled "A Charge, Delievered to the African Lodge." Printed in 1792 and 1797, Hall's essays exhorted black Masons to focus on education, piety, communal support, and egalitarianism as the keys to collective black uplift. Hall's work also reminded his brethren that they were descendants of a noble ancestry, for Africa, and not Europe, had been the cradle of civilization.

Hall's essays addressed white citizens too. Expressing anger at the uncivil behavior of white Bostonians toward their fellow black citizens, Hall envisioned African Americans as both freedom fighters and modern nation builders. "In the late war," he counseled, blacks "had marched shoulder to shoulder, brother soldier and brother soldier, to the field of battle" with whites. Despite risking their lives for American liberty, people of color now faced a hostile racial climate in the new republic, including "daily insults . . . in the streets of Boston," as Hall put it. Nevertheless, he counseled forbearance, hoping that this policy would prove free blacks' dedication to biracial democracy. Still, neither of Hall's "Charge" pamphlets advised timidity among free blacks. Referring to the slave rebellion in St. Domingue, Hall urged African Americans to band together and struggle mightily against racial oppression. "Let us not be cast down under these and many other abuses we at present labour under," he thundered, "for the darkest is before the break of day." Enslaved people's struggle in St. Domingue reminded Hall that blacks could be a revolutionary and liberating force so long as they stood up for their rights and remained united.[5]

By the time of Prince Hall's death in 1807, Boston's African-American community had made significant strides toward self-empowerment (if not full equality). One sign was the founding of the African Baptist Church in 1805, followed by the building of the African Meeting House a year later. More broadly, Hall's generation of free black Bostonians created a tradition of political activism that would impress subsequent generations of American abolitionists, from the radical black pamphleteer David Walker (who joined Prince Hall's African Lodge in the 1820s before authoring his famous *Appeal*) to William Lloyd Garrison (who adopted Hall's brand of biracial egalitarianism as his own in the 1830s). Hall's name itself lived on when the African Lodge became the Grand Lodge of Prince Hall Masons in the early nineteenth century, a label that now characterizes black Masons everywhere.

Richard Allen's Dream

Like Prince Hall, Richard Allen dreamed of black redemption. But for Allen, the independent church, rather than the Masonic lodge, was the center of black community life. Allen also viewed the black church as a powerful platform from which to launch the national struggle for freedom and equality.

A generation younger than his Massachusetts counterpart (Allen was born in 1760), he expressed similar concerns about black liberty in Revolutionary America. When Hall's first abolitionist petition reached the Massachusetts legislature, the teenaged Allen was stuck on a Delaware plantation, worrying about a lifetime in "bitter bondage."[6] Looking for ways out of this brutal existence, he found evangelical religion and then a pathway to freedom. By the time he was in his twenties, Allen had secured not only liberty but a rising reputation on the mid-Atlantic revival circuit. He adopted Psalm 68—"Princes shall come out of Egypt and Ethiopia shall stretch forth its hands to God"—as a veritable injunction to redeem not only himself but the American nation too.

Allen found Methodism at a moment of personal crisis around 1777, when his second master sold his mother. Young Allen rallied by setting up a meeting between his second master, Stokeley Sturgis, and a Methodist preacher named Freeborn Garrettson. A former slaveholder, Garrettson gave stern sermons about Christian morality. "Thou art weighed in the balance and found wanting" (Daniel 5:27), he lectured Allen's master.[7] Deeply shaken, Sturgis accepted Allen and his brother's offer to purchase their liberty. With his master's approval, Allen took to the road to earn money and preach the gospel. Working as a bricklayer, cartman, sawyer, and butcher, among other jobs, he paid off his freedom agreement early. In 1783, the same year that the United States signed a peace treaty with Great Britain, Allen was free.

Allen's conversion experience connected him to antislavery religion. Methodist preachers roaming the countryside declared all souls equal before God. Initially a dissenting faith within the Anglican Church, Methodism grew on both sides of the Atlantic precisely because its sense of spiritual egalitarianism appealed to marginalized people, from enslaved blacks to laboring whites. Methodists' plain speaking and massive revivals brought thousands of new converts into the American branch of the church by the end of the Revolutionary Era. Black men and women drew particular inspiration from revivalism, whose emotive, interactive meetings recalled African call-and-response traditions. African Americans also appreciated founder John Wesley's increasingly well-known antislavery stand. In turn, Methodist ministers viewed African Americans as a powerful, largely untapped, religious constituency.

Over his long life, Allen cultivated a nearly unrivaled national leadership position among people of color, surpassing even the hallowed Prince Hall. A year after moving to Philadelphia in 1786, he helped inaugurate the Free African Society, the first black benevolent group in Pennsylvania. Already preaching in the streets and swelling the congregation at the mostly white St. George's (Methodist) Church, Allen was saddened to find segregated seating policies in the House of the Lord. He joined fellow blacks who wished, as he put it later, to "sit under their own vine and fig tree." They departed from St. George's, proudly proclaiming that "we never entered it again."[8]

Even before this galvanizing exodus, Allen and his friend Absalom Jones imagined launching independent black churches. Jones eventually headed St. Thomas's African Episcopal Church, while Allen would lead the African Methodist Episcopal Church. Known as Bethel ("House of God"), Allen's church grew from several dozen congregants in the 1790s to nearly fifteen hundred by the 1820s. The church became an emblem of racial and ancestral pride nationally. The very sight of Allen's preachers inspired African Americans. "See his ministers in the states of New York, New Jersey, Pennsylvania, Delaware, and Maryland carrying the gladsome tidings of free and full salvation to the colored people," David Walker declared in his *Appeal*.[9]

From the founding of Bethel onward, Allen remained an activist minister.

R*ev. Richard Allen* was drawn in 1813 by an unknown artist. Perhaps the most familiar of his three portraits, this image depicts Allen only a few years before he was named the first bishop of the newly formed African Methodist Episcopal Church. He points to a Bible to illustrate not only black literacy but African Americans' moral sense. Allen believed that both the Bible and the Declaration of Independence mandated universal freedom and equality.

He authored several pamphlets of protest, lobbied political officials to support black equality, and crafted the first autobiography by a Black Founding figure. "Rome had her Caesar . . . Germany her illustrious Luther . . . America her Washington, Jefferson and Abraham Lincoln," Philadelphia bishop A. M. Wyman proclaimed during the Civil War. African Americans had their own "illustrious hero" in Allen.[10]

The rising black preacher also articulated philosophical notions about black identity that would influence nearly every major African-American leader following in his wake, particularly the idea that racial and civic allegiances were compatible. In Allen's eyes, blacks must be seen as cofounders of the American nation. As he observed in 1827, enslaved people created American prosperity. "Africans have made fortunes for thousands," he wrote in *Freedom's Journal*, "who are yet unwilling to part with their services." Now African Americans would expand the ideological meaning of the American Revolution, linking racial liberation to the nation's founding mission. For these reasons, Allen argued, the United States was a black homeland. "This land which we have watered with our tears and our blood," he wrote, "is now our mother country and we are well satisfied to stay where wisdom abounds, and the Gospel is free."[11]

Like Massachusetts, Pennsylvania struggled with the contradiction of slavery in the land of liberty. In 1780 the state passed the Western world's inaugural gradual abolition law, liberating enslaved people born after its passage when they turned twenty-eight. Though none of the roughly seven thousand enslaved people in the Quaker State would be freed by the law, the abolition act spurred black restiveness. Pennsylvania's enslaved population ran away, complained, and compelled white figures to address their immediate desires for liberty. A wave of freedom agreements between masters and slaves during the 1780s and 1790s—much like the one Richard Allen had signed—reduced slavery's size. By the early 1800s only a few hundred slaves remained in Pennsylvania, and African Americans viewed its borders as a potential sanctuary.

Yet Pennsylvania was no haven for people of color. In Philadelphia most white workers feared competition from free black laborers and tried to freeze them out of well-paying work. Others maligned black Philadelphians, resented their independent churches, and tried to pass legislation depriving them of voting rights. If blacks earned legal freedom in Pennsylvania, they did not get social and political equality.

In the midst of growing racial hostility, Philadelphia's autonomous black churches, like Boston's African Lodge, served as communal sanctuaries for people of color. Evidence came in the form of grassroots support of

Allen's church by African-American women, who helped build Bethel by running benevolent societies, raising funds, and espousing racial uplift as a community-wide goal. Allen's first and second wives—Flora, who died in 1801, and Sarah, who lived until 1849—donated their own wages to Bethel and cosigned property deeds for the fledgling church. With women and families supporting them, free black churches prospered in Philadelphia. By the 1810s African Methodist, Episcopal, Presbyterian, and Baptist churches dotted the city.

Though black churches led the struggle for justice in Philadelphia, Allen and Jones formed a Masonic lodge in 1797 after they were rebuffed by white Masons. Fittingly, Jones and Allen summoned Prince Hall himself to install the first officers of Philadelphia's African Lodge of Pennsylvania. Over the next several years, black leaders built a black Masonic hall and formed three new lodges in the city, all bustling with men striving for economic and educational advancement and searching for fraternity and equality in a hostile world.

But the black church remained Allen's primary concern. With autonomous religious groups appearing all along the Atlantic coast, black leaders joined Allen to form the African Methodist Episcopal (AME) denomination in 1816—the first national organization created by blacks and sanctioned by white authorities. The AME emphasized racial pride, piety, and educational uplift. An inspiration to generations of African Americans, it became the largest black church by the Civil War. It also became a key site of political protest. Within their secure confines at Sixth and Lombard streets, Bethelites organized abolitionist petition drives, celebrated the end of the international slave trade in 1808, sponsored prominent African-American lecturers, and underwrote the publication of several important pamphlets on issues ranging from Haitian emigration to the rise of discriminatory practices in the North.

A genial and modest man whose physical presence appeared anything but intimidating, Allen possessed a legendary determination to succeed. When aroused by some issue, black activist Henry Highland Garnet recalled, Allen's piercing eyes "seemed to blaze with a fire that attracted the attention of all who beheld them."[12] Allen hoped to become a national race leader capable of both mobilizing people of color and confronting white statesmen about racial injustice. Alluding to writings by Franklin, Jefferson, and Washington, Allen published over half a dozen pamphlets and essays and participated in nearly every black petition drive in Philadelphia. In 1792 he joined the first petition drive to Congress urging American leaders to pass a federal abolition law. In 1799 he was one of more than seventy people of color who signed a similar petition to Congress.

His first publication, coauthored with Absalom Jones, came in 1794: "A Narrative of the Black People During the Late Awful Calamity in Philadelphia." A searing indictment of white racism, it defended blacks against accusations that they had plundered white homes during the recent yellow fever disaster. Not so, Allen countered, for African Americans had volunteered to aid the city when many white figures fled. Allen added an antislavery address challenging national statesmen to liberate enslaved people and incorporate them into the body politic. "If you love your children, if you love your country, if you love the God of love, clear your hands from slaves, burden not your children or country with them," he wrote. After publishing the document, Allen marched into a federal office, where a clerk notarized it as the first copyrighted pamphlet by a person of color.[13]

Five years later Allen published twin eulogies of white men who had taken his abolitionist message to heart. The first honored Warner Mifflin, a slaveholding Delawarean who emancipated his slaves before becoming an itinerant abolitionist; the second heralded George Washington as an antislavery icon. In both cases, Allen hoped to validate abolitionism as purifying and patriotic.

Like Prince Hall, Allen eventually entertained emigration as a key strategic response to rising racism. Worried that young blacks would rebel against community leaders, as well as white citizens, if more and better economic opportunities did not arise, Allen began to consider emigration as a means of channeling African Americans' anger. Though free blacks faced the common problem of racial discrimination in early national Philadelphia, leaders and community members often disagreed on emigration plans. Though a backer of black sea captain Paul Cuffee, who sought to create international trade networks between Western and African societies, Allen discovered that many free black Philadelphians opposed African colonization. In fact, in 1817 the black masses rejected black leaders' support of the slaveholder-dominated American Colonization Society (ACS). Community opposition to the ACS at Allen's own Mother Bethel Church compelled black leaders to oppose colonization as a slaveholding front.

Yet the aging Allen continued to worry about class divisions within Philadelphia's black community. While some blacks had risen from their servile status, Allen knew, many others had not. The top 5 percent of the free black population was composed of an economic elite. Below them was a middling group of small property owners who practiced trades and ran small shops. At the bottom simmered a much larger group who rented squalid homes in alleys and courtyards and possessed negligible personal property. In stark statistical terms, there were roughly one thousand black worthies and fourteen thousand "poor people" of color in Philadelphia by the time of the first major abolitionist census in the 1830s. A decade before that, some members of the underclass had already begun turning away from Allen's lectures on moral rectitude, piety, and temperance. In 1820 a group of parishioners actually departed Bethel Church, alleging that Allen had acted in a haughty manner.[14]

By the mid-1820s, a frustrated Allen supported Haitian emigration as a means of realizing African Americans' freedom dreams. With southern slavery expanding and racism intensifying in the North, Allen thought that people of color needed a safety valve beyond U.S. borders. Though he had long hoped Americans would embrace racial reform, Allen despaired of achieving it in a land seemingly devoted to slaveholders' rights. After considering and rejecting African colonization, he turned to Haiti as a possible asylum. When that dream failed, he recommended black migration to British Canada (where slavery had been banned). By arguing that Canada would allow blacks to achieve universal equality and economic uplift, Allen indicated that his faith in American liberty was nearly at an end.

Still, Allen remained in Philadelphia for his entire life, constantly battling against white hostility and discrimination. He even rekindled his faith in interracial democracy within the United States by joining the Free Produce Movement (which boycotted slave-made products) in the 1830s. And prior to his death in March 1831, he returned to the twin revolutions that had initially inspired his freedom dreams: the American Revolution, which spawned the Declaration of Independence, and the evangelical revolution, which declared all humanity equal before God. Arranging his personal affairs in 1830, Allen prepared a manuscript that recounted his struggles to speed black redemption. Excising all allusions to emigration, his autobiography told African Americans that the United States was a black homeland. Published in 1833, it became a prized possession in many black households. As Frederick Douglass later observed, Allen's dedication to egalitarianism secured his rank "among the remarkable men whose names have found deserved place in American annals."[15]

Daniel Coker's Journey

Daniel Coker was the youngest member of the Black Founding trio. Born in 1780 in Frederick County, Maryland, to an indentured white mother and an enslaved father, he secured his freedom by running away to New York. Returning to Baltimore in 1801, he joined Sharp Street Methodist Church, where both whites and blacks worshipped. As at St. George's in Philadelphia, racial friction led to a breakaway movement akin to Allen's celebrated departure (though most of the black Sharp Street Church congregants did not follow Coker). Still, he became Baltimore's leading advocate of independent black churches and, at age twenty-one, the first black teacher at the African Academy. Though the white Methodist church would not sanction his breakaway group or ordain him, Coker served in a ministerial capacity at the new church, also known as Bethel, where he advocated spiritual and educational uplift. He was soon in contact with black leaders throughout American society. He rose so fast that he was briefly elevated to bishop of the African Methodist Episcopal denomination in 1816.

Believing that abolitionism was a natural extension of both American Revolutionary ideology and evangelical doctrine, Coker made his Baltimore church and school centers of black reform. In 1810 he told a public gathering that, contrary to the "extraordinary opinion of some philosophers," black students were not "inferior to the whites in the organization of body and mind."[16]

That same year Coker issued a pamphlet urging white southerners to embrace emancipation and racial equality. Published in Baltimore, it confronted an unyielding white population. Although northern abolition laws had curtailed bondage above the Mason-Dixon Line, reformers had no such victories in the heart of slave country. By 1800 Marylanders and Virginians still held well over 300,000 slaves. Still, there had been some hopeful trends. In Virginia a liberalized manumission law of 1782 had prompted the freedom of between 6,000 and 10,000 slaves by 1806, when the state changed the law. In Maryland, black runaways made such substantial inroads against bondage that many masters reduced slavery to indentured servitude (in exchange for pledges not to flee again). These deals, combined with other manumission deeds and migration from various parts of the South, created a vibrant free black population of over 10,000 persons in Baltimore by the 1830s.

Yet Baltimore's free blacks endured constant discrimination, facing a much less favorable economic and political environment than their brethren in Philadelphia. With attenuated economic opportunity, class divisions were less pronounced among the city's free population. Coker and community members in his church and school responded to antiblack hostility by coming together to consider a range of strategic options to racial injustice, from literary protest to emigration overseas.

Coker fervently hoped his abolitionist pamphlet would spawn a southern abolitionist revival. Titled "A Dialogue Between a Virginian and an African Minister" (1810), it was the first black abolitionist essay published in the Upper South since Benjamin Banneker's letter to Thomas Jefferson in the early 1790s. Though Baltimore's racial climate remained moderate relative to other locales, Coker's pamphlet was risky. To gain a white audience, Coker had to balance abolitionist pronouncements against mainstream racial sensitivities. Thus he constructed his pamphlet as a dispassionate scholarly essay rather than an abolitionist harangue.

Drawing freely on Scripture, Lockean natural rights philosophy, and Revolutionary ideology, Coker's pamphlet featured a slaveholding Virginian and a free black minister who engage in a wide-ranging discussion of southern abolition. "Sir," the Virginia master asks at the outset, "I have understood that you have advanced an opinion that it would be just in our legislature to enact a law for the emancipation of our slaves that we hold as our property[,] and I think I can convince you that it would be wrong in the highest degree." "Sir," the African minister replies deferentially, "I will hear you with pleasure."[17]

These niceties established, Coker's morality play then counters every objection to abolition. What about masters' property rights? What about biblical justifications of bondage? What about black vengeance against white masters? The African minister replies authoritatively to the master's queries, illustrating not only blacks' firm grasp of abolitionist philosophy but the principles of rational discourse. If African Americans could argue effectively, Coker implied, then they must be considered equal citizens rather than beasts of burden. On biblical justifications of slavery, for example, Coker demolished slaveholders' favorite dictum—"servants obey your masters"— by referring to other sections of the Bible that contradict it, such as the book of Exodus ("Let my people go") and Acts of the Apostles ("the Lord hath made of one blood all nations of the earth"). So dazzled is the Virginian by this display of black genius that he vows to liberate his slaves.[18]

Coker's happy ending was of course fiction. Few masters embraced his abolitionist call to arms. By the 1820s even private emancipation stalled in the Upper South, and a younger generation of white leaders began to label free blacks everywhere—not southern bondage—as the nation's enduring problem. Moreover, he had traveled a rough road after forming his independent black church. Coker and his followers fitted out a rented brick building while convening camp meetings to increase their number. Still, most of the city's black Christians preferred to remain in the white-controlled Methodist church, seeing it as their best chance for advancement. Coker's tribulations increased in 1818, when the AME Conference, organized by Allen in Philadelphia, suspended him from the ministry for a year for allegedly speaking ill of some members. The collapse of his personal finances also led to a new plan in 1820: Coker would take the struggle for freedom and justice overseas, leaving American oppression and inequality far behind.

Under the aegis of the American Colonization Society, Coker journeyed to the land of his ancestors. With family and scores of devotees in train, he settled in Sherbro, a colony of ex-slaves in Liberia, on the west coast of Africa. Wearied by what he termed "these divisions in America," Coker would spend the rest of his life in Africa (where his descendants still reside).[19] Coker's journey remained the exception, not the rule, among people of color, who still overwhelmingly rejected colonization. Indeed, the ACS's harsh language about free blacks (both northern and southern colonizationists pictured African Americans as a scourge) drew scorn from generations of African-American leaders. Nevertheless, Coker's African departure spoke to the frustrations of some southern slaves (and free blacks) who came to view African colonization as their only means of attaining equal liberty. Since the Revolutionary Era, disaffected people of color had revisited exodus from time to time. Both Hall and Allen had flirted with emigrationist schemes. But neither man ever departed the United States. Coker did, and he viewed his African journey as more than just a missionary endeavor—it was, he believed, a form of black self-determination. Though underwritten by the ACS, Coker's African plan allowed him to exert control over his life and destiny. He hoped that other people of color would follow him back across the Atlantic.

Though emigrants did continually trickle into Liberia, no steady stream of converts followed. Yet when he died in 1846, Coker remained convinced of the righteousness of his American departure. He had founded the West African Methodist Church (in British Sierra Leone, where he eventually moved). He also left an emigrationist legacy that compelled subsequent African-American leaders to consider the merits of black exodus.

Revolutionary Black Communities, Revolutionary Black Leaders

Hall, Allen, and Coker exerted a profound influence on black reform. Well before the rise of Frederick Douglass, Sojourner Truth, and other well-known antebellum black activists, these Black Founders recognized that racial redemption depended on communal, not just individual, empowerment. In this manner Hall, Allen, and Coker all became fierce advocates of group economic advancement, universal liberty, and communal pride. Each man also believed that African Americans as a whole, from enslaved people to free blacks, had equal claims on the American Revolution. For them, liberty and justice for all did not stop at the color line.

But Black Founders did much more than that. In an era of nation building, Hall, Allen, and Coker helped inaugurate some of the earliest and most successful communal institutions in free black society: the African Lodge, Bethel Church, and the AME denomination. Here too Black Founders were often the most visible faces of a process with deep community roots. In Boston, Philadelphia, New York, Baltimore, and a range of other locales, unheralded men and women joined in the effort to create schools, Masonic lodges, benevolent societies, churches, and insurance organizations. Yet Hall, Allen, and Coker added important dimensions to free black institutional life. By publicly celebrating African ancestry, they grounded black identity in a noble preslavery past; by utilizing print culture to argue that slavery and racism violated both secular and sacred creeds, they brought black dissent into mainstream culture.

It is little wonder, then, that Hall, Allen, and Coker were icons of black activism. Their lives ennobled the struggles of countless people of color. Even in the twenty-first century, we are still trying to catch up with their revolutionary activism.

FOR FURTHER READING

On struggles against slavery and racial injustice in the American Revolutionary Era, see in particular Gary B. Nash, *The Forgotten Fifth: African Americans in the Revolutionary Era* (Cambridge, Mass., 2006), and Douglas R. Egerton, *Death or Liberty: African Americans and Revolutionary America* (New York, 2009). Benjamin Quarles's classic book, *The Negro in the American Revolution* (Williamsburg, Va., 1961), also remains a good source on the subject. On recent scholarly understandings of Black Founders, see Richard S. Newman and Roy Finkenbine, "Black Founders and the New Republic: An Introduction," *William and Mary Quarterly,* 3rd ser., 64, no. 1 (January 2007): 83–94. On Prince Hall, Charles H. Wesley's *Prince Hall: Life and Legacy,* 2nd ed. (Washington, D.C., 1983), remains useful. On Revolutionary Era blacks, see especially Sidney Kaplan and Emma Nogrady Kaplan, *The Black Presence in the Era of the American Revolution* (Amherst, Mass., 1989). On free blacks in the early republic, the best work is James Oliver Horton and Lois E. Horton, *In Hope of Liberty: Culture, Community, and Protest Among Northern Free Blacks, 1700–1860* (New York, 1997). See also Joanne Melish, *Disowning Slavery: Gradual Emancipation and Race in New England, 1780–1860* (Ithaca, N.Y., 1998). For an analysis of free black membership in Prince Hall's African Lodge (and related organizations), see Peter P. Hinks, *To Awaken My Afflicted Brethren: David Walker and the Problem of Antebellum Slave Resistance* (University Park, Pa., 1997). There are now many fine books on eighteenth-century African-American figures, including John Saillant, *Black Puritan, Black Republican: The Life and*

Thought of Lemuel Haynes, 1753–1833 (New York, 2002); Julie Winch, *A Gentleman of Color: The Life of James Forten* (New York, 2002); and Jon F. Sensbach, *Rebecca's Revival: Creating Black Christianity in the Atlantic World* (Cambridge, Mass., 2005). For a new look at Richard Allen, see Richard S. Newman, *Freedom's Prophet: Bishop Richard Allen, the AME Church, and the Black Founding Fathers* (New York, 2008).

CHAPTER NINETEEN

Richard and Judith Randolph, St. George Tucker, George Wythe, Syphax Brown, and Hercules White: Racial Equality and the Snares of Prejudice

Melvin Patrick Ely

Richard Randolph sat down at the mahogany desk in his Virginia plantation house in 1796 and committed an unusual act for a man of twenty-five: he wrote a will. More striking still, he filled the first half of the document not with detailed instructions for the disposition of his many worldly goods but with a blistering attack on slavery—the very institution on which his family based its wealth and prestige. Randolph addressed part of his testament to the 150 bondpeople he had unwillingly inherited from his father five years earlier, "*humbly* beg[ging] their forgivness, for the manifold injuries I have too often inhumanly, unjustly, & mercilessly inflicted on them."[1]

Randolph had absorbed racially egalitarian precepts from the stepfather who reared him, St. George Tucker, and from George Wythe, his teacher at the College of William and Mary, and he now called for his slaves to go free after his death. Unlike most others who granted liberty to African Americans during the years after the American Revolution, Randolph also directed that his former slaves receive a sizable portion of his own plantation as a base on which to build new lives as free people. Randolph's late father had made a quick mass emancipation legally impossible by using almost all his enslaved people as collateral for loans he had taken out, and Richard himself died only a few months after he wrote his will. Nearly a decade and a half would pass before Richard's widow, Judith, made his vision of freedom real at Christmastime 1810.

Two of the enslaved persons Randolph proposed to liberate, and perhaps the most impressive of the lot, were Syphax Brown and Hercules White, both born by the mid-eighteenth century and thus older than Richard himself by a generation or more. These two black men and the young white aristocrat who owned them enacted a bold experiment: Richard's will made possible, and Syphax's and Hercules' actions helped create, a community of liberated Afro-Virginians which embodied the most radical principle of the American Revolution—that all people are created equal.

Randolph wrote his will nearly fifteen years after the American victory at Yorktown, but the document captured in writing the heartfelt cry of a devout child of the Revolution. Richard's stepfather, the prominent attorney and jurist St. George Tucker, had fought alongside the Marquis de Lafayette in the Yorktown campaign. Young "Dickey," who was about eleven at that time, had invested all his emotion and his precocious intellect in the patriot struggle against both Great Britain and her supporters in his own neighborhood. "I wish the british may meet with destruction & their attempts be baffled in every instance," he wrote to his warrior "Papa." "Which I make no doubt they would if the Tories did not give them such good intelligence." "I wish I was big enough to turn out" for army service, the boy added. Dickey followed military campaigns assiduously and even shared his own tactical and strategic assessments with Tucker.[2]

In that summer of 1781 patriots in Dickey Randolph's neighborhood—his family lived on a plantation named Bizarre on the Appomattox River in south-central Virginia—were sacrificing food and fiber for the troops. In July the British colonel Banastre Tarleton led a force of cavalry and mounted infantry into the Appomattox Valley, burning, looting, and taking local men prisoner. Richard's mother, Frances (Fanny) Tucker, prepared to evacuate Bizarre, readying her five children and her slaves for the trip and putting a "steel hilted dagger into her stays" for protection.[3] The family's flight was delayed for a couple of days by a disabled wagon and ultimately was rendered unnecessary when Tarleton's men veered away from Bizarre and headed back east.

During those tense hours, as at other times, the African Americans belonging to the Randolph-Tucker family played a role in the Revolutionary War that Dickey would never forget. Slavery robbed black people of liberty but not of will, and the crisis had presented some new options to bondpeople. Early in the war the British had offered freedom to American slaves who would join them, and thousands fled from their masters during the conflict. The Tuckers acknowledged that the enslaved had good reason not to stand by those white Americans who deprived them of liberty. At the time of Tarleton's raid, the family's fate rested for a time in the hands of the black wheel-wright who had the ability to fix their wagon, and Fanny felt fortunate that, as she prepared her escape from the war zone, "my faithful Servants are every thing I cou'd wish them, & are willing to follow my fortune."[4]

The Tarleton scare had not been the first experience that subtly demon-strated to Dickey Randolph how thoroughly his stepfather's dream of Amer-ican liberty, and the family's well-being overall, depended on the labor and even the goodwill of enslaved black people. In July of that same year young Richard had been confronted with a frightening scene: a man leading two riderless horses—one of them his Papa's mount, Hob—up the lane toward the Randolph-Tucker mansion. Richard instantly concluded that St. George Tucker had been killed in battle. The boy soon realized, however, that if Tucker were dead, his formidable black valet, Syphax, should be astride the second horse, bringing home both Hob and the mournful news of Tucker's

Eleven-year-old Richard Randolph expressed his patriotic fervor in a letter to his stepfather, St. George Tucker, who was serving in the military campaign of 1781 that would lead to the American victory at Yorktown. The ideals of the Revolution, rein-forced by Randolph's great teacher, George Wythe, would remain at the core of the young man's consciousness, prompting him to denounce American slavery in the harsh-est terms and to offer his own slaves both their liberty and a parcel of Randolph land on which to build new lives.

demise. Syphax was nowhere to be seen—which could only mean that his services were still required in camp by a very-much-alive St. George Tucker.[5] For young Richard Randolph, the presence or absence of this black man, so integral to the life of the Randolph-Tucker family, literally embodied the difference between life and death—of Tucker and, metaphorically, of the patriot cause.

Tucker, a native of Bermuda who had moved to Virginia to attend the College of William and Mary, owned scores of slaves; he entrusted Syphax with sensitive missions such as transporting money between the Tucker home and Lafayette's encampment. Tucker had tutored young Richard in the principles of the Enlightenment as asserted in the American Revolution. Dependent though he would always be on enslaved labor, the older man thought deeply about the way American slavery contradicted those Revolutionary ideals and corrupted everyone who benefited from the institution. Defying the stereotype of the great planter as a self-indulgent drone, Tucker—like Richard's mother and the boy's late father—constantly demanded industry and "Improvement" of their sons.[6] Richard sometimes chafed under the family regime, but he also came to see that slavery flouted the Randolph-Tuckers' work ethic by exacting labor through force rather than by appeals to character and internal motivation.

Tucker conveyed his antislavery principles not merely to his sons but also to the world in 1796—about the same time Richard Randolph wrote similar ideas into his will. In his *Dissertation on Slavery: With a Proposal for the Gradual Abolition of It in the State of Virginia,* and again in another work he published in 1803, Tucker admitted that even as he and other white Americans made their Revolution, "we were imposing upon our fellow men, who differ in complexion from us, a *slavery,* ten thousand times more cruel than the utmost extremity of those grievances and oppressions, of which we complained." Tucker was not content merely to deplore "the tyrannical and iniquitous policy which holds so many human creatures in a state of grievous bondage"; other American and European revolutionaries, including Thomas Jefferson, did that much, lamenting the practice of keeping other persons in slavery, but assuming that blacks were intellectually and morally inferior to whites. St. George Tucker explicitly declared the African race "our fellow men, and equals." His stepson Richard likewise called African Americans "our fellow creatures, equally entitled with ourselves to the enjoyment of Liberty and happiness." For Randolph as for Tucker, it followed ineluctably that slavery was "the most lawless and monstrous tyranny," in which white Americans acted "in contradiction of their own declaration of rights, and in violation of every sacred Law of nature; of the inherent, unalienable & imprescriptible rights of man; and of every principle of moral & political honesty."[7]

Richard Randolph drew not only on the ideas he had absorbed at his stepfather's knee but also on principles he had learned from his mentor at William and Mary, George Wythe, who had instructed young Dick in Greek, Latin, and mathematics in 1786 and 1787. A signer of the Declaration of Independence and by many reckonings America's first true professor of law, Wythe also carried out, with Thomas Jefferson and Edmund Pendleton, a thorough reform of Virginia's law code after the Revolution. Remarkably, however, Wythe (whose surname was pronounced like the preposition *with*) had become perhaps the most esteemed man in Virginia other than George Washington largely through his talent as a teacher. One of Randolph's contemporaries wrote that "nothing would advance me faster in the world, than the reputation of having been educated by Mr. Wythe, for such a man as he, casts a light upon all around him." Richard Randolph himself called Wythe "that best of Men!"—"the brightest ornament of human nature."[8]

If George Wythe, whose Quaker mother may have influenced his view of slavery, wrote much about that institution, few of his words have survived. With Jefferson, he did draft a proposal shortly after the Revolutionary War under which Virginia's slaves would gradually have been emancipated; needless to say, that measure was not adopted. As chancellor of Virginia (a high court judge), Wythe wrote a legal opinion in 1805 or 1806 stating that, when the status of a person of color was in doubt, the burden of proof that he or she was a slave lay on the individual who claimed ownership; Wythe explicitly based his opinion partly on the first article of Virginia's Declaration of Rights, which asserts that "all men are by nature equally free." Some feared that Wythe's decision called into question the entire legal basis for racial slavery in Virginia.

It is doubtful that Wythe, in deciding this case, *Hudgins v. Wrights,* had any thought of destroying slavery; the slaves in that specific instance had asserted the relatively narrow claim that, as descendants of an American Indian woman, they and their forebears had been wrongly enslaved under a body of law that permitted only people of matrilineal African descent to be held in bondage. Most owners of African Americans presumably could substantiate both the race of their slaves and their legal title to own those people. Wythe himself issued rulings in other cases involving slave property without challenging the right of white persons to own black human beings. Moreover, Virginia's highest court, in an opinion written by none other than St. George Tucker, soon rejected Wythe's suggestion that the personal freedoms guaranteed by the Declaration of Rights might trump the prerogatives of people who owned property in the form of slaves.[9] Still, Wythe's opinion at least hinted at the truly revolutionary implications that could flow from white Virginians' professed ideals.

More impressive are Wythe's views on the subject of race and human rights in general. His pronouncements as a professor at William and Mary come down to us through his students. One of those men recalled that his teacher had rejected a cardinal racial axiom of the old South—the idea that, in the event large numbers of African Americans were ever set free, they would have to be deported to some location far away from white American society. "Mr. Wythe, to the day of his death," this student remembered, "was for *simple abolition,* considering the objection to color as founded in prejudice." Jefferson reported that Wythe's "sentiments on the subject of slavery [were] unequivocal."[10]

Wythe, like Tucker and Randolph after him, not only condemned bondage but also asserted the actual equality of the races, an idea that found concrete expression under his own roof. In the years around the turn of the eighteenth century, Wythe was rearing a mulatto boy named Michael Brown almost as a son—even though, contrary to statements many have made since, Brown was probably not Wythe's natural son or other blood relative. The older man taught Brown Latin, Greek, and natural science, just as he would have instructed a favored white boy; he wrote a will in which he left the young man a substantial part of his estate and placed Brown under the protection of Thomas Jefferson. Wythe and Brown soon paid for the older man's racial open-mindedness with their very lives: Wythe's grandnephew, who apparently resented the old man's love for and legacy to Brown, poisoned both men. The nephew was never punished for the murders; the only potential witnesses against him were people of color, who, under the laws of Virginia and many other American states, were barred from testifying against white defendants.

Wythe's fate offers an extreme example of the resistance that any serious challenge to the idea of white supremacy might face in the post-Revolutionary South. The thoughts and actions of Wythe's student St. George Tucker illustrate other obstacles. Tucker, having asserted the equality of white and black and recognized that American slaves possessed a right of revolution surpassing that which their masters had invoked against Great Britain, sought in his *Dissertation on Slavery* in 1796 to find a way to eliminate slavery in Virginia that the propertied classes would accept. His plan of liberation would have taken effect over a period of many years, applying only to blacks born after a certain date; even those who would gain freedom under Tucker's scheme would have to remain in service to their white masters until age twenty-eight.

Tucker sought not only to ensure that no white person would suffer an economic loss but also to ease the minds of the many whites who feared living alongside the sizable free black populace that a general emancipation would produce. Tucker had no doubt that, should large numbers of blacks ever go free, white animosity would prevent the two races from living in harmony. Moreover, he bowed to the popular conviction that "these [enslaved] people, accustomed to be ruled with a rod of iron, will not easily submit to milder restraints" such as the sort of policing that was adequate to control the behavior of European immigrants. Freed blacks "would become hordes of vagabonds, robbers and murderers," Tucker wrote in 1803—partly, perhaps, to win over those who might otherwise accuse him of softness or naïveté.

"Whoever proposes any plan for the abolition of slavery, must either encounter, or accommodate himself, to prejudice," Tucker admitted. "I have preferred the latter; not that I pretend to be wholly exempt from it, but that I might avoid as many obstacles as possible."[11] Tucker saw no moral or legal justification for the forcible deportation of liberated African Americans, but his plan aimed indirectly to achieve essentially the same end: it denied blacks the right to own property, bring lawsuits, make wills, or otherwise expand their liberty beyond simple freedom from chattel slavery and security in life and limb. Most slaves liberated under his program, Tucker suggested, would emigrate—supposedly of their own volition.

‿℮

Even as Tucker labored over his *Dissertation on Slavery*, Richard Randolph composed his will, which challenged, at least in a small way, stepfather Tucker's belief that emancipated blacks would have to move to some distant place in order to avoid perpetual racial conflict. Richard fully shared Tucker's worries about the burdens white racism imposed on free blacks in America. Yet where certain other masters—Richard's brother, John Randolph, for one—would ultimately emancipate enslaved blacks and provide for their transportation to free territory within the United States or in Africa, Richard called for a four-hundred-acre swath of his plantation to be apportioned among the slaves he wanted to go free after his death, as reparations for their years in bondage. The farms they would establish on that land would give them a chance to carve out lives as free people, not in faraway exile but in their own homeland—Virginia.

Randolph's radical sensibility had been whetted by the French Revolution, of which he became an avid partisan. In the early 1790s he and his circle began addressing one another as "Citizen" rather than as "Mr.," "Mrs.," or "Miss." Again imitating French Revolutionary practice, Randolph dated his will in "the twentieth year of american Independence" rather than in the traditional "year of our Lord" (A.D.). And in the spirit of the French Left, Richard used his last testament to embrace his "first and greatest duty"—"to befriend the miserable & persecuted of whatsoever nation[,] colors or degree."

For all its idealism, Richard's will also exuded a corrosive cynicism. He despaired of the American Revolution's proud legacy; through slaveholding, he believed, "every principle of moral & political honesty" had melted away before "sordid . . . avarice and the lust of power." Many slaves in Virginia, Richard noted, including almost all those he himself had inherited at age twenty-one from his long-dead father, were mortgaged to "british Harpies"—"rapacious creditors" whose claims on slaves as collateral for outstanding loans raised a legal barrier to the liberation of those people. Far worse, Randolph, the child of the Revolution, felt betrayed by his own countrymen—slaveholders who continued to practice the very sort of exploitation they had supposedly rebelled against twenty years earlier. In Richard's mind, those people had become a new generation of the very Tories he had so loathed during the war, exploiting and mortgaging enslaved human beings in pursuit of "money to gratify pride & pamper sensuality." Randolph responded "with an indignation too great for utterance at the tyrants of the Earth—from the throned Despot of a whole nation, to the more despicable [and] not less infamous petty tormentor of single wretched slaves, whose torture constitutes his wealth and enjoyment."

The factors that might turn a southern republican into an emancipator and defender of racial equality could be highly personal. Most people who declared that all men were created equal—including the author of the Declaration of Independence himself—did not free their slaves, while some Federalists who detested the French Revolution and the very idea of equality did liberate bondpeople. Richard Randolph himself led a complicated if brief life. Some four years before he wrote his will, he had been accused of impregnating his wife's sister and of either killing the baby or concealing its stillborn corpse. Richard's wife, Judith, and St. George Tucker defended his good name, and the young man hired John Marshall and Patrick Henry to defend him; he avoided trial on the charges.

The modern observer may be tempted to see Randolph's emancipatory will as an expression of displaced guilt over what he may have done with his sister-in-law. But he can hardly have believed that creating a community of free Afro-Virginians in Prince Edward County would change the opinion of his individual character that either his friends or his enemies held. Richard's will did amount to a tortured cri de coeur, and suicide cannot entirely be ruled out as the cause of his sudden death mere months after he wrote the document. Yet in that very testament he had declared his determination to live long enough to liberate his slaves.

In fact, however, Richard Randolph died without having emancipated a single enslaved African American. Strikingly, he apparently failed to liberate even the five individuals who were not mortgaged to secure the family debt. Richard's hatred of self-indulgence and hypocrisy in others was the more intense precisely because he considered *himself* self-indulgent and hypocritical. While making the antislavery case perhaps more eloquently than any other American of his generation, he still led the life of a great Virginia planter—a situation that he said he despised but that he did little or nothing to change, other than to write a heartrendingly eloquent will.

Slavery indeed made hypocrites of those who reaped its rewards, turning American Revolutionaries into tyrants and transforming self-professed Christians into oppressors. At the same time, the institution required the enslaved to dissemble and humble themselves in order to make their way. Slavery besmirched even the most radical egalitarians, George Wythe and St. George Tucker. Tucker, who lived until 1827, remained a major slaveholder throughout his life; Wythe owned seventeen blacks in 1784, though a few years later he conveyed thirteen people to his late wife's family and set five others free.[12] At one point in 1781 Wythe even offered to keep an eye out for certain fugitive slaves claimed by none other than Thomas Jefferson.[13] By 1803 Tucker was prepared to concede, at least for public consumption, that Jefferson might be right about the inherent superiority of the white race, though he still noted that there were "many powerful arguments" to the contrary.[14] And in 1806 it was Tucker, in the role of jurist, who overturned Wythe's legal opinion that seemed to expand the scope of the Virginia Declaration of Rights.

If actions count more than ideas, then the most steadfastly radical white figure in the Wythe-Tucker-Randolph circle turned out to be Citizen Judith Randolph, Richard's widow. Richard's cousin as well as his wife, Judith was a bright and urbane woman from a wealthy home. The couple were intellectually and ideologically compatible; Judith quoted the classics and commented on politics in her letters. But she did not inveigh against slavery so far as we know. When Judith professed her determination to implement the emancipation that her late husband's will called for, she framed her intentions not as an enactment of universal principles but rather as a token of love and respect for him. Even then it took Judith fourteen years to put Richard's last testament into effect—years in which her slaves repeatedly protested, through work slowdowns and at least one demonstration en masse, the delay in tendering them the freedom Richard had called for them to receive.

In the winter of 1800–01 Judith was complaining to St. George Tucker—

who had offered her his protection after Richard's death—that "subordination was entirely out of the question" among her slaves, and that it "required [her] continual mediation, & temporizing offices, to keep even tolerable peace between the Negroes & their Overseer."[15] She apparently sold some of Richard's bondpeople in order to remain solvent and ultimately pay off the mortgages that prevented the liberation of the rest. Finally, at the end of the year 1810, Judith executed the manumission of ninety-some enslaved blacks, saying that she "owed to the memory of the best of men, & most indulgent of husbands, to assume a willingness I could not feel, to fulfil the task his will had rendered necessary."[16] And then, after setting those people free, she purchased a few slaves in her own right to serve the wants of her much-diminished household.

For all her shortcomings as a liberator, however, Judith Randolph did in the end keep faith with nearly a hundred Afro-Virginians and with her egalitarian husband. She not only gave the group their freedom; much as Richard had wished, she parceled out 350 acres of the Randolphs' own land among the newly emancipated people, who would possess it as their own forever. Judith pronounced herself "unable to express how much that conviction cost me."[17] The price is clear, however; she sacrificed all of her husband's human property and a sizable minority of his landed estate—the two principal bases of wealth in the old South. And she did so even though she had two sons whose potential inheritance was greatly reduced by her actions.

Judith lacked her husband's fiery indignation over human bondage. Like him, she never weaned herself from the comforts that personal servants could provide. She declined to make still heavier sacrifices that might have shortened the captivity of those Randolph slaves who eventually went free. But if husband Richard had lived into middle age on a debt-ridden plantation, he might well have joined in some of his wife's vacillations. In the end, Judith did what Richard never had time to do, and perhaps never actually would have done: she gave up a large part of the only world she had ever known, and the only one to which she could imagine belonging.

Judith Randolph overcame one mental obstacle to the emancipation with the help of her husband's slaves themselves. In his will Richard had recognized that he or his heirs could render his slaves only "as free as the illiberal laws will permit them to be." Virginia, like most other states both North and South, barred free African Americans from voting, serving on juries or in the militia, and testifying against white defendants in courts of law. Free blacks had to carry documentation of their right to liberty, and in some years they had to pay special taxes. In short, the law consigned them to second-class citizenship or worse.

The few enslaved black people whom Judith Randolph set on the road to emancipation before 1810 helped allay her fear that legal freedom would entail little but hardship for Afro-Virginians. Syphax Brown, the former valet to Richard Randolph and to St. George Tucker, went free shortly after Richard's will was proved. He became a waiter; his wife was a clothes washer and midwife. By 1808 Brown had saved money from his earnings and acquired a small herd of hogs; some of the animals strayed into the garden of a white neighbor, James Bennett, who promptly shot them.

Loyal as he had been to the Randolph-Tucker family, Syphax, as a free man, neither turned to Judith Randolph for protection nor conceded anything to white supremacy. Free black Virginians did possess certain important rights: unlike slaves, they had control of their own persons; they could hold, buy, sell, and bequeath property, including land; and they could file civil suits, even if the defendant was white. Syphax Brown sued James Bennett, alleging that the white man had fenced his garden inadequately and fired on the invading hogs without justification. An all-white jury awarded Brown more than $13—enough to buy four of the largest and best hogs in the county, or as many as a dozen hogs of middling size and quality.

Judith Randolph allowed Hercules White, whom she still owned, to operate as a virtual free agent in the first years of the nineteenth century. He worked as a carpenter, a cooper, a tiller of other people's land, a hauler of cargo, and a slaughterer and dresser of hogs. At a time when young white men of the yeoman farmer class considered $1.00 a day to be a good wage, the industrious Hercules White sometimes earned $1.50 or even $2.00 in a day. He grew corn and tobacco, presumably on Judith Randolph's land, and he sold his crops. By 1810 White was dealing in substantial sums, apparently borrowing to take advantage of opportunities that arose and then paying back the loans rapidly—which he could have done only after reaping a good return on his investments. One white man, George Backus, frequently did business with Hercules White, at one point selling the black man a good rifled musket for $20.00, a hefty sum at the time. When Backus defaulted on a large debt to White—more than $70.00—Hercules, like Syphax Brown, did not hesitate to sue the white man. White died before the case came to court, but the authorities took his suit seriously, sending a deputy to serve a writ on the white defendant in a distant county.

Despite the pervasive racism of slaveholding Virginia, white individuals hired Hercules White's services, paid him at least what they paid men of their own color for similar work, and did other business with him. And when push came to shove, White did not hesitate to ask that the courts vindicate him against a white man. Even before his formal manumission and the filing of his lawsuit, Hercules was comporting himself essentially as a free person. Judith Randolph never fully convinced herself that the slaves she liberated would be allowed to prosper in a white-controlled society, but the assertiveness and the successes of Syphax Brown and especially of Hercules White, in both the economic and the legal arenas, may have helped her believe that at least some of those she set free would hold their own.

When Judith executed her mass emancipation and parceled out the land that its new black residents would name Israel Hill, Hercules White was by common consent the most prominent and influential of the settlers. Years later another man formerly owned by the Randolphs would remember White as "a great favourite with his former marster & mistress, as well as [with] the slaves emancipated" by Judith in 1810.[18] An enslaved person could alienate his black peers by trying too hard to earn his owners' approval; that Hercules won the esteem of both groups testifies to his character as vividly as do his concrete accomplishments.

White died only a year or two after Israel Hill was settled, his economic dealings with white people having remained many and varied. Younger members of his family went on to buy, sell, and sometimes develop lots in the nearby town of Farmville, and to cooperate with white Christian believers in establishing the first Baptist church in that place. Other "Israelites" (as free black residents of Israel Hill sometimes called themselves) likewise conducted business with white people during the half century before the Civil War, as did various free Afro-Virginians in the area who had no connection to the Randolphs. Free men of color occasionally even settled down with white wives, and one newly freed black family migrated west in concert with white neighbors. Israel Hill itself would continue to exist as a viable black community well into the twentieth century. A variety of factors made these developments possible, not least among them the self-respecting demeanor and industriousness of free blacks such as Hercules White, who lived as if he believed himself the peer of everyone he dealt with of whatever color.

By 1821 George Wythe, Richard and Judith Randolph, and Hercules White were dead. St. George Tucker, a quarter century after his first proposal to wean his home state from slavery, was still trying to devise a scheme that would make gradual emancipation politically acceptable to his fellow white men. He looked westward toward the Louisiana Purchase. Between the Mississippi River and the Pacific coast, he thought that newly established black townships, interspersed with many more townships to be settled by whites, could absorb more than half a million liberated African Americans, and that perhaps a million or two additional blacks could be located in the West if his scheme were expanded over the years. He suggested that each free black family receive a farm of twenty to forty acres rent-free for life.

Each free black township would center on a village; these hamlets, Tucker proposed, would boast schools and churches led by whites for the instruction of blacks, and would house white justices of the peace to keep order, perhaps with the aid of black constables. Tucker's "object," he wrote, was "to emancipate the Slave, and afford him an asylum against poverty, and wretchedness, without inviting him to stay within the [already settled] territories of the United States, if he can find a happier, or more comfortable Situation in any other Country."[19] Tucker's revised plan, however sincerely and articulately formulated, never saw the light of day. In the end, it would take a great civil war to liberate African Americans in their millions, and much longer than that to afford many of them "an asylum against poverty, and wretchedness."

It is important to recognize Tucker, and the others whose ideas or actions helped produce the Randolph emancipation and the free black community of Israel Hill, for what they were, and were not. George Wythe and St. George Tucker had been soldiers of the American Revolution, the former in councils of state and the latter on the battlefield. Richard and Judith Randolph were children of that Revolution in the fullest sense. Syphax Brown and Hercules White owed their freedom to the Revolutionary ideology of Wythe, Tucker, and the Randolphs and in no small part to their own initiative. But none of these six Americans was a revolutionary in the realm of race, slavery, and freedom, though each was a radical in some significant way.

Wythe and Tucker made no progress toward eradicating the system under which some Americans claimed the right to own others, and Tucker in particular flourished under that very regime. Yet both men dared to espouse an idea that most whites would continue to resist for nearly two centuries to come—that all people, of all colors, truly are created equal and endowed with the same rights. Richard Randolph, though he died a slaveholder, gave eloquent voice to that radical concept and laid out a plan of liberation that aimed to make the idea real, albeit on a small scale. Judith Randolph, with all her self-proclaimed reluctance, actually carried out Richard's bold wish—something that very few in the old South would have had the fortitude to do. All four sought to remedy the violations of human liberty that white racism had produced, but none found a way to liberate their country from those snares of "prejudice" that Tucker so poignantly recognized.

Syphax Brown and Hercules White, for their part, could not *afford* to behave like radicals or to "fight the power" in a white supremacist system that declared them chattels until late in life, and that even then imposed serious limitations on their prerogatives as free men. Yet Brown's and White's very lives—their dignified carriage and their defense of their rights—in themselves constituted a quietly radical statement of the doctrine of racial equality, as did the lives of many other African Americans both free and enslaved. Whatever the failings of Wythe, Tucker, and the two Randolphs—each of whom benefited from a system whose morality they denied—they shared with Syphax Brown and Hercules White, and proclaimed openly, the idea that the American Declaration of Independence actually meant what it said about human equality.

FOR FURTHER READING

Richard and Judith Randolph's emancipatory legacy, the influence of George Wythe and St. George Tucker on Richard's ideology, and the history of Hercules White, Syphax Brown, and other free African Americans on Israel Hill and in the surrounding area are related in Melvin Patrick Ely, *Israel on the Appomattox: A Southern Experiment in Black Freedom* (New York, 2004). Two iterations of Tucker's proposal for ending slavery are readily available today: Tucker, *A Dissertation on Slavery: With a Proposal for the Gradual Abolition of It, in the State of Virginia* (1796; rpt., Westport, Conn., 1970); and Tucker, *Blackstone's Commentaries, with notes . . . to the constitution and laws . . . of the United States and of . . . Virginia*, vol. 1, pt. 2 (1803; rpt., Union, N.J., 1996). A discussion of Tucker that emphasizes his complicity in the slaveholding system is Phillip Hamilton, "Revolutionary Principles and Family Loyalties: Slavery's Transformation in the St. George Tucker Household of Early National Virginia," *William and Mary Quarterly*, 3rd ser., 55 (1998): 531–56. John T. Noonan Jr., *Persons and Masks of the Law* (Berkeley and Los Angeles, 1976), treats George Wythe in a somewhat similar vein. Among writings about Wythe and slavery, the most useful are Wythe Holt, "George Wythe: Early Modern Judge," *Alabama Law Review* 58 (2006–07): 1009–39, and Philip D. Morgan, "Interracial Sex in the Chesapeake and the British Atlantic World, c. 1700–1820," in *Sally Hemings and Thomas Jefferson: History, Memory, and Civic Culture*, ed. Jan Ellen Lewis and Peter S. Onuf (Charlottesville, Va., 1999), 56–60.

CHAPTER TWENTY

"Every Man Should Have Property": Robert Coram and the American Revolution's Legacy of Economic Populism

Seth Cotlar

On March 5, 1791, Robert Coram excitedly walked a few blocks from the Wilmington print shop of Brynberg and Andrews to the small rented home that doubled as his schoolhouse. In his hands was a newly bound copy of his first (and, though he did not know it at the time, only) publication, *Political Inquiries, to which is Added a Plan for the Establishment of Schools Throughout the United States.* After proudly showing his wife, Rhoda, the 107-page pamphlet—the fruits of several hard months of reading and writing undertaken with a newborn in the house— he sat down to write a letter to the nation's president. Only four years later Coram organized angry public meetings to protest what he regarded as the quasi-aristocratic and antidemocratic policies of George Washington's administration, but in this one-sentence missive he struck a tone of polite respect. He simply asked the president to accept a copy of his pamphlet "on the Subject of Education," written "chiefly with a design of being useful to my country."[1]

Coram probably suspected that Washington would never respond, let alone read his pamphlet, but the thirty-year-old veteran had his reasons for writing that letter. After all, both he and the president had risked their lives in the American Revolution, and the experience had profoundly transformed them, though in very different ways. While Washington had emerged from the war a cautious political leader who valued social stability and political tranquillity above all else, the war had fired Coram's political imagination and inspired him to dedicate his life to the cause of universal equality and democracy. Now, only a few years after the new nation had begun its

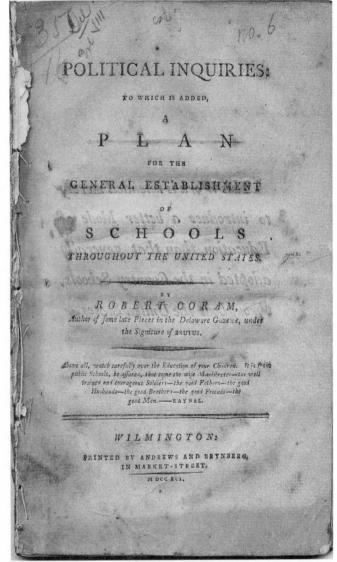

POLITICAL INQUIRIES:

TO WHICH IS ADDED,

A

P L A N

FOR THE

GENERAL ESTABLISHMENT

OF

S C H O O L S

THROUGHOUT THE UNITED STATES.

BY

ROBERT CORAM,

*Author of some late Pieces in the Delaware Gazette, under
the Signature of* BRUTUS.

*Above all, watch carefully over the Education of your Children. It is from
public Schools, be assured, that come the wise Magistrates—the well
trained and courageous Soldiers—the good Fathers—the good
Husbands—the good Brothers—the good Friends—the
good Men.*——RAYNAL.

WILMINGTON:

PRINTED BY ANDREWS AND BRYNBERG,
IN MARKET-STREET.

M DCC XCI.

This 107-page pamphlet inaugurated the public political career of thirty-year-old Robert Coram. The schoolteacher and Revolutionary War veteran was elected in late 1791 to help rewrite the Delaware state constitution, and by 1794 he had become a key figure in Delaware's emerging democratic opposition. The pamphlet developed the argument that only a well-funded system of public education could create the level of economic opportunity and equality necessary to sustain a democratic political system.

experiment in self-rule, Coram the idealist felt it was his duty to remind Washington the pragmatist that they had fought for something grander than mere national self-determination. If the nation were to fulfill its promise to its citizens and the world, Coram argued in his pamphlet, then it was obliged to guarantee that every citizen could live free of the burdens of poverty and personal dependence. To achieve this goal, Coram called upon the government to ensure that "every man should have property," in the form of either land or sufficient training in a trade.[2]

Knowing that many readers would resist this visionary proposition, Coram took pains to show that his plan was practical and thoroughly congruent with the nation's founding principles. He was an idealist, but he was not politically naïve. He explicitly rejected a governmental redistribution of wealth or "an equal division of lands"; rather, he called upon the nation to create the world's first publicly funded, universal system of education.[3] In the more pragmatic sections of the pamphlet, Coram offered some calculations demonstrating that such a plan could be implemented within the existing system of county and state governance and with relatively little cost to taxpayers. More important, he argued that only such a system could fulfill the Revolution's promise to create a robustly democratic nation comprised of intellectually and economically independent citizens.

Coram and his pamphlet were largely forgotten after his death in 1796. In the few instances when writers or politicians have mentioned or reprinted his pamphlet, they have praised it as a prescient treatise on educational reform. But that greatly understates the extent of Coram's intellectual and political ambitions. Both his pamphlet and his subsequent career as a democratic activist in Wilmington show that for Coram, building public schools was not an end in itself but merely one solution for what he saw as the modern world's most shameful and increasingly pressing problem—the widening gap between the wealthy few and the impoverished many.

Coram's life experiences had convinced him that despite the political promise of his revolutionary age, the so-called civilized world was in crisis. He spent his teenage years in the booming and violently exploitative slave society of Charleston; his young adulthood as a petty naval officer passing through the turbulent ports of the Caribbean and Europe and on shipboard fighting alongside dispossessed men from many nations; and then an abbreviated adulthood as an advocate for the poor and the enslaved in the commercializing port town of Wilmington. These experiences taught him that with the exception of a privileged elite, virtually all citizens of "civilized" nations were systematically denied either the property in land or the training in a trade necessary to ensure them lives of dignity and self-determination.

While "the birds have nests [and] the foxes have holes, . . . the civilized man has nowhere to lay his head: he has neither habitation nor food, but forlorn and outcast, he perishes for want and starves in the midst of universal plenty."[4]

While leaders like George Washington and Alexander Hamilton dreamed of building a modern nation that could rival Europe in its commercial splendor and cultural refinement, Coram found the allure of such societies limited. Unlike Washington or Hamilton, Coram had actually seen Europe. He found the benefits of modern "civilization . . . not sufficiently solid, numerous, nor splendid; we everywhere perceive that degradation and distress which thy daughter poverty has entailed upon our race."[5] He had seen slaves beaten and hanged in Charleston while their masters poured their ill-gotten fortunes into lavish new theaters and exchange houses. He had seen both the palaces and the overflowing workhouses of Europe and spent countless hours conversing with sailors and dockworkers who had developed a scathing critique of the exploitation and corruption that made such extremes possible. Like many of his nonelite contemporaries, Coram wanted to live in a prosperous society, but he considered prosperity useless, even immoral, if it was not widely shared. Coram wrote in 1791 with a sense of urgency, for the world he saw emerging around him in both Europe and America—one in which a few were becoming splendidly wealthy and comfortable while the majority lived perpetually on the edge of economic ruin—looked to him like a repudiation of the Revolution for which he had risked his life. In his estimation, it was the duty of the people's government, not just the people in their individual capacities, to foster widespread prosperity.

⤜ℯ

Nothing was predictable about Robert Coram's embrace of democratic radicalism. He was raised in a Charleston merchant family of modest means and unremarkable politics. His parents, John and Ann Coram, had emigrated from Bristol, England, in 1765, bringing with them their seven young children, including four-year-old Robert. John Coram was one of many immigrants to Charleston—a city on the eve of Revolution where nearly half the twelve thousand inhabitants were slaves—who sought to take advantage of South Carolina's booming economy built around the exportation of slave-produced goods and the importation of luxury items for the enjoyment of an increasingly confident planter elite. For a short while John Coram occupied a comfortable niche within Charleston's middling ranks, forming partnerships with a few of the city's established merchants and setting up a popular store that offered imported consumer goods.

Over the course of the 1770s, however, the family's fortunes took a turn for the worse. Ann Coram died in 1770, and her young daughter followed in 1773. At the time of his wife's death, John Coram had decided to test the waters of the lucrative but risky slave trade, importing and selling nine Africans. For reasons that are not clear, these slaves were eventually seized by government authorities, and Coram was unable to recover his substantial investment in the venture. In 1775 John tried to make a fresh start when he opened a small secondhand-goods store and took on extra work as a justice of the peace. But as the colonies moved toward declaring independence, he was forced to acknowledge that his personal pursuit of happiness and economic independence in the new world had come up short.

Despite the difficulties he experienced in his business dealings, John seems to have succeeded in providing a good education for his children. Of the three Coram descendants who left a trace in the historical record, all took up careers that required a facility with the pen. Francis Coram worked as a scrivener in post-Revolutionary Charleston, and Thomas became a prominent engraver and artist in that same city. Robert, meanwhile, established himself as a teacher, author, and eventually a newspaper editor in Wilmington.

Aside from paying to educate their sons, John and Ann Coram also instilled in them a profound belief in the broader importance of education. In the early 1800s Francis helped lead a movement to build institutions of higher education in South Carolina, while Thomas was a generous benefactor of Charleston's home for orphaned children. Despite these similarities, the fact that Francis and Thomas stayed behind in Charleston after the war and accommodated themselves to that planter-dominated slave society indicates that they did not share the radically egalitarian politics that underlay their brother Robert's ideas about education. Indeed, given what we know about the nature of private education in pre-Revolutionary Charleston, Robert's schooling was designed primarily to provide him with the social graces necessary to ensure his integration into the city's elite circles. If it was in Charleston that Robert learned the intellectual independence and political assertiveness that marked the rest of his life, then he acquired those habits of mind outside the hours of instruction funded by his parents.

Robert's first lessons in political theory and practice were almost certainly provided by the small community of Charleston's patriot radicals who played a central role in the city's politics in the mid-1770s. These populist radicals—men like merchant Christopher Gadsden, newspaper editor Peter Timothy, and scores of middling artisans—mobilized large numbers of ordinary citizens to protest the increasingly ominous actions of the British government and to force the hand of the wealthy, conservative patriots, who until that point had dominated the city's politics. This coalition of radicals organized a series of public demonstrations, filled Charleston's taverns and public spaces with heated political argument, and gathered crowds of young men to prevent local officials from implementing policies they regarded as tyrannical. It is easy to imagine that as an intellectually curious and politically minded teenager, Robert Coram enthusiastically listened to these debates and joined in these crowd actions. In 1769, when Robert was only eight, his father was among those merchants who circulated petitions in support of Charleston's nonimportation agreements. As late as 1776 John served as a justice of the peace in Charleston, suggesting that he was not actively opposed to the patriots who had taken control of the city's governance. Perhaps John cooperated with the patriot movement for self-interested reasons, to allay suspicions that his neighbors may have harbored about the allegiance of this English émigré, or perhaps his was one of those many households in Revolutionary America that swam with daily conversation about political theory and events. Regardless, given John's ongoing, if modest, support for the patriot cause, he probably did not discourage Robert's budding political interests.

The turning point for both John and Robert came in the summer of 1778. Whatever ardor John may have felt for the patriot cause, it cooled, for that summer he refused to take an oath to the new South Carolina government, fled North America, and filed a Loyalist claim with the British. Within weeks of his father's departure, seventeen-year-old Robert signed on as a petty naval officer with Alexander Gillon, a wealthy merchant and slaveholder who had come late to the patriot movement but quickly earned the trust and support of the city's radical white artisans. While many of South Carolina's wealthiest men moved cautiously toward war in 1775–76 and worried that lesser white men would challenge their power, Gillon seized the opportunity to establish his populist credentials.

Why Coram cast his lot with Gillon in 1778 is not known. He may have become acquainted with Gillon by participating in the heady street politics of 1776–78. Or perhaps he wanted to send a message to his Loyalist father by heading off on a dangerous adventure on behalf of the patriot cause. Since there is no evidence that Robert ever reestablished contact with his father after their parting in 1778, political differences likely inspired young Robert to declare his own independence from his family and pursue unknown adventures in the Revolutionary Atlantic.

Coram shipped out on the *Gustave* under Gillon's command in August 1778, and after a brief stop in Havana they arrived in France at the end of

December. Gillon's mission was to acquire three ships for the South Carolina navy, but his hopes for accomplishing this were quickly dashed. As Gillon traveled around Europe fruitlessly searching for willing investors and available ships, Coram found himself stranded in Nantes and Paris for six months. Getting wind that John Paul Jones was looking for men to join his naval forays against the British, Coram tracked down Benjamin Franklin in Passy on May 9, 1779, and secured a letter of recommendation addressed to Captain Jones. A month later Coram signed up as an unpaid midshipman on the *Bonhomme Richard.* He sailed on two missions that summer, and in the last one he commanded the mizzentop in the battle against the *Serapis,* one of the most bloody and dramatic engagements of Jones's illustrious career. Young Coram apparently acquitted himself well, for Jones later commended him as "a brave, steady officer" who "behaved gallantly from the beginning to the end of the action."[6]

Coram's service under Captain Jones ended in October 1779, when he rejoined Gillon, who had just secured a ship at Texel, an island off the northern coast of Holland renowned among sailors and ship captains as a good place to put together a crew and provision a ship. But it took Gillon twenty months to prepare the newly renamed *South Carolina* for battle. For this entire time Coram was again stranded in a European port town, probably helping to recruit some one hundred French sailors who eventually served with him and perhaps contributing to transforming the former commercial vessel into a battle-ready ship.

In August 1781 Coram was finally able to reinitiate his military career when the *South Carolina* headed out into the Atlantic to join the fight against the British. Between January and May 1782—several months after the decisive Battle of Yorktown had essentially guaranteed an American victory in the War for Independence—the *South Carolina* joined in a series of Spanish expeditions that captured numerous British ships in the Caribbean. At the end of this expedition, the *South Carolina* sailed to Philadelphia to dispose of its newly won bounty. After a six-month stay, Coram and the *South Carolina* finally headed home for Charleston on December 20, 1782. Twenty-one-year-old Robert Coram must have looked forward to telling his brothers and other childhood friends about his experiences at sea, but as his ship rounded the cape of New Jersey, it was captured by a British man-of-war. Coram and his fellow prisoners of war were then transported to New York City and locked beneath the decks of the notoriously foul-smelling and disease-ridden prison ships that had claimed the lives of thousands of American soldiers. Coram's suffering was mercifully cut short, however, when he was freed by the armistice of April 1783.

His naval career having come to an inglorious end, Robert spent the next four years casting about for the purpose that would define the next chapter of his life. For reasons we will probably never know, sometime between 1784 and 1787 he decided that his future lay not in Charleston but in a small northern port that he had perhaps briefly passed through in 1782.

༄

When an articulate, worldly, and idealistic young stranger named Robert Coram arrived in Wilmington, Delaware, all he had to his credit was the proceeds from the sale of his veteran's bounty (a three-hundred-acre tract of land in the South Carolina backcountry) and perhaps some remaining prize money from the *South Carolina*'s successful exploits in the spring of 1782. Supporting himself by teaching school, he soon married a young woman from an old, though not particularly prominent, Wilmington family. At some point in 1790 Robert decided to write a treatise that would both encapsulate what he had learned over the past decade and offer a utopian vision for the new nation's future.

To accomplish this task, he needed books, so he joined the Wilmington Library Company and offered to serve as the custodian of the group's collection of approximately eight hundred volumes. On May 26, 1790, he transported the entire library to his home. Over the next seven months he worked his way through several histories of the new world's indigenous peoples, Sir William Blackstone's *Commentary on the Common Law,* Catharine Macaulay's *History of England,* Adam Smith's *Wealth of Nations,* Charles Dupaty's *Letters on Italy,* Cesare Beccaria's *Of Crimes and Punishments,* Noah Webster's recent publications on education, and multiple works by French philosophes Buffon, Raynal, and Gouget. In December 1790, having completed his self-appointed course of study and arrived at his own judgment on these materials, Coram stepped down from his post as librarian and carted the Library Company's books to John Webster's apothecary shop.

Coram clearly coveted the Library Company's extensive and expensive collection of books, but the organization was valuable to him in other ways as well. By joining the Library Company, he got to know scores of local artisans, merchants, and farmers who paid a small amount every year for the privilege of borrowing the library's books. Joining this self-selected group enabled Coram to find other intellectually curious, if not always like-minded, people in his adopted hometown. Indeed, it is no coincidence that the Library Company's membership rolls contain the names of about a dozen people who would later become Coram's closest political associates. These relationships formed, in part, during the two hours every week that

Coram was obliged to open the collection to borrowers. These visits provided Coram with his first audience, and he undoubtedly took advantage of the opportunity to share his latest discoveries and insights with his fellow readers. In turn, the democratically inclined citizens of Wilmington were elated to discover a new neighbor with such finely honed political and intellectual skills.

Coram's interlocutors soon discovered that while educational reform may have been his top political priority and the putative subject of his pamphlet, his deepest passion revolved around a much larger intellectual question: the origins and questionable legitimacy of "the right to exclusive property." Like many reform-minded people around the Atlantic basin—from political thinkers like Thomas Jefferson, Thomas Paine, and Joel Barlow to agrarian radicals like Herman Husband—Coram regarded the existing distribution of property in Europe and America as a problem of "great importance" that "deserves [a] most candid and equitable solution."[7] Coram drew much of his inspiration from the work of Cesare Beccaria, whose *Of Crimes and Punishments* had become a canonical text among the radicals of the late eighteenth century. Coram endorsed Beccaria's central argument that the "terrible and perhaps unnecessary . . . right of exclusive property" was responsible for much of the poverty, crime, and misery that marked modern commercial societies.[8] Knowing that many American readers would be unfamiliar with this argument, which he had first encountered during his European travels, Coram devoted much of his pamphlet to developing and defending it.

Coram opened with a contrast between Native American societies and those of "civilized" Europe. His study of Native American history had convinced him that they were a "happier" and "infinitely more virtuous" people "than the inhabitants of the most polished nations of Europe."[9] While no Native Americans lived in the sort of splendor that a few Europeans enjoyed, their societies lacked Europe's rampant crime, crippling diseases, and deep poverty. Contrary to the belief prevailing among his fellow citizens, Coram demonstrated that North America's original inhabitants used sophisticated agricultural techniques to produce more than enough food to sustain themselves. They lived in a world of plenty, even though they did not seek wealth as an end in itself and held their lands in common. Criticizing the many writers whose "prejudice against the Indians" had led them to produce "monstrous caricatures" of these people as violent, antisocial savages, Coram marshaled an array of evidence to demonstrate how "their equality of condition, manners, and privileges . . . animates them with a pure and truly patriotic spirit which tends to the general good of . . . society."[10] Drawing on both his critical reading of the available historical works and an extended conversation he had had with a Creek traveling companion in the summer of 1790, Coram came to a stark conclusion. The differences between "the civilized man and the savage" could be attributed to one key factor, "the division of property. To the one, it is the source of all his happiness; to the other, the fountain of all his misery."[11]

European society had taken its wrong turn when it deviated from the "law of nature" and God's will by "parceling out to individuals what was intended for the general stock of society." The Bible clearly stated "that God gave to man dominion over the earth, the living creatures, and the herbs," yet "human laws have . . . limited this jurisdiction to certain orders or classes of men; the rest are to feed upon air if they can or fly to another world for subsistence."[12] Civilized nations may "boast of having established the . . . happiness of man," but "at every corner of your streets [lay] some wretched object with tattered garments, squalid look, and hopeless eye . . . expostulating with heaven and asking what he had done, that he should deserve to be born in an indigent and dependent station." Whereas Native American societies, with their communal patterns of land ownership, ensured that everyone's right to property was honored, in civilized nations "poor men [have] no rights."[13]

Coram closely studied the text that put forward the most fully developed justification for the Anglo-American system of exclusive property rights, William Blackstone's *Commentaries on the Common Law.* Blackstone's canonical work was "much celebrated," but Coram found it filled with "downright nonsense."[14] In salty language reminiscent of the assertive and sarcastic tone of eighteenth-century tavern talk, Coram suggested that Blackstone's "crazy theories" were little more than an "artfully contrived" apology for "the monopoly of lands as held in Europe." Had Blackstone honestly inquired into the origins of Europe's concentrated landholdings, he would have discovered that there was nothing natural or legitimate about them: "Exclusive property in lands originated with government; but most of the governments that we have any knowledge of were founded by conquest: property therefore in its origin seems to have been arbitrary." Had Blackstone admitted this, it would have saved him "much sophistry and absurdity and not a little impiety: for it is surely blasphemy to say that there is a necessity of abrogating the divine law contained in the text of Genesis to make room for human laws which starve and degrade one half of mankind to pamper and intoxicate the rest."[15]

Coram did not call for the abolition of private property; rather, he urged the American government to reverse the civilized world's history of dispossession by restoring each citizen's natural right to property: "Society should . . . furnish the people with [the] means of subsistence, and those means should be an inherent quality in the nature of the government, universal, permanent, and uniform, because their natural means were so." His proposed system of universal, public education was intended to serve this end, but he intimated that this reform alone would not be sufficient. In a society where 90 percent of citizens earned their living from the soil, "it is much to be wished that *every citizen could possess a freehold*."[16] Coram expected that this two-pronged solution would create a nation of roughly equal and politically empowered citizens, thus building "a foundation for laws which will totally eradicate from civilized man a very large portion of those vices which such legislators as Dr. Blackstone pretend to be natural to the human race." Like most radicals of his day, Coram believed that democratically organized governments would produce economically just societies. He considered existing inequalities to be the artificial products of unequal laws that systematically punished the poor and privileged the wealthy. As he saw it, for centuries humans had created "an artificial inequality among themselves and then cr[ied] out it is all natural." Coram hoped that his generation, by establishing a more "rational" property regime, could begin building a more egalitarian and inclusive society.[17]

Such visions of using government power to foster a more equitable distribution of property soon became tainted by their association with Jacobinism (and later socialism or communism), but in the early 1790s Coram's ideas seem to have resonated with a large number of his neighbors. His egalitarian argument that "a man has a right to as much land as he cultivates and no more" was frequently echoed by American farmers in the 1790s as they agitated for policies that would open up the western lands to small proprietors and prevent the consolidation of those lands into the hands of a few wealthy speculators.[18] Closer to home, two local newspapers published favorable reviews of his pamphlet, and there is no evidence that his reputation in Wilmington suffered. In September 1791 the other members of the Library Company selected Coram to be one of their directors and put him in charge of purchasing new books for the coming year. His proudest moment came later that same month when more than sixteen hundred citizens in New Castle County voted him to serve in their ten-member delegation to Delaware's state constitutional convention. After spilling so much ink criticizing the laws that others had made, Coram finally got his chance to participate in the process himself.

The experience of lawmaking almost certainly fell short of his expectations. Coram was the youngest and one of the poorest delegates at the convention convened to bring Delaware's antiquated constitution into conformity with the new state and federal charters. Soon after his arrival in Dover it became clear that he would spend most of his time working with a small coalition of democrats to resist a powerful majority comprised of wealthy, conservative delegates eager to preserve their long-standing control over Delaware's society and politics. While Coram's opponents sought to restrict suffrage and preserve the power of Delaware's governor and small senate, Coram countered by proposing universal suffrage and a unicameral legislature that would augment the power of Delaware's ordinary citizens. The democratic minority made some gains in the convention, but for the most part their efforts fell short. For example, over his and only five other dissenting votes, the convention implemented a new requirement that one must possess either a two-hundred-acre freehold or an estate worth £1000 to serve as a state senator.

Coram's votes at the convention also illustrate his efforts to defend the interests of poor and middling farmers who had fallen into debt. Due largely to a shortage of specie, farmers in the 1780s found it increasingly difficult to pay their private debts and public taxes. Across the country rates of foreclosure skyrocketed, and many debtors complained that the legal system was stacked in the interests of creditors and so expensive as to make it inaccessible to all but the wealthiest citizens. Farmers in many localities found creative ways to protect their property against the claims of their creditors. Local juries frequently rejected the advice of judges and decided on behalf of their indebted neighbors. Many communities set up informal boards comprised of local citizens that took responsibility for adjudicating small debts, thus saving the debtors the cost of going through the formal legal system. These practices cut into creditors' profits, and they lobbied the conservative majority at the constitutional convention to take measures that would protect their interests. Coram resisted these efforts at every step. He voted against a provision that allowed debt cases to be moved to distant jurisdictions in the name of providing a supposedly fairer trial. He proposed that all debts under £120 be subject to adjudication through informal citizen boards, and he supported a plan that would forbid foreclosure if an inquest of "four judicious and substantial landholders" found that a defendant's debts amounted to less than the expected yearly rents and profits from their property for the ensuing seven years. Despite Coram's efforts, all of these proposals designed to help small farmers and debtors were voted down.

Given the subtle understanding of the relationship between wealth and power articulated in Coram's pamphlet, he was probably not surprised by his many defeats at the constitutional convention. His democratic coalition won a few concessions, and on several occasions he had voted with the majority, including one case where the delegates rejected an article declaring that only white people could be freeholders in the state. The fact that Coram never ran for public office again indicates that this experience had soured him on the possibilities of effecting change from within the formal political system. He did not disengage from politics, however. He turned his attentions instead to organizing his fellow citizens to pressure their legislators into taking actions that would benefit those whose voices were rarely heard in the halls of power.

For a brief period from the end of the constitutional convention in May 1792 until the summer of 1794, Coram seems to have retreated from public life. At some point in the early 1790s he stopped working as a schoolteacher, and over the following years he pursued several lines of work, none of which ever materialized into a steady and lucrative vocation. The difficulty of supporting his growing family in such circumstances may have consumed so much of his time that he had little left over to devote to his political passions. He still found time, however, to write occasional pieces on education and other political matters for the local newspaper. Evidence also suggests that he became involved with Wilmington's abolitionists, though the extent of his engagement is impossible to assess. All we know is that in 1792 he signed a petition calling for authorities to more vigorously pursue and prosecute people who kidnapped free blacks and sold them into slavery; and in January 1794 he traveled to a meeting of the Abolition Societies of the United States in Philadelphia as a delegate from the Wilmington society.

Coram's understated role in Wilmington's public affairs would change in the politically charged summer of 1794. Over the preceding two years, democrats like him had become increasingly worried that the ruling Federalists' animosity toward the French Revolution was symptomatic of a broader, counterrevolutionary design. In over forty localities across the country, Americans who supported the French cause and advocated for continued democratization at home organized political clubs designed to articulate and publicize their criticisms of the Washington administration. On August 9, 1794, two days after Washington declared martial law and sent federal troops marching into western Pennsylvania to put down the Whiskey Rebellion, Coram attended a meeting of Wilmington's newly formed Patriotic Society. From that point forward the society met bimonthly to discuss current political developments and craft a range of proclamations and petitions that they then submitted to local newspapers, the Delaware legislature, and eventually even the president. It speaks volumes of Coram's influence in Wilmington's opposition community that the first petition drafted by the Patriotic Society called for a state-funded system of free public education.

In November 1794 Coram was elected to the Patriotic Society's committee of correspondence responsible for coordinating local efforts with like-minded groups across the country. Henceforth he extended his influence beyond the confines of Wilmington. In spring 1795 he traveled into the rural areas west of the city to help organize the Amicable Association, a group devoted to assisting indebted farmers and supporting the same political principles articulated by the Patriotic Society. That summer he served as the secretary of a public meeting in Wilmington called to express opposition to the Jay Treaty. More than five hundred people gathered to hear the treaty read aloud and to approve a resolution (coauthored by Coram) protesting the pro-British nature of the treaty and calling for stronger ties between America and her sister republic in France. Perhaps thanks to Coram's work corresponding and building connections with democratic activists around the country, this resolution was reprinted in almost a dozen newspapers across the country, from Portland, Maine, to Charleston.

Coram initiated the next, and final, stage of his political career on September 8, 1795, when he published the first edition of the *Delaware Gazette* under his editorship. For the past year, the Patriotic Society had argued that Federalist actions such as the suppression of the Whiskey Rebellion and the negotiation of the Jay Treaty had gained public assent only because the people were denied accurate information. Coram's was one of nine new democratic newspapers that started up between 1794 and 1796 with the goal of giving voice to what democrats hoped would be a rising tide of dissent. If they could reach the American citizenry with their positions on contemporary political events, then they had no doubt that the Federalists would soon be voted out of office. As did the nation's other like-minded newspapers, Coram's *Delaware Gazette* printed a wide range of articles that developed the central arguments of the emerging democratic party—that the ruling Federalists favored the wealthy over the poor, preferred to rule over a passive and ignorant citizenry, and ultimately aspired to replicate Britain's aristocratic hierarchy in the United States.

The level of partisan vitriol in Coram's paper was typical, but Coram wanted to do far more than play the role of party mouthpiece. He hoped that his newspaper would affect how his fellow citizens voted, but he also used his new platform to publicize the loftier and more controversial ideas he had articulated in his 1791 pamphlet. In 1794 he had purchased a copy of William Godwin's six-hundred-page tome, *On Political Justice.* In the work of this British radical (best known today as the husband of Mary Wollstonecraft and the father of Mary Shelley), Coram found a kindred spirit. Like Coram, Godwin invested great hopes in the power of education and regarded gross inequalities of wealth as one of the key obstacles that stood in the way of creating a more just and democratic society. Coram contracted with a local printer to bring out an American edition of Godwin's work. He also inserted excerpts from Godwin in virtually every one of his biweekly newspapers, using the words of this respected thinker to communicate both his own systemic critique of injustice and his optimistic sense that a change for the better was imminent.

The first excerpt from *Political Justice* that Coram offered his readers, for example, contained Godwin's scathing indictment of the "insolence and usurpation of the rich," who, through their control of the government, "are perpetually reducing oppression into a system." Later excerpts developed Godwin's argument that despite this long history of oppression, human societies were capable of "perpetual improvement." Echoing Coram's reformist zeal, Godwin chastised his contemporaries who considered "change impracticable" and failed to "incessantly" look "forward to its accomplishment."[19] In other sections of his newspaper, Coram supplemented these inspirational dispatches from the avant-garde of British radicalism with reports about other European radicals' latest efforts to demolish the centuries-old inequalities that democrats feared were being slowly rebuilt in America.

For the first several months Coram poured himself into the work, scouring other newspapers for good material to share with his readers and regularly producing pieces of his own composition. In November, however, the tenor of the paper started to change. By late December the excerpts from Godwin ceased, and Coram's voice vanished from the paper. On December 29, 1795, Coram signed his name to an unusually large bundle of public documents. It appears that he was taking care of unfinished business, knowing that the sickness that had drawn him away from his editorial duties in November would likely end his life.

On March 11, 1796, one of the nation's most widely read democratic newspapers, *The New-York Journal,* printed an obituary that memorialized Coram as a "great man (for such he certainly was)" whose "writings have sometimes been contradicted, but never refuted."[20] His wife, Rhoda, who never remarried and listed Robert's name on her tombstone when she was buried in the 1840s, kept his memory alive for their four small children. In 1941 Coram's great-great-granddaughter, Mabel Talbott Owen, wrote a letter to a Federal Writers' Project researcher recounting how her "frail old" grandmother would fill "my childish ears with tales of *her* Grandfather Robert Coram who having died fairly young, was a glamorous youthful figure to her." According to Mrs. Owen, Rhoda and then her daughter had carefully preserved and passed down Coram's "sword, and parts of an old uniform," which her grandmother used as props to illustrate her stories.[21]

Coram's memory and legacy were not cherished as dearly by his fellow citizens. In February 1796, after years of protesting and petitioning led by Coram, the state of Delaware finally passed a School Fund Act, one of the first in the nation designed to provide free public education to every young citizen of the state. The bill was drastically underfunded, however, and did little to improve the state of education in Delaware. Perhaps if Coram had lived to continue advocating for the cause, it would not have taken until 1829 for Delaware to build a functioning public school system.

Coram's broader arguments about the government's duty to protect the rights of the poor and foster greater economic equality, however, continued to occupy an important place in America's political culture. While the nation's dominant political language took on an increasingly antistatist cast in the nineteenth century, many of Coram's political descendants—whether they be agrarian populists, reformist thinkers, or labor radicals—echoed the claim he put forward in 1791 that personal liberty and state power were not mutually exclusive. Though few of those descendants would have traced their genealogies to this son of the American Revolution, they voiced the same Revolutionary Era aspirations that shaped Coram's lifework. Although much of that work remained undone, Coram's unstinting devotion to equality—for African Americans, Native Americans, and the poor—would continue to be a part of the Revolution's legacy for generations to come.

FOR FURTHER READING

Robert Coram's pamphlet *Political Inquiries* is publicly available in "The Online Library of Liberty" (http://oll.libertyfund.org/) sponsored, ironically enough, by the Liberty Fund, a libertarian organization devoted to defending the right to property and limiting state power. An extensive analysis and contextualization of Coram's pamphlet appears in Seth Cotlar, *Tom Paine's America: The Rise and Fall of Trans-Atlantic Radicalism in the Early Republic* (Charlottesville, Va., 2011), chap. 4. For more on the Revolutionary Era in Charleston, see Richard Walsh, *Charleston's Sons of Liberty* (Columbia, S.C., 1968), and Emma Hart, *Building Charleston* (Charlottesville, Va., 2009). James A. Lewis, *Neptune's Militia: The Frigate* South Carolina *During the American Revolution* (Kent, Ohio, 1999), provides an excellent history of Alexander Gillon's mission and the ship on which Robert Coram served. The broader Revolutionary currents of the late eighteenth century that shaped Coram's political outlook are eloquently evoked in Marcus Rediker and Peter Linebaugh, *The Many-Headed Hydra: The Hidden History of the Revolutionary Atlantic* (Boston, 2001). The partisan politics of America's 1790s, and particularly the role of groups like the Patriotic Society, are judiciously treated in Sean Wilentz, *The Rise of American Democracy* (New York, 2006), chap. 2. The economic difficulties that ordinary farmers faced in the 1780s and 1790s, as well as the creative tactics they employed to defend their interests, are discussed in Terry Bouton, *Taming Democracy: "The People," the Founders, and the Troubled Ending of the American Revolution* (New York, 2007). On Delaware's politics in that era, see John A. Munroe, *Federalist Delaware* (New Brunswick, N.J., 1954).

CHAPTER TWENTY-ONE

Thomas Greenleaf: Printers and the Struggle for Democratic Politics and Freedom of the Press

Jeffrey L. Pasley

According to *The New-York Journal*, the summer of 1788 would be the most critical "that America ever saw," but not because Thomas Greenleaf and his contributors were worried that the new Constitution might not be ratified. Rather, they were worried that it *would* be ratified. As one of the tiny handful of American newspaper editors who allowed any criticism of the document in his pages, and a committed antifederalist, Greenleaf had no doubt that his own role would be crucial. He upgraded the *Journal* to a daily, one of America's first, and planned to foster a vigorous debate. "Newspapers will become more important . . . than they have ever been," he wrote, in an item others reprinted more than twenty times. "In a free country," the *Journal* argued, every "member of the community" needed to "be informed of its political manouvres [*sic*]," and what was more, each needed to develop his own position and take a stand on it. "Rouse then . . . NEWSPAPERS ARE THE GUARDIAN OF FREEDOM; by NEWSPAPERS only are ye made acquainted with . . . the Freedom or the Slavery of your own species."[1]

Greenleaf's suspicions of the new Constitution were plain and defiant enough to earn him the long-term enmity of certain powerful men in his state, notably one Alexander Hamilton. In the shorter term, his stance drew nasty epithets and physical danger at the hands of a temporarily outraged populace. On the day New York State finally ratified the Constitution, July 26, 1788, the city's typical Saturday-night festivities expanded to include the sacking of Greenleaf's home and business on Pine Street. Most of the city's workingmen had been convinced that the new regime would cure the postwar economic depression, and they were encouraged to vent their frustration on a publication that was seen for the moment as an enemy of the people. Throughout the day the Greenleaf establishment was periodically terrorized. By the evening the printer had dismissed his journeymen and apprentices for their own safety, while he and one stalwart who refused to leave stood guard.

When the streets had finally quieted around midnight, Greenleaf and the lone apprentice dozed in a room above the front door with two loaded pistols at hand. An hour or so later they awoke to the sound of a marching corps of men being halted in front of the house. A hail of rocks greeted the printer when he opened the window to see what was happening. Someone shouted, "Brake in my boys [*sic*]," and pieces of door and glass went flying as the mob rushed the front of the house. They then smashed all the way in, wrecking Greenleaf's shop and making off with enough of his type to prevent the *Journal* from continuing as a daily publication. Only the intervention of some of Greenleaf's neighbors and political allies prevented something much worse.[2]

Greenleaf was publishing again on the thirty-first. He shrugged off what later free press theorists would call the "chilling effect" on journalism that threats of prosecution and violence were meant to engender. Giving in would have been a dereliction of what Greenleaf conceived to be his most basic duty as a printer of newspapers: "When a Printer . . . rejects decent discussions upon important topics" and thus "voluntarily FETTERS [his press], then—if ever, in a republican country . . . is the time to fear." Defiantly the editor declared that he was guilty of "no other crime than that of having ACTED THE PART OF AN INDEPENDENT CITIZEN. . . . This freedom, which we have been taught to distinguish as the FREEDOM of the PRESS, has hitherto been conceived the 'PALLADIUM OF LIBERTY,' in America." If that changed, then "farewell to all political virtue—farewell to justice."[3]

Greenleaf was a pioneer and pillar of a group of printers and publishers whose actions and continued existence established the freedom of political communication that allowed American democracy to develop and function. The Bill of Rights that popular resistance forced into the Constitution may have barred any law abridging freedom of the press, but that was a term that jurists of the time commonly interpreted to mean only freedom from press licensing laws and other forms of prepublication censorship and "prior restraint." There was no guarantee of the crucial right to publicly criticize a sitting government or politically organize against it from the outside free from reprisal. On the contrary, when such an opposition did emerge, the Washington and Adams administrations and their supporters tried to suppress it, a campaign that culminated in the infamous Alien and Sedition Acts of 1798.

The right to democratic opposition would be vindicated only by the successful exercise of it in the face of repression, by maintaining a steady stream of criticism and then marshaling that critique and its exponents to vote the existing regime out of office. The Democratic-Republican supporters of Thomas Jefferson would pull this off in the election of 1800, but their success was rooted in the determination of the printers who maintained the network of newspapers that formed the backbone of the opposition through the 1790s. Initially this was a small group of journals, and Greenleaf's New York paper was one of the oldest and most widely read. Only the Philadelphia *Aurora* was more influential or better circulated. Greenleaf was the mainstay and role model of the group, continuing to publish and keeping up his political fire despite the mobbings, boycotts, inquisitions, and eventually prosecutions. With no sympathetic courts to defend the constitutional rights of publishers, opposition politicians, or dissenting citizens, it was only by such tenacity that a politically meaningful form of press freedom was ever won in the United States.

~e

In many ways, Thomas Greenleaf's life encapsulated the history of the early American political press. Like another primary target of the Sedition Act, Philadelphia *Aurora* editor Benjamin Franklin Bache (his namesake's favorite grandson), Greenleaf had a family background that imbued him with a far less submissive attitude toward the men in power than was true of most eighteenth-century printers. And Greenleaf could make one claim Bache could not: he wrote and edited from direct experience of political publishing that dated back to the beginnings of the Revolution.

Political activism was a relatively new and rare thing in the American printing trade during the Revolutionary Era. Printing had been jealously guarded by the colonial authorities, and the few newspapers that existed were treated as public utilities for local officials and lawyers. Most successful printers avoided politics and controversy whenever they could. Ship arrivals, official documents, and polite verse were much safer. Operating in tiny, underdeveloped local markets, they could not afford to alienate any potential customers. "Freedom of the press" in this sort of environment meant freedom of access to print, not protection for publishers. It was emblematic of the colonial printing experience that the printer most renowned today for his heroic political stand, John Peter Zenger, was put on trial in 1730s New York for material written by his lawyer contributors to advance their own political goals. Most colonial printers were smarter than that.

American newspapers suddenly exploded into political prominence during the 1760s, when the Stamp Act's effort to tax the colonies without their consent filled the colonists with outrage. Educated radicals like Samuel and young John Adams turned to newspapers as their "political Engine!" The British and colonial tradition of anonymous and pseudonymous writing in newspapers afforded a measure of insulation from reprisals and prosecution. The printer's was often the only authorial name given in the pages of newspapers, so the printer was the only party who could be held legally responsible.

Patriot newspaper offices became not just the ideological but also the physical centers of the resistance movement, places where leaders "frequently convened . . . and concocted many of the measures of opposition . . . which led to, and terminated in the independence of our country," *Massachusetts Spy* printer Isaiah Thomas remembered. Sam Adams and John Hancock were among the habitués of his and *The Boston Gazette*'s offices. In 1771 Isaiah Thomas was joined by a teenaged Thomas Greenleaf and his father, Joseph.[4]

A local justice of the peace in rural Abington, Massachusetts, Joseph Greenleaf was known to the British government as a troublemaker. Joseph came suddenly to political prominence when he was credited as the author of Abington's 1770 town resolves, a "flaming and rash" piece that declared British parliamentary taxes on the colonies "a mere nullity" that the colonists could resist by force. The acclaim his resolves received from Boston radicals inspired Joseph to make a sudden career change at the age of fifty-one. He sold the family's house and farm in Abington and used the proceeds to become a partner in *The Massachusetts Spy*. His son Thomas became an apprentice in the printing office that published the *Spy*.[5]

It was an unusual move for a well-connected colonial official like Joseph Greenleaf to have his son "bred a printer." Though printers enjoyed a higher status in their communities than most workers, they were still tradesmen and manual laborers. The early American printing office operated only on human power: each page of each copy of every book, pamphlet, or newspaper had to be hand-cranked on heavy, oily machinery. As a man who worked with his hands for a living, "a meer mechanic in the art of setting and blacking types," a printer was socially beneath the notice of any educated gentleman, be he lawyer, merchant, or college freshman.[6]

Printers' "mechanical" status was reinforced by the hardscrabble economic conditions that prevailed in their trade. Even if a printer was lucky enough to move up through the craft system and become master of his own shop, a printing office was a shoestring, low-margin business requiring the owner's close, year-round management and continued labor alongside his handful of apprentices and journeymen and all the other members of his household.

The Greenleaf family discovered almost immediately the depth of the difficulties that partisan journalists faced. Joseph delivered a series of scabrous articles over the signature of "Mucius Scaevola" that enraged the royal authorities. Governor Thomas Hutchinson summoned him to answer for one of these publications, and when the elder Greenleaf refused to show—on the advice of his patriot friends—Hutchinson had him fired from his job as a justice of the peace. As would happen in Thomas Greenleaf's later career, the repression backfired, only making the victimized journalist a martyr for his cause while leaving him free and motivated to write more.[7]

With the quixotic optimism common to the political publishers of early America, who often let their ideological hopes trump their business judgment, Joseph Greenleaf decided in 1773 to open a printing office of his own and take over a struggling literary magazine, the dissonantly named *Royal American Magazine,* in the process. He dragooned his now-journeyman-printer son Thomas to handle the actual pressing of ink on paper. The Greenleafs published a new issue of their magazine in March 1775, at a time when Joseph was already on a list of subversives the British military was to round up or kill if rebellion broke out. It was little wonder that the Sedition Act would hold few terrors for his son.[8]

In 1775 the Greenleafs would have to temporarily flee Boston along with other prominent patriots on the list. But while the Adamses, John Hancock, and other surviving ringleaders were soon rewarded with seats in the Continental Congress and the state house, their faithful printers were left to become refugees and make their ways as best they could. Thomas Greenleaf was sent off south to find work as a journeyman printer. He later joined the army, serving as a lieutenant of artillery stationed in Nantasket before botched smallpox inoculations forced him out of the service.

The newly independent American Republic's rulers preferred newspapers to act as their handy conduits to the people rather than as in-house critics, and most printers complied, following their long-ingrained commercialism. Thomas Greenleaf was different. He had learned the practical and commercial aspects of the trade well in the *Massachusetts Spy* shop, but he was continually attracted to working on journals that spoke trenchant if sometimes extreme criticism of whoever happened to be in power. Back in Boston toward the end of the war, he found formative work as a printer and "sub-editor" in the office of the Boston *Independent Chronicle.* During the 1780s and 1790s, the *Chronicle* heaped charges of counterrevolution and corruption on the city's elites, and it would become one of the very few New England papers to espouse the antifederalist cause, against the Constitution.[9]

The opportunity of Greenleaf's lifetime came in September 1785, when he answered an ad in *The New-York Journal* seeking "an active, industrious Person" to take over "management and direction" of the paper and its attached print shop. The *Journal* belonged to Elizabeth Holt, widow of New York's Revolutionary printer John Holt. Her son-in-law Eleazer Oswald had been trying to run her operation long-distance and his own *Independent Gazetteer* in Philadelphia at the same time. Oswald wanted out of his mother-in-law's business but placed a high priority on maintaining the paper's critical stance toward the men in power. His ad promised favorable terms if the applicant could demonstrate "an unshaken attachment to independent and revolution principles." Thomas Greenleaf must have been an obvious choice.[10]

Subscribing heartily to the antiauthoritarian ideology of his father and Oswald, yet taking a more indirect and businesslike approach, Greenleaf was soon calmly but firmly challenging the bulk of his new city's political and social establishment. He bought out the paper in January 1787 and started the antifederalist daily that put him on a collision course with the constitutional vigilantes of July 1788.

⁓

Physically, the early American newspaper was not a very impressive specimen, consisting of four poorly differentiated pages dominated by advertising. There were no illustrations beyond crude standardized woodcuts and precious little news that the modern reader would recognize as such. Instead, a mass of tiny type without descriptive headlines presented what would be considered the raw material of news as we know it today: not "stories" but speeches, government documents, letters, and political essays. Most printers were too poor to pay their writers and too busy getting ink on paper to do any systematic newsgathering themselves. Always in need of material, they clipped from or summarized what they read in other newspapers, and they not infrequently published articles that had been dropped off in the dead of night, signed only by a fictional character. Thomas Greenleaf had a letterbox in the window of his office for just this purpose.

But as unprepossessing as these rags could seem, they came to be regarded as "immense moral and political engines" with no equal as a "mode of communicating knowledge among the bulk of mankind." They proved especially crucial to the building of political movements like the American and French revolutions. As the Reverend Samuel Miller put it, newspapers made it possible to spread information, "to sow the seeds of civil discord, or to produce a spirit of union and co-operation through an extensive community . . . with a celerity, and to an extent of which our ancestors had no conception."[11]

The movement that occasioned Miller's worried comments was the Democratic-Republican opposition of the 1790s, which built the beginnings of a democratic political system in the United States through newspapers like Thomas Greenleaf's. Fearful of even the most basic kind of electoral democracy and worried that political divisions might break up their infant republic if they became too bitter and ingrained, the framers of the Constitution designed the new government to prevent the development of national parties and insulate the national leadership from local voters as much as possible. One of their explicit aims was to elevate the status of the men who made key national decisions, in hopes that the broader views of those who had enjoyed the advantages of wealth, education, and travel would counteract the marked tendency toward partisanship, particularism, and populism that had been notable among the relatively plebeian state-level leaders who had emerged after the Revolution.

The plan to avoid party divisions quickly ran aground on criticism of the Washington administration policies that came from within the governing elite of planters, lawyers, and merchants, and also from outside it: over what many saw as President Washington's kingly style (he made some of the first claims of executive privilege to keep presidential secrets); over Alexander Hamilton's trickle-down financial plans; and finally over a foreign policy that tilted increasingly away from America's old ally, France, and toward the British Empire. These debates spun out from Congress and Washington's cabinet and took "out of doors" form first in the press and then in electoral competition. Poet Philip Freneau was handpicked by Thomas Jefferson and James Madison themselves to edit the Philadelphia *National Gazette,* the first new journal created specifically for the opposition. Freneau was soon joined, and then replaced, by a small network of printer-editors who picked *themselves* as Democratic-Republican partisans. Thomas Greenleaf was one of these: not necessarily the group's cleverest or nastiest writer, but perhaps the shrewdest businessman among them, with the most stable and reliable publication.

‿℮

Giving printers a prominent, if inadvertent, political role helped doom the Constitutional framers' plans for a more quiescent and elitist politics. Neither Greenleaf nor his readers were proletarian revolutionaries (and the New York Democratic-Republican leadership was replete with Revolutionary War heroes and members of the manorial Livingston family). Yet the tradesmen, mechanics, and small farmers who formed their base of support were a newly assertive factor in American politics, at a time when the basic issue was whether opponents of the government were going to be allowed to express any opinions at all.

Greenleaf's paper functioned as the local center of a nationwide political movement, but one that was always sustained and guided by the local community rather than by any national party organization or leaders. Long before organized political parties emerged, Greenleaf had established himself in his adopted city and used his press to promote the institutions of its civic life, especially the new associations that sought the participation and came to the aid of working- and middle-class men. In his capacity as a community leader and small businessman, Greenleaf was a cofounder of an immigrant aid society and an early "sachem" of the Tammany Society, originally a patriotic fraternal organization.

Like most successful periodicals, Thomas Greenleaf's newspaper was itself a community for its like-minded readers, in a way that promoted their political participation and the growth of his party's support. Reading a partisan newspaper was the only form of political party "membership" most Americans would ever experience. An effective political printer had to be a true editor, selecting a variety of materials that together formed a coherent message. Greenleaf did not put himself forward in his pages, as many of his fellow Democratic-Republican editors did; he did not promote his own political ambitions, pick arguments with rivals, or dominate the proceedings with his own opinions. Instead, Greenleaf culled the most incisive articles from his exchange papers (newspapers that the post office allowed to be mailed between printers free of charge) and published extensive original content, most of it probably contributed, anonymously or pseudonymously, by his crew of local political allies. A standing back-page notice announced that "Letters of Intelligence, occasional paragraphs, speculative pieces" would be "gratefully received" and informed readers of the letterbox in the office window for "the greater convenience and safety" (read: anonymity) of their contributions. Preserving his writers' deniability in this way was actually an act of courageous political self-sacrifice for Greenleaf, as he was the only one who could be held responsible for such articles in court or in the streets. He had proven he could take the heat, so his writers kept their communications coming.[12]

Greenleaf was considered unusually effective in circulating his paper among the city's tradesmen and the farmers of the surrounding counties. He always published a semiweekly edition for half the usual subscription price, either as his primary journal or a cheaper alternative. Carriers distributed papers in the city, and post riders were sold sets of discounted copies so they could resell subscriptions to the farmers on their routes. Ordinary people pored over his daily in the "Taverns and Hair-Dresser's Shops," Federalists complained, and his semiweekly *Patriotic Register* seemed to be the only city paper that poor farmers in the rural Hudson River counties ever saw.[13]

Political newspaper readership among common folk was a disturbing development for the Federalists, whose writers constantly inveighed against social mobility and the broadening of political participation. Some working-class and middle-class politicians found their animus for joining the opposition in the resentment they felt at being sniffed over by self-styled aristocrats and native-born elitists.[14]

Federalist elitism and Democratic-Republican resentment of it broke into the open with the controversy over the creation of the French Republic and the U.S. foreign policy decisions toward it. A network of political clubs usually called Democratic Societies sprang up in support of the French cause and its principles, especially to see "the EQUAL RIGHTS OF MAN" firmly established in America, Europe, and the world, and "to erect the Temple of LIBERTY on the ruins of *Palaces* and *Thrones*." While eminently respectable from their own point of view, the societies also contained plenty of men the Federalists considered social upstarts: tradesmen, mechanics, immigrants, and social-climbing lawyers. Greenleaf was not only a leading member of the New York Democratic Society but also used his newspaper to disseminate the group's statements in a way that allowed them to have a political impact beyond its own membership.[15]

The main purpose of the Democratic Societies was to be a vehicle for effective popular political expression, one that would not only be critical of government actions that deserved criticism but also work to defeat miscreant officials at polls if necessary. Elementary as that sounds today, even such a basic democratic function seemed almost revolutionary in a society where the ruling elites saw political parties as near-treasonous conspiracies. The Democratic Societies were predicated on the idea that it was the duty of ordinary citizens to be jealous of their rights and vigilantly "guard . . . against every encroachment on the equality of freemen." Greenleaf's New York Democratic Society promised to "constantly express our sentiments as well of our PUBLIC OFFICERS, as of their MEASURES." As America's first self-identified practitioners of democracy, the popular societies faced some serious backlash from those above.[16]

One Saturday in late December 1793, after a long day at the paper, Greenleaf handed over a submitted article to his compositors without reading it, because it was in the handwriting of one of his usual contributors. The piece turned out to be a particularly offensive squib against President Washington that even Greenleaf professed to find distasteful. Seizing the opportunity to curb the local opposition's leading printer, Federalist William Willcocks convened a meeting at the Tontine Coffee House a few days later that called on Greenleaf to give up the name of the author of the offending article, make a public apology, and cease "tending to convert the liberty of the press into an engine of sedition" by publishing articles critical of government officers and policies. If he failed to meet these conditions, Greenleaf would be "considered unworthy to be a member of" the national community and his newspaper would be condemned as "a common nuisance" that it would be "the duty of every honest man . . . to endeavor to suppress." A subscription boycott commenced, and Greenleaf was called to answer for his offenses at another meeting.[17]

The printer Greenleaf willingly apologized for the tone of the article but, like his father twenty years earlier, rejected the effort to discipline him as a dangerous (attempted) blow against freedom of the press. A group of Greenleaf's supporters and contributors gathered at Corre's Hotel for a countermeeting; a young lawyer and budding free-press theorist named Tunis Wortman sat as secretary and most likely penned the meeting's statement. Their arguments formed the beginnings of a principled case for political free expression that Wortman would later turn into a seminal book in American legal thought. "Freedom of enquiry through the medium of an unrestrained press" was crucial to maintaining the republican equality between rulers and ruled, the pro-Greenleaf committee argued. "Though it is to be lamented that the Freedom of the Press is sometimes abused by being made the vehicle of licentious personal scurrility . . . this evil is the necessary effect of that freedom." The meeting resolved that "no limitation or restriction of the Liberty of the Press, intended to correct such abuse, can ever accomplish this desirable purpose, without producing with it a train of evils infinitely more to be dreaded, than those which may sometimes be the consequence of its unlimited freedom."[18]

It was this same meeting defending Thomas Greenleaf that led directly to the founding of New York City's local Democratic Society. The society's constitution, framed by Tunis Wortman, was published in Greenleaf's newspaper and also issued as a separate pamphlet. Like the 1788 incident earlier and the Sedition Act later, the whole situation seemed to boomerang on the Federalists. Greenleaf's circulation shot up to its highest level yet, probably around two thousand per issue, among the largest circulation figures cited anywhere in the nation. Increased circulation enabled Greenleaf to buy new type, and with 1794's first issue, he added his own name to the paper's title and expanded the format, with no price increase. The front page of the first new issue contained a fierce libertarian quotation on freedom of the press from British opposition politician Lord Lyttelton: "to argue against any branch of liberty from the ill use that may be made of it, is to argue against liberty itself." Using a logic particular to the partisan press, Greenleaf saw his increased sales as a public referendum approving himself and his cause.[19]

The Democratic Societies themselves withered somewhat when President Washington publicly denounced them, but the nascent opposition party actually reached a new and more powerful stage by 1795; its flagship newspapers seemed to grow in influence, and its street- and tavern-level organization continued with or without the aid of political clubs. Young politicians associated with the clubs began to be elected to office: in New York City the most notable instance was Edward Livingston's election to Congress. The Democratic Society took over the formerly nonpartisan Tammany Society. In 1795 and 1796, fueled by a leaked text that Greenleaf and other printers disseminated, the opposition mounted massive street demonstrations in all the major cities and almost defeated the Washington administration's Jay Treaty with Great Britain. The Jay Treaty angered many Americans by giving in to the mother country's demands that the United States abide by British trade regulations but failing to defend the rights of American ships and sailors seized by the British navy.

At the time of the Jay Treaty demonstrations, Greenleaf pioneered another journalistic trend of tremendous importance to the social and political changes of the next century: the explicit dedication of new newspapers to the cause of a political party or movement. (Radical abolitionism, for instance, began with a newspaper, *The Liberator.*) In June 1795 Greenleaf relaunched his new daily newspaper under the title *Argus,* after the hundred-eyed giant of Greek myth who could penetrate "the most tenebrous shades . . . with his fifty *wakeful* eyes." The *Argus*'s "address," or mission statement, to readers made it perhaps the first American newspaper to frankly embrace its role as a party organ. The printer saw his partisan stance as one that showed his political independence and republican virtue rather than compromising it. Greenleaf noted from his own experience that any American who tried to express and foster "opinions that do not accord with the wishes of those in power" was "reviled as an enemy to his country, sedi-

SEVEN DOL. PER AN.] | - WEDNESDAY, AUGUST 3, 1796. [NUMBER '387.

This nameplate from *Argus, or Greenleaf's New Daily Advertiser*, is dated August 3, 1796. After upgrading his newspaper to a daily, Greenleaf adopted the name and symbol of the all-seeing watchman of Greek myth, and added a new motto that invoked the iconoclastic radicalism of Thomas Paine and the French Revolution: "We Guard the Rights of Man."

tious, turbulent, wishing to destroy the government." The only safe mode of opposition was banding together with like-minded people in a party, an organization that could defend its ideas and personnel and peacefully compete for power.

As Greenleaf saw it, condemnations of both partisanship and press freedom were based on a related fallacy that scholars of press law have labeled the "bad tendency" argument; namely, that certain statements were so offensive and incendiary that they tended to inspire retaliatory violence or other disturbances of the peace. This bad tendency was legally culpable under the British common law. Stealing a march on better-known party theorists like Martin Van Buren by several decades, Greenleaf argued that parties, and partisan newspapers, were essential to the preservation of liberty. "Parties, say some, are abominable; they destroy the peace of society, &c.," Greenleaf wrote, yet it seemed to him "that *liberty*, without parties, can never be maintained."[20]

By the time the Democratic-Republicans first contested the presidency in 1796, Thomas Greenleaf somewhat accidentally found himself the elder statesman of a growing and increasingly feared fraternity of printers. *Journal* writers minced no words about the local and national elections of 1796. The choice was between having "GENUINE PATRIOTS" like Jefferson and Aaron Burr "at the head of our government" or having men like John Adams, "*white-washed whigs*" and "*venal slaves to a despotic and foreign King.*"[21]

In 1798, fearing a nonexistent internal revolution and an equally farfetched French land invasion, congressional Federalists enacted a sweeping security program that included a home-front military buildup and the infamous Alien and Sedition Acts. The primary goal of the laws was to shut down the opposition press or intimidate it into silence until after the next election in 1800. The Alien Acts were aimed at the immigrant radicals working in the opposition press; the laws made it easier for the president to deport noncitizens he deemed to be threats and lengthened the delay for immigrants seeking citizenship rights. The Sedition Act made criticism of the government a criminal offense, imposing penalties of up to $2,000 and two years in prison on anyone who should "write, print, utter, or publish, or shall cause or procure to be written, printed, uttered, or published . . . any false, scandalous and malicious writing or writings against the government of the United States, or either house of the Congress . . . or the President of the United States . . . with intent to defame the said government . . . or to bring them . . . into contempt or disrepute; or to excite against . . . either of them the hatred of the good people of the United States."[22]

The Sedition Act's architects told themselves that printers were mercenary wretches who would give up their political activity as soon the government made it too hot and expensive for them. The crackdown was part of a general Federalist effort to discipline benighted common people who gave or accepted the wrong political advice. "It is a mortifying observation," Judge Alexander Addison wrote, "that boys, blockheads, and ruffians, are often listened to, in preference to men of integrity, skill, and understanding." In rural New York one of the specific complaints was that country people were putting up liberty poles ("wooden Gods of sedition") in town squares. In New York City an unruly "class of Cartmen and Mechanics" were tearing the Federalist black cock's feathers out of gentlemen's hats in the streets. All these "knaves and fools" were Greenleaf readers, Federalists told each other.[23]

True to his own heritage, Thomas Greenleaf responded to the Sedition Act by printing one of the bitterest essays that had yet appeared in his paper. "Government, as it has hitherto been administered, has been universally in all ages and in all countries more or less, a conspiracy of the few against the many," despaired an unsigned letter. "What an awful lesson is our own government at this very moment reading to us on this head," by passing what seemed to most Democratic-Republican printers a flagrantly unconstitutional measure. In his own editorial voice, Greenleaf promised, tongue only a bit in cheek, that "*by it, we shall scrupulously regulate our conduct as Editor,* and consider ourselves as amenable to it as to all other laws."[24]

The Federalists had tried to deflect the charge that their sedition law violated the Bill of Rights by allowing a defense based on the most progressive legal standard of press freedom then available in case law or legal treatises, the one from the Zenger case of 1735 holding that defendants could exonerate themselves if they could prove to the jury that their charges were true. The Zenger standard was wholly inadequate for the functioning democracy that emerged in the 1790s. While the Sedition Act was more lenient than similar laws in Europe, it nonetheless criminalized almost any criticism that might be made in protesting government policy or campaigning against an incumbent officer. It opened editors of opposition newspapers to court actions for almost any political essay or comment they might print, even a reprint from another paper or a report of a public meeting. Pleading truth as a defense was useless when dealing with opinions expressed in a political firefight. How would a defendant prove in court, to name two statements deemed prosecution-worthy, that John Adams was a man "without patriotism, without philosophy" and a "mock Monarch"?[25]

In practice, few Sedition Act defendants had much opportunity to even try. Federalist judges dominated the federal and northern state courts, and they conducted sedition proceedings in a bitterly partisan manner. Orations denouncing the Republicans and warning about the dangers of unchecked political criticism were delivered from the bench, with juries present. If defense attorneys made an effort to actually prove their clients' accusations, the judges commonly disallowed the evidence and witnesses on grounds that they would not have such vile slander aired in their courts.

The Sedition Act was vigorously enforced. Every major opposition newspaper was hit in some fashion, along with many of the minor ones. Some twenty-five people were arrested under the Sedition Act, and they and other opposition journalists and speakers were harassed in other ways as well, including boycotts, beatings, floggings, and private lawsuits. Nor was the repression limited to the press. A sitting congressman, former printer Matthew Lyon of Vermont, got a $1,000 fine and four months in jail for reading a letter against Federalist foreign policy during his campaign for re-election.

Crucially, Greenleaf and his fellow Democratic-Republican journalists dealt with the Sedition Act like a political opposition rather than as innocent nonpartisans seeking legal vindication. They had done nothing that *ought* to be legally culpable, but they had little faith that innocence alone would see them through. Like many other papers, the *Argus* printed the text of the First Amendment as proof, but an old antifederalist like Greenleaf knew that it was "egregious folly to expect that men, if they have the power, will be restrained from prosecuting schemes of self-aggrandizement, by mere paper and parchment."[26] While Democratic-Republicans defended themselves in court, they had no expectation that the courts were the venue in which the Sedition Act could be defeated, and not simply because partial Federalist judges controlled them. Judicial review of federal laws had not yet been attempted in 1798: the architect of that procedure, John Marshall, was a Federalist politician from Virginia who would not even be appointed to the Supreme Court until 1801.

More fundamentally, in the 1790s courts were simply not considered, especially by Democratic-Republicans, to be the only or even the most likely means of enforcing the Constitution. Constitutions had chiefly been considered popular documents, enacted by the people and policed by their representatives. If the latter failed or refused to do their job, then public opinion would express its disapproval in popular voting. Officials and regimes that violated constitutional principles would be thrown out of office. It would be many decades before courts and lawyers seized sole control of constitutional interpretation. In the meantime constitutional boundaries were set by whoever could win out in principled political battles for the hearts and minds of the voters.

Astute partisan editors like Thomas Greenleaf recognized the Sedition Act and the rest of the Federalist repression campaign as a golden political opportunity. The Federalists had finally gone too far, providing incontestable proof of the authoritarianism that Democratic-Republicans had always accused them of, replete with columns of ready-made copy in the form of trial transcripts, legislative protests, and their brother editors' sagas of suffering. So rather than shrinking in the face of the Sedition Act, the opposition press responded by redoubling its efforts, in greater numbers and with more intensity than before, despite the threat and reality of prosecution.

༺༂༻

Thomas Greenleaf was on John Adams's enemy list from the beginning of his administration. Unfortunately, in the case of both Greenleaf and his ally in Philadelphia, Benjamin Franklin Bache, yellow fever got them before the federal government could. The almost-yearly late-summer outbreak of the disease in the mid-Atlantic cities was particularly virulent in 1798. While wealthier people and most other politicians fled to the country, the two printers stayed at their posts. By mid-September two-thirds of Greenleaf's customers had moved and all of his apprentices had deserted, and Thomas worked himself to the point of exhaustion printing and distributing the paper almost on his own. Not surprisingly, he fell ill, then died hours later, on the afternoon of September 14, 1798. Greenleaf's friends and allies eulogized him in a widely republished notice that highlighted his political commitment: Greenleaf was hailed as "a steady uniform zealous supporter of the Rights of Humanity; a warm friend to civil and religious liberty, unawed by persecution or prosecution, both of which it has not unfrequently been his lot to experience."[27]

As it turned out, death could stop neither the *Argus* nor the Federalist vendetta against it. Like most traditional craftsmen's shops, the early American printing office was a family affair, a household as well as a workplace. The printer's apprentices (and sometimes journeymen) lived under the same roof as his children and ate at the same table. A printer's wife thus had the job of feeding, clothing, and co-managing the workforce. It was difficult for a printer to manage very long without a close working partner, and the evidence suggests that a printer's wife and the other women of the household commonly shared fully in his political commitments—and took them over if circumstances dictated. Thomas Greenleaf had first bought the *Journal* shop from John Holt's widow, Elizabeth, who had been the named proprietor for three years and who made sure that the paper ended up in politically congenial hands. Greenleaf's own widow would repeat the pattern.

Ritsana (Ann) Quackenbos Greenleaf had been Thomas's wife since 1791. A poor relation of Governor George Clinton, she came from good antifederalist stock. Facing life with several small children, a business, and no husband, a distraught Ann was forced to suspend the paper for several weeks after Thomas's death. But her political "inclination" as much as her "duty and interest," she said, resolved her to "resume our Daily Task" as soon as possible. Like Benjamin Franklin Bache's wife in Philadelphia, she revived her husband's newspaper a few weeks after his death, with no cessation or moderation of its political content. The daily *Argus* and its companion *Journal* reappeared in early November 1798 bearing Ann Greenleaf's imprint and a sad but defiant face. To the "friends of genuine republicanism" who sympathized with her loss and honored the memory of Thomas Greenleaf, she took pleasure in announcing that the "same principles which have hitherto distinguished these papers, will be invariably adhered to—the Rights of the People, and the Constitution of our country founded on those rights . . . To this grand object, our Political labors shall tend." Regular contributors were asked to submit their articles as usual, in the hopes that the "favours of the friends of the late Mister Greenleaf, will be extended to his Widow and Children." With their help, the *Argus* continued much as before.[28]

At the same time, the *Argus* publicized increasingly successful efforts to organize the opposition electorally under the leadership of Aaron Burr. The state legislative elections in the spring of 1800 would determine the winner of New York's crucial swing electoral votes and, most likely, the winner of the rematch between Jefferson and Adams. Alexander Hamilton, still the primary Federalist leader despite being long out of office, was concerned that the opposition press stood firm and, worse, that its barrages were having some effect on popular opinion. Federalist authorities cracked down hard in advance of the New York state elections.

The plight of "Jacobin" widows and orphans inspired no sympathy in officials who thought they were putting down a revolution. In the summer of 1799 Secretary of State Timothy Pickering ordered New York federal district attorney Richard Harison to find something seditious to prosecute in the *Argus,* and Harison had an indictment ready by fall. Among other things, Ann Greenleaf was indicted for reporting on liberty poles and complaining about the sedition law under which she was being prosecuted. Harison also made Ann the first and at that point the only woman to be "accused of being a wicked and malicious person seeking to stir up sedition 'with Force and Arms.' "[29] Unfortunately for Harison, when Ann fell ill in that year's follow-up yellow fever epidemic, the trial had to be postponed.

Not to be denied, Alexander Hamilton personally requested that the State of New York go after Ann Greenleaf and her paper. The *Argus* had reprinted a widely published article out of Boston that accused Hamilton of being the prime mover behind a Federalist effort to buy out the Philadelphia *Aurora* office from Benjamin Franklin Bache's widow and brought up, by way of analogy, Hamilton's self-admitted history of paying blackmail in the case of his affair with Mrs. Maria Reynolds. Hamilton haughtily claimed that only "public motives" had impelled him to legally notice the publication. Green-leaf was endangering society by having the nerve to print articles that might make readers think that "the Independence and liberty of the press are endangered by the intrigues of ambitious citizens." What a notion! "In so fla-grant a case the force of the laws must be tried."[30]

With Ann still too sick to stand trial, the New York State attorney general Josiah Ogden Hoffman decided to pick on one of her employees, David Frothingham, a printer she had recently hired as a foreman to help manage the shop and edit the paper. Frothingham was charged with criminal libel, tried, and convicted in November; he was sentenced to a $100 fine (on a salary of $8 a week) and four months in Bridewell prison. When Frothing-ham finally got out of jail, he dropped out of the printing trade. The local rumor was that he had fled to sea.

In the meantime, Ann Greenleaf found a way both to uphold her hus-band's legacy and to get herself and her children out of the Federalists' sights. In March 1800 she sold the *Argus* and *The New-York Journal* to David Denniston, a Democratic-Republican printer from Newburgh, New York. The new ownership rebranded Greenleafs' two newspapers in more aggressively partisan form, as the daily *American Citizen* and its semiweekly "country edition," the *Republican Watch-Tower.* Soon Denniston was joined by editor James Cheetham, a refugee radical journalist from England who quickly showed himself to be far more voluble and strident than Thomas

Greenleaf. The Federalists had not suppressed the Greenleafs' opposition newspaper; they had managed to turn it into something far worse.

Selling the offending journal did not cancel Ann Greenleaf's postponed sedition trial, set for April 1800, but in the meantime Federalists began to catch up with the new political culture. More than a year of nonstop prosecutions and terrible publicity had only dug them into a deeper and deeper political hole. District Attorney Harison decided that publicly persecuting a young Democratic-Republican widow just before the state election might not be the wisest course, and he shelved the Greenleaf prosecution.

It was too late for the Federalists as a party. The *American Citizen* was only one of a wave of new Democratic-Republican newspapers, most of them much more bombastically and thoroughly partisan than anything Thomas Greenleaf would have published; they popped up at the rate of seven or eight per month as the 1800 elections approached. The Federalists lost the presidency, Congress, and most of the non–New England states in that round of contests and almost everywhere else in the 1802 and 1804 election cycles. The competitive, relatively democratic party politics that street and tavern politicians like printer Thomas Greenleaf had helped foster and found was permanently established, whether the Founders wanted it or not.

While printers' behavior and voters' choice did more than anything to repudiate seditious libel prosecutions and secure freedom of the press, the political thought underpinning that freedom also took a leap forward in 1800. One prominent aspect of the campaign was a series of writings condemning the Sedition Act and defending freedom of political expression on constitutional and theoretical grounds. One book set out the first full-scale theory of American press freedom: *A Treatise Concerning Political Enquiry and the Liberty of the Press,* written by Thomas Greenleaf's longtime contributor and colleague in the Democratic and Tammany societies, Tunis Wortman.

The book's origins, even the original formulation of certain passages, can be found in Wortman's defense of Greenleaf in 1793–94. Embedding press freedom in fully developed Enlightenment theories of knowledge, government, and social improvement, Wortman denied that punishing seditious libel—criminal harm of the government by speech or writing—was wise, necessary, or even possible. Government had "no legitimate empire over opinion . . . no equitable jurisdiction over the operations of the mind." No good government needed protection from any threats short of mass violence. "Freedom of investigation," as Wortman called the right of citizens to speak and write critically of a ruling regime, was a necessity if a free, republican government were to be maintained. It was far more dangerous to "damp the ardour of Political Enquiry" with threats and punishments, than to risk that critics might be occasionally overzealous or misinformed. The power to restrict political opinion was "incessantly liable to be prostituted to the most invidious and oppressive purposes" and thus likely to bring on corruption, despotism, or rebellion. Hence government should abandon all efforts to police political opinion. "Shall we, then, to prevent an inferior and almost imaginary evil," the alleged danger to social order presented by scurrilous journalism, "resort to the introduction of a system which may be accompanied with such formidable calamities?" The argument was hardly settled in 1800, but the rudiments of the modern libertarian approach to press freedom were put in place then, partly by Thomas Greenleaf's example and sacrifice.[31]

FOR FURTHER READING

The essential work on the political world Thomas Greenleaf lived in, and the source of much of background information used in this article, is Alfred F. Young, *The Democratic Republicans of New York: The Origins, 1763–1797* (Chapel Hill, N.C., 1967). There are no biographies, but there is much information on Greenleaf's early life in Massachusetts in the published correspondence of his father's brother-in-law, *The Papers of Robert Treat Paine* (Boston, 1992, 2005), vols. 2 and 3.

The broad interpretation of early American printing and politics that informs this article has been presented at length in Jeffrey L. Pasley, *"The Tyranny of Printers": Newspaper Politics in the Early American Republic* (Charlottesville, Va., 2001). On the Revolutionary printing trade and other matters, see Bernard Bailyn and John B. Hench, eds., *The Press and the American Revolution* (Boston, 1981). On the Democratic-Republican newspapers of the 1790s, see Donald H. Stewart, *The Opposition Press of the Federalist Period* (Albany, N.Y., 1969).

The starting point for any study of freedom of the press in early America is Leonard W. Levy's *Emergence of a Free Press* (New York, 1985), which should be supplemented with Norman L. Rosenberg, *Protecting the Best Men: An Interpretive History of the Law of Libel* (Chapel Hill, N.C., 1986), and Jeffery A. Smith, *Printers and Press Freedom: The Ideology of Early American Journalism* (New York, 1988). On the Alien and Sedition Acts, no work has surpassed James Morton Smith, *Freedom's Fetters: The Alien and Sedition Laws and American Civil Liberties* (Ithaca, N.Y., 1956).

CHAPTER TWENTY-TWO

The Plough-Jogger:
Jedediah Peck and the Democratic Revolution

Alan Taylor

I n September 1799 a magistrate arrested Jedediah Peck at his farm in Otsego County in New York. Clapped into iron handcuffs, Peck was taken south to New York City for arraignment. He stood accused of sedition against the federal government for maligning the very law used to arrest him. A farmer, preacher, state legislator, and former judge, Peck vigorously promoted a democratic style that antagonized the Federalists, who dominated the state and the nation. Instead of discrediting him, however, the arrest confirmed his warnings that the Sedition Act imperiled freedom in America. A veteran of the Revolution and a man of slight and hunched stature, Peck evoked popular sympathy and outrage as he passed in irons through the countryside. Jabez D. Hammond recalled, "A hundred missionaries in the cause of democracy stationed between New-York and Coopers-town, could not have done so much for the republican cause as this journey of Judge Peck, as a prisoner, from Otsego to the capital of the state." In the spring, the prosecution collapsed for want of witnesses, and the Federalists belatedly recognized that a trial would only compound the debacle in public relations created by Peck's arrest.[1]

Born in Connecticut in 1748, Peck was one of thirteen children raised by an obscure farmer. Lacking the means for a formal education beyond a country grammar school, he taught himself by reading and memorizing the Bible. Seeking "a hope of Ever Lasting Salvation," he developed an evangelical faith shared by most of his rural neighbors. During the American Revolutionary War, Peck served as an enlisted man in the Continental Army, where he experienced "the horrors of war and . . . long and tedious marches, summer heat, and winter's frost, perils, hunger, thirst, and nakedness." Shared with fellow soldiers, those sufferings deepened his commitment to the new republic and heightened his zeal to detect and defeat would-be aristocrats allegedly bent on counterrevolution.[2]

After the war Peck migrated westward to settle at Burlington, in Otsego County. A frontier jack-of-all-trades, he was an evangelical preacher as well as a farmer, surveyor, carpenter, millwright, judge, and politician. Untrained in any theology and unaffiliated with any denomination, he preached as an independent itinerant paid by contributions. A friend recalled:

> Judge Peck, although a clear-headed, sensible man, was an uneducated emigrant from Connecticut. His appearance was diminutive and almost disgusting. In religion he was fanatical, but in his political views, he was sincere, persevering and bold; and although meek and humble in his demeanor, he was by no means destitute of personal ambition . . . He would survey your farm in the day time, exhort and pray in your family at night, and talk on politics the rest part of the time. Perhaps on Sunday, or some evening in the week, he would preach a sermon in your school house.

His nimble mind and keen political instincts compensated for his unappealing appearance: short, heavy, and slightly hunched. Peck personified the stereotypical Yankee: resourceful, versatile, shrewd, pious, and opportunistic.[3]

Peck combined political populism with his evangelical faith to extol the democratic purpose, divine origin, and global mission of the American Revolution. He preached:

> Monarchical Government is the literal kingdom of Satan, and the antichrist or the image of the beast. Representative government is the literal and peaceable kingdom of the Messiah . . . So Representative Government shall chase, break and destroy Monarchical Government and spread itself over the earth.

Although nominally a Federalist, Peck enthusiastically endorsed the radical French Revolution, which he hoped would transform the world: "May the fire of liberty, that is now burning in France spread over Europe, Asia, and Africa and destroy tyranny and despotism."[4]

At first Peck's popularity at Burlington endeared him to the county's premier judge and wealthiest landlord, William Cooper. A poorly educated, former wheelwright from New Jersey, Cooper became wealthy by shrewdly speculating in land on New York's rapidly settling frontier. Retailing farm-sized lots to settlers from New England, Cooper founded Otsego County and the new village at Cooperstown, at the head of the Susquehanna River, about eighty miles southwest of Albany. Those settlers included Peck, who praised Cooper as "the poor man's benefactor and the widow's support— the Father of his County." In 1791 Cooper became the new county's presiding judge, and he secured Peck's appointment as one of the three associate judges. In return, Peck supported Cooper's election to Congress in 1794.[5]

During the early 1790s the Federalists dominated politics in New York State and in the nation, where they had secured and administered the national government mandated by the federal Constitution of 1787. In New York they were led by Stephen Van Rensselaer, the Harvard-educated landlord who owned most of three counties, and by his brother-in-law, Alexander Hamilton, the great lawyer. Both had married sisters who belonged to another great landed family, the Schuylers. The Federalists sought to limit the recent Revolution by regulating social mobility and by consolidating economic, social, political, and cultural authority in an order of wealthy and learned gentlemen, like the interlocking Van Rensselaer, Schuyler, and Hamilton families.

By underestimating the democratic potential of the American Revolution, the Federalists provoked, at mid-decade, a growing challenge from opponents who called themselves Republicans and sometimes Democratic-Republicans (but who should not be confused with the Republican Party of our own time). Appealing to ambitious common people, the Republicans cast themselves as egalitarian "Friends of the People"—in contrast to the Federalists, who posed as paternalistic "Fathers of the People." The New York Republicans sought a liberal society in which an impartial government would secure equal opportunity for all by refusing to countenance superior privileges for the elite. They promised voters that equal rights and equal opportunity would free the market to reward the industrious poor rather than perpetuate the idle rich. This process would eliminate the colonial vestiges of hierarchy from American politics, society, and culture.[6]

Ill educated, rough-hewn, and self-made, Cooper could have been a Republican if his timing had been better, his perception keener, and his politics more agile. But he longed to overcome his humble origins and crude manners by winning acceptance from the wealthy and educated men who led the Federalist Party in New York. By trying to impress an elitist social circle, Cooper gradually lost touch with the common settlers who had been his base of support. He tragically reached for a genteel persona and an elite acceptance that lay just beyond his grasp—at a moment when both were becoming devalued by the rise of the democratic politics promoted by the more nimble and opportunistic Jedediah Peck.[7]

In the spring of 1796, while Cooper was away in Congress, Peck launched a bid for the state senate, challenging Cooper's preferred candidate. Lacking genteel manners and great property, Peck could not practice the traditional politics, known as "making interest," which relied on electioneering by surrogates. So he defied convention by promoting his own candidacy while traveling through the county as a preacher. A friend recalled, "He always had his saddle bags with him, filled with political papers and scraps, that he distributed whenever he went from home, and then at night and frequently on Sundays, would hold meeting and preach." Peck also penned his own pieces for the local newspaper. Unlike his elitist foils, who preferred classical pseudonyms, Peck published under his own name or his well-known nickname, "the Plough-Jogger." Instead of writing in the obscure, wordy, and pretentious style of his learned foes, he mastered a colloquial voice, rich in vivid metaphor, rural humor, and Yankee sagacity.[8]

Where traditional politicians avoided issues and campaigned by flaunting their largesse and influence, Peck sought to persuade common voters. He was constructing public opinion: a mass of common readers paying critical attention to public measures. He championed popular sovereignty, moral families, and mixed metaphors: "Let us all shout with one voice the sovereignty of the people; long live the Law which is king, Liberty and Equality . . . Then we will disband, and each of us walk peaceably home, and set our houses in order." Making a virtue of his commonality, Peck cast himself as the farmer's candidate, as the populist champion of the country towns rebelling against the proud and propertied villagers of Cooperstown. Denouncing the village's genteel lawyers as irreligious, card-playing, and heavy-drinking, he posed as the candidate devoted to "good family government, which is the basis of civil [government]."[9]

Although he called himself a Federalist, Peck vigorously championed the democracy that his party strove to contain. He rejected the elitist notion of the legislator as a superior gentleman who knew better than did public opinion. Peck exhorted the common people to assert their sovereign power over their legislators: "In Representative governments, the people are master, all their officers from the highest to the lowest are servants to the people." He insisted that only tireless and suspicious vigilance by common people could preserve the republic from plots by crypto-aristocrats: "Fellow-citizens, you are the only guardians and pilots of your ship LIBERTY, and if you do not watch her course, by small degrees she will depart from the small hemisphere of republicanism, and find herself involved in the frozen ocean of monarchy, bound down with the icy bars of despotism."[10]

Defending the traditional notion of the proper legislator as a well-educated gentleman, the Federalist lawyers ridiculed Peck's pretensions. Abraham C. Ten Broeck likened Peck to a frog, an "insignificant animal that just so vainly imagined its little self swelled, or about to be, to the size of an ox." But this elitist contempt antagonized the Otsego farmers, who identified with Peck as a fellow commoner who spoke and wrote as they did. Writing to the county's newspaper, the *Otsego Herald,* a Peck supporter named David Goff reminded the lawyers that nine-tenths of the county voters were "steady, industrious Farmers who know but little about *twistification, ambiguity,* etc., in comparison to you." Goff advised them "not to be so haughty, neither wise in your own conceits. Consider that your whole dependence is upon those Farmers, whom you look upon with so much disdain."[11]

Peck won popular applause as a common man who could provoke and outwit the lawyers in a medium that they had dominated: the newspaper. With every exchange, he grew more self-assured and sharp-witted. When an elitist denounced him as an "ambitious, mean, and grovelling demagogue," Peck serenely replied: "Where did you learn these compliments you have returned to me for my polite letter, in the college or assembly?" Nothing so infuriated a gentleman than to appear less composed in public than a Yankee so common as Jedediah Peck.[12]

Although he lost his first race for the senate in the spring of 1796, Peck kept his campaign alive in the press through the next summer and fall. Delighting in the open debate that so unhinged his rivals, he published a collection of his essays (and of his foes' intemperate replies) entitled *The Political Wars of Otsego.* The book enraged a genteel Federalist landlord, Jacob Morris. On October 5, during a court session in Cooperstown, Morris "snouted" Peck by seizing and twisting his nose: a physical humiliation publicly inflicted by a gentleman to show his contempt for a man of lower status. Peck's foes exulted in the newspaper: "The great Political Plough of this County is rendered unfit for service, having by the phrenzy of its owner encountered a sound stump by which it had its nose twisted." But Peck quickly secured grand jury indictments against Morris for assault and against one of the lawyers, Joseph Strong, for forgery. Then Peck returned to print: "It is true [that] the nose of the Plough at first twisted a little, but by a sudden jerk of the Plough-jogger and the elastic nature of the nose, it vibrated with double force, and threw the stumps slap against the Grand Jury." No matter what his foes did or wrote, Peck had the last and best word, winning the battle to shape public opinion.[13]

Cooper disliked the political contention that roiled Otsego in his absence, but he primarily blamed the village lawyers, who more openly and contemptuously defied his wishes. They helped another Federalist to defeat

Cooper's bid for reelection to Congress in 1796, and they opposed his political comeback two years later. Their opposition forced Cooper and Peck to make common cause in the election of 1798, when Cooper returned to Congress while Peck at last won the seat in the state legislature that he had so long coveted.[14]

But their reconciliation proved short-lived owing to a political crisis that pushed Peck into the Republican ranks and would drive Cooper to reaffirm his Federalism. In 1798 a diplomatic crisis with France emboldened the Federalists to suppress their domestic critics. When the French foreign minister demanded bribes and tribute from American diplomats, popular opinion in America favored preparations for war by the Federalist administration led by John Adams. Demonizing their Republican opponents as subversive anarchists in cahoots with the French, the Federalists in Congress passed a Sedition Act that criminalized public criticism of the federal government.[15]

Both parties were so edgy because the American Republic was so new, so tenuous, so risky, and its powers still so undefined and subject to debate. Moreover, with the perversion of the French Republic into a militarist oligarchy, the United States was the only substantial republic in a world dominated by monarchies and empires hostile to popular government. Federalists and Republicans alike recognized that all previous republics had been unstable and short-lived. Consequently, both parties saw the republic as threatened by powerful and insidious foes from within as well as from without.[16]

The Republicans insisted that the American Revolution had been a social movement to secure equal rights, liberties, and opportunities for common men who had defied colonial aristocrats as well as British rule. The Republicans argued that the Revolution's legacy was threatened by the Federalists, cast as latter-day Loyalists longing to replicate the British system of monarchy and aristocracy. By enlarging and centralizing power funded by increased taxes, the Federalists allegedly meant to impoverish and subdue the common people, subverting their republic. For the republic to survive, the Revolution had to be permanent, as a vigilant people continuously detected and cast out the internal enemies to equal rights and popular sovereignty.[17]

But the Federalists delimited the Revolution as a brief, orderly, and consensual affair that had ended once national independence had been secured and the Constitution ratified. By defining the Revolution as limited and conservative, the Federalists insisted that the people should fear attacks on order rather than inroads on their liberties. The true danger to the republic allegedly came from insidious malcontents eager to replicate the radicalism of the French Revolution. The Federalists appealed to "every man who is desirous of a settled order of things, and averse from continual innovation and revolution." They depicted the ideal republic as at rest, in stable and harmonious equilibrium as the common people deferred to the gentlemen whom they had elected to political office. In sum, the Federalists and Republicans competed to determine the legacy of the American Revolution.[18]

Although nominally a Federalist, Peck had risen by defying Otsego's leading Federalists (with the partial exception of William Cooper). As a state legislator, he became a maverick, frequently breaking party ranks to vote with the Republicans led by Aaron Burr. Peck's Otsego foes accused him of mental instability, compulsive ambition, religious hypocrisy, and thorough vulgarity. They regarded him as further proof that common men should not be entrusted with high office. "No minds are more susceptible of envy than those whose birth, education & merit are beneath the dignity of their station," insisted one Otsego Federalist.[19]

In response, Peck attacked his foes on moral and cultural grounds, assailing their gentility as hostile to the plain style and evangelical Christianity of their country constituents. He denounced his Federalist colleagues in the assembly for denying biblical revelation and for keeping late hours to gamble at cards and to drink wine and brandy. Peck vigorously opposed a bill to increase the pay of state legislators, which he insisted "causes a cry to be heard from the poor in all parts of our county." His populism was simultaneously economic and cultural: a defense of small farmers' property as well as of their morals and manners. His accusations delineated the divide, of both class and culture, that separated the leading villagers from the hinterland farmers.[20]

Republican leaders hoped to deploy Peck as their wedge to split the rural Yankee constituency that had voted so staunchly Federalist in upstate New York. With Peck's help, the Republicans could expand their base beyond the Hudson and Mohawk valleys into the hilly and Yankee-populated counties of central and western New York. In February 1799 the Republican legislators pushed Peck's proposals for decentralizing and democratizing New York's political structures. He proposed subdividing the large, multicounty, and multimember senatorial districts into individual county districts. He also urged the popular election of the state's presidential electors, rather than allowing the Federalist state legislature to choose them. On February 16 Peck voted with Burr and the other Republicans to denounce the Sedition Act as "contrary to the dearest interests of Freemen." But his Otsego Federalist colleagues voted with the majority to endorse that act.[21]

To punish Peck, the Federalists sacked him as a county judge on March 9, 1799. Defiant, he ran for reelection to the assembly as a Republican in April. Confident that judicial removal had disgraced him, the Federalists continued to ridicule Peck as an unworthy bumpkin, without considering that country voters might resent attacks on a man for thinking and speaking as they did. Exploiting the Federalists' miscalculation, the *Albany Register* pointedly asked voters: "Are those men who despise Plough-Joggers fit to rule in a Republican state? . . . How then will the enlightened yeomanry of Otsego relish the Aristocratical notion that the profession of a plough-jogger is beneath the *dignity* of a Judge?" Republican support combined with Federalist ridicule to make a folk hero of Peck, who handily won reelection.[22]

Peck's victory embarrassed Cooper, who had promised to secure his defeat. During the election campaign Cooper published a warning: "Every man who circulates two seditious printed Papers, disseminated by Jedediah Peck, through this County, is liable to two years imprisonment, and a fine of two thousand dollars, at the discretion of the Court." Defying Cooper, Peck continued to circulate a Republican petition demanding repeal of the Sedition Act. One day Cooper caught Peck "in the act," confiscated his parcel of petitions, and sent them to the federal attorney for New York, Richard Harison. Deeming the petition seditious, Harison secured a grand jury indictment in New York City. A federal judge issued a warrant for Peck's arrest, which Cooper arranged in late September 1799 in Burlington. To compound Peck's woes, Cooper also brought a civil suit against him for an unpaid and overdue land debt, winning a $220 judgment from the Otsego County court on October 17. Forgetting all past friendship and alliance, Cooper pursued Peck with a grim determination.[23]

But the arrest made Peck into a Republican hero, which led the district attorney to drop the prosecution in the spring in New York City. Meanwhile, Judge Cooper had fallen in Otsego County. On October 25, 1799, the state supreme court rebuked Cooper for an arbitrary ruling against a lawyer who had criticized him. Humiliated, Cooper resigned as judge and announced that he would not run for reelection to Congress. He hoped that his double withdrawal would permit Otsego voters to rally around less controversial Federalists in the next round of elections. Likening the county to his infant, Cooper explained that he had "rather the child should be Nursed by a stranger, than that it should be hewn in pieces" by the "Great Violence of Party amongst us." By resigning, Cooper claimed that he remained Otsego's self-sacrificing father.[24]

Cooper's resignation failed to undo the damage wrought by his arrest of Peck. In the April 1800 election the New York Republicans won a stunning victory, capturing a great majority in the assembly and making gains in the state senate. In Otsego County, previously a Federalist stronghold, the Republicans won a state senate seat and captured three of the four seats in the assembly. Running for reelection, Peck was the county's leading vote-getter, for the first time in his career, which attests to his role in leading the Republican surge.[25]

The Republican triumph in New York State had national consequences. By securing control of the assembly, which would dominate the smaller state senate in jointly choosing the state's twelve presidential electors in the fall, the New York Republicans provided the critical margin of victory for Thomas Jefferson over the incumbent John Adams. Overestimating his power as a Father of the People, Cooper had tried to suppress the Republican challenge led by his former client, Jedediah Peck. That miscalculation contributed mightily to the Federalist downfall, not merely in Otsego County but in the state and then in the nation.[26]

In April 1801 the New York Republicans consolidated their triumph by capturing the governorship, electing George Clinton to replace John Jay. Otsego County delivered a narrow majority for Clinton (51 percent), and Peck again led the pack as the Republicans captured all four assembly seats with an average of 58 percent of the vote. That the Republicans scored even larger majorities in the assembly races than in the gubernatorial voting indicates their special appeal to poor men: to the tenants and marginal freeholders who met the property requirement to vote for assemblymen but not the higher requirement to vote for governor. Four-fifths of the Otsego men who voted for the assembly, but not for governor, cast Republican ballots. In Otsego County Republicanism was primarily a movement of smallholding farmers (possessing farms worth less than $250).[27]

Having won both houses of the legislature as well as the governor's seat, the Republicans seized control of the Council of Appointment, the great machine for building or destroying political coalitions in New York. Beginning in August 1801, the council systematically purged Federalists from county as well as state posts, installing Republican replacements as a reward for their electioneering efforts. In Otsego the council replaced 69 percent of the civil officeholders, including ten of the eleven major positions: sheriff, clerk, surrogate, four judges, and four assistant justices. Comparing the new appointees with the ousted men reveals the transformation wrought by the electoral revolution. Most of the Republican appointees were farmers markedly poorer and less cosmopolitan than the Federalists whom they displaced. According to tax lists, the average new officer possessed only half as much property as his ousted counterpart: a mean of $1,143 for the new compared with $2,262 for the displaced. Shocked by the turnover, the Federalist *Otsego Herald* mocked the new justices as virtual illiterates.[28]

Worst of all in Federalist eyes, the Council of Appointment restored Jedediah Peck to the Otsego bench and promoted him to first judge. Worth a modest $1,325, according to Burlington's tax list, Peck owned a mere hundredth of the riches possessed by Otsego's original first judge, William Cooper ($131,720). Elevation to the county's preeminent post was a sweet triumph for a common man summarily dismissed by his Federalist foes just two years earlier. The Father of the People had given way to the Friend of the People.[29]

In April 1804 Peck won a seat in the state senate by garnering 61 percent of the vote in the county. The Republican legislators promptly placed Peck on the Council of Appointment, the great instrument of power in the state. As first judge, state senator, and councilor, Peck had become the most powerful man in Otsego County. "For many years he controlled the politics of the county, put up and put down who he pleased," Levi Beardsley recalled.[30]

In power, Peck remained a committed democrat, both honest and tireless in his dedication to the common people. In the legislature he pressed vigorously for the popular election of presidential electors, the subdivision of the

No portrait of Jedediah Peck survives in the public domain, but this painting, *Justice's Court in the Backwoods* (1852), represents his legacy: the ascendancy of middling farmers and artisans to political authority. Doubling as a justice, the shoemaker has set aside his tools but remains attired in his leather work apron as he hears a case, assisted by a jury of fellow commoners and harangued by two country lawyers. The court meets in a tavern that doubles as the local post office. The artist, Tompkins Harrison Matteson (1813–84), grew up in Peck's hometown of Burlington in Otsego County. *Courtesy of the New York State Historical Association, Cooperstown.*

vast state senatorial districts, the abolition of imprisonment for debt, the emancipation of slaves in the state, and protection for the settlers in the state's military tract from eviction by land speculators with suspect titles. An evangelical moralist, he also proposed legislation to require daily Bible readings in the schools and to stiffen the criminal penalties for adultery and for dueling. In 1805 he defiantly resisted the bribes proffered by the lobbyist for a bank seeking legislative incorporation, in contrast to his more venal colleagues who eagerly accepted the offers and passed the bill.[31]

Peck's greatest cause was to secure state funding for common schools. Public education would "bring improvement within the reach and power of the humblest citizen," for he regarded widespread, free access to education as essential for the republic to survive. Peck reasoned that European monarchs and aristocrats dominated and exploited their common people by keeping them poor and ignorant: "In all countries, where education is confined to a few people, we always find arbitrary governments and abject slavery." Only an educated people would protect and sustain the republican government that alone could protect their prosperity and liberty. Almost every year, Peck sponsored bills to increase state subsidies for common schools. His triumph came in 1812 when the legislature passed a comprehensive program for public financing based on Peck's report.[32]

In 1824, three years after Peck's death, the state's geographer, Horatio Gates Spafford, paid tribute to his late friend:

> Judge Peck was a man of humble pretensions to talents, and still more humble learning; but of principles as firm and incorruptible, uniformly, through a long life, as ever any man possessed, in any country or in any age. There was a pure principle of honest patriotism about him, that made him quite obnoxious to certain dictators; and the youth of this republic should be reminded of the sneers of a class of politicians, anxious to put him out of their way, who vainly strove to fix all sorts of imputations and odium on [his] character . . . Youth of the Republic! He enjoyed a complete triumph, lived to see it, and his memory lives in honor, committed to your safe keeping, an instructive lesson for your remembrance.

The modern cult of the Founding Fathers implies that we owe the revolution primarily to well-born and well-educated gentlemen. That cult obscures the role of Jedediah Peck, who refused to compromise his democratic principles by settling for an elitist version of the republic. If we forget Peck (and his like), we will settle for a tepid and limited vision of our Revolution as complete by 1788, with the ratification of the Constitution. If so, we'll distort the experience of people who regarded the 1800–01 transfer of power from Federalists to Republicans as a profound social and political revolution. An

Albany resident remembered, "So great was the change, and so sudden the turn of the executive wheel, that the event was felt through all the ramifications of society, and the period became as memorable as that of the birth of the nation."[33]

Most historians describe the Republican movement of the 1790s as the top-down creation of the Virginia planters Thomas Jefferson and James Madison. But in the northern states, the Republican insurgency owed less to Jefferson and Madison than to the many local challenges to Federalist gentlemen by ambitious democrats. By mobilizing common voters, local insurgents like Peck built the popular constituency that the national leaders attached themselves to. Only by looking beyond Jefferson and Madison can we recover the social significance of Republicanism as a democratic movement.[34]

Lacking the private wealth essential to constructing a traditional interest, the Republicans had created a party framework of committees and conventions to determine candidates and to rally voters. And they persuaded the people that professed friendship for the people was the proper and fundamental basis for authority. Where the Federalists had upheld gentility as a prerequisite for office, the Republicans persuaded the people that wealth, birth, connections, and manners tended to menace the republic of common men. In 1800–01 elections came to turn on who could best depict the opposition as crypto-aristocrats out to subvert the republic. That political revolution depended on Peck and his peers.

A classic American populist, Peck mixed attributes that we now ascribe to the left and to the right. On the one hand, he wanted to employ the state to enforce Christian morality, and he waged a culture war against cosmopolitan gentlemen. On the other hand, he promoted public education for all as essential to protect the class interests of the common majority of tradesmen and farmers against exploitation by the wealthy and powerful. In an age of diminishing support for public education, Peck warns us that we imperil the very foundation of our republic and risk succumbing to the rule of a latter-day aristocracy by the wealthy. If we forget Peck, we will sacrifice his great insight: that the republic is what we, the citizens, make of it, for without our vigorous, daily defense, it will become a hollow shell.

FOR FURTHER READING

The New York State Historical Association in Cooperstown has a very limited collection of Jedediah Peck's papers. Hartwick College, in Oneonta, has a substantial collection of William Cooper's papers, which have been microfilmed. For Peck's published writings, see the *Otsego Herald* for 1795–1801, and Peck, *The Political Wars of Otsego: or Downfall of Jacobinism and Despotism* (Cooperstown, N.Y., 1796). For Peck's political context, see Jabez D. Hammond, *The History of Political Parties in the State of New-York,* 2 vols. (Albany, N.Y., 1842); Alan Taylor, *William Cooper's Town: Power and Persuasion on the Frontier of the Early American Republic* (New York, 1996); Alan Taylor, "From Fathers to Friends of the People: Political Personas in the Early Republic," *Journal of the Early Republic* 11 (Winter 1991): 465–91; Throop Wilder, "Jedediah Peck: Statesman, Soldier, Preacher," *New York History* 22 (July 1941): 290–300; Sherman Williams, "Jedediah Peck, the Father of the Public School System of the State of New York," New York State Historical Association *Quarterly Journal* 1 (July 1920): 219–40; and Alfred F. Young, *The Democratic Republicans of New York: The Origins, 1763–1797* (Chapel Hill, N.C., 1967).

Afterword

Eric Foner

Among the numerous pieces of correspondence produced during the American Revolution, few have been more frequently cited in recent years than Abigail Adams's plea in the spring of 1776 to her husband, John, to "remember the ladies" when the Continental Congress drew up laws for an independent America. Less familiar is John Adams's response: "We have been told that our struggle has loosened the bonds of government everywhere; that children and apprentices were disobedient; that schools and colleges were grown turbulent; that Indians slighted their guardians, and negroes grew insolent to their masters." John Adams's fervent desire to cast off the rule of the British Crown did not affect his strong belief in social hierarchy, and he viewed these developments with alarm. But inadvertently his letter identified one of the most enduring results of the struggle for independence: an upsurge of egalitarian sentiment that threw into question not only monarchical rule but inequalities of every sort. This was the essence of the American Revolution.

The essays in *Revolutionary Founders* go a long way toward illuminating this upsurge and making it central to our understanding of that turbulent era. They bring to life a remarkable cast of characters—ordinary Americans who helped to shape the dual struggles for American independence and over what kind of society an independent United States was to be. They challenge us to expand the study of the Revolution beyond the realm of a few Founding Fathers, where it has resided, at least in popular historical consciousness, despite decades of scholarship on the era's social history. This book helps us to understand the social conflicts unleashed by the struggle for independence, the Revolution's achievements, and the unfinished agendas it left for future generations to confront.

A few of the individuals highlighted in these twenty-two essays are already well known, although not necessarily well understood. Jill Lepore points out that mainstream historians still treat Thomas Paine, whose great pamphlet *Common Sense* is universally acknowledged as a key catalyst of the decision for independence, with condescension. Abigail Adams is widely appreciated for her long, sparkling exchange of letters with her husband, but as Woody Holton shows, she also engaged in her own private rebellion, engaging in business independently and writing her own will. These actions challenged the common law of coverture that defined married women as legal appendages of their husbands. Most of the subjects in *Revolutionary Founders*, however, will be unfamiliar not simply to general readers and students but also to scholars. Taken together, their stories shed new light on the broad historical themes of that turbulent era.

Some of the essays suggest that we need to revise what we think we know of Revolutionary America. Gregory Nobles shows that we err in attributing the 1786 "rebellion" that now bears his name to the instigation or leadership of Daniel Shays. In fact, this was a loosely organized, largely spontaneous protest against economic inequality that engaged the energies of thousands of citizens of western Massachusetts. Terry Bouton writes that calling the Pennsylvania antitax uprising of 1794 the Whiskey Rebellion is to legitimate the pejorative label assigned to it by Alexander Hamilton. Both authors suggest that these uprisings might better be called regulations, to connect them with pre-independence popular movements that sought through direct action to "regulate" the policies of government.

This call for renaming, in fact, highlights one of the main themes that unite these essays—how the era's popular radicalism built upon long-established traditions, grievances, and modes of organization. Alfred Young demonstrates that the Boston shoemaker Ebenezer Mackintosh used the pre-existing committees that organized for Pope's Day activities in Boston to mobilize crowd opposition to the Stamp Act. In Worcester, Massachusetts, according to Ray Raphael's portrait of radical blacksmith Timothy Bigelow, mass mobilizations in 1774 that shut down local government and forced Crown officials to resign built on traditional structures such as militia gatherings, town meetings, and even tavern political discussions. Other essays delineate how long-standing ethnic conflicts (Scots-Irish vs. English, for example) and class hostilities fed into resistance to British rule. These divisions, moreover, long outlived the War of Independence. Indeed, one lesson of *Revolutionary Founders* is that like scholars of the "long civil rights movement," who have pushed the chronological boundaries of the struggles of the 1960s back to the 1930s and forward to our own time, we ought to be thinking of a Long American Revolution. The War of Independence was relatively brief; the transformation of American society it unleashed and the struggle over the fruits of independence lasted for decades.

If the social ferment of the war and its aftermath fed on pre-existing grievances, the struggle for independence nonetheless created a radically new situation. The idea of liberty became a Revolutionary rallying cry, a standard by which to judge and challenge homegrown institutions as well as imperial ones. As Jon Butler points out, the ideology of liberty galvanized by political independence made possible the achievement of the long-suppressed popular demand for religious freedom. Baptists in Virginia had been persecuted, assaulted, and imprisoned before the war and had repeatedly petitioned for the right to worship as they pleased. They aligned themselves with the movement toward independence even while their demands for toleration intensified. The eventual result was the landmark law disestablishing the Anglican Church in Virginia, which set the stage for the first amendment to the U.S. Constitution.

Revolutionary Virginia was clearly a volatile place. In Boston, according to Young, "the class feeling of the poor against the rich" was absorbed into and mitigated by the conflict with Great Britain. But as Michael McDonnell shows, the "spirit of levelling" that had long inspired poorer Virginians to protest unequal taxation and lack of political power did not abate during the War of Independence. McDonnell relates how James Cleveland, a tenant farmer who had been employed by George Washington before the war to help shore up Washington's claim to western lands, organized opposition to Virginia's policy of financing the war through regressive poll taxes and the exemption of one overseer from military service for every four slaves (a measure that anticipated the controversial "twenty-negro" exemption enacted by the Confederacy ninety years later). The demands for social equity and greater democracy by ordinary Virginians like Cleveland continued after the achievement of independence.

Indeed, the expansion of political democracy was one of the era's signal achievements. Most radical was Pennsylvania, which did away entirely with property qualifications for voting, substituting a taxpaying requirement that enfranchised virtually all white males except for apprentices and the extremely poor. This was a far cry from the prewar situation in which every colony required some kind of property ownership to vote. As Gary Nash shows, the movement that produced the forward-looking Pennsylvania Constitution of 1776 was spearheaded by a group of political radicals who had enjoyed little influence before that year. Their social composition would not be surprising to anyone familiar with democratic movements in contemporary England and France—professionals (teachers, a druggist, a physician), artisans, middling merchants, and an itinerant pamphleteer, Thomas Paine.

Other essays also show how progress toward political democracy arose from pressure from below, and how controversial the idea of a vital, critical public sphere embracing ordinary citizens remained throughout this era. Opponents of independence in the 1770s complained that men like the blacksmith Timothy Bigelow were "spending their time in discoursing of matters they do not understand." The same charge was hurled two decades later against the Democratic-Republican Societies, which criticized the domestic and foreign policies of the Washington administration. As Jeffrey Pasley demonstrates, it took time for the idea to sink deep roots that ordinary people had a right not simply to vote but to engage in continual oversight and criticism of government. When President Washington condemned the societies as "self-created," he was invoking the time-honored tradition that political organization and public discourse should be structured from the top down. The prosecutions of newspapers critical of John Adams's administration under the Sedition Act of 1798 reflected the same idea. But the very volatility of these post-Revolutionary years, with popular "regulations," the proliferation of opposition newspapers, and feverish public debate, illustrates that ordinary Americans no longer felt they needed the sanction of their betters to engage in public debate or to subject the workings of their government to scrutiny.

Indeed, the Revolutionary Era emerges in these pages as a time of free-wheeling debate, of intense discussion at every level of society of the fundamentals of political and economic life. It is remarkable how many common folk depicted here felt moved to express in print their views on government and society. Probably the most prolific was Herman Husband, a deeply religious farmer and lay preacher. As described by Wythe Holt, Husband's long career illustrates both the chronological scope of the "long revolution" and the combination of religious and secular egalitarianism that underpinned much of the era's radicalism. Before the War of Independence, Husband had been involved in the North Carolina Regulation of the 1760s and was powerfully influenced by the religious revivals known as the Great Awakening. In 1779 he had a vision of a New Jerusalem, an intensely democratic and egalitarian organization of society that he spent the remainder of his life promoting in articles, pamphlets, and speeches. Husband was one of the countless Americans who felt empowered to have their say on political and social matters in the era of the Revolution.

The real American Revolution, Thomas Paine wrote, was intellectual and not military: "We see with other eyes; we hear with other ears; and think with other thoughts, than those we formerly used." The repudiation of monarchy and hereditary aristocracy, the expansion of the public sphere, and the insistent claims for greater equality all underscore Paine's point. Yet these essays also reveal the limits of change and the persistence of inherited notions even in this turbulent era. As Nash notes, despite the widespread belief that economic equality must provide a social underpinning for republican government, efforts in Pennsylvania to empower the legislature to limit the amount of property an individual could own were rejected by the constitutional convention. Abigail Adams could flout the law by conducting business independently, but for most women the Revolution offered few changes in status. Judith Sargent Murray wrote powerful essays in the 1790s asserting the intellectual equality of women with men and praising the radical feminism of Mary Wollstonecraft. But as Sheila Skemp shows, Murray, trapped within the confines of late-eighteenth-century womanhood, remained dependent on her two husbands and failed to find an audience for her writings. Indeed, Skemp argues, the political reaction against the French Revolution as well as revelations about Wollstonecraft's less-than-conventional personal life produced a backlash that closed off further discussion of women's rights for this generation.

For Native Americans, the independence of the United States was a disaster (partly because the British in the Treaty of Paris abandoned their Indian allies by recognizing American sovereignty over the entire region east of the Mississippi River, completely ignoring the Indian presence). As Colin Calloway and James Martin relate, there was no single Indian response to the War of Independence. Like white Americans, Indians divided in allegiance; indeed, the Revolution produced civil wars among native nations. Calloway explores the split between established Cherokee chiefs who followed a policy of cautious accommodation and a younger generation of warriors, led by Dragging Canoe, who rejected land-cession treaties and launched a war against the Americans that proved disastrous, leading to further erosion of Cherokee landholdings. The unity of the Six Nations of the Iroquois Confederacy also shattered, as some tribes sided with the British while the Oneidas, led by Han Yerry, took up arms alongside the Americans. Yerry even led a group of Oneida warriors to assist George Washington's army when it was encamped at Valley Forge. The Oneidas thus escaped the forced land cessions to which the other Iroquois tribes were subjected following American independence. But this did not prevent the continuing intrusion of white settlers onto their land. Indeed, the problem went deeper than overt violations of Indian sovereignty. Almost all white Americans saw westward expansion as crucial to the new nation's political and social development. Even Herman Husband based his blueprint for a perfect society on the availability of cheap western land, thus unconsciously writing into his utopian project a recipe for war, conquest, and dispossession of the Native Americans.

The era's greatest contradiction, of course, was the continued existence of slavery in a nation ostensibly devoted to universal freedom. Fought in the name of liberty, the Revolution for a time threw into question the future of slavery in British North America. Beginning in 1777, when Vermont forbade slavery in its new constitution (which Thomas Young, an architect of the Pennsylvania Constitution of the previous year, helped to write), every northern state enacted measures to abolish the institution. These were the first legal steps toward emancipation in the new world. Some individuals, like the Virginian Richard Randolph, as Melvin Patrick Ely relates, voluntarily liberated their slaves. At the same time, with the British offering freedom to slaves who fled their patriot owners, thousands of blacks sought liberty within British lines. Several of George Washington's slaves ran away, and more, his kinsman Lund Washington reported, would do so "if they could." For blacks as well as whites, Lund Washington recognized, "liberty is sweet." As Cassandra Pybus notes, when the British evacuated cities like New York, Charleston, and Savannah at the end of the war, they took thousands of slaves with them, rejecting American demands for the return of their human property. Many of these fugitives ended up in Sierra Leone in West Africa.

The career of the poet Phillis Wheatley reflects the crosscurrents of black sentiment during the Revolutionary Era. Committed to the freedom of her people, yet torn, as David Waldstreicher shows, between allegiance to the Crown and support for American independence, Wheatley urged both sides to act to put an end to slavery. Once independence had been achieved, black leaders struggled to prove their patriotism and to find an equal place in the new nation. As Richard Newman notes, a group of black Masons led by Prince Hall offered their services to the government of Massachusetts to help suppress the Regulation of 1786 known today as Shays's Rebellion. The governor rejected their offer. Blacks had never been fully accepted by the patriotic movement in Massachusetts. As Young relates, while "Negroes" took part in Boston crowd activities, the Pope's Day companies warned them to "stay away from the parade" during the Stamp Act crisis of 1765.

The British philosopher and economist Adam Smith once warned that the democratization of politics could make the abolition of slavery more, not less, difficult, since in a government based on the popular will, "the persons who make all the laws . . . are persons who have slaves themselves." Thus the "freedom of the free" could readily intensify the "oppression of the slaves." The post-independence United States illustrates Smith's point. White democracy went hand in hand with the strengthening of slavery and the intensification of racism. Despite the disruptions of the War of Independence, the first census, in 1790, revealed that the slave population, around five hundred thousand when Jefferson wrote the Declaration of Independence, had grown to seven hundred thousand. Even as Americans celebrated their freedom, the contours of American nationality that emerged from the Revolution—the definition of those entitled to enjoy the "blessings of liberty" protected by the Constitution—increasingly came to be defined by race. After 1800 every state that entered the Union, with the single exception of Maine in 1821, limited the right to vote to white men. Blacks who obtained freedom in the North found themselves subjected to discrimination in every phase of their lives. Eventually early black leaders like Prince Hall, Richard Allen, and Daniel Coker, whose careers Richard Newman outlines, despaired of achieving equality in the United States and embraced emigration as a way to achieve freedom and equality. It is an ironic commentary on the limits of the American Revolution that such men felt they were more likely to achieve freedom in monarchical Great Britain than in the republican United States. However, as Newman notes, most ordinary black Americans preferred to struggle for equality in the United States rather than leave the land of their birth.

In 1830, as Philip Mead relates, Joseph Plumb Martin, a Revolutionary War veteran from Connecticut, published his memoirs. He was one of several hundred soldiers who recorded their experiences in print for posterity. Martin offered a remarkably accurate account of the battles in which he had participated and complained of subsequent neglect by his countrymen, especially his inability to obtain land that had been promised to soldiers. But beyond personal grievances, his aim was to rectify what he considered a faulty historical record. "Great men," Martin wrote, "get great praise; little men nothing." So it has too often remained in the writing of history. Let us hope that *Revolutionary Founders* finally succeeds in setting the record straight about the American Revolution and the ongoing struggle it unleashed for liberty and equality.

Acknowledgments

We are especially indebted to Keith Goldsmith, our editor at Knopf, whose enthusiasm, knowledge, editorial skills, and, not least of all, patience made possible the completion of a complex project involving as it did three editors and eighteen contributing authors. We are grateful for the work of our copy editor, Janet Biehl, and for the attention of Lydia Buechler and Ellen Feldman at Knopf.

We appreciate the efforts of our supportive and knowledgeable agent, Sandra Dijkstra, and of Elizabeth James of the Dijkstra Agency in coordinating the paperwork with authors.

Marian Olivas, Program Coordinator at the National Center for History in the Schools, and Laura Mills, an intern at the Center, expedited photo research and copyright clearance.

—A.Y., G.N., and R.R.

Notes

Full titles for works cited in the notes with short titles may be found in the For Further Reading section at the end of each essay.

INTRODUCTION· *"To Begin the World Over Again"*

1. Thomas Paine, *Common Sense* (1775), in *The Complete Writings of Thomas Paine,* ed. Philip S. Foner, 2 vols. (New York, 1945), 1:45; Paine, *The Forester's Letters No. 3* (1776), in *Complete Writings,* 2:81–82.
2. Paine, *The Age of Reason* (1794), in *Complete Writings,* 1:464.
3. Abigail Adams to John Adams, Mar. 31, 1776, in *Adams Family Correspondence,* ed. Lyman H. Butterfield et al., 10 vols. to date (Cambridge, Mass., 1963–), 1:369–71.
4. *The Records of the Federal Convention of 1787,* ed. Max Farrand, 4 vols. (New Haven, Conn., 1937), 1:48, 50, 131, 153, 201 ("the genius of the people").
5. Joseph Plumb Martin, *Private Yankee Doodle, Being a Narrative of Some of the Adventures, Dangers, and Sufferings of a Revolutionary Soldier,* ed. George F. Scheer (Hallowell, Me., 1830; rpt., Boston, 1963), 283.
6. Herman Husband, Manuscript Sermons [1793?], 47–48, Scull Collection, Historical Society of Western Pennsylvania.
7. John Adams, *Diary and Autobiography of John Adams,* ed. Lyman H. Butterfield et al., 4 vols. (Cambridge, Mass., 1961), 3:333.
8. John Adams to Benjamin Waterhouse, Oct. 29, 1805, in *The Selected Writings of John and John Quincy Adams,* ed. Adrienne Koch and William Peden (New York, 1946), 147–48.
9. Seneca Falls Declaration of Sentiments, July 19, 1848, in *Documents of American History,* ed. Henry Steele Commager (New York, 1968), document 172.
10. Frederick Douglass, Oration, July 5, 1852, in *Life and Writings of Frederick Douglass,* ed. Philip Foner, 5 vols. (New York, 1950–75), 2:189.

ONE· *Ebenezer Mackintosh: Boston's Captain General of the Liberty Tree*

1. Francis Bernard to the Earl of Halifax, Aug. 15, 16, 1765, Sparks Mss., Letterbooks, IV:137–41, 141–43, Houghton Library, Harvard University; Malcolm Freiberg, ed., "An Unknown Stamp Act Letter, Aug. 15, 1765," *Proceedings of the Massachusetts Historical Society* 78 (1967): 138–42; Cyrus Baldwin [to his brother], Aug. 15, 19, 1765, Misc. Bound Mss., Massachusetts Historical Society (hereafter MHS).
2. Thomas Hutchinson to Thomas Pownall, Mar. 8, 1766, Hutchinson Letterbooks, 26, MHS.

3. Hutchinson to Pownall, Mar. 6, 8, 1766, Hutchinson Letterbooks, 26, MHS; Francis Bernard to Earl of Halifax, Aug. 15, 16, Sparks Mss., Letterbooks, IV:137–41, 141–43; Hutchinson, *Diary and Letters,* ed. Peter Orlando Hutchinson, 2 vols. (Boston, 1884–86), 1:71; Young, *Liberty Tree,* 346–54.

4. Adair and Schutz, *Oliver's Origins and Progress,* 65.

5. Allan Kulikoff, "Progress of Inequality in Revolutionary Boston," *William and Mary Quarterly,* 3d ser., 28 (1971): 411–12, appendix, "Occupation of Boston Males, 1790." I have adjusted the 1790 census numbers for 1765; J. L. Bell, "From Saucy Boys to Sons of Liberty," in *Children in Colonial America,* ed. James Marten (New York, 2007), 205.

6. For Tony and Daly, two ship carpenters, see Jesse Lemisch, *Jack Tar vs. John Bull: The Role of New York's Seamen in Precipitating the Revolution* (New York, 2007), 101.

7. Cited in Anderson, "Ebenezer Mackintosh," 20.

8. Schuler Merrill, Haverhill, N.H., c. 1812, in Francis S. Drake, *Tea Leaves* (Boston, 1884), 61.

9. Carp, "Fire of Liberty," 786–87, 791–92, 794–96.

10. Nash, *Urban Crucible,* chaps. 7, 9 (poverty), 297 (Otis and Hutchinson); Robert St. George, *Conversing by Signs: Poetics of Implication in Colonial New England* (Chapel Hill, N.C., 1998), 206–18 (artisan exodus).

11. For recent interpretations: Peter Benes, "Night Processions: Celebrating the Gunpowder Plot in England and New England," in *The Worlds of Children, 1620–1920, Annal Proceedings of the Dublin Seminar for New England Forklife,* ed. Peter Benes and Jane M Benes, eds. (Boston, 2000), 9–28; Brendan McConville, "Pope's Day Revisited," *Explorations in Early American History* 3 (2000): 258–80; Francis D. Cogliano, *No King, No Popery: Anti-Catholicism in Revolutionary New England* (Westport, Conn., 1996).

12. Bell, "Du Simitiere's Sketches of Pope's Day," 207–15.

13. Hutchinson to Pownall, Mar. 6, 1766; Adair and Schutz, *Oliver's Origins and Progress,* 54; John Rowe, *Letters and Diary,* ed. Anne Rowe Cunningham (Boston, 1903), Jan. 24, 1765.

14. *Massachusetts Acts and Resolves,* III, chap. 14 (1756–67), chap. 18 (1752–53); *Boston Evening Post,* Nov. 11, 1745 ("Protestant mob").

15. *Boston News-Letter,* Nov. 8, 1764; J. Quincy Jr., *Reports of the Cases of the Superior Court of Judicature,* ed. Samuel M. Quincy (Boston, 1865), 112–13 (Hutchinson charge); and Suffolk County Court Records, Files 100480, 100493 (Grand Jury indictments, warrants, recognizances) in Supreme Judicial Court Archives.

16. *Records of the Town of Braintree,* ed. Samuel A Bates (Randolph, Mass., 1886), 404–6.

17. Henry Bass to Samuel P. Savage, Dec. 19, 1765, *Proceedings of the Massachusetts Historical Society* 14 (1910–11): 688–89.

18. Hoerder, *Crowd Action in Revolutionary Massachusetts,* 90–110; Nash, *Urban Crucible,* 292–96; Morgan, *Stamp Act Crisis,* chap. 8.

19. Hutchinson to Richard Jackson, Aug. 30, 1765; Hutchinson to William Bollan, Aug. 20, 1765, Massachusetts Archives, 26, 146–47; Thomas Hutchinson, *History of Colony and Province of Massachusetts Bay,* 3 vols. (Cambridge, Mass., 1938), 3:89–93; Hutchinson, *Diary and Letters,* 2:70–72.

20. Hutchinson to R. J. Jackson, Aug. 16, 30, 1765; Hutchinson to William Bollan, Aug. 20, 1765; Petition to the King, Oct. 25, 1765, Tyler, ed., Hutchinson Transcripts, Colonial Society of Massachusetts.

21. Bernard to Earl of Halifax, Aug. 31, 1765, British Public Record office, C.O. 5/755, reprinted in *English Historical Documents,* ed. Merrill Jensen (New York, 1955), 675–80; Bernard to John Pownall, Nov. 1, 26, 1765, Sparks Mss., Letterbooks, V:18–23, 43–45.

22. Young, *Liberty Tree,* 327–29.

23. Hutchinson to Pownall, Nov. 26, 1765; Bernard to Pownall, Nov. 1, 26, 1765, Sparks Mss., Letterbooks, V:18–23, 43–45.

24. Bernard to Halifax, Aug. 31, 1765, in Jensen, *English Historical Documents,* 675–80; Bernard to Pownall, Nov. 1, 5, 1765, Sparks Mss., Letterbooks, V:6–23, 43–46, Harvard; Hutchinson, *Diary and Letters,* 2:71; John Boyle, "Journal of Occurrences in Boston," Nov. 1, 1765, *New England History General Register* 84 (1930): 170–71.

25. Bernard to Pownall, Nov. 5, 1765, Sparks Mss., Letterbooks, V:18–23; Adair and Schutz, *Oliver's Origins and Progress,* 54–55.

26. Bernard to Pownall, Nov. 26, 1765, Sparks Mss., Letterbooks, V:43–45; Hutchinson to Benjamin Franklin, Nov. 18, 1765, Misc. Bd. Mss., MHS.

27. Bernard to Pownall, Nov. 26, 1765, Sparks Mss., Letterbooks, V:43–45; Young, *Liberty Tree,* 327–46.

28. Walter Wallace, " 'A Lion with Nails and Fangs': Masaniello of Naples and the Folklore of Political Violence" (Milan Group in Early American History, 1990) in *Communitas* [Italian] (1992): 191–218.

29. John Adams, *Diary and Autobiography of John Adams,* ed. Lyman H. Butterfield, 4 vols. (Cambridge, Mass., 1961), 1:300; Thomas Paine, *Common Sense,* in *Complete Writings of Thomas Paine,* ed. Philip Foner, 2 vols. (New York, 1945), 1:29–30.

30. Pauline Maier, *The Old Revolutionaries* (New York, 1980), 101–8; Ray Raphael, *Founders: The People Who Brought You a Nation* (New York, 2009), 80–83, 97–99, 108–10, 118–21.

31. George Mason to Joseph Harrison, Oct. 20, 1769, cited in Anderson, "Note on Ebenezer Mackintosh," 361; Anderson, "Pascal Paoli: An Inspiration to the Sons of Liberty," *Publications of the Colonial Society of Massachusetts* 26 (1924–26): 199–204.

32. Suffolk County Court, File 101432: *Ruth Thompson vs. Ebenezer McIntosh et al.,* Mar. 1769; Superior Court of Judicature (acknowledgment of a debt to Thompson, an appeal, March, 1769, and recovered judgment of £9), File 98740: "A True List of Prisoners in Suffolk County Jail," July 9, 1770.

33. Adair and Schutz, *Oliver's Origins and Progress,* 54–55.

34. *Legal Papers of John Adams,* ed. L. Kinvin Wroth and Hiller Zobel, 3 vols. (Cambridge, Mass., 1965), 3:266; Hutchinson to Lord Dartmouth, Dec. 3, 1773, Hutchinson, Letterbook 27:577–78, Massachusetts Archives.

35. Schuler Merrill in Drake, *Tea Leaves,* 61; Benjamin Thatcher, *Traits of the Tea Party* (New York, 1835), appendix.

36. William Gordon, *History of the Rise . . . of the United States,* 4 vols. (London, 1788), 1:230–35; Young, "Tar and Feathers," in Young, *Liberty Tree,* 150–56; Adair and Schutz, *Oliver's Origins and Progress,* 94.

37. Nathaniel Coffin to Charles Steuart, May 23, 1770, Charles Steuart Papers, 5026:56–59, National Library of Scotland, brought to my attention by Benjamin Carp; *Massachusetts Spy,* Apr. 7, 1774; "Extract of a Letter from Boston, Nov. 24, 1774," in *Letters on the American Revolution,* ed. Margaret Willard (Boston, 1925), 31.

38. Anderson, "Ebenezer Mackintosh," 63.

39. William Henry Drayton, *The Letters of Freeman, etc.: Essays on the Nonimportation Movement in Souuth Carolina,* ed. R. Weir (Columbia, S.C. 1977), 31; Young, "The Mechanics of the Revolution," in Young, *Liberty Tree,* 53.

40. "Crispin," *Massachusetts Spy,* Jan. 17, 1772; Isaiah Thomas, *History of Printing in America,* ed. Marcus McCorison (New York, 1980), 265; Young, *Shoemaker and Tea Party,* pt. 1, chaps. 5–8; Bostonian cited in Eric Foner, *The Story of American Freedom* (New York, 1998), 7.

41. Adams, *Diary and Autobiography,* Aug. 15, Dec. 18, 1765, 1:259–60, 263–65; Pauline Maier, "Samuel Adams," *American National Biography* (New York, 1999), 121–26; Ronald P. Formisano, *The Transformation of Political Culture: Massachusetts Parties, 1790s–1840s* (New York, 1983), 31–33 (Hancock); John W. Tyler, *Smugglers and Patriots: Boston Merchants and the Advent of the American Revolution* (Boston, 1986), 242; Nash, *Urban Crucible,* 362.

T W O · *Blacksmith Timothy Bigelow and the Massachusetts Revolution of 1774*

1. Nutt, *History of Worcester,* 74–79; Moynihan, *History of Worcester,* 61.

2. *Worcester Town Records,* 199–202.

3. Nutt, *History of Worcester,* 56–59; *Worcester Town Records,* 87, 131, 162, 180; Moynihan, *History of Worcester,* 65; Izard, "Andrews-Bigelow Site."

4. *Worcester Town Records,* 205; Johnson, *Worcester in War for Independence,* 41.

5. American Political Society (hereafter APS), Minutes; Lovell, *Worcester in the Revolution,* 21–26; Moynihan, *History of Worcester,* 67.

6. Hersey, *Col. Timothy Bigelow,* 8–9.

7. *Worcester Town Records,* 230–33; *Boston News-Letter and Massachusetts Gazette,* June 30, 1774; *Boston Gazette,* July 4, 1774.

8. APS, Minutes; French, *General Gage's Informers,* 15; "General Gage's Instructions, of 22d February 1775, to Captain Brown and Ensign D'Bernicre," and "Narrative, &c.," Massachusetts Historical Society *Collections* 4 (1916): 204–18.

9. *Massachusetts Gazette,* Sept. 15, 1774; *Boston Evening-Post,* Sept. 19, 1774; APS, Minutes; *Worcester Town Records,* 234, 238–39; Lincoln, *History of Worcester,* 83; Lovell, *Worcester in Revolution,* 38, 41.

10. Wroth, *Province in Rebellion,* 877–80; Lincoln, *Journals of Provincial Congress/County Conventions,* 627–31.

11. Parkman, Diary; Wroth, *Province in Rebellion,* 528–31; *Boston Evening-Post,* Aug. 29 and Sept. 5, 1774; Raphael, *First American Revolution,* 70–71, 75–82.

12. Gage to Dartmouth, Aug. 27, 1774, in *Correspondence of General Thomas Gage,* ed. Clarence E. Carter (New Haven, Conn., 1931), 1:366.

13. Thomas Young to Samuel Adams, Aug. 19, 1774, Samuel Adams Papers, New York Public Library; Wroth, *Province in Rebellion,* 808, 812; Raphael, *First American Revolution,* 82, 237.

14. Wroth, *Province in Rebellion,* 689–92; Boston Committee of Correspondence, Correspondence and Proceedings, reel 1, New York Public Library.

15. Wroth, *Province in Rebellion,* 894–97; Lincoln, *Journals of Provincial Congress/County Conventions,* 631–35.

16. Wroth, *Province in Rebellion,* 525; Thomas Young to Samuel Adams, Sept. 4, 1774, Samuel Adams Papers, New York Public Library; Gage to Dartmouth, Sept. 2, 1774, in Carter, *Correspondence of Gage,* 1:370. For a narrative account of the Powder Alarm, see Raphael, *First American Revolution,* 112–30.

17. Parkman, Diary; APS, Minutes.

18. Parkman, Diary.

19. Ibid.; Lincoln, *Journals of Provincial Congress/County Conventions,* 635–37.

20. Raphael, *First American Revolution,* 130–38; Lincoln, *Journals of Provincial Congress/County Conventions,* 637.

21. Andrew Davis, *The Confiscation of John Chandler's Estate* (Boston, 1903), 224.

22. The "List of Voters for the Year 1779 in Worcester" (Worcester Society of Antiquity, *Proceedings,* 16 (1899): 451–52; reproduced on Documents page, rayraphael.com), presented to the town in that year by Worcester selectmen and assessors, includes eight women and eleven estates. We do not know how these were represented at the meetings.

23. Lincoln, *Journals of Provincial Congress/County Conventions,* 641–44.

24. David Conroy, *In Public Houses: Drink and the Revolution of Authority in Colonial Massachusetts* (Chapel Hill, N.C., 1995), 147–49.

25. For the dramatic relocation of Thomas's press, see Raphael, *Founders,* 176–78.

26. *Boston Gazette,* Nov. 28, 1774. Worcester blacksmiths met on September 8 and November 8, but the resolution must have originated at the earlier date, since it cited the authority of the August 26 multicounty convention rather than the Provincial Congress.

27. APS, Minutes, Oct. 3, 1774; *Worcester Town Records,* 244; Lincoln, *History of Worcester,* 91–92; Nutt, *History of Worcester,* 538.

28. Raphael, *First American Revolution,* 63–156. The Revolution did not extend to the island counties (Dukes and Nantucket) or to the sparsely populated counties in Maine (York, Cumberland, and Lincoln).

29. John Adams, *Diary and Autobiography,* 2:134–35.

30. Ibid., 2:140–41; John Adams to Joseph Palmer, Sept. 27, 1774, and John Adams to William Tudor, Oct. 7, 1774, John Adams, *Papers,* 2:173, 187–88.

31. Samuel Adams to Joseph Warren, Sept. 25, 1774, Samuel Adams, *Writings,* 3:159; Wroth, *Province in Rebellion,* 81–82. Wroth calculates that twenty-three out of thirty-four men who served on key committees or held multiple committee assignments came from Boston and other "major trading towns" in the East, even though these towns accounted for only 20 percent of the delegates.

THREE · *Samuel Thompson's War: The Career of an American Insurgent*

1. *Massachusetts Spy,* June 21, 1775.

2. This theme is developed in some detail in Breen, *American Insurgents, American*

Patriots. Also see Michael Rose, *Washington's War: From Independence to Iraq* (London, 2007).

3. Nathan Fiske, *The Importance of Righteousness to the Happiness and the Tendency of Oppression to the Misery of the People . . .* (Boston, 1774). He delivered this sermon on July 14, 1774.

4. *Common Sense* in *The Complete Writings of Thomas Paine,* ed. Philip S. Foner, 2 vols. (New York, 1945), 1:22–23.

5. A splendid exception is Leamon, *Revolution Downeast,* 62–80, 157–62, and 198–208.

6. Cited in Yerxa, *Burning of Falmouth,* 130.

7. Cited in Jack P. Greene, *Imperatives, Behaviors, and Identities: Essays in Early American Cultural History* (Charlottesville, Va., 1992), 236.

8. Cited in George Augustus Wheeler and Henry Warren Wheeler, *History of Brunswick, Topsham, and Harpswell, Maine . . .* (Boston, 1878), 812.

9. Cited in Nathan Goold, "General Samuel Thompson of Brunswick and Topsham, Maine," Maine Historical Society *Collections* 1 (1904): 423, 427.

10. Wheeler and Wheeler, *History of Brunswick,* 813.

11. Ibid.

12. *Virginia Gazette* (Pinkney), May 18, 1775.

13. Cited in David Doyle, *Ireland, Irishmen and Revolutionary America, 1760–1820* (Dublin, 1981), 110.

14. See, for example, Edward L. Parker, *History of Londonderry, Comprising the Towns of Derry and Londonderry, New Hampshire* (Boston, 1851), chap. 1.

15. Andrew Sherman, *The O'Briens of Machias, Me., Patriots of the American Revolution* (Boston, 1904), 15. Also, [no author.] "Exertions of the O'Brien Family . . . Carefully Taken Down from the Life of Captain John O'Brien, of Brunswick for the Maine Historical Collections," Maine Historical Society *Collections,* 1st ser., 2 (1847): 229–37.

16. Andrew Sherman, *Life of Captain Jeremiah O'Brien: Machias, Maine* (Morristown, N.J., 1902), 16.

17. Goold, "Samuel Thompson," 427.

18. Josiah Pierce, *A History of the Town of Gorham, Maine* (Portland, Me., 1862), 117.

19. Leamon, *Revolution Downeast,* 63.

20. Ibid.

21. Cited ibid., 64–65.

22. Cited in Goold, "Samuel Thompson," 435.

23. Ibid., 439.

24. Cited in Leamon, *Revolution Downeast,* 66.

25. Ibid., 67.

26. *New-England Chronicle,* Nov. 23, 1775.

27. *Boston Gazette,* Mar. 17, 1777.

28. Cited in Goold, "Samuel Thompson," 455.

29. *Documentary History of the Ratification of the Constitution,* ed. John P. Kaminski and George J. Saladino, 23 vols. to date (Madison, Wisc., 2000–), 4:1354.

30. Goold, "Samuel Thompson," 424–25.

FOUR· *Philadelphia's Radical Caucus That Propelled Pennsylvania
to Independence and Democracy*

1. Selsam, *Pennsylvania Constitution of 1776,* 148–49; William Smith from Bedford County, quoted in Burton A. Konkle, *The Life and Times of Thomas Smith, 1745–1809* (Philadelphia, 1904), 75.

2. *To the Free and Patriotic Inhabitants of the City of Philadelphia and Province of Pennsylvania* (1770), quoted in Charles S. Olton, *Artisans for Independence: Philadelphia Mechanics and the American Revolution* (Syracuse, N.Y., 1975), 43, 53; *Pennsylvania Gazette,* Sept. 27, 1770.

3. Quoted from *Life and Times of Thomas Smith,* in Burton A. Konkle, *George Bryan and the Constitution of Pennsylvania, 1731–1791* (Philadelphia, 1922), 66.

4. William Duane, ed., *Extracts from the Diary of Christopher Marshall, 1774–1781* (Albany, N.Y., 1877), for Cannon going "to [the] State House Yard to help consult and regulate the forming of the militia."

5. *Arms, Country, and Class,* 54.

6. *Pennsylvania Gazette,* Feb. 28, 1776, for "Rationalis" 's attack on *Common Sense;* Mar. 9, 1776, for "Cato" 's attack on Cannon.

7. *Marshall Diary,* 62–65.

8. *The Complete Writings of Thomas Paine,* ed. Philip S. Foner, 2 vols. (New York, 1945), 2:81–82; *Pennsylvania Gazette,* Feb. 28; Mar. 6, 13, 20, and 27; Apr. 3, 10, and 24; May 1 and 15, 1776.

9. Quoted in David Hawke, *In the Midst of Revolution: The Politics of Confrontation in Colonial America* (Philadelphia, 1961), 118.

10. Quoted in Ryerson, *Revolution Is Now Begun,* 215.

11. "Philadelphia Committee to the Committees of the Several Counties," in Peter Force, *American Archives,* 4th ser. (Washington, D.C., 1846), 6:520–21.

12. *Pennsylvania Magazine of History and Biography* 22 (1898): 469.

13. Quoted in Rosswurm, *Arms, Country, and Class,* 97.

14. "The Address of the Deputies from the Committees of Pennsylvania, assembled in Provincial Conference, June 22," in Force, *American Archives,* 4th ser., 6:962.

15. "To the Several Battalions of Military Associators," broadside at Historical Society of Pennsylvania, Philadelphia.

16. *Marshall Diary,* 81.

17. Ibid., 84.

18. At another point Franklin argued that governing bodies should have the power "of limiting the Quantity and the Uses of it [wealth]"; quoted in Edmund S. Morgan, *American Heroes: Profiles of Men and Women Who Shaped Early America* (New York, 2009), 216–17.

19. William Hooper (North Carolina), quoted in Kruman, *Between Liberty and Authority,* 32.

20. Selsam, *Pennsylvania Constitution of 1776,* 199.

21. Ronald Schultz, *The Republic of Labor: Philadelphia Artisans and the Politics of Class, 1720–1830* (New York, 1993), 54; Benjamin Rush to Anthony Wayne, Sept. 24, 1776, in *Letters of Benjamin Rush,* ed. L. H. Butterfield, 2 vols. (Philadelphia, 1951), 1:114–15, 137, 148.

22. Attributed to Adams by Rush in his letter to Adams, Oct. 12, 1779, *Letters of Rush,* 1:240.

23. *Pennsylvania Evening Post,* Oct. 24, 1776.

24. "Consideration," in *Pennsylvania Gazette,* Oct. 30, 1776; and "John Trusshoop," ibid., Nov. 13, 1776; "The Considerate Freeman to the People," ibid., Nov. 20, 1776.

25. The thirty-one resolutions of the anticonstitutionalists were printed in *Pennsylvania Gazette,* Oct. 23, 1776, and in most other Philadelphia newspapers.

26. Quoted in Esmond Wright, *Franklin of Philadelphia* (Cambridge, Mass., 1986), 251.

27. Foner, *Writings of Paine,* 2:956.

FIVE · *A World of Paine*

1. Foner, *Writings of Paine,* 1:3, 17.

2. *The Papers of John Adams,* ed. Robert J. Taylor, 13 vols. (Cambridge, Mass., 1977–), 4:37, 41, 53, 29.

3. Nelson, *Thomas Paine,* 49.

4. Foner, *Writings of Paine,* 1:19.

5. *Diary and Autobiography of John Adams,* ed. Lyman H. Butterfield, 4 vols. (Cambridge, Mass., 1961), 3:330–41.

6. Collins, *Trouble with Tom,* 22.

7. Foner, *Writings of Paine,* 1:49–50; Nelson, *Thomas Paine,* 108.

8. Nelson, *Thomas Paine,* 203.

9. Ibid., 9.

10. Mercy Otis Warren, *History of the Rise, Progress, and Termination of the American Revolution,* 3 vols. (Boston, 1805), 1:378–80.

11. E. Foner, *Paine and Revolutionary America,* 264.

12. Collins, *Trouble with Tom,* 29.

13. Perry Miller, *The Nation,* February 23, 1946, 232; Sean Wilentz, "The Air Around Tom Paine," *New Republic,* April 24, 1995, 38; Bernard Bailyn, *Faces of Revolution* (New York, 1992), n.p.

14. Keane, *Tom Paine,* xiii.

15. Foner, *Writings of Paine,* 1:286, 344, 404–05.

16. Nelson, *Thomas Paine,* 202, 220, 228.

17. Ibid., 229–30.

18. Ibid., 241.

19. Ibid., 248, 274–75, 281.

20. Ibid., 285.

21. Foner, *Paine and Revolutionary America,* xii.

22. Foner, *Writings of Paine,* 1:464, 599.

23. "Plea for a Patriot," *Galaxy* 21 (May 1876): 593.

24. Wilentz, "Air Around Paine," 38.

25. Kaye, *Paine and Promise of America,* 171.

26. Collins, *Trouble with Tom,* 53, 57, 62, 64.

27. Nelson, *Thomas Paine,* 270, 308, 306; "Sketch of the Life of Thomas Paine," *Spirit of the Pilgrims* 4 (June 1931): 341.

28. Colllins, *Trouble with Tom*, 15.

29. Foner, *Paine and Revolutionary America*, 257.

30. Warren, *History of . . . American Revolution*, 1:379.

31. Foner, *Writings of Paine*, 1:601, 465.

32. Nelson, *Thomas Paine*, 9.

S I X · *Phillis Wheatley: The Poet Who Challenged the American Revolutionaries*

1. *New-York Journal,* June 3, 1773, Thomas Woolridge to Lord Dartmouth, Nov. 24, 1772, in *Phillis Wheatley and Her Writings* [hereafter *PWW*], ed. William H. Robinson (New York, 1984), 388, 454.

2. Phillis Wheatley, *Complete Writings* [hereafter *CW*], ed. Vincent Carretta (New York, 2001), 128–29.

3. B. D. Barger, *Lord Dartmouth and the American Revolution* (Columbia, S.C., 1965), 10.

4. *PWW,* 30–31, 316, 385–87.

5. Margaretta Odell, "Memoir," in *Memoir and Poems of Phillis Wheatley, a Native African and a Slave* (Boston, 1838), 7–10.

6. Oliver Morton Dickerson, ed., *Boston Under Military Rule, 1768–1769, as Revealed in a Journal of the Times* (1936; rpt. New York, 1970), 3, 6, 16–17; Hoerder, *Crowd Action,* 191–92.

7. Zobel, *Boston Massacre,* 182.

8. *PWW,* 139, 455; Hoerder, *Crowd Action,* 223. Robinson includes a poem from the newspaper that he believes Wheatley wrote, but Mason and Carretta do not include it in their editions for lack of positive proof. Wheatley included a Boston Massacre poem in her 1772 proposals; *The Poems of Phillis Wheatley,* ed. Julius Mason, 2nd ed. (Chapel Hill, N.C., 1989), 188n2.

9. Peter Linebaugh and Marcus Rediker, *The Many-Headed Hydra: Sailors, Slaves, Commoners, and the Hidden History of the Revolutionary Atlantic* (Boston, 2000), 232; Bradley, *Slavery, Propaganda,* 59–61.

10. *CW,* 75–76.

11. *CW,* 114, 116; *PWW,* 370, 372.

12. Carretta, "Introduction," *CW,* xxiii–xxv.

13. Waldstreicher, *Runaway America,* 195–97, 202–3; Franklin to Jonathan Williams Sr., July 7, 1773, Williams to Franklin, Oct. 17, 1773, in *The Papers of Benjamin Franklin,* ed. Leonard Woods Labaree et al., 39 vols. (New Haven, Conn, 1959–), 20:291–92, 445.

14. Mukhtar Ali Isani, ed., "The British Reception of Wheatley's *Poems on Various Subjects," Journal of Negro History* 66 (Summer 1981): 144–49.

15. Wheatley to David Wooster, Oct. 18, 1773, in *CW,* 146–47; John Andrews to William Barrell, Jan. 28, 1774, Andrews-Eliot Correspondence, Massachusetts Historical Society.

16. *Connecticut Gazette,* Mar. 11, 1774, in *CW,* 152–53.

17. *CW,* 83–88; *PWW,* 49–50.

18. *CW,* 88–90.

19. *CW,* 90–92; Wheatley to Obour Tanner, Feb. 14, 1776, in "The Hand of America's First Black Female Poet," National Public Radio online, http://www.npr.org/templates/story/story.php?storyId=5021077, accessed Aug. 10, 2009; Christopher Leslie Brown, *Moral Capital: Foundations of British Abolitionism* (Chapel Hill, N.C., 2006), 169.

20. *PWW,* 288–91; Washington to Joseph Reed, Washington to Phillis Wheatley, in *PWW,* 451–52; M. A. Richmond, *Bid the Vassal Soar: Interpretive Essays on the Life and Poetry of Phillis Wheatley and George Moses Horton* (Washington, D.C., 1974), 3–9; Henry Wiencek, *An Imperfect God: George Washington, His Slaves, and the Creation of America* (New York, 2003), 205–14; Frank Shuffleton, "On Her Own Footing: Phillis Wheatley in Freedom," in *Genius in Bondage: Literature of the Early Black Atlantic,* ed. Vincent Carretta and Phillip Gould (Lexington, Ky., 2001), 186–87.

21. *PWW,* 347–48.

22. Odell, "Memoir," 20, 23, 29.

23. William H. Robinson, *Phillis Wheatley: A Bio-Bibliography* (Boston, 1981), 30, 32.

24. *CW,* 101–2.

25. Thomas Jefferson, *Notes on the State of Virginia with Related Documents,* ed. David Waldstreicher (Boston, 2002), 178.

S E V E N · *"Adventures, Dangers and Sufferings": The Betrayals of
Private Joseph Plumb Martin, Continental Soldier*

1. Martin, *Private Yankee Doodle,* 85, 92–93.

2. Ibid., 95.

3. Dexter, *Graduates of Yale College,* 2:421–22; Martin, *Private Yankee Doodle,* 5; William Burdick, *The Massachusetts Manual: or Political and historical register, for the political year from June 1814, to June 1815,* vol. 1 (Boston: 1814).

4. Martin, *Private Yankee Doodle,* 292–93.

5. Ibid., 128; Daniel M. Sivilich and Gary Wheeler Stone, "The Battle of Monmouth: The Archaeology of Molly Pitcher, the Royal Highland Regiment and Colonel Cilley's Light Infantry," http://www.saa.org/Portals/0/SAA/Public/resources/MonmouthBravo.pdf; Mount Holly maps are compliments of John Naggy, Oct. 10, 2005.

6. Martin, *Private Yankee Doodle,* 115; Thomas J. McGuire, *The Philadelphia Campaign: Brandywine and the Fall of Philadelphia* (Mechanicsburg, Pa., 2006), 187–88.

7. Martin, *Private Yankee Doodle,* 220–21; Angus McFee petition, American Loyalist Claims, 13/26/264–65, Connecticut Adjutant General's Office, *Record of Service of Connecticut Men in the War of the Revolution, War of 1812, Mexican War,* ed. Henry P. Johnson (Hartford, Conn., 1889), 44, 213, 408.

8. Martin, *Private Yankee Doodle,* xxiv.

9. Ibid., 14, 7.

10. Ibid., 9, 7.

11. Ibid., 5, 14, 17.

12. Ibid., 19, 24, 39, 41.

13. Ibid., 60–61.

14. Ibid., 284–85, 68, 50, 181.

15. Ibid., 285, 100–1; on food shortages, see Richard Buel Jr., *In Irons: Britain's Naval Supremacy and the American Revolutionary Economy* (New Haven, Conn., 1998).

16. Martin, *Private Yankee Doodle,* 105, 167; for more on the "moral economy" idea, see Alan Kulikoff, "The Transition to Capitalism in Rural America," *William and Mary Quarterly,* 3rd ser., 46, no. 1 (1989): 120–40.

17. Martin, *Private Yankee Doodle,* 136, 122, 147–48, 165.

18. Ibid., 150; Fred Anderson, *A People's Army: Massachusetts Soldiers and Society in the Seven Years' War* (Chapel Hill, N.C., 1984).

19. Martin, *Private Yankee Doodle,* 172, 182; Nathanael Greene to William Greene, May 27, 1780, in *The Papers of General Nathanael Greene,* ed. Richard K. Showman, 13 vols. (Chapel Hill, N.C., 1976–), 5:582.

20. Martin, *Private Yankee Doodle,* 194, 196.

21. Ibid., 265, 280–81.

22. Ibid., 281.

23. Ibid., 283.

24. *Resolutions, Laws, and Ordinances, Relating to the Pay, Half Pay, Commutation of Half Pay, Bounty Lands, and Other Promises Made by Congress to the Officers and Soldiers of the Revolution* (Washington, D.C., 1838; rpt., New York, 1970), 22.

25. Martin, *Narrative* (1830), title page; Jonathan Shay, *Achilles in Vietnam: Combat Trauma and the Undoing of Character* (New York, 1995).

26. Prospect Land Committee to the Waldo Patent Commissioners, Feb. 16, 1790, Massachusetts State Archives, quoted in Taylor, *Liberty Men,* 103.

27. Joseph P. Martin to Henry Knox, Dec. 22, 1801, ms, Gilder Lehrman Institute; also quoted in Taylor, *Liberty Men,* 247–48.

28. *Resolves of the Commonwealth of Massachusetts the 26th May, 1812 to the 2d March, 1815* (Boston, 1812–15), 15; William Burdick, *The Massachusetts manual, for the political year from June 1814, to June 1815* (Boston, 1814), 50.

29. Joseph P. Martin, Revolutionary War Pension File, NARA M805, W1629. On pension financing, see Resch, *Suffering Soldiers,* chaps. 4 and 5; Martin, *Private Yankee Doodle,* 292.

30. William D. Williamson, *The History of the State of Maine from Its First Discovery, A.D., 1602, to the Separation, A.D. 1820, Inclusive* (Hallowell, Me., 1832), 556; Martin, *Private Yankee Doodle,* 287–88; John Dwelly, Revolutionary War Pension File, NARA M805, W17738, pp. 34 and 35.

31. Martin, *Private Yankee Doodle,* 287–88.

32. On the competing narratives, see Resch, *Suffering Soldiers.*

33. Joseph P. Martin to the Committee on State Lands, Feb. 1, 1833; Petition of Joseph P. Martin for a grant of 200 acres of land to the Joint Standing Committee on State Lands, Jan. 12, 1836, ms, Maine State Archives, Maine Land Office Revolutionary War Land Bounty Applications Box 12; Petition of J. P. Martin to the amount of taxes overpaid by him, refunded to him, House of Representatives, June 14, 1848, ms, Maine State Archives, Legislative Records, Resolves 1848, Box 93, Chapter 10.

34. [Joseph Williamson,] *Republican Journal* (Belfast, Me.), May 10, 1850; "List of Deaths in 1830," MS Transc., Stockton Springs Historical Society, Stockton Springs, Me.

E I G H T · *"The Spirit of Levelling": James Cleveland, Edward Wright,*
and the Militiamen's Struggle for Equality in Revolutionary Virginia

1. Cresswell, *Journal,* Feb. 12, 1776, 138; McDonnell, *Politics of War,* 194.
2. Lund Washington to George Washington, Feb. 29, 1776, in Abbot, *Washington Papers, Revolutionary War Series,* 3:395–96.
3. McDonnell, *Politics of War,* 198–99.
4. Scribner, *Revolutionary Virginia,* 6:474–77, 7:114–15, 236–37.
5. Lund Washington to George Washington, Feb. 29, 1776.
6. Scribner, *Revolutionary Virginia,* 6:474–77, 7:114–15, 236–37.
7. Lund Washington to George Washington, Feb. 29, 1776.
8. McDonnell, *Politics of War,* 194.
9. Cresswell, *Journal,* Jan. 15, 19, 22, 26, 1776, 135–36; McDonnell, *Politics of War,* 198–99, 211.
10. McDonnell, *Politics of War,* 202, 204.
11. Ibid., 210.
12. Ibid., 211.
13. Ibid., 217–18.
14. Ibid., 239.
15. Ibid., 236.
16. Ibid., 280.
17. Ibid., 285.
18. Charlotte County Petition, [Oct. 15, 1779,] Library of Virginia; McDonnell, *Politics of War,* 290–91.
19. Proceedings of a General Court Martial, June 18–19, 1781.
20. Charlotte County Petition, [May 26, 1780,] Library of Virginia; McDonnell, *Politics of War,* 370–71.
21. Proceedings of a General Court Martial, June 18–19, 1781.
22. McDonnell, *Politics of War,* 423–24; Cumberland County Petition, [Mar. 5, 1781,] Library of Virginia.
23. The account of Wright's conspiracy here and in the following paragraphs is drawn from Proceedings of a General Court Martial, June 18–19, 1781.
24. McDonnell, *Politics of War,* 469.
25. Ibid., 454, 468.
26. Ibid., 465.
27. McDonnell, "Class War," 338.
28. McDonnell, *Politics of War,* 442–43.

N I N E · *Mary Perth, Harry Washington, and Moses Wilkinson:*
Black Methodists Who Escaped from Slavery and Founded a Nation

1. Reverend Clarke, the chaplain in Sierra Leone, letter of July 29, 1796, *Evangelical Magazine* 4 (London, 1796), 460–64.
2. William Warren Sweet, *Virginia Methodism: A History* (Richmond, Va., 1955), 51.
3. *The Journal of Joseph Pilmore, Methodist Itinerant for the Years August 1, 1769, to*

January 2, 1774, ed. Frederick Maser and Howard Maag (Philadelphia, 1969), 148–54.

4. Thomas Ludwell to Richard Henry Lee, Dec. 23, 1775, Lee Papers, University of Virginia.

5. Lund Washington to George Washington, Dec. 3, 1775, in *The Papers of George Washington, Revolutionary War Series,* ed. W. W. Abbot and Dorothy Twohig (Charlottesville, Va., 1988), 2:571, 481–82.

6. Log of HMS *Roebuck, Naval Documents of the American Revolution,* ed. William Bell Clark, William James Morgan, and Michael J. Crawford (Washington, D.C., 1970), 5:1250–51.

7. For the original draft treaty with amendments, see Oswald to Melbourne, Nov. 30, 1782, CO 5/110, 377, National Archives of the United Kingdom.

8. *Memoirs of the Life of Boston King: A black preacher, written by himself during his residence at Kingswood School,* ed. Ruth Holmes Whitehead and Carmelita Robertson (1796), 157.

9. "Substance of a Conference Between General Washington and Sir Guy Carleton, 6 May 1783," *The Writings of George Washington,* ed. John C. Fitzpatrick, 39 vols. (Washington, D.C., 1938), 26:402–6.

10. Methodist preacher William Black quoted in Wilson, *Loyal Blacks,* 124.

11. J. B. Elliott, *Lady Huntingdon's Connection in Sierra Leone* (London, 1851), 15; John Clarkson's Journal of his Mission to America, Mar. 11, 1792, New York Public Library.

12. Clarkson's Journal of his Mission, Apr. 11, 1792.

13. Anna Maria Falconbridge, *Two Voyages to Sierra Leone* (1794), in *Maiden Voyages and Infant Colonies,* ed. Deirdre Coleman (London, 1999), 102.

14. Ibid., 122.

15. Clarkson's Journal of his Mission, May 19, 1792.

16. Petition to Clarkson in *"Our Children Free and Happy": Letters from Black Settlers in Africa in the 1790s,* ed. Christopher Fyfe (Edinburgh, 1991), 25–26.

17. Jordan, Willkinson, et al. to Clarkson, Nov. 19, 1794, ibid., 47.

18. Zachary Macaulay, "Journal 1793–99," entry for Sept. 13, 1793, Macaulay Papers, Huntington Library, San Marino, Calif.

19. Macaulay, Journal, May 8, 1796, Macaulay Papers.

20. Macaulay to Mills, Feb. 4, 1797, Macaulay Papers.

21. Wilberforce to Dundas, Apr. 1, 1800, Melville Papers, Add. Mss. 41085, British Library.

TEN· *James Ireland, John Leland, John "Swearing Jack" Waller, and the Baptist Campaign for Religious Freedom in Revolutionary Virginia*

1. Isaac, *Transformation of Virginia,* 149.

2. Semple, *Rise and Progress of Baptists,* 403–5.

3. Harper and Jacumin, *Esteemed Reproach,* 19, 25, 35–36.

4. Ibid., 42, 96–97, 107. The King James version of Revelation 6:4 states, "And there went out another horse that was red: and power was given to him that sat thereon to

take peace from the earth, and that they should kill one another: and there was given unto him a great sword."

5. Harper and Jacumin, *Esteemed Reproach,* 108–9, 121, 127–28.
6. Lewis Peyton Little, *Imprisoned Preachers and Religious Liberty in Virginia* (Lynchburg, Va., 1938), 516–20.
7. Semple, *Rise and Progress of Baptists,* 410.
8. Fristoe, *Ketocton Baptist Association,* 64–65.
9. Ibid., 65; Isaac, *Transformation of Virginia,* 174, 238, 286.
10. Rhys Isaac, "Evangelical Revolt," *William and Mary Quarterly,* 3rd ser., 31 (1974): 353; Fristoe, *Ketocton Baptist Association,* 66.
11. Isaac, *Transformation of Virginia,* 162.
12. Little, *Imprisoned Preachers,* 283; Spangler, *Virginians Reborn,* 200.
13. Garrett Ryland, *The Baptists of Virginia, 1699–1926* (Richmond, Va., 1810), 93–95.
14. Ibid., 92, 93.
15. Ibid., 96.
16. Ibid., 98.
17. James Madison, *Memorial and Remonstrance Against Religious Assessments* (1785).
18. Ryland, *Baptists of Virginia,* 124–25.
19. Buckley, *Church and State in Revolutionary Virginia,* 136.
20. *Virginia Statute for Religious Freedom* (1786).
21. Semple, *Rise and Progress of Baptists,* 158.
22. Scarberry, "John Leland and James Madison," 760, 763.
23. Ibid., 788.
24. Ibid., 790.
25. Semple, *Rise and Progress of Baptists,* 303, 304.

ELEVEN· *Declaring Independence and Rebuilding a Nation: Dragging Canoe and the Chickamauga Revolution*

1. *American State Papers, Class II: Indian Affairs,* ed. Walter Lowrie and Matthew St. Clair Clarke, 2 vols. (Washington, D.C., 1832–34), 1:432.
2. Tom Hatley, *The Dividing Paths: Cherokees and South Carolinians Through the Era of Revolution* (New York, 1992), 228, 231.
3. Davies, *Documents of the American Revolution,* 3:72.
4. *The Colonial and State Records of North Carolina,* ed. William L. Saunders and Walter Clark, 30 vols. (Raleigh, N.C., 1886–1914), 10:764.
5. Davies, *Documents of the American Revolution,* 12:189.
6. Ibid., 12:131.
7. Ibid., 12:192; *Colonial and State Records of North Carolina,* 10:764.
8. Davies, *Documents of the American Revolution,* 12:194.
9. Ibid., 12:198–200; *Colonial and State Records of North Carolina,* 10:773–74.
10. Davies, *Documents of the American Revolution,* 12:203–4; *Colonial and State Records of North Carolina,* 10:777–80.
11. Justice, *Our Fire Survives the Storm,* 31–33, 38–40; italics in original.
12. Drayton quoted in Hatley, *Dividing Paths,* 192; *The Papers of Thomas Jefferson,* ed. Julian P. Boyd, 37 vols. to date (Princeton, N.J., 1950–), 1:494.

13. Cumfer, *Separate Peoples,* 103.

14. Lyman Copeland Draper Manuscripts, State Historical Society of Wisconsin (on microfilm), 4QQ, 96–97, 143; Brown, *Old Frontiers,* 161 (Dragging Canoe for King George).

15. Draper Mss., 4QQ, 151–54.

16. *American State Papers, Class II: Indian Affairs,* 1:431.

17. *Colonial and State Records of North Carolina,* 11:428, 14:243–45.

18. *American State Papers, Class II: Indian Affairs,* 1:432.

19. Quoted in James H. O'Donnell III, *Southern Indians in the American Revolution* (Knoxville, Tenn., 1973), 118–19.

20. Cumfer, *Separate Peoples,* 37.

21. "Dragging Canoe in a Publick Talk of July 12, 1779," British Museum, Papers of Governor-General Sir Frederick Haldimand, Add. Mss. 21777: 170–71, and quoted in Evans, "Dragging Canoe," 184.

22. Quoted in Colin G. Calloway, *The American Revolution in Indian Country* (New York, 1995), 209.

23. *Colonial and State Records of North Carolina,* 13:500.

24. Cumfer, *Separate Peoples,* 111.

25. Quoted in Calloway, *American Revolution in Indian Country,* 210.

26. "Journal of the Grand Cherokee National Council, 27 June 1792," *American State Papers, Class II: Indian Affairs,* 1:271.

27. *American State Papers, Class II: Indian Affairs,* 1:255, 262–63.

28. *The Journal of Major John Norton, 1816,* ed. Karl F. Klinck and James J. Talman (Toronto, 1970), 149.

29. Justice, *Our Fire Survives the Storm,* 155.

T W E L V E · *Forgotten Heroes of the Revolution:*
Han Yerry and Tyona Doxtader of the Oneida Indian Nation

1. Testimony of Mrs. Jacob Doxtader, Henry Powless, and Cornelius Doxtader, Lyman Draper Mss., 11 U 191–94, 200 (microfilm edition, 1980, reel 57), State Historical Society of Wisconsin (SHSW); Declarations of Peter Doxtader and Jinney Doxtader, in Maryly B. Penrose, ed., *Indian Affairs Papers: American Revolution* (Franklin Park, N.J., 1981), 350–55. I am indebted to Caroline K. Andler, former tribal genealogist of the Brothertown Indian Nation, for sharing with me her unpublished ms., "Descendants of Cornelius Dockstader"; see pp. 1–6. I am also grateful to historian Joseph T. Glatthaar, who first introduced me to the lives of Han Yerry and Tyona Doxtader. Extant documents vary widely in the spelling of Han's names. For consistency and clarity, I use Han Yerry Doxtader throughout this essay. Spelling in all quotations has been updated to conform to modern usage.

2. Testimony of Theresa Swamp, Mrs. Jacob Doxtader, and Cornelius Wheelock, Draper Mss., 11 U 191, 210–11 (microfilm edition, 1980, reel 57), SHSW.

3. Andler, "Descendants of Cornelius Dockstader," 7.

4. Speech to the Six Nations from the Twelve Colonies, July 13, 1775, in *American Archives,* ed. Peter Force, 9 vols. (Washington, D.C., 1837–1853), 4th ser., 2:1880–83.

5. Declaration of Peter Doxtader, in Penrose, *Indian Affairs Papers,* 350–55. See also

John Hadcock to Lyman Draper, Draper Mss., Feb. 6, 1878, 11 U 242–43 (microfilm edition, 1980, reel 57), SHSW.

6. Message contained in Edward Foy to Alexander Fraser, Apr. 7, 1777, Add. Mss., Ms 21699, reel 15, Frederick Haldimand Papers, Public Archives of Canada.

7. Testimony of Cornelius Wheelock, Draper Mss., 11 U 191, 210 (microfilm edition, 1980, reel 57), SHSW.

8. Daniel Claus to William Knox, Nov. 6, 1777, in *Documents Relative to the Colonial History of the State of New-York,* ed. Edmund B. O'Callaghan et al., 15 vols. (Albany, N.Y., 1853–87), 8:725.

9. Timothy Edwards to Horatio Gates, Sept. 22, 1777, reel 5, Horatio Gates Papers, New-York Historical Society. See also Letter from Albany, Sept. 27, 1777, *New-York Journal,* Oct. 6, 1777.

10. Isaac Pierce to Peter Gansevoort, Sept. 26, 1777, Box 18, Gansevoort-Lansing Coll., New York Public Library (NYPL).

11. George Washington to Commissioners of Indian Affairs, Mar. 13, 1778, in *The Papers of George Washington, Revolutionary War Series,* ed. Philander D. Chase et al., 18 vols. to date (Charlottesville, Va., 1985–2008), 14:76–77.

12. George Washington to Philip Schuyler, May 15, 1778, ibid., 15:128–31. See also Philip Schuyler to James Dean, reel 29, Schuyler Papers, NYPL.

13. Speech from the Continental Congress to the Oneida Indians, Dec. 3, 1777, in *Journals of the Continental Congress, 1774–1789,* ed. Worthington C. Ford et al., 34 vols. (Washington, D.C., 1904–37), 9:996.

14. Philip Schuyler to the Oneidas, May 11, 1778, in Penrose, *Indian Affairs Papers,* 135–37.

15. Speech of George Clinton, Sept. 4, 1784, in *Public Papers of George Clinton,* ed. Hugh Hastings et al., 10 vols. (Albany, N.Y., 1899–1914), 8:348.

16. Speech of Marquis de Lafayette, Oct. 3, 1784, *New Jersey Gazette,* Nov. 28, 1784. See also Account of Lafayette's Meeting with the Six Nations, Oct. 3–4, 1784, and Lafayette to his Wife, Oct. 4, 1784, in *Lafayette in the Age of the American Revolution,* ed. Stanley J. Idzerda, 5 vols. to date (Ithaca, N.Y., 1977–83), 5:255–62.

17. Speech of Good Peter, Apr. 11, 1792, f. 128, 15, reel 60, Timothy Pickering Papers, Massachusetts Historical Society.

T H I R T E E N · *"Satan, Smith, Shattuck, and Shays":*
The People's Leaders in the Massachusetts Regulation of 1786

1. *Bickerstaff's Boston Almanack for 1787,* National Portrait Gallery.

2. *New Jersey Journal,* Jan. 17, 1787, Library of Congress.

3. For the military background of Shays and Shattuck, see Feer, "Shays's Rebellion," 205, 220–21.

4. The characterization of Shattuck comes from the Reverend Grindall Reynolds, "Concord," in Drake, *History of Middlesex County,* 1:392. For a brief summary of Shattuck's postwar political positions, see Feer, "Shays's Rebellion," 205.

5. For the political background of Pelham, see Gregory H. Nobles, "Shays's Neighbors: The Context of Rebellion in Pelham, Massachusetts," in Gross, *In Debt to Shays;* the quotations are from 195–96.

6. Ibid., 193–94, 198; Feer, "Shays's Rebellion," 222–23.

7. Minot, *History of the Insurrections.* For a brief portrait of Minot, see Richards, *Shays's Rebellion,* 159–62.

8. Minot, *History of the Insurrections,* 11, 16, 28.

9. The description of the events in Concord comes from Reynolds, "Concord," in Drake, *History of Middlesex County,* 1:392–93; see also Feer, "Shays's Rebellion," 202–7.

10. Minot, *History of the Insurrections,* 42; Reynolds, "Concord," in Drake, *History of Middlesex County,* 392.

11. Reynolds, "Concord," in Drake, *History of Middlesex County,* 393.

12. Minot, *History of the Insurrections,* 46.

13. Ibid., 47–48; Feer, "Shays's Rebellion," 225.

14. Minot, *History of the Insurrections,* 48–49.

15. Justus Forward Diary, September 28, 1786, quoted in Nobles, "Shays's Neighbors," 201. Forward's use of the term "Laboratory" here refers to the Springfield Arsenal's *elaboratory,* a worksite for manufacturing cartridges and other munitions.

16. *Regulators* is the term now used by most historians. For a sustained discussion of the use of the term *regulation,* see Formisano, "Teaching Shays/The Regulation." Robert Gross also provides a brief background on the term in "A Yankee Rebellion? The Regulators, New England, and the New Nation," *New England Quarterly* 82, no. 1 (March 2009): 120–21. Richards puts the term in a comparative regional context for eighteenth-century America in *Shays's Rebellion,* 63–68.

17. For the various explanations of the patterns of participation in the insurrection, see Szatmary, *Shays' Rebellion,* and Richards, *Shays's Rebellion.* For other works that explore participation at the local level, see Nobles, "Shays's Neighbors," and John L. Brooke, "A Deacon's Orthodoxy: Religion, Class, and the Moral Economy of Shays's Rebellion," both in Gross, *In Debt to Shays,* 185–203, 205–38. See also Brooke, "To the Quiet of the People: Revolutionary Settlements and Civil Unrest in Western Massachusetts, 1774–1789," *William and Mary Quarterly,* 3rd ser., 46, no. 3 (July 1989): 425–62.

18. For the events of 1774 in Massachusetts as a whole, see Raphael, *First American Revolution;* for the particular case of Hampshire County, see Nobles, *Divisions Throughout the Whole,* 166–69.

19. Samuel Ely's activities in western Massachusetts receive extensive treatment in Taylor, *Western Massachusetts,* 111–27. See also Feer, "Shays's Rebellion," 142–64.

20. For Shattuck's arrest, see Feer, "Shays's Rebellion," 319–23; Richards, *Shays's Rebellion,* 19–21.

21. Feer, "Shays's Rebellion," 361.

22. Shepard to Lincoln, January 24, 1787, quoted in Feer, "Shays's Rebellion," 365.

23. This account of Day's unilateral action in Springfield draws upon Szatmary, *Shays' Rebellion,* 101–2, and Richards, *Shays's Rebellion,* 28–29.

24. Feer, "Shays's Rebellion," 367–68; Richards, *Shays's Rebellion,* 28–30; Szatmary, *Shays' Rebellion,* 101–2.

25. For the last days of Shays's activities as leader of the insurrection, see Feer, "Shays's Rebellion," 370–80; Richards, *Shays's Rebellion,* 30–35; Szatmary, *Shays' Rebellion,* 103–6.

26. Taylor, *Western Massachusetts,* 165–67.

27. Only two of the men condemned for being participants did hang; they had been found guilty of theft, not insurrection. I have addressed the question of official mercy elsewhere: see Gregory H. Nobles, "The Politics of Patriarchy in Shays's Rebellion: The Case of Henry McCullough," in *Families and Children, Annual Proceedings of the Dublin Seminar for New England Folklife,* ed. Peter Benes (Boston, 1987), 37–47; and " 'Yet the Old Republicans Still Persevere': Samuel Adams, John Hancock, and the Crisis of Popular Leadership in Revolutionary Massachusetts, 1775–1790," in *The Transforming Hand of Revolution: Reconsidering the American Revolution as a Social Movement,* ed. Ronald Hoffman and Peter J. Albert (Charlottesville, Va., 1995), 258–85.

28. What about Nathan Smith? Most famously Job Shattuck's outspoken counterpart at the Concord court closing in September 1786, he had apparently escaped capture when the government men came after him later that fall; according to local lore, he had a secret closet in his house, and he either disappeared from town or perhaps hid at home for the duration of the insurrection. After it was over, he came back to Shirley to live for a few years, but "his dissipated habits clung to him . . . [and] he died in miserable poverty" sometime in the 1790s. See Reynolds, "Concord," in Drake, *History of Middlesex County,* 392.

FOURTEEN· *William Findley, David Bradford,*
and the Pennsylvania Regulation of 1794

1. *Debates and Proceedings of the General Assembly, on the Memorial Praying a Repeal or Suspension of the Law Annulling the Charter of the Bank,* ed. Mathew Carey (Philadelphia, 1786), 125, 66, 130.

2. Ibid., 65–66, 69.

3. Edmund Randolph, May 29, 1787, in *The Records of the Federal Convention of 1787,* ed. Max Farrand, 3 vols. (New Haven, Conn., 1911), 1:27. Alexander Hamilton, June 18, 1787, ibid., 299; "To the Corresponding Committee of Kentucky for the Meeting of Fayette in Lexington," Apr. 8, 1794, quoted in "The Democratic Societies of 1793 and 1794 in Kentucky, Pennsylvania, and Virginia," *William and Mary Quarterly* 2, no. 4 (October 1922): 248–49.

4. William Findley, *A Review of the Revenue System Adopted by the First Congress Under the Federal Constitution: Wherein the Principles and Tendency of the Funding System and the Second Congress Are Examined. In Thirteen Letters to a Friend. By a Citizen* (Philadelphia, 1794), 113–30.

5. Ibid., 105, 40, 125.

6. Constitution of the Society of United Freemen, Rawle Papers, Historical Society of Pennsylvania, Philadelphia; Brackenridge, *Incidents of the Insurrection,* 1:86; Depostion of William Faulkner, Allegheny County, Sept. 28, 1792, Pennsylvania Whiskey Rebellion Collection, Library of Congress, Washington, D.C. (hereafter WRLC); Deposition of Daniel DePew, Nov. 19, 1794, Rawle Papers; *Pittsburgh Gazette,* Feb. 17, 1787, Oct. 10, 1793.

7. Constitution of the Society of United Freemen; Minutes of the Meeting at Pittsburgh, 1792, *Pennsylvania Archives,* ser. 2, vol. 4, 30–31.

8. Minutes of the Meeting at Pittsburgh, 1792.
9. William Findley to John Hamilton, Nov. 28, 1792, John Hamilton Papers, Westmoreland County Historical Society, Greensburg, Pa.; Findley to Alexander Addison, Nov. 30, 1792, Alexander Addison Papers, Darlington Library, University of Pittsburgh, Pittsburgh.
10. Brackenridge, *Incidents of the Insurrection*, 1:122.
11. Alexander Fulton to George Washington, 1794, WRLC.
12. *Pittsburgh Gazette*, Sept. 24, 1794; Brackenridge, *Incidents of the Insurrection*, 1:99, 3:26; Dorothy Elaine Fennell, "From Rebelliousness to Insurrection: A Social History of the Whiskey Rebellion, 1765–1802" (Ph.D. diss., University of Pittsburgh, 1981), 183–86.
13. Ross, Yeates, and Bradford to the Secretary of State, Aug. 30, 1794, WRLC.
14. Anna Bradford Miles to Boyd Crumrine, Apr. 26, 1883, Boyd Crumrine Papers, Historical Collections, U. Grant Miller Library, Washington and Jefferson College, Washington, Pa.
15. Findley, *History of the Insurrection*, 53–54, 309–10.
16. Minutes of the Meeting at Pittsburgh, Sept. 7, 1791, *Pennsylvania Archives,* ser. 2, vol. 4, 20–22; Minutes of the Meeting at Pittsburgh, 1792.

FIFTEEN· *The New Jerusalem: Herman Husband's Egalitarian Alternative to the United States Constitution*

1. Lycurgus III [pseud. Herman Husband], *XIV Sermons on the Characters of Jacob's Fourteen Sons* (Philadelphia, 1789), 45; A Common Farmer in the Western Country [pseud. Herman Husband], [*Manuscript Sermons*] (unpublished untitled manuscript, 1793?), Scull Collection, Historical Society of Western Pennsylvania, 8.
2. Ibid., 21, 34.
3. Ibid., 47–48.
4. Husband, *XIV Sermons,* 12.
5. Husband, *Manuscript Sermons,* 103.
6. Ibid., 24, 33.
7. Jones, "Herman Husband," 19; Herman Husband, Letter to John Earl Granville Viscount Carteret, "8 mo. 9th" 1756, in A. Roger Ekirch, " 'A New Government of Liberty': Hermon Husband's Vision of Backcountry North Carolina, 1755," *William and Mary Quarterly,* 3d ser., 34 (October 1977): 646, 643.
8. Herman Husband, *A Continuation of the Impartial Relation* . . . (n.p., 1770), ed. Archibald Henderson, in *North Carolina Historical Review* 18 (1941): 64, 68n; Herman Husband, *An Impartial Relation of the First Rise and Cause* . . . (n.p., 1770), in *Some Eighteenth-Century Tracts Concerning North Carolina,* ed. William K. Boyd (Raleigh, N.C., 1927), 329, 317, 268.
9. Kars, *Breaking Loose Together,* 121.
10. Husband, *Impartial Relation,* 285.
11. Kars, *Breaking Loose Together,* 173.
12. Husband, *Impartial Relation,* 309; Regulators' Advertisement No. 5, Mar. 22, 1768, quoted ibid., 265; Husband, *Continuation,* 64.

13. William Tryon, Proclamation of June 21, 1768, quoted in Husband, *Impartial Relation,* 271; Husband, *Impartial Relation,* 280.

14. [Herman Husband], *Proposals to Amend and Perfect the Policy of the Government of the United States of America* (n.p., 1782), 8–9; Husband, *Manuscript Sermons,* 24; Report of Husband's Revolutionary War speech to former Regulators imprisoned for Toryism at Staunton, Va., in *The Regulators in North Carolina: A Documentary History, 1759–1776,* ed. William S. Powell et al. (Raleigh, N.C., 1971), 566; [Herman Husband,] *A Proposal, or a General Plan and Mode of Taxation* . . . (n.p., 1778), inserted within Husband, *Proposals to Amend and Perfect,* 32–33.

15. Herman Husband, Address to the Quakers, in Assembly (draft, 1780), Historical Society of Pennsylvania, 5 (see Jones, "Herman Husband," 257n13).

16. Husband, Address to the Quakers, 4; Husband, *Proposals to Amend and Perfect,* 7, 3.

17. Jones, "Herman Husband," 262. The vision is most fully described in Husband, *Proposals to Amend and Perfect,* 35–36; Husband, *Manuscript Sermons,* 150–52.

18. Ibid., 4, 150; Husband, *Proposals to Amend and Perfect,* 11, 36.

19. Lycurgus III [pseud. Herman Husband], *A Sermon to the Bucks and Hinds of America* (Philadelphia, 1788), 9.

20. Hugh H. Brackenridge, *Incidents of the Insurrection in the Western Parts of Pennsylvania* (Philadelphia, 1795), 1:95; Johann David Schoepf, *Travels in the Confederation,* trans. Alfred J. Morrison (Philadelphia, 1911), 1:297; Albert Gallatin to Hannah Gallatin, May 15, 1795, Albert Gallatin Papers, New-York Historical Society; Testimony of Robert Smiley [*sic*], June 3, 1795, (trial of Husbands [*sic*] and Filson [*sic*]), (Justice William Paterson's bench notes of testimony given at the sedition trial of Herman Husband and Robert Philson), William Paterson Papers, Askew Library, William Paterson University.

21. Testimony of James Wilson, June 4, 1795 (Paterson's notes), Paterson Papers.

22. Husband, *Manuscript Sermons,* 47.

23. Husband, *XIV Sermons,* viii.

24. Bloch, *Visionary Republic,* 183, 184; [Herman Husband,] *A Dialogue Between an Assembly-Man and a Convention-Man* (Philadelphia, 1790), 5, 6.

25. Ibid., 9, 10.

26. Husband, *Manuscript Sermons,* 19–20.

27. Husband, *Proposals to Amend and Perfect,* 10; Husband, *Manuscript Sermons,* 118; Husband, *XIV Sermons,* vii.

28. Husband, *Proposals to Amend and Perfect,* 9; Husband, *Sermon to Bucks and Hinds,* 19, 20; Husband, *Manuscript Sermons,* 72.

29. Husband, *Sermon to Bucks and Hinds,* 23, 25.

30. Husband, *XIV Sermons,* viii, 19, 20, 27; Husband, *Sermon to Bucks and Hinds,* 24.

31. Husband, *Proposals to Amend and Perfect,* 12.

32. Husband, *A Dialogue,* 11.

33. Husband, *XIV Sermons,* viii, 45–46.

34. Husband, *Sermon to Bucks and Hinds,* 16; Husband, *Proposals to Amend and Perfect,* 21, 16, 17.

35. Ibid., 20.

36. [Herman Husband,] *The Common Farmer (Number 2),* in James P. Whittenburg,

" 'The Common Farmer (Number 2)': Herman Husband's Plan for Peace Between the United States and the Indians, 1792," *William and Mary Quarterly*, 3rd ser., 34 (Oct. 1977): 650.

37. Husband to Granville, 641, 643.

38. Husband, *Manuscript Sermons*, 122.

39. Hill, *World Turned Upside Down*, 115; Winstanley quoted ibid., 135.

40. Husband, *XIV Sermons*, Sermon 10 [separately paginated], 17; Husband, *Dialogue*, 12.

41. Husband, *Sermon to Bucks and Hinds*, 28; Husband, *XIV Sermons*, 33, 25.

42. Husband, *XIV Sermons*, 34; Husband, *Dialogue*, 11, 4; Husband, *Sermon to Bucks and Hinds*, 2.

43. Fennell, "From Rebelliousness to Insurrection," 194, 202.

44. Brackenridge, *Incidents*, 1:95; Testimony of Albert Gallatin, June 3, 1795 (Paterson's notes), Paterson Papers.

45. Bloch, *Visionary Republic*, 184; Fennell, "From Rebelliousness to Insurrection," 192–226; Hogeland, *Whiskey Rebellion*, 93–95, 117, 172, 179, 182–83, 203; Jones, "Herman Husband," 350–59. See also Bouton, *Taming Democracy*, 9, 219, 242.

46. Bloch, *Visionary Republic*, 184.

47. *The Diaries of George Washington*, ed. Donald Jackson et al., 6 vols. (Charlottesville, Va., 1976–79), 6:185; George Washington to Alexander Hamilton, Oct. 26, Oct. 31, 1794, in *The Papers of Alexander Hamilton*, ed. Harold C. Syrett et al., 27 vols. (New York, 1961–87), 17:344, 350; Herman Husband to Emy Husband, Oct. 22, 1794, quoted in E. Howard Blackburn and William H. Welfley, *The History of Bedford and Somerset Counties, Pennsylvania*, 3 vols. (New York, 1906), 2:153.

SIXTEEN· *The Battle Against Patriarchy That Abigail Adams Won*

1. "Abigail Adams's Disposition of Her Property," Jan. 18, 1816, *Microfilms of the Adams Papers*, reel 607 (microfilms from this collection hereafter designated in the form AP#607).

2. Adams employed a half-dozen imperative verbs in her 1776 statement—and none in the slightly longer passage she wrote in 1782. AA to JA, Mar. 31–Apr. 5, 1776, June 17, 1782, *Adams Family Correspondence* [hereafter *AFC*], ed. Lyman H. Butterfield et al., 10 vols. to date (Cambridge, Mass., 1963–), 1:370, 4:328.

3. AA to JA, ca. July 15, 1778, *AFC*, 3:61.

4. JA to AA, Nov. 6, 1778, AA to JA, Dec. 13, [1778,] Mar. 20–Apr. 23, [1779,] *AFC*, 3:115, 136, 192.

5. JA to AA, Feb. 16, June 17, 1780, *AFC*, 3:275, 366; [Benjamin Waterhouse,] *A Journal, of a Young Man of Massachusetts, Late a Surgeon on Board an American Privateer, Who Was Captured at Sea by the British . . .* (Boston, 1816), 10; Gardoqui & Sons, "Invoice of Sundries shipp'd Per the Phenix James Babson master for Newburyport on Acct. of the Honble. John Adams Esq. . . . 31st Jany. 1780," *AFC*, 3:facing p. 117.

6. JA to AA, [ante March 15, 1780,] *AFC*, 3:301.

7. AA to JA, [ca. July 15, 1778,] *AFC*, 3:62.

8. AA to JA, July 24, 1780, *AFC,* 3:381.

9. JA to AA, March 15, 1780, AA to JA, Sept. 3, 1780, Mercy Otis Warren to AA, Dec. 21, 1780, *AFC,* 3:302, 406, 4:42.

10. AA to JA, April 25, 1782, *AFC,* 4:315.

11. JA to AA, July 1, 1782, *AFC,* 4:337.

12. AA to JA, July 17–18, 1782, *AFC,* 4:345.

13. AA to JA, July 17–18, 1782, JA to AA, Oct. 12, 1782, *AFC,* 4:345, 5:15.

14. AA to JA, Dec. 27, 1783, *AFC,* 5:286.

15. Ibid.

16. AA to JA, Jan. 3, 1784, *AFC,* 5:292.

17. AA to JA, Nov. 11, 1783, *AFC,* 5:269.

18. AA to CT, Sept. 8, 1784, JA to CT, Apr. 24, 1785, *AFC,* 5:458, 6:88–90.

19. AA to CT, [April 26]–May 10, 1785, *AFC,* 6:108.

20. AA to CT, [April 26]–May 10, 1785, CT to AA, Jan. 5, 1786, *AFC,* 6:108, 7:5–6.

21. AA to Mary Smith Cranch, July 12, 1789, *AFC,* 8:389.

22. Ibid.

23. AA to CT, Aug. 2, Oct. 3, 1790 (excerpt), CT to JA, Jan. 7, 1791, *AFC,* 9:84, 84n, 176; CT ("Trustee to Mrs. Abigl. Adams"), receipt for U.S. Treasury bonds, Aug. 21, 1792, in Jeremiah Colburn autograph collection, 7:243, property of the Bostonian Society, on deposit with the Massachusetts Historical Society; CT ("for John Adams Esq"), receipt for U.S. Treasury bonds, Dec. 23, 1790, ibid., 7:241.

24. AA to John Quincy Adams, Dec. 24, 1815, AP#428.

25. AA to Thomas Boylston Adams, Feb. 28, 1802, AP#401.

26. AA to John Quincy Adams, Dec. 24, 1815, AP#428.

27. "Abigail Adams's Disposition of Her Property," AP#607; AA and JA, deed to John Quincy Adams, Aug. 18, 1803, Quincy, Wendell, Holmes, and Upham Family Papers, Massachusetts Historical Society, reel 35.

28. "Abigail Adams's Disposition of Her Property," Jan. 18, 1816, AP#607.

29. Ibid.

30. Louisa Catherine Adams to Thomas Boylston Adams, Jan. 7, March 14, 1819, AP#446.

SEVENTEEN· *America's Mary Wollstonecraft: Judith Sargent Murray's Case for the Equal Rights of Women*

1. Judith Sargent Murray, *The Gleaner* (rpt., Schenectady, N.Y., 1992), 702, 703.

2. Ibid., 727.

3. Ibid., 705.

4. Judith Stevens to Winthrop Sargent, July 2, 1778, Murray Letter Book 1:122; Murray to Mr. Redding of Falmouth, England, May 7, 1801, Murray Letter Book 11:287, Mississippi Archives, Jackson.

5. Ibid., 705, 709, 710.

6. Murray to Mr. Redding of Falmouth, England, May 7, 1801, Murray Letter Book 11:288.

7. Murray to Esther Ellery, Apr. 22, 1797, Murray Letter Book 10:102; Murray to Mrs. Barrell of York, Nov. 25, 1800, Murray Letter Book 11:227–29.

8. Judith Stevens to Mary (Maria) Sargent, Mar. 16, 1783, Murray Letter Book 2:100, 103.

9. Murray, *Gleaner,* 729.

10. Judith Stevens to Winthrop Sargent, Nov. 28, 1784, Murray Letter Book 2:296.

11. Murray, *Gleaner,* 728; Constantia, "Desultory Thoughts," *Gentleman's and Lady's Town and Country Magazine* (June 1784), n.p.

12. Judith Stevens to Mrs. Barrell of Old York, Jan. 31, 1784, Murray Letter Book 2:193.

13. Murray, *Gleaner,* 150.

14. Ibid., 38.

15. Judith Stevens to Mr. Sewell, July 15, 1781, Murray Letter Book 1:339, 340.

16. John Murray to Winthrop Sargent, Dec. 7, 1798, Winthrop Sargent Papers, Reel 4, Massachusetts Historical Society, Boston.

17. Murray to C. D. Ebeling, July 22, 1799, Murray Letter Book 11:38, 39.

18. Murray, *Gleaner,* 726.

19. See Zagarri, *Revolutionary Backlash.*

20. *A Wollstonecraft Anthology,* ed. Janet M. Todd (Bloomington, Ind., 1977), 1; Emily W. Sunstein, *A Different Face: The Life of Mary Wollstonecraft* (New York, 1975), 351.

21. Murray to Mrs. Barrell of York, Nov. 25, 1800, Murray Letter Book 11:229, 232.

22. Murray to Mrs. K, Apr. 21, 1802, Murray Letter Book 11:343, 353.

23. Judith Stevens to Fitz William Sargent, May 25, 1782, Murray Letter Book 2:9; Murray to Miss Mary Parker of Portsmouth, Sept. 8, 1784, Murray Letter Book 2:276.

24. Murray, *Gleaner,* 36.

E I G H T E E N · *Prince Hall, Richard Allen, and Daniel Coker: Revolutionary Black Founders, Revolutionary Black Communities*

1. *Philadelphia Gazette,* Dec. 31, 1799.

2. "To the Honorable Counsel & House of Representatives for the State of Massachusetts . . . ," petition submitted by Prince Hall and eight African Americans on Jan. 13, 1777, online at http://www.pbs.org/wgbh/aia/part2/2h32.html.

3. Ibid.

4. "To the Honorable Counsel & House of Representatives for the State of Massachusetts . . . ," Jan. 4, 1787, Massachusetts State Archives.

5. Prince Hall, *A Charge to the Brethren of the African Lodge* (Boston, 1792); Hall, *A Charge Delivered to the African Lodge* (Boston, 1797), in *"Face Zion Forward": First Writers of the Black Atlantic, 1785–1798,* ed. Joanna Brooks and John Saillant (Boston, 2002), 197, 203–4.

6. *Life, Experience and Gospel Labors of the Right Reverend Richard Allen* (Philadelphia, 1833), 7–8.

7. Ibid., 6–7.

8. See this reminiscence of Allen's departure in the *Colored American* (New York City), October 14, 1837.

9. Walker's *Appeal* is partially reprinted in *Pamphlets of Protest: An Anthology of African American Protest Writing, 1790–1860,* ed. Richard Newman, Philip Lapsansky, and Patrick Rael (New York, 2001), quotation on 97–99.

10. *The Christian Recorder,* Feb. 8, 1865.

11. *Freedom's Journal,* Nov. 2, 1827.

12. Garnet's recollections are reprinted in *The Christian Recorder,* Feb. 20, 1869.

13. Allen, "Address to Those Who Keep Slaves and Approve the Practice," reprinted in Newman et al., *Pamphlets of Protest,* 42.

14. See Emma Lapsansky, " 'Since They Got Those Separate Churches,' " *American Quarterly* 32, no. 1 (Spring 1980): 54–78. On class divisions in northern free black communities, see also Leslie Harris, *In the Shadow of Slavery: African Americans in New York City, 1626–1863* (Chicago, 2003). The key primary source remains the Pennsylvania Abolition Society's economic and social "Report on the Condition of the People of Color" (Philadelphia, 1838).

15. See Douglass, "Richard Allen's Place in History," unpublished speech at the Chicago World's Fair Congress of Religions, Sept. 22, 24, 26, 1893, Frederick Douglass Papers, Library of Congress, Box 31, Reel 19, 1, 3.

16. Coker quoted in Christopher Phillips, *Freedom's Port: The African American Community of Baltimore, 1790–1860* (Urbana, Ill., 1997), 132.

17. "A Dialogue Between a Virginian and an African Minister" (Baltimore, 1810), reprinted in Newman et al., *Pamphlets of Protest,* 52–65.

18. Ibid.

19. Phillips, *Freedom's Port,* 138.

NINETEEN· *Richard and Judith Randolph, St. George Tucker, George Wythe, Syphax Brown, and Hercules White: Racial Equality and the Snares of Prejudice*

The author gratefully acknowledges the assistance of Edward Maris-Wolf, Susan A. Riggs, Margaret Cook, and Jennifer R. Loux.

1. The text of Randolph's will is found in Ely, *Israel on the Appomattox,* 447–50.

2. Ibid., 17.

3. Ibid., 18.

4. Ibid., 18.

5. Ibid., 17.

6. Ibid., 21–22.

7. Tucker, *Dissertation on Slavery,* 10; Tucker, *Blackstone's Commentaries,* vol. 1, pt. 2, appendix, note H, 76; Tucker, *Dissertation on Slavery,* 51.

8. Ely, *Israel on the Appomattox,* 23.

9. *Hudgins v. Wrights,* in *Judicial Cases Concerning American Slavery and the Negro,* ed. Helen T. Catterall, 5 vols. (1926; rpt. New York, 1968), 1:112–13; Holt, "George Wythe," 1031–33.

10. Ely, *Israel on the Appomattox,* 24; Thomas Jefferson to Richard Price, Aug. 7, 1785, in *The Papers of Thomas Jefferson,* ed. Julian P. Boyd, 36 vols. (Princeton, N.J., 1950–2009), 8:357.

11. Tucker, *Blackstone's Commentaries,* vol. 1, pt. 2, appendix, note H, 74 and 78–79.

12. Holt, "George Wythe," 1026.

13. Wythe to Jefferson, Dec. 31, 1781, in *Wythe, George, Letters to Thomas Jefferson, 1775–1806, The Papers of Thomas Jefferson,* Library of Congress (Washington, D.C., 1920), microfilm, Library of Virginia.

14. Tucker, *Blackstone's Commentaries,* vol. 1, pt. 2, appendix, note H, 75.

15. Ely, *Israel on the Appomattox,* 39.

16. Ibid., 45.

17. Ibid.

18. Ibid., 5.

19. Supplement to Note H, in a printed copy of Tucker, *Blackstone's Commentaries* (1803), vol. 1, pt. 2, appendix, note H, which is interleaved with Tucker's handwritten additions and revisions c. 1821, Special Collections, Swem Library, College of William and Mary.

TWENTY · *"Every Man Should Have Property": Robert Coram and the American Revolution's Legacy of Economic Populism*

1. Robert Coram to George Washington, Mar. 5, 1791, in *The Papers of George Washington, Presidential Series,* ed. Jack D. Warren, 13 vols. (Charlottesville, Va., 1998), 7:512–23.

2. Coram, *Political Inquiries,* 106.

3. Ibid., 22.

4. Ibid., viii.

5. Ibid., 74.

6. Coram reprinted this commendation from Captain Jones in the *Delaware Gazette* of Nov. 17, 1795, in order to defend himself against Federalist accusations that he was unpatriotic.

7. Coram, *Political Inquiries,* 25.

8. Ibid., 54.

9. Ibid., 10.

10. Ibid., 12, 17.

11. Ibid., 21.

12. Ibid., 30, 21–22.

13. Ibid., 47, 60–61.

14. Ibid., 51, 29.

15. Ibid., 44, 50–15.

16. Ibid., 56, 106.

17. Ibid., 25, 85, 30.

18. Ibid., 49.

19. *Delaware Gazette,* 6, 9, Oct. 16, 1795.

20. *New-York Journal,* Mar. 11, 1796.

21. Jeanette Eckman Papers, Box 16, Delaware Historical Society.

TWENTY-ONE · *Thomas Greenleaf: Printers and the Struggle for Democratic Politics and Freedom of the Press*

1. *The New-York Journal, and Weekly Register,* May 29, 1788; *The Documentary History of the Ratification of the Constitution,* ed. Merrill Jensen, John P. Kaminski, Gaspare J. Saladino, et al., 23 vols. to date (Madison, Wisc., 1976–), 18:375.

2. *New-York Journal,* July 31, Aug. 7, 1788.; Paul A. Gilje, *The Road to Mobocracy: Popular Disorder in New York City, 1763–1834* (Chapel Hill, N.C., 1987), 97–99.

3. *New-York Journal,* Aug. 7, 1788.

4. John Adams diary, Sept. 3, 1769, *Adams Family Papers: An Electronic Archive,* Massachusetts Historical Society, http://www.masshist.org/digitaladams/; Isaiah Thomas, *The History of Printing in America,* ed. Marcus A. McCorison (New York, 1970), 258–59n.

5. Benjamin Hobart, *History of the Town of Abington, Plymouth County, Massachusetts from Its First Settlement* (Boston, 1866), 269–73.

6. James Edward Greenleaf, *Genealogy of the Greenleaf Family* (Boston, 1896), 152; Stephen Botein, " 'Meer Mechanics' and an Open Press: The Business and Political Strategies of Colonial American Printers," *Perspectives in American History* 9 (1975): 127–225, quotation on 158.

7. Bernard Bailyn, *The Ordeal of Thomas Hutchinson* (Cambridge, Mass., 1974), 197–99. The quote is from "Centinel, No. XXVIII," (Boston) *Massachusetts Spy,* Jan. 2, 1772.

8. Lyon N. Richardson, *A History of Early American Magazines, 1741–1789* (1931; rpt., New York, 1966), 166–68.

9. *Papers of Robert Treat Paine,* 3:98–99, 137–38, 278.

10. *The New-York Journal, and the Weekly Register,* Sept. 1, 1785; Leona M. Hudak, *Early American Women Printers and Publishers, 1639–1820* (Metuchen, N.J., 1978), 513–14.

11. "Advantages of Newspapers," *The Green Mountain Patriot* (Peacham, Vt.), Oct. 26, 1796; Samuel Miller, *A Brief Retrospect of the Eighteenth Century,* 2 vols. (New York, 1803), 2:251–52.

12. *Greenleaf's New York Journal & Patriotic Register* (shortened hereafter), Jan. 1, 1794ff. This was the semi-weekly edition that Greenleaf published for the rest of his life. All further quotations are from this edition unless otherwise noted.

13. *Commercial Advertiser* (New York), July 12, 13, 14, Aug. 11, 1798.

14. *The Democratic-Republican Societies, 1790–1800: A Documentary Sourcebook of Constitutions, Declarations, Addresses, Resolutions, and Toasts,* ed. Philip S. Foner (Westport, Conn., 1976), 24, 154–55.

15. Ibid., 64, 151.

16. Ibid., 54, 151, 154.

17. *American Minerva* (New York), Dec. 10, 1793; *Daily Advertiser* (New York), Dec. 11, 12, 1793.

18. *Diary, or Loudon's Register* (New York), Dec. 21, 1793.

19. Foner, *Democratic-Republican Societies,* 151–54; *Greenleaf's New York Journal,* Jan. 1, 1794.

20. *Argus & Greenleaf's New Daily Advertiser* (New York), June 2, 1795.

21. *Greenleaf's New York Journal,* Dec. 27, Apr. 22, 1796.

22. Library of Congress, "Primary Documents in American History: Alien and Sedition Acts," http://www.loc.gov/rr/program/bib/ourdocs/Alien.html.

23. Smith, *Freedom's Fetters,* 398–99; Alexander Addison, *Reports of Cases in the County Courts of the Fifth Circuit, and in the High Court of Errors and Appeals, of the State of Pennsylvania, and Charges to the Grand Juries of Those County Courts*

(Washington, Pa., 1800), 202; *Albany Centinel,* Aug. 10, 1798; *Commercial Advertiser* (New York), July 12, 13, Aug. 11, 1798.

24. *Greenleaf's New York Journal,* July 14, 18, 1798.

25. *Annals of Congress,* House of Reps., 5th Cong., 2d sess., 2097; Joseph I. Shulim, *John Daly Burk: Irish Revolutionist and American Patriot* (Philadelphia, 1964), 30.

26. "Communication," *Greenleaf's New York Journal,* July 18, 1798.

27. *Greenleaf's New York Journal,* Sept. 15, 1798; Frederic Hudson, *Journalism in the United States, from 1690 to 1872* (1873; rpt., New York, 1968), 145; Joseph T. Buckingham, *Specimens of Newspaper Literature: With Personal Memoirs, Anecdotes, and Reminiscences,* 2 vols. (Boston, 1850), 1:248–87, quotation on 281.

28. *Greenleaf's New York Journal,* Sept. 15, Nov. 7, 1798; Hudak, *Early American Women Printers and Publishers,* 576–89.

29. Quotation from Smith, *Freedom's Letters,* 400 n. 50.

30. Alexander Hamilton to Josiah O. Hoffman, Nov. 6, 1799, in *The Papers of Alexander Hamilton,* ed. Harold C. Syrett et al., 27 vols. (New York, 1961–87), 24:5–6.

31. Tunis Wortman, *A Treatise Concerning Political Enquiry and the Liberty of the Press* (New York, 1800), 163, 168–69.

TWENTY-TWO · *The Plough-Jogger: Jedediah Peck and the Democratic Revolution*

1. James Morton Smith, "The Sedition Law of 1798 and the Right of Petition: The Attempted Prosecution of Jedediah Peck," *New York History* 35 (Jan. 1954): 65; *Albany Register,* Oct. 1, 1799; "Albany," *New London Bee,* Oct. 16, 1799; Hammond, *History of Political Parties,* 1:132 ("hundred missionaries"); Richard Harison to Timothy Pickering, Apr. 10, 1800, Pickering Papers, 26:77, Massachusetts Historical Society.

2. Jedediah Peck, "Account of the Peck Family," Misc. Mss. P, New York State Historical Association (hereafter NYSHA); Peck, "Journal of a Voyage," Aug. 15, Sept. 25, Oct. 8, 1771, NYSHA; Peck, "The Copy of a Letter from a Son of Liberty," *Otsego Herald,* Apr. 21, 1796.

3. Hammond, *History of Political Parties,* 1:123–24 ("Judge Peck"); Levi Beardsley, *Reminiscences; Personal and Other Incidents; Early Settlement of Otsego County* (New York, 1852), 71–72.

4. Jedediah Peck, "Monarchical and Representative Government Contrasted," *Otsego Herald,* Apr. 21, 1796 ("Monarchical Government"); [Peck,] "J. P. Americus," *Albany Gazette,* Jan. 17, 1793 ("May the fire"); Peck, *The Political Wars of Otsego: or Downfall of Jacobinism and Despotism* (Cooperstown, N.Y., 1796), 9.

5. Peck quoted in Young, *Democratic Republicans,* 264; Council of Appointment, Record Book 2 (1786–1792), NYSA.

6. Taylor, *William Cooper's Town,* 256–57.

7. Peter Van Schaack to Abraham Van Vechten, Aug. 5, 1797, C. E. French Collection, Massachusetts Historical Society; Taylor, *William Cooper's Town,* 257.

8. Beardsley, *Reminiscences,* 72 ("saddle bags"); [Jedediah Peck,] "Plough-Jogger," and "Copy of a Letter from a Son of Liberty," *Otsego Herald,* Apr. 14 and 21, 1796.

9. [Jedediah Peck,] "Advice to Farmers, Mechanics, & Traders," and "A Plough Jog-

ger," *Otsego Herald,* Apr. 14, 1796 ("good family"); [Peck,] "Copy of a Letter from a Son of Liberty," *Otsego Herald,* Apr. 21, 1796 ("Let us").

10. [Jedediah Peck,] "Philo-Virtutus," *Otsego Herald,* Apr. 21, 1796 ("Representative government"); [Peck,] "Observer," *Albany Gazette,* Apr. 25, 1796 ("Fellow-citizens").

11. Abraham C. Ten Broeck, "To J. Peck, Esq," *Otsego Herald,* Apr. 21, 1796; David Goff, "To the Pretended Friends to Cooperstown and the County," *Otsego Herald,* June 23, 1796.

12. Jedediah Peck to Jacob Morris, Apr. 29, 1796, and Morris to Elihu Phinney, May 6, 1796 ("ambitious"), *Otsego Herald,* May 12, 1796; Peck to Morris, *Otsego Herald,* May 26, 1796 ("Where did").

13. Peck, "Proposals for Printing by Subscription," *Otsego Herald,* May 26, 1796; Peck, *Political Wars of Otsego;* "Communication," *Otsego Herald,* Oct. 6, 1796 ("great Political Plough"); Jedediah Peck, "Re-Communication from the Plough-Jogger's Journal," *Otsego Herald,* Oct. 13, 1796 ("It is true").

14. Burlington nomination meeting, Apr. 3, 1798, *Otsego Herald,* Apr. 12, 1798; Otsego County voting returns, *Otsego Herald,* May 31, 1798; Taylor, *William Cooper's Town,* 263 and 496n14.

15. John C. Miller, *Crisis in Freedom: The Alien and Sedition Acts* (Boston, 1951).

16. "Marcellus," *Albany Centinel,* Apr. 1, 1800; Howe, "Republican Thought," 147–65.

17. "A Republican," "Albany," and "Address to the Electors of New York," *Albany Register,* Mar. 25, 1799, Mar. 12, 1800, and Mar. 13, 1801.

18. "Marcus Brutus," *Albany Gazette,* May 14, 1798; "To the Electors of the State of New York," *Albany Centinel,* Apr. 12, 1799 ("every man").

19. Benjamin Gilbert, Joshua Dewey, and Francis Henry to Jedediah Peck, Sept. 10, 1798, and "Otsegonius," *Otsego Herald,* Sept. 20, 1798, and Jan. 3, 1799 ("No minds").

20. Jedediah Peck to Benjamin Gilbert, Joshua Dewey, and Francis Henry, *Otsego Herald,* Oct. 11, 1798; Peck to Dewey, and Peck to Henry, *Albany Register,* Feb. 1, and Feb. 18, 1799 ("causes").

21. "An Elector," and "Legislature of New York," *Albany Register,* Feb. 11 and 15, 1799; "Assembly Debate," *Otsego Herald,* Feb. 28, 1799; Hammond, *History of Political Parties,* 1:123–24.

22. Daniel Hale to William Cooper, Jan. 9, 1799, William Cooper Papers, Hartwick College Archives; Council of Appointment Records, vol. 4, 135, and 150, NYSA; *Otsego Herald,* Mar. 7, 1799; *Albany Register,* Mar. 15, 1799 ("Plough-Joggers"); Hammond, *History of Political Parties,* 1:130–31. For the voting returns, see *Albany Centinel,* June 14, 1799.

23. William Cooper, "Caution!" *Albany Centinel,* Apr. 23, 1799; William Cooper to Oliver Wolcott, Aug. 20, 1799 ("in the act"), and Sept. 16, 1799, Wolcott Papers, 15:43 and 59, Connecticut Historical Society; Hammond, *History of Political Parties,* 1:131–32; *William Cooper v. Jedediah Peck,* Otsego County Court of Common Pleas Records, vol. 1, June 27 and Oct. 17, 1799, Otsego County Clerk's Office.

24. William Cooper to John Jay, Oct. 25, 1799, document #1550, New York State Library.

25. "Albany," *Albany Centinel,* May 27, 1800; Stephen Van Rensselaer to William

Cooper, Apr. 28, 1800, William Cooper Papers, Hartwick College Archives. For the voting returns, see *Otsego Herald,* May 15, 1800.

26. Hammond, *History of Political Parties,* 1:137–39, 144–45; Taylor, *William Cooper's Town,* 257.

27. Hammond, *History of Political Parties,* 1:154–55; Taylor, *William Cooper's Town,* 280–83 and 501n65; *Otsego Herald,* May 14, 1801.

28. Hammond, *History of Political Parties,* 1:167–80; Council of Appointment Records, 4:255 and 273, and 6:1, 76, and 106, NYSA; Otsego County, Tax Assessment Rolls, 1800, Series B-0950–85, Box 37, NYSA; Taylor, *William Cooper's Town,* 283–84, 501n67, 501n68.

29. See the Burlington tax return for Peck's property and see Burlington, Butternuts, Milford, Otego, Otsego, and Pittsfield returns for Cooper's properties in Otsego County, Tax Assessment Rolls, 1800, Series B-0950–85, Box 37, NYSA.

30. *Otsego Herald,* May 10, 1804; Hammond, *History of the Political Parties,* 1:218; Beardsley, *Reminiscences,* 71 ("For many years").

31. Throop Wilder, "Jedediah Peck: Statesman, Soldier, Preacher," *New York History* 22 (July 1941): 290–300; "Assembly Proceedings," *Otsego Herald,* Mar. 24, 1803; Jedediah Peck, affidavit, Mar. 27, 1805, *Albany Register,* Mar. 16, 1807.

32. [Jedediah Peck,] "Thoughts on Public Schools," *Albany Register,* Feb. 18, 1799 ("bring improvement" and "In all countries"); Wilder, "Jedediah Peck," 298–99; Sherman Williams, "Jedediah Peck, the Father of the Public School System of the State of New York," New York State Historical Association, *Quarterly Journal* 1 (July 1920): 219–40; Hammond, *History of the Political Parties,* 1:158–59.

33. Horatio Gates Spafford, *A Gazetteer of the State of New-York* (Albany, N.Y., 1824), 69 ("Judge Peck"); Gorham A. Worth, *Random Recollections of Albany from 1800 to 1808* (Albany, N.Y., 1866), 3 ("So great").

34. Richard E. Ellis, *The Jeffersonian Crisis: Courts and Politics in the Young Republic* (New York, 1971); Taylor, *William Cooper's Town,* 257–58.

Contributors

TERRY BOUTON is an associate professor of history at University of Maryland, Baltimore County, and the author of *Taming Democracy: "The People," the Founders, and the Troubled Ending of the American Revolution.*

T. H. BREEN is director of the Nicholas D. Chabraja Center for Historical Studies and the William Smith Mason Professor of American History at Northwestern University. His most recent book is *American Insurgents, American Patriots: The Revolution of the People.*

JON BUTLER, the Howard R. Lamar Professor of American Studies, History, and Religious Studies at Yale University, writes on colonial America and the history of American religion. Among his books are *Awash in a Sea of Faith: Christianizing the American People* and *Becoming America: The Revolution Before 1776.*

COLIN G. CALLOWAY is the John Kimball Jr. 1943 Professor of History and Professor of Native American Studies at Dartmouth College. His many books include *One Vast Winter Count: The Native American West Before Lewis and Clark,* which won six "best book" awards, and *The American Revolution in Indian Country.*

SETH COTLAR is an associate professor of history at Willamette University. He is the author of *Tom Paine's America: The Rise and Fall of Trans-Atlantic Radicalism in the Early Republic.*

MELVIN PATRICK ELY is the author of *Israel on the Appomattox: A Southern Experiment in Black Freedom from the 1790s Through the Civil War,* which won the Bancroft, Beveridge, and Wesley-Logan prizes, and of *The Adventures of Amos 'n' Andy: A Social History of an American Phenomenon.* He teaches at the College of William and Mary.

ERIC FONER, the DeWitt Clinton Professor of History at Columbia University, is the author of many books on American history, including *Tom Paine and Revolutionary America* and, most recently, *The Fiery Trial: Abraham Lincoln and Slavery.*

WYTHE HOLT is University Research Professor of Law Emeritus at the University of Alabama School of Law. His essays have appeared in leading American and Canadian law journals. He has recently completed a book on the federal criminal trials arising from the Whiskey Rebellion.

WOODY HOLTON is the author of *Abigail Adams,* which was awarded the Bancroft Prize; *Unruly Americans and the Origins of the Constitution,* a finalist for the National Book Award; and *Forced Founders: Indians, Debtors, Slaves, and the Making of the American Revolution in Virginia,* winner of the Merle Curti Award. He teaches at the University of Richmond.

JILL LEPORE is the David Woods Kemper '41 Professor of American History at Harvard, where she is chair of the History and Literature Program. She is also a staff writer at *The New Yorker.* Her most recent book is *The Whites of Their Eyes: The Tea Party's Revolution and the Battle over American History.*

JAMES KIRBY MARTIN is the Hugh Roy and Lillie Cranz Cullen University Professor of History at the University of Houston. He is the author or editor of twelve books, many dealing with Revolutionary America. His current writing interests include the Six Nations as they dealt with the War for American Independence.

PHILIP MEAD is the author of " 'Melancholy Landscapes': Soldier Narratives and the Limits of American Revolutionary Nationhood" (Ph.D. diss., Harvard, 2010). He teaches in the Literature and History Program at Harvard and is currently working on a book-length biography of Joseph Plumb Martin.

MICHAEL A. McDONNELL lectures at the University of Sydney, Australia, and has written extensively on the American Revolution. His book, *The Politics of War: Race, Class, and Conflict in Revolutionary Virginia,* won the New South Wales Premier's History Award in 2008.

RICHARD S. NEWMAN, professor of history at Rochester Institute of Technology, specializes in the study of the abolitionist movement and African-American reformers. He is the author of *Freedom's Prophet: Bishop Richard Allen, the AME Church, and the Black Founding Fathers* and *The Transformation of American Abolitionism: Fighting Slavery in the Early Republic.*

GREGORY NOBLES is a professor of history at Georgia Tech, where he also directs the university's honors program. He has written extensively about agrarian movements in the Revolutionary Era, most recently in a book coauthored with Alfred F. Young, *Whose American Revolution Was It? Historians Interpret the Founding.*

JEFFREY L. PASLEY, associate professor of history at the University of Missouri–Columbia, is the author of the prize-winning "*The Tyranny of Printers*": *Newspaper Politics in the Early American Republic.* A journalist and speechwriter before entering academia, Pasley also writes the politics and history blog "Publick Occurrences" for the online magazine *Common-Place* (http://www.common-place.org/pasley/).

CASSANDRA PYBUS is the Australian Research Council Professor of History, University of Sydney, Australia. Her most recent book is *Epic Journeys of Freedom: Runaway Slaves of the American Revolution and Their Global Quest for Liberty.*

SHEILA SKEMP is the Clare Leslie Marquette Professor in American History at the University of Mississippi. Her most recent book is *First Lady of Letters: Judith Sargent Murray and the Struggle for Female Independence.*

ALAN TAYLOR is a professor of history at the University of California at Davis. His books include *The Divided Ground: Indians, Settlers, and the Northern Borderland of the American Revolution; American Colonies: The Settlement of North America;* and *William Cooper's Town: Power and Persuasion on the Frontier of the Early American Republic,* winner of the Bancroft, Beveridge, and Pulitzer prizes.

DAVID WALDSTREICHER is the author of *In the Midst of Perpetual Fetes: The Making of American Nationalism, 1776–1820; Runaway America: Benjamin Franklin, Slavery, and the American Revolution;* and *Slavery's Constitution: From Revolution to Ratification.* He teaches at Temple University.

Editors

GARY B. NASH is professor of history emeritus and director of the National Center for History in the Schools at UCLA. He is the former president of the Organization of American Historians (1994–95) and an elected member of the American Academy of Arts and Sciences, the American Philosophical Society, the American Antiquarian Society, and the Society of American Historians. He has published many books and essays on the Colonial and Revolutionary eras of American history. His latest book is *Liberty Bell,* published in Yale University Press's Icons of America series.

RAY RAPHAEL's fifteen books include *A People's History of the American Revolution* and *Founding Myths: Stories That Hide Our Patriotic Past.* His most recent work is *Founders: The People Who Brought You a Nation,* a sweeping narrative history based on the lives of seven diverse participants. A lifelong teacher at the middle school, high school, and college levels, he now leads workshops for history teachers. His forthcoming book, *Inventing the American President,* will be published early in 2012.

ALFRED F. YOUNG's 1976 edited volume, *The American Revolution: Explorations in the History of American Radicalism,* is known for its essays opening up the subject, as is the 1993 sequel, *Beyond the American Revolution.* He continues this exploration in two biographies, *The Shoemaker and the Tea Party: Memory and the American Revolution* and *Masquerade: The Life and Times of Deborah Samson, Continental Soldier. Liberty Tree: Ordinary People and the American Revolution* is a volume of his own interpretive essays.

Index

Page numbers in *italics* refer to illustrations.

Copyright Information